Domaine Weinbach

Domaine Grosbot-Barbara

Domaine Joseph Voillot

Domaine Lucien Crochet

Savignola Paolina

Champagne Roses de Jeanne

Arianna Occhipinti

Domaine La Grange Tiphaine

Azienda Agricola Nicolis

Castello di Radda

THE
WINE TABLE

THE
WINE TABLE

RECIPES AND PAIRINGS FROM WINEMAKERS' KITCHENS

VICKIE REH

Skyhorse Publishing

Skyhorse Publishing books may be purchased in bulk at special discounts for sales promotion, corporate gifts, fund-raising, or educational purposes. Special editions can also be created to specifications. For details, contact the Special Sales Department, Skyhorse Publishing, 307 West 36th Street, 11th Floor, New York, NY 10018 or info@skyhorsepublishing.com.

Skyhorse® and Skyhorse Publishing® are registered trademarks of Skyhorse Publishing, Inc.®, a Delaware corporation.

Visit our website at www.skyhorsepublishing.com.

10 9 8 7 6 5 4 3 2 1

Library of Congress Cataloging-in-Publication Data

Names: Reh, Vickie, author.
Title: The wine table : recipes and pairings from winemakers' kitchens / Vickie Reh.
Description: New York, NY : Skyhorse Publishing, [2018] | Includes index.
Identifiers: LCCN 2017050974| ISBN 9781510730830 (hardcover : alk. paper) | ISBN 9781510730847 (Ebook)
Subjects: LCSH: Food and wine pairing. | Cooking. | LCGFT: Cookbooks.
Classification: LCC TX911.3.M45 R44 2018 | DDC 641--dc23 LC record available at https://lccn.loc.gov/2017050974

Cover design by Jenny Zemanek
Cover photograph by Michael Boudot, courtesy of Champagne Legras & Haas

Print ISBN: 978-1-5107-3083-0
Ebook ISBN: 978-1-5107-3084-7

Printed in China

For Devin

TABLE OF CONTENTS

INTRODUCTION
What Does the Winemaker's Family Eat?

Food before Wine? Chicken or Egg?

It's the classic question. What came first—the chicken or the egg? Food or wine?

Well, not really. Obviously food came first, but early references to wine can be found in the Book of Genesis in the Bible. So, let's just say it's been quite some time since man discovered that grapes left too long in an enclosed container fermented into wine.

As for myself, growing up in a rather abstemious military family with a professional cook for a grandmother and a mother, aunts, and a paternal grandfather who were all great cooks, it's little wonder that I'm obsessed with food. I remember rolling lumpia with our Filipina neighbors in Angeles City, Philippines, when I was seven; learning to make refried beans from scratch as an eighth grader with the cooks at Sacred Heart Catholic School in Del Rio, Texas; and making homemade cottage cheese with my grandmother on summer vacations to Kansas.

My grandmother Grace was an inspiration to me. At a time when few women worked outside of the home, my grandmother drove thirteen miles from the family farm to the nearest town of Concordia, Kansas, to work as a restaurant cook, and that was after she cooked for her family of eight plus the farmhands, raised her own chickens, tended her acre-large farm garden, and canned the results. Her cooking was so well respected that clients called to make sure she was in the kitchen before coming to the restaurant and patrons sent tips back to her—unheard of in Kansas at the time. I like to think I inherited my cooking genes from her, although the thought of what her schedule must have been like exhausts me.

And then I discovered wine. Now, I'm confident I was not the first to fall in love with French wine on a college exchange trip to France, and I guarantee you that I will not be the last. I know you can picture it: young girl from Kansas travels to France, sips wine at sidewalk cafés, nibbles cheese and other delicacies, practices her French accent and her beret-wearing skills, and tumbles head over heels in love with a country and a culture—statistically, it was almost a given (I should know; I was a statistician in a former life). The wine love affair endured. Thank heavens the statistician gig did not. Since that time, wine has fascinated me. I remember smuggling a bottle of Muscadet home from my first trip to France and as a college student springing for the "expensive" Mouton Cadet that was the best wine available in Manhattan, Kansas, at the time while all of my other friends and some of my professors were drinking Gallo Hearty Burgundy. I was a horrible wine snob back then. As for now, I'll plead the fifth except to say that I don't look for points or big names when I buy wine. In fact, with very few exceptions, I'm almost antiestablishment in my wine taste.

For years, I have had a somewhat dual personality professionally. I'm happy working on either side of the kitchen door. When I'm working in the front of the house or retail, I want to be cooking; and when I'm in the kitchen, I want to run out and pour the perfect glass of wine to compliment my dish.

I finally realized that mine is not a split personality at all. I'm not *either* fascinated with wine *or* obsessed with food. Rather, I am devoted to the combination, the thought that one without the other is lacking—a concept that I like to call *The Wine Table*.

When I first started traveling on wine trips, I loved learning about wine—seeing the vineyards where the grapes were grown, the winery where the wine was made, talking to the winemakers—and yet the food fascinated me. I remember on my first professional wine trip to Spain, slipping away every chance I got with Tim McKee, the James Beard Award-winning Chef of La Belle Vie in Stillwater, Minnesota. While everyone else was taking a smoke break or stretching their legs, we would jump off the bus and race into the town butcher shops and grocery stores to see what they were selling. We perused the menus of every restaurant we passed and asked endless questions. It's a habit that still defines my behavior when I travel and is the basis for this book, the quest to answer the questions: What are they serving with this? What is authentic? What is classic? What makes sense? What goes with what?

And finally, what does the winemaker's family eat? There are many factors at play when answering that question. Some are as basic as who does the cooking in the family. Growing grapes and making wine is hard, physical labor, and feeding the family at the end of the day can be as much a chore for them as it is for any working family. In remote areas, even shopping for food can be time-consuming and require considerable planning. I remember visiting a family in Corbières, France, where the grocery truck came to town for two hours one day a week. Obviously, they grew a significant amount of their own food and purchased local meat and cheese, etc., from neighbors, but if you can only buy flour one day a week, you had better plan well. I must confess I just got back from the grocery store before sitting down to write this and now realize that I forgot to buy lemons—I could not go a week between visits from the grocery truck. And yet, they take it in stride.

Other factors involve the location of the vineyards and what grows around it. What is blowing in the wind, and does it affect the flavors of the grapes? Can you taste it in the wine, and is it also incorporated in the food of the region?

Perched high on a Tuscan hill near Gaiole in Chianti, the San Vincenti property is lined with rows of rosemary bushes taller than most men. The wine tastes of rosemary because the wind blows the scent from the rosemary leaves onto the grapes, and notes of rosemary are redolent in the Braised Wild Boar dish that Marilena Pucci served us when we visited.

The wines of Muscadet in the Loire-Atlantique department of France have pronounced salinity due to their proximity to the Atlantic Ocean and the strong maritime winds. So too does the bounty of regional seafood. Chablis and Sancerre often have chalky marine-like flavors owing to the sea fossils trapped in their Kimmeridgian soils. The cheeses of the both regions, particularly those of Sancerre, have chalky, salty notes that mirror the wines. *I like this. Wine should taste like where it is grown, and so should the food.*

Most of the winemakers I know are committed to the local food movement. Many work organically in the fields with some adhering to the more stringent rules of biodynamics. This concern for organic and healthy plants and animals almost always extends to their food culture, as well.

For me, both wine and food need to convey authenticity and a sense of place. I am adamantly opposed to the globalization of food and wine. I have no interest in wines that taste alike, modern-style Bordeaux that evokes California Cabernet, which in turn tastes Australian. Along the same vein, it has gotten to the point where luxury restaurants almost anywhere in the world serve the same high-level ingredients—truffles, foie gras, and caviar—whether they make sense or not given the restaurant's theme or location. Sure, it's luxurious, but do we crave that? Do we dream about that? Or does the architecturally interesting dish with uncountable ingredients and flashy technique fade rapidly from your memory? Does it touch your soul with its simplicity, its finesse, its natural complexity? For me, the answer is no. For me, it is the simple roast chicken, the pristine Belon oyster, the perfectly grilled prawn that haunts me.

One of the keys to *The Wine Table* is restraint—few ingredients in food, few ingredients in wine. Restraint in cooking, noninterventionist winemaking, they are basically the same thing applied to a different métier. It is all about the quality of the raw materials. For farmers, whether their crop is grapes or another product, the work should be done in the fields—then the harvest, the vintage, the products shine. We should shop and cook the same way.

There are very few rules to Wine Table cooking.

1. Buy the best, freshest ingredients you can find and get out of the way.
2. Practice restraint. Use as few ingredients as possible (why use four ingredients when three will do?).
3. Just because you can doesn't mean you should. Complicated techniques for technique's sake are meaningless and rarely enhance flavor.

Frankly, Rules #2 and #3 are just offshoots of Rule #1.

Wine Table cooking doesn't require fancy equipment, a culinary degree, or an enormous food budget. The beauty of having so few rules is that anyone can do it.

Some of the best times in my life have been spent around a table at a winery, drinking good, honest wine and sharing food I've prepared with a winemaker and his or her family—Dover sole in Sancerre with Laurence Crochet, Pompe aux Grattons with Monique Barbara in Saint Pourçain, Pork Rillettes with Damien Delecheneau in Montlouis, Choucroute with the Faller ladies of Domaine Weinbach in Alsace, and a blow-out "festa" at Savignola Paolina on a balcony overlooking Ludo's Chianti vineyards. I've shared a wonderful meal with Mrs. Monique Gussalli Beretta showcasing Beretta family recipes. I've cooked for harvest workers and winery employees during the harvest in Provence, Champagne, and Alsace. Along the way, I have amassed recipes and wonderful memories, and I have honed the concept of *The Wine Table*.

I invite you to pull up a chair at my table and let me share these experiences with you.

WINE TABLE BASICS

FOOD

Where to Find It and How to Buy It

Ok, this is the fun part. Well, at least it's fun to me. I know that for some folks, grocery shopping is a chore. Hopefully, we can liven that up and make it less a task that needs to be accomplished and more a fun field trip.

We are lucky in the US. For the most part, we have multiple grocery stores close by, many of which are open round the clock. Our stores are stocked with fruits and vegetables from around the world. You can buy tomatoes, blueberries, and asparagus all year round. I'm just not sure you *should*. In fact, I am pretty adamant that you shouldn't. Some things just don't travel well and at the very least are lacking in flavor when they finally get here.

Remember Wine Table Rule #1. Buy the best, freshest ingredients you can find and get out of their way.

Why is this important? The fresher the food, the more recently it has been picked, the better it tastes. So how do you find the best, freshest ingredients? You buy as locally as you can because that means your food has had to travel less distance to get to you. Hopefully, you have a farmers' market or farm stand in your vicinity. Make friends with the farmers who grow your food. Not only is it a rewarding emotional connection, it makes it easier for you to be sure that your food is grown and raised the way you want. This is what many of my winemaker friends do.

Take Damien Delecheneau of La Grange-Tiphaine in Amboise, France, for example. When we were cooking lunch together at his winery home, we tossed vegetable scraps directly through the open window to his chickens grazing in the yard outside. What he doesn't grow in his garden, he shops for at the local farmers' market. He barters with other organic farmers and even purchases an organically raised pig every year from a friend, butchering it himself so that he, his wife Coralie, and their boys, Paul and Camille, can have organic, local pork all year round. The pork rillettes made from that pig were delicious. *Trust me. I know.* Pork rillettes are kind of my thing.

Likewise, Guilliaume and Karina Lefèvre of Domaine de Sulauze in Provence, France, grow their own organic wheat and hops, raise their own chickens, and have an amazing kitchen garden that furnishes organic produce for them for much of the year. They barter their wine with their next-door neighbor for meat from the famed *Taureau de Camargue,* a breed of cattle from the region; serve it with their own vegetables and bread made with their own organic wheat and baked in their ancient stone oven; and wash it down with their own biodynamic wine or the organic beer brewed from their own grain at the brasserie on the Domaine. These people are walking the walk.

Meet Your Local Farmer

Make a habit of stopping by the farmer's market or farm stand when you get a chance. Strike up a conversation with a farmer the next time you are there. Meet the people who grow your food. Ask them to refer you to their friends. Is it easier to go to your big box grocery store? Yes. Is the food anywhere near as good? No. I mean seriously, when was the last time you felt like bragging about going to a big box store? But putting a dish on the table and saying, "I got this at the farmers' market this morning"—that is something you want to brag about.

I'm not suggesting you never eat anything that isn't grown nearby. Take citrus fruit, for example. I live in Virginia. We do not have local lemons, but I could not cook without them. I like a good black truffle as much as the next girl and am completely obsessed with saffron. I'm not telling you to stop using avocados or artichokes. I'm just saying that if the food you are eating is grown locally, you should buy it locally. It will taste better.

Local versus Organic Hierarchy

This topic could be the subject of a whole other book, so I'll make my explanation short. Ideally, we would all have the time and talents to grow our own organic food, but since that is not realistic for most of us, I have a purchasing hierarchy when it comes to buying food, especially produce and meats.

1. *If your choice is between local or organic, buy locally.* The blueberries that you buy at the farmers' market are going to taste better than the organic ones from Chile that you can get year-round. Also, although I am not a food scientist, I cannot help but think that fruits and vegetables flown here by airplane have to absorb some exhaust fumes which cannot a) be healthy or b) taste good, not to mention the carbon footprint ramifications. And don't get me started on my trust issues with regards to organic certification in the US, let alone in far-off lands.
2. If you do not have a farmers' market and your grocery store doesn't feature local produce, your next-best bet is to buy organic from a reputable store. At least that way there has been an effort to limit chemical treatments in your food that are at the same time unhealthy and mute the flavor.
3. *Support your local bodega.* Finally, if you cannot buy local or organic, I advocate supporting small individual stores. Make friends with the shopkeepers. They will steer you to the best products.

Fresh versus Pantry Staples

Fresh

There are certain foods that I always have on hand. For the most part, these aren't all that perishable, but even if they are, I still have to have them.

Eggs:

Whitmore Farm: My friends Will Morrow and Kent Ozkum of Whitmore Farm in Emmitsburg, Maryland, have the best eggs ever! *The yolks are thick and viscous, so dark gold, they look as if they've been soaked in saffron. The whites stand up high and firm, a fitting pillow for the lovely dark gold yolk. And they taste amazing!* They are so good that they routinely win awards at every fair they enter; so good that I limit the number of people I tell about them; so good, that I drive all the way up to the farm (an hour and a half each way) during the winter to buy a case and then I don't tell people I have them, doling them out as presents or discreetly selling a few dozen to a select few. If they know which chicken laid the egg, they even write the name of the chicken on the egg. I cannot imagine not having these eggs. Try to find your own Will and Kent.

Normal Free-Range Eggs: As good as Will and Kent's eggs are, I do have to purchase other eggs from time to time. First of all, the yolk is so thick in a Whitmore Farm egg, they don't work well for baking. Also, if I am only going to use the whites and need a lot, I don't use their eggs, either. It seems a shame to waste those yolks. When not using Whitmore Farm eggs, I prefer free-range eggs from a local producer.

Dairy

Butter: I always have both salted and unsalted butter on hand. I use unsalted butter in cooking and bak-

Whitmore Farm eggs and truffles

ing. That way, it is easier to control the salt content in the dish. I use salted butter for finishing. For example, if I am sautéing something, making a butter sauce, or baking something, I use unsalted butter. If I am adding butter as a final note to vegetables or slathering butter on a freshly baked biscuit, I use salted butter. I usually have everyday salted butter for, well, everyday use, and a higher-quality butter—like the Sea Salt Crystal Cultured Butter from Vermont Creamery—when I want to treat myself or my guests.

Milk and Cream: I stock small quantities of 2 percent and whole milk to cook with. I always have at least a pint of heavy cream in the fridge to finish soups and sauces. I also keep a small container of crème fraîche on hand.

Cheese: Oh cheese, how I love thee. I always have tons of cheese in my fridge. At the very least, I have Parmigiano Reggiano, Pecorino Romano, and a mild cheddar. Generally, there are also pieces of Loire Valley goat cheese and whatever cheese strikes my fancy at Arrowine and Cheese, my favorite local wine and cheese shop. I am a huge fan of sheep cheese from the Pyrenees and I love good Raclette. My poor husband, Jeff, who is allergic to cheese, suffers through my obsession.

Fruits, Vegetables, and Herbs

Lemons and Limes: I like other citrus fruits, but I can't cook without lemons and, to a slightly lesser extent, limes.

Flat Leaf Parsley: This is my go-to herb to brighten up a dish, both for its vibrant color and for its flavor that I can only describe as clean and green. Try making a little salad with parsley, thinly sliced shallots, lemon juice, extra-virgin oil, and Fleur de Sel. It's a symphony of brightness.

Thyme and Rosemary: Dry is okay. Fresh is amazing. Luckily, I live in a fairly moderate climate, so my thyme and rosemary tend to live all year round in the minuscule courtyard right outside my kitchen door.

Garlic, Shallots, Chives, Leeks, Yellow, Red, and Green Onions: All part of the allium family, all indispensable.

Carrots and Celery: For stocks and soups.

Potatoes: Russets for baking, mashing, and French fries. Baby potatoes of all colors for boiling, sautéing, or roasting.

Pantry Staples

Oil

Extra-virgin olive oil: finishing oil,
    cooking oil
Neutral oil: i.e., canola or peanut
oil
Walnut oil
Sesame oil

Vinegar

Apple cider vinegar
Sherry vinegar
White wine vinegar
Red wine vinegar
Distilled
Balsamic vinegar

Salt

I'm a salt freak. Anyone who knows me will attest to that. It's not exactly unusual for a chef to love salt, but I have taken it a bit further, going so far as to plan a family vacation around salt—spending a week in Brittany, France, visiting salt ponds and buying so much salt that I had to purchase an extra suitcase to tote it all home (my husband, Jeff, was thrilled, by the way). If there is sea, wind, and sun, I'll be searching for salt to buy.

Kosher salt
Fleur de Sel (white and gray)
Maldon salt
Fine sea salt
Table salt
Pink curing salt

Flavored salts
    Piment d'Espelette
    Saffron
Colored salts
    Pink Australian salt
    Black salt

Trapani Salt Ponds, Sicily

Salt: For the purposes of determining salt quantities for the recipes in this book, the following are the types of salt that I use regularly. Using the right salt is key because each salt has a different sodium content. As a general rule, Diamond Crystals salt is half as strong as table salt. If in doubt, weigh the salt, as the sodium content is equal between two salts of equal weight.

Kosher Salt (Diamond—1 tsp. = 1120 mg. sodium; Morton's—1 tsp. = 1920 mg. sodium): I'll start with the salt that I use the most. When it comes to basic cooking, I use kosher salt. Kosher salt does not mean Jewish salt. It comes from the word Koshering (or curing) because it is ideally suited to curing and preserving meats. It has no additives, and because its crystals are larger, they cover more area and dissolve more slowly, which means it absorbs fluids and sinks into the meat more slowly. Chefs like it because it is dry and the crystals are large; it doesn't stick to your fingers, and it is easier to control sodium content. Kosher salt is not as good for baking, as the larger crystals do not dissolve well in the limited amount of liquid of baked goods. If a recipe doesn't specify, assume that it calls for Diamond Crystals Kosher salt.

Table Salt (1 tsp. = 2360 mg. sodium): Table salt is very fine-grained and is treated with iodine for health reasons and an anticaking additive to prevent clumping. Table salt works well in baking and in salt shakers.

Maldon Flakes (1 tsp. = 2320 mg. sodium): Maldon salt is from England, and I love using it as a garnish. It is light, flaky, and very crunchy, and I adore the pyramidal shape of it. The crystals are like snowflakes—no two are alike. I often use flavored Maldon salts that I mix myself as a garnish on dishes.

Sea Salt (sodium content varies depending on the size of the crystals): Sea salt is produced in salt ponds with an evaporation process that takes between one to five years. After harvesting, it is sorted, cleaned, and processed. The care needed for this takes time and increases the cost of the salt. Fleur de Sel is the highest, finest grade of sea salt.

Pink Curing Salt (also known as Prague Curing Powder #1 and #2): This salt is used in making pâtés and sausages and in meat curing. It is dyed pink to blend better with the meat and to prevent it from being confused with common table salt. #1 contains table salt and a small amount of sodium nitrite. #2 contains table salt, sodium nitrites, and sodium nitrates. #2 is more frequently used in long-term curing.

Sugar

Granulated sugar
Confectioner's sugar (powdered)
Light brown sugar

Stock—Bouillon Cubes/Canned Stock

Neither of these is an ingredient that I use in everyday cooking. I prefer to use my own homemade stocks, but I can certainly understand the convenience factor. Bouillon cubes especially are frequently used in French home cooking. I prefer Knorr brand, available in chicken, beef, vegetable, and fish flavors. These cubes contain significant amounts of salt, so be careful when using them.

As with bouillon cubes, canned stock is a great convenience frequently used in home cooking. Just like with bouillon cubes, canned stock has varying levels of sodium. Exercise caution when adding salt to a recipe if using canned stock.

Flour/Meals/Breadcrumbs/Croutons

All-purpose flour
Bread flour
00 Pasta flour
Wondra flour
Chickpea flour
Corn meal
    Coarse
    Fine

Breadcrumbs: If you are like me, I always have leftover bread. Why throw it out when you can make breadcrumbs or croutons?
    Fresh
    Dried
    Croutons
    Panko

Spices

Pepper
    Black peppercorns
    White pepper
    Green peppercorns
    Piment d'Espelette

Cayenne pepper

Dried red pepper flakes

Saffron is a spice consisting of the stigma of the saffron crocus. Although it is extremely expensive, I find myself using it in quite a few recipes. Luckily, you don't have to use much to reap the benefits.

Pimentón de la Vera: Ground smoked paprika from Spain's Extremadura region—another absolute must for me.

Bay leaves

Rubbed sage

Dried oregano

Dried thyme

Cumin seeds

Fennel seeds

Whole coriander

Whole nutmeg

Whole allspice

Cinnamon

Whole cloves

Curry powder

Turmeric

Canned Foods

Beans: Beans are one of the few foods that I think are really good canned.

San Marzano tomatoes DOP: These deep red tomatoes are Italian plum tomatoes with a pedigree. With their low acidity, high pulp-to-seed ratio, and their sweet ripe flavor, San Marzano DOP (*Denominazione di Origine Protetta*) tomatoes grown in the volcanic soils at the foot of Mount Vesuvius are universally recognized as fantastic sauce tomatoes. Unfortunately, there are a lot of fake San Marzanos on the market. Make sure the tomatoes you buy actually say San Marzano DOP on the label.

Tuna: Pay extra for high-quality tuna packed in oil.

Anchovies in olive oil

Pickled/Jarred Foods

Capers (both in brine and in salt)

Cornichons
Cocktail onions
Pepperoncini
Piquillo peppers

Guindilla peppers: These cute little Basque peppers are not too hot, not too sweet. Available in some gourmet stores or online through Amazon.

Condiments

Dijon mustard (smooth and coarse)
Soy sauce
Mayonnaise: I know, shocking, but there are times when I want to make mayonnaise and times when the recipe works better with store-bought mayonnaise. I prefer Duke's brand.
Hot sauces:
    Light-bodied hot sauce: Tabasco or the equivalent
    Sriracha

Pasta

I like to make fresh pasta (or to buy good, fresh, locally made pasta, not that chemical-filled stuff you can get in the dairy section of the grocery store—please!) and there are dishes where it is a necessity, but I really love dried pastas of all types. If it is good enough for the Italians, it is good enough for me. Try to buy pasta that is made from durum wheat semolina. I prefer pasta with a rougher texture rather than a smooth texture. The sauce sticks better. I always have boxes or bags of the following types of dried pasta around (it drives my husband crazy!):

Spaghetti
Linguine
Radiatore
Orzo/Riso
Orecchiette
Penne
Small shells
Large shells
Pappardelle

Pici: A very thick, long pasta from Siena. It is hard to find, but delicious.

Rice/Grains

Basmati
Medium grain
Arborio
Wild rice—which isn't really rice. It is a grass seed, but whatever.
Quinoa
Lentils (Umbrian or de Puy)
Cannellini beans

Nuts

Walnuts
Almonds
Pine nuts
Pistachios

WINE

What Is Wine?

In the simplest of terms, wine is grape juice that has undergone alcoholic fermentation. Alcoholic fermentation occurs when yeast converts sugar to produce alcohol and CO_2. That's it. It seems basic because it is. The complexity arises in making it taste good.

How Is Wine Made?

There are many books written about the process of making wine. Here are the basics.

The largest fruit crop on earth, grapes are grown in vineyards located predominantly between the latitudes of 30 and 50 degrees in each hemisphere. Ninety percent of the grapes grown for consumption are *vitis vinifera* grapes.

Grapes need several factors to thrive. Climate-wise, they need warm, dry summers, mild winters, at least seven hours of direct sunlight per day, and sufficient

Viticulturist: he/she who grows the grapes.

Winemaker: he/she who takes said grapes and makes the wine.

Oenologist: One who is an expert in the science of wine and winemaking.

water to keep the plant hydrated. While there are many types of soil suitable for growing grapes, good drainage is of paramount importance, as the vines need their roots to be able to reach water without being constantly immersed in it. Low fertility soil is best because it forces the roots to drive deep in their search for nutrients. The old adage about grapes needing to be stressed is true. After that, grape variety, the type of training and pruning that is done, and what kind of pest and disease treatments are used depend on the terroir, the philosophy of the viticulturist, and, often, the laws of the region.

Terroir: I like the definition on the Guild Somm website: "The complete system of the living vine." This takes into account: location, topography, soil, climate, and aspect (degree and direction of the slope).

Harvesting can be done by hand or machine although most critics agree that hand harvesting is better for higher-quality wine. There are many levels of selection and sorting, most of which are better achieved when you hand harvest. In the winery, the grapes are crushed, and in the case of most white wine, the skins, stems, and seeds are removed before fermentation. Red wines remain on their grape skins during fermentation.

After fermentation, wine can be fined and filtered to remove sediments and impurities. It is then placed in a tank or barrel to age before being bottled. Decisions regarding fining, filtration, and racking, as well as aging regimen (tank or barrel, size of barrel, wood type and age, and length of aging), depend on the winemaker, the traditions of the region, and the regulations of the local governing body. (See Wine Terms, page 472.)

The makings of an ideal year include: cool, wet winter months, no frost after spring, pruning to manage potential crop size, moderate days and cool nights throughout the summer, minimal rain, no excessive heat, and a warm and dry autumn with only small amounts of rain leading up to harvest.

How to Buy Wine

Meet Your Local Wine Salesperson, i.e., Get Thee to Thy Local Wine Store

I cannot stress enough how much better you will drink for the same amount of money if you frequent your local wine shop. Make friends with the salespeople and take their advice. Of course, it helps to give them some hints as to your taste and budget. Answers to the following questions will go a long way toward improving your drinking experience.

Red or White? (And Let's Not Forget Rosé.)

Red, white, or rosé is up to you, but keep an open mind. Some people think they only like one type of wine, but when they try a different kind, they find they really like it. Do not fall into the trap of eschewing rosés as a matter of course. They pair super well with food!

Still or Sparkling?

Still wines make up the majority of the wines we drink, but don't rule out sparkling wine too hastily. Many people think sparkling wines are only for celebrations, but the lively acidity, vibrant fruit, and palate-cleansing bubbles make sparkling wine an ideal candidate for a myriad of different foods. For example, sparkling wine is delicious with oysters and a great accompaniment for salty snacks.

Dry or Sweet?

Not to be insulting, but many people say they like really dry wines when in reality, some of the wines they drink have a bit of residual sugar. Brut Sparkling wines have a slight amount of sugar to balance out the racy acidity. Likewise, some Shiraz from Australia and definitely California Chardonnays have a bit of residual sugar hiding behind all of that fruit. This isn't necessarily a bad thing. Some foods pair better with wines that have a little sugar. In fact, you'll find that spicy cuisines like Indian or Thai taste incredibly good when paired with a moderately sweet Riesling. Just remember, the wine must always be sweeter than the food. If it isn't, the wine will taste sour and astringent.

What Kind of Wine Have You Liked in the Past?

This is a key piece of information. It helps inform your wine salesperson about your habits and gives them a magic decoder ring of sorts to aid them in deciphering your taste in wine. Say you like Pinot Grigio from Northern Italy but are looking to change things up a little bit. You might also enjoy a Garganega/Trebbiano blend from the neighboring region of Soave or a Spanish Albariño. Both wines have similar acidity, fruit profiles, and alcohol levels as Pinot Grigio, so it is a fairly safe bet that you will enjoy them. If you like high-tannin, oak-aged California Cabernets, your salesperson can comfortably recommend a Washington State Cabernet/Merlot blend or possibly an Australian Shiraz. These wines would suit your taste much better than a delicate

Red Burgundy. Also helpful is what you have not liked. Information, in this case, never hurts your cause.

How Do You Drink Wine? With Food? As a Cocktail? Or Both?

This is sort of a continuation of the previous question. The kinds of wines you have liked in the past and how you drink those wines map out your wine taste in a way that can be read quite clearly. You like to drink wine with food; therefore, you most likely prefer wines that are relatively high in acidity and not overpowering. These are the wines that will most likely compliment food. But on the days when you want to have wine as a cocktail, you may wish to choose something a little less mineral driven, a wine with more fruit—one with a certain quaffable quality like a New World Pinot Noir, for example. You can certainly do both. You just need to determine which wine you want for which occasion.

New World or Old World?

For the most part, this question can be answered by analyzing the previous two questions. If you drink wine with food, you will most likely lean toward the Old World, and if you like wine as a cocktail, you will skew New World. However, many good food wines can be found in the New World, and there are some delicious "cocktail" wines in the Old World. There are also those who, for political reasons, prefer wines from one region or the other. I'm not very political myself, so I don't go there, but it is important to some folks, so it needs to be considered.

Price Range?

Do not be shy about answering this last question. I think as a culture we are taught to never tell our price range for fear we will be overcharged. I call it the Curse of the Car Salesman. Seriously though, I have never met anyone in wine retail who works on commission. They do not make more money if they sell you a higher-priced bottle of wine. They are there to help you, to increase your wine enjoyment, to provide you with the best bottle of wine in your price range. And please don't say inexpensive, moderate, etc. Your salesperson doesn't know your economic status, so they have no clue what your idea of moderate is. One person's moderate is another person's inexpensive.

If possible, **buy in quantity**. Most wine shops and even many supermarkets give you a discount if you buy a certain number of bottles—usually a case. Twelve of the same wine means you are buying a solid case. Twelve different wines equal a mixed case. If you are just starting out, I think a mixed case makes more sense. Mix in a few more expensive bottles with your "budget" buys, or split a case with a friend. You'll save money so you can buy either more or better wine.

Remember what wines you bought and liked. **Take photos!** I used to tell customers to write down the names of wines they liked, but in our current culture almost everyone has a smartphone with a camera. Even my Mom has one! Take photos of the wines you liked so you can show your wine salesperson. Even if they don't have that wine, it gives them a hint about your palate and enables them to direct you to something you will like.

What Should You Do if There Isn't a Wine Shop in Your Town?

Other than the obvious solution of moving, there are a few things you can do:

1. If you buy wine at your local grocery store and don't know what kind of wine you like, try wines from different countries, regions, and styles. Read up on the wines, take photos, and remember what you did and did not like. Unlike my previous advice, in this case I would not buy wine in bulk until I learned what I liked. Also, contrary to my direction to only take photos of wines you like, you will also need to document the ones you do not like so you don't just keep buying the same disappointing wine over and over again. You will begin to recognize a pattern, (e.g., you like white wines from Italy and red wines from Argentina), and you will be able to tailor your purchases to your tastes. *This will be more work for you, but you were the one who didn't want to move.*

2. Follow a few basic wine/food pairing rules and see how they work with your taste. (See the Section on Wine and Food Pairing Tips below, page 23).

3. Use visits to other towns as an opportunity to visit wine shops and purchase wine.

4. Beg friends to bring you wine when they come from out of town.

5. See if your state allows you to buy wine online, although I don't recommend you do that until you have some idea of your wine tastes. I would hate for you to pay to have a case of wine shipped to you, only to find out you don't like the wine.

Wine Tasting Basics

There are countless books and videos devoted to the subject of tasting wine, including in-depth analyses of the structure, aromas, flavors, age, and origin of the wine.

For the purposes of this book, we want to determine if the wine is sound (without flaws) and if you like it. To do this, you should pour your glass about one quarter full (at a restaurant the server will pour you a small amount to taste). Swirl the glass to release the aromas. It should smell clean.

What is clean? Fruit, baking spices, leaves, herbs, all of these things are clean. Even stoniness is clean. Damp wet basement, wet cardboard or newspaper, ammonia, or a pronounced smell of wet animal are flaws in a wine. If you are in a restaurant and smell these, tell your server that the wine is bad and that you would like another bottle. If you are at home, replace the cork in the bottle of wine and if possible return it to the store where you purchased it. The first time you do this it is nerve-racking, but *it is your right as a consumer to get a sound bottle of wine*. Any reputable wine shop or restaurant should make this process easy and painless for you.

After smelling the wine, you should taste it, swirling it in your mouth to get the full effect. If you are tasting a lot of wines, you should probably spit the wine into a separate glass or container. This is what the professionals do. It enables them to taste multiple wines without feeling the effects of the alcohol. If you are at home or out to dinner and the wine is sound, I suggest you swallow it. I mean, that's the whole point, right?

Unless you are a wine professional at an industry tasting, I do not believe in spitting wine at a restaurant during dinner. I find it unsightly. If you do not want to imbibe a lot of alcohol, take a small sip, but spitting at a restaurant in polite company (which, and I say this with love, almost by definition means *not* with wine professionals) is just gross.

And now for the difficult question—*What do you do if the wine is sound and you just do not like it?*

That's a tough one. If you are at a restaurant, you can tell your server that you believe there is nothing wrong with the wine, but that you just do not like it. Depending on the level of the restaurant, they may allow you to replace it with another wine. I would hope that they would.

If you have purchased the wine from a wine shop, it is a little stickier.

- If there is nothing wrong with the wine and you have purchased only one bottle of that wine, I do not recommend taking it back to the store.
- If, however, you have purchased multiple bottles of the same wine that you do not like, I would advise taking the unopened bottles back to the wine shop where you purchased them. Most reputable shops will allow you to exchange them for another wine, although liquor regulations in some states do not allow this.
- Either way, if you definitely do not like a wine, you may want to take a photo of it on your phone with a notation that you did not like it. That way you can show it to your salesperson the next time you are at your wine shop to

help them better understand your wine taste. This is contrary to my previous instruction to only take photos of wines you like, but in this case you do not just "not prefer" this wine, you actively do not like it and you will want to remember that fact.

How to Store Wine

All wine storage needs are not created equal. For some people, no storage is necessary. These folks stop by the store and pick up whatever tasty little beverage they are going to drink that evening or the next night. Storing this wine is as simple as taking it out of the bag and, in the case of white and rosé wine, placing it in the refrigerator (remember: once a white wine is thoroughly chilled, you should take it out of the refrigerator about 15 minutes before serving it. I generally like my rosé wines very cold and for the most part do not take them out of the refrigerator ahead of time). Red wine can be left upright on the counter as long as it isn't close to a source of heat or light. (If it is summertime or your kitchen is at all warm, don't forget to pop it in the refrigerator for 15–30 minutes before you plan on serving it.)

At the opposite end of the spectrum are those collectors with massive cellars in their basement complete with labels and/or a complex computerized inventory. These cellars are often decorated in a style matching their wine tastes—French Château, Napa Chic, or Italian Villa—and frequently have tasting tables and expensive glassware, etc.

Middle ground is the real estate most of us inhabit. This middle ground can be a dark cool closet in the basement or bedroom, a shaded cool cabinet in the dining room or kitchen, or a small climate-controlled wine refrigerator. You'll note that the leitmotif here is the lack of sun and relative coolness of the storage area. The other must-have is the ability to store the wines on their side. This prevents the cork from drying out and protects the wine. Wine racks are an ideal solution, but I had a friend who just stored his wine cases in such a way that the bottles rested on their sides.

When I moved into my current house, the kitchen was quite lovely with nice decorative touches, including a wrought-iron wine rack built on top of a cabinet in the alcove adjacent to the stove. It was also right next to a large west-facing window perfectly situated to receive lots of afternoon sun. It looked amazing. I ripped it out immediately (well, to be honest, Jeff ripped it out immediately). Pretty is nice, but it's not the first, second, or even third consideration when storing wine. It's about keeping the wines relatively cool, on their side, and away from the sun.

Follow these simple rules, and you won't go wrong. Again with the simple rules! Isn't *The Wine Table* easy?

Wine Glasses and Utensils

As with wine storage, this can run the gamut from a basic jelly jar and the corkscrew attachment on your Swiss Army Knife, to a different very expensive glass for each type of wine and a collection of antique corkscrews. And as before, most of us reside in the middle ground somewhere.

Glassware

If you are first starting out, I recommend that you purchase an all-purpose glass—one that is suitable for both red and white wines. My all-purpose glass of choice is the Riedel Chianti glass. It is medium-sized with a tapered rim and a good balance for swirling. I find it works well for red, white, and rosé wines. It could even serve as your sparkling wine glass. (In fact, most of my friends who make Champagne insist on using regular stemware for their wines.) Personally, I like a real Champagne flute for some Champagnes, especially if I'm in a celebratory mood. The one I use is quite similar to the shape of my all-purpose glass. It is just slightly more slender. For more expensive or more serious Champagnes, I use my Riedel Chianti glass.

From there, you can purchase glasses based on your favorite wine style if you wish, but given a choice between a fancy glass or a nicer bottle of wine, my money always lands on the "buy nice wine" side of the equation.

Wine Openers

Once again, the choice depends on your means and wine budget. You can splurge on an extremely expensive wine opener built into your countertop and adorned with 14K. gold engravings if you wish. For me, a simple waiter's wine key is my preference. For once, however, I *am* super picky about the kind I like. I prefer one with a knife that isn't serrated and is sharp enough to easily cut the foil from around the bottom lip of the bottle. Ideally, the knife is the perfect length that when you snap it closed one-handed, it doesn't knick your finger (I hate when that happens!). The worm (or screw) should be smooth for ease of entry into the cork. The pull mechanism should be two-part, with a screw bevel in the center to make it easier to extract the cork. That's it, no fancy wings, etc. You should experiment until you find the type you prefer and then stick with it.

Decanters, Aerators, etc.

Decanters are nice to have, but unless you are really fancy or are lucky enough to score some older vintages, you probably won't need them. Again, spend your money on the wine. If you progress to the point where you want a decanter, pick one that is well balanced for ease of pouring.

The one exception to this is if you frequently drink wines that are meant to be aged while they are still very young. In this case, you may want to decant the wine and swirl it around for a while to help it open up. Unless you really have no storage space or actually *need* to open the wine early (say, for example, you are moving and can't take it with you), I recommend exercising a little restraint and letting it age. I apologize if that sounds snotty, but since you have spent your hard-earned money to buy a wine suitable for aging, why not let it age? That being said, I am the queen of letting a wine age the recommended amount of time and then popping the cork the minute it reaches maturity. I mean seriously, self-control only goes so far.

Grape Names: When discussing certain international grape varieties, I struggle with what to call them. Is it Pinot Noir? Or Pinot Nero? Since this book covers wineries in France and Italy, grape varieties will be labeled in the language of the country where the winery is located. Therefore when I describe Pinot Noir in France, it will be designated Pinot Noir. For the same grape in Italy, I will use Pinot Nero. The same goes for Pinot Blanc/Bianco and Pinot Gris/Grigio.

Wine and Food Pairing Tips

There are many different wine and food pairing tips. Here are the ones I find most useful. Keep in mind that no rules are set in stone. *Ultimately, you should drink what you like.*

I guess it is time to address the elephant in the room. I have been quite open about my views on eating as locally as possible. Strangely enough, I don't feel the same about wine. I started drinking wine as a student in France, and for many years French wine was all that I drank. Since then, following trips to Italy, Spain, and Portugal, and subsequent trips to France, my main wine tastes have expanded to include Italian, Spanish, Portuguese, and German wines. It could be because my cooking style is strongly rooted in French, Italian, and Spanish cuisines, or it could be because Old World wines tend to pair well with food. In any case, it is what I know and where the majority of my wine dollars are spent. I am quite lucky, however. Living in Virginia, I am exposed to some very good regional wines like those made by Rutger de Vink of RDV, Jim Law of Linden, and Jeff White of Glen Manor. I drink those and enjoy them immensely. I also enjoy New Zealand and Oregon Pinot Noirs and New Zealand Sauvignon Blancs from time to time. In this way, I am following my own advice and drinking what I like.

Pair Wines with Cuisine of the Region

As I said, I tend to cook French, Italian, and Spanish dishes. To me it just makes sense to pair these dishes with wines from that country or region. *Cinghiale in Umido,* the classic Braised Wild Boar dish from Tuscany, is best cooked in and served with Chianti Classico. Bouillabaisse, the famed seafood stew from Marseille (or Cassis, depending on whom you believe—and that could be the subject of a whole other book), pairs superbly with Provençal Rosé. Cassoulet? Minervois or Cahors. Choucroute Garnie? Alsatian Pinot Gris or Riesling. You get my drift.

I never understand restaurants with a specific regional cuisine that serve wine from a different country or region. For example, a French Bistro in Washington, DC that serves Argentine Malbec or Australian Shiraz doesn't make sense to me. I have nothing against those two wines. I just think that they have a place and that place is in an Argentinian or Australian restaurant. It is about authenticity, and serving those wines at a French bistro makes no more sense than decorating a French bistro with koala bears and boomerangs.

On the other hand, when I travel, I drink 100 percent locally. For example, while vacationing in the Adriatic beach town of Senigallia in Italy's Marche region, I drank only wines from the Marche, mostly Verdicchio dei Castelli di Jesi—exquisite with the bounty of just-caught seafood. Likewise, when I am in California's Napa Valley, I drink wines from Napa. I wait until I'm in Sonoma to drink wines from Sonoma.

Phew! Now that I've gotten that off my chest, let's move on.

Basics of Wine and Food Pairing

When pairing, you need to consider the structure of the wine and the food. Structure in wine is determined by the levels of acidity, alcohol, and tannin. A fuller-bodied wine tends to be higher in alcohol and tannin. Lighter-bodied wines tend to be more delicate. You should match the body and structure of the food to the wine. Is the food light and delicate? If so, you should pick a wine whose structure is light and delicate. Likewise, a powerful wine can stand up to more robust dishes.

Pair Based on Flavor Notes

When considering what wine to go with a dish, remember that you need to pair based on the predominant flavors of the dish, as that can radically impact what wine you choose. The predominant flavors are often the sauce, rather than the main ingredient, but they can also include the cooking method. The wine choice for a simple roast chicken might be wrong for a spicy dish like Szechuan Chicken.

Cooking Method: Poached, Roasted, Sautéed, Braised, Fried, or Grilled?

Poaching, roasting, and sautéing chicken are the simplest cooking methods flavor-wise, which is not to imply that chicken cooked in any of those ways is flavorless, but those methods change the basic flavors of the chicken the least. Granted, a crispy-skinned roast chicken can be deliciously flavorful (as anyone who has eaten the Roast Chicken at the Zuni Café in San Francisco can attest), but the predominant flavor is still chicken. The same holds true for a simple sautéed piece of chicken. Poached chicken relies on the poaching liquid for added flavor, but even so, it tastes like chicken. Foods prepared this way pair well with beautiful complex whites with moderate or no use of oak, such as a Chablis or Alsatian Pinot Gris, or lighter reds like a young Red Burgundy, Alsatian Pinot Noir, or well-made Beaujolais.

Braising involves adding a liquid, usually a mixture of wine and broth, to browned chicken and cooking the meat half immersed in the braising liquid in a covered pot. Here the contents of the braising liquid and flavoring components used when browning flavor the dish. Coq au Vin is a fine example of this method, where the earthiness of the mushrooms, the sweetness of the pearl onions, and the light porkiness of the lardons simmering away with a good red wine change the focus from the chicken to the sauce, with its darkly earthy components necessitating a more complex, earthier wine. Now is the time to up the ante on Red Burgundy and pour something with a little bottle age from a good Village or splurge on a Premier or Grand Cru.

Grilling imparts a charred smoky flavor to the food. This is an important flavor note to consider. For example, Syrah from the Northern Rhône exhibits a smoky, meaty characteristic that is killer with grilled steak or lamb.

Finally, frying does not necessarily change the basic flavor of a dish, e.g., fried chicken (unless the batter or breading preparation is strongly flavored) still ranks chicken as the main flavor. It is the fat in the dish that comes from frying that you must consider when selecting a wine. See the section below on fat vs. acidity for more details, but I always serve fried chicken with a wine with good levels of acidity. I particularly like Champagne, Provençal Rosé, Beaujolais, or young Chianti. Add a stout beer to the batter or cayenne to the breading? You've got a completely different situation. Beer batter adds a creamy yet yeasty characteristic to the chicken that calls for something a little yeastier yet a with punch of acidity, like lees-aged Cru Communal Muscadet. Spicy cayenne sends us directly to a Mosel Riesling or a Demi-Sec Vouvray whose sweetness can tame the spice, while the high acidity levels balance the fat. As you can see, what you add to the dish is a game changer.

Which Leads Us to the Sauce . . .

As with cooking method, a sauce frequently has ingredients that assume the role of predominant flavor component. Pair according to that component.

Paired to Match

You've heard of the brides who dye their shoes to match their dress? DTM equals Dyed to Match. Well, think of this as PTM, Paired to Match.

Earthy to Earthy: Earthy foods taste great with earthy wines. That's why Burgundy both red and white spring to mind when I think of pairing a dish with mushrooms.

Fruity to Fruity: I make a shrimp salad with cold poached shrimp and a lightly spicy fruit salsa, using whatever fruit is in season. It is particularly good with peaches or nectarines. Add a Halbtrocken Mosel Riesling and plop me down under a shady umbrella on my back patio, and I'm in heaven. Want to make it even better? Relocate my umbrella (and my wine) to a pink sand beach in Bermuda.

Salty to Salty: Briny oysters, anyone? Paired to match with . . . Survey says? Chablis, Sancerre, or Champagne from the Aube region of Champagne because of the salinity found in their ancient Kimmeridgian soils. What do you find in Kimmeridgian soils? Ammonite and Exogyra Virgule Fossils, ancient sea creatures from the Kimmeridgian age in the late Jurassic period. (See Soil and Soul, page 431.) Remember one of my first rules of wine pairing is to pair foods and wine based on what is present in the region. Could anything be more present than the content of the soil where vines are planted? Possibly the salt content in the Atlantic Ocean breezes near the French port city of Nantes, in which case, I nominate Muscadet as the perfect oyster wine.

Creamy to Creamy: One classic pairing is lobster with a high-quality California Chardonnay, as the creaminess of the wine enhances the sweet richness of the lobster.

Bitter to Bitter: White Italian wines often have a bitter flavor component to them. In small amounts, this is not a flaw, but rather a flavor enhancer. Think about the addition of bitters to a mixed drink. That bitterness is an essential component without which the drink would likely taste a little flat. A lovely hint of bitterness works very well with foods with a bitter component, like oven-roasted radicchio or fennel.

Acidity to Acidity: Tomatoes and Chianti, enough said.

And then there are the contrasts

Fat vs. acidity: Fat and acidity are also a delicious match. Acidity cuts through fat and fat tames acidity. One of my favorite examples is Pork Rillettes with Vouvray; the fatty delicious savory meat spread achieves perfect balance with the high acidity of Vouvray's Chenin Blanc. Conversely, Viognier's low acidity is a fitting foil for a summery fruit salad, which is . . . low in fat. See how easy this is?

Tannin and Alcohol vs. Spice: Wines that are high in tannins and alcohol emphasize the spiciness of foods, so care should be taken when pairing foods with high levels of either. *So . . . what does one serve with spicy food?* There are several ways to deal with the question of spice and wine. Since, as noted above, alcohol makes the spiciness of a food more pronounced, high spice levels can be tamed by a wine with reduced alcohol content.

Increase the sugar level. Just as alcohol emphasizes spiciness, sugar mutes it. Aromatic sweet wines like Rieslings are delicious with spicy foods, although you still need to keep in mind the weight of the wine and food. As a general rule, sweeter wines are lower in alcohol, so they have that going for them—which is nice. (And you don't even have to thank the Dalai Lama for it.)

Spice to Spice: Pair spicy food with a spicy wine like a Zinfandel or a Shiraz. This is a PTM comparison where I recommend you proceed with caution. Remember these are wines that tend to be high in alcohol and tannins, and you know what that means. Your food will taste spicier—perfect if that is what you are going for.

Avoid delicate wines with spicy foods. Whether your wine is white or red, a delicate wine will be overshadowed by a dish with heavy spices, so choose wines with vibrant flavors.

Don't Overshadow Your Trophy Wine

This is a personal recommendation and one I doubt you will find in many wine tasting/pairing books. Say you have an old bottle of something really special that you have carefully stored for years. You have decided to open it, possibly for a special occasion, or maybe just because you think it is time.

For argument's sake, let's say this is a bottle of 2002 Clos de Tart. This is a highly collectable Monopole Grand Cru from Morey-St-Denis in France's Burgundy region— expensive, worth every penny and all the care you have put into storing it. Do not pull out all the stops and make an elaborate dish with strong flavors. Your main course should emphasize simple preparation and flavors so that the wine itself can shine. Ideally, the most complex flavors on your table that night should come from that bottle of Clos de Tart. I promise you, when you finally uncork that wine, you are going to want something that enhances the wine, without overshadowing it. My go-to dish of choice in the case of old Burgundy is always roast chicken and in the case of old Bordeaux, standing rib roast. You get the picture!

Cooking with Wine

It is a tried-and-true rule that you should never use a wine to cook with that you wouldn't drink. While it is not always economically feasible to cook with the same wine you are planning on serving, sticking to the same grape variety or wine region is a good idea. As noted above, I recommend splurging on as good a bottle of Burgundy as you can afford when serving Coq au Vin, but I certainly can't afford to cook with a 2009 Roumier Bonnes Mares Grand Cru. So, I use an inexpensive (not that there are many left) Red Burgundy to make the chicken and pour the more expensive wine with dinner. Likewise, if you are making *Brasato in Barolo* (beef braised in Barolo wine), braise your beef in a *relatively* affordable Langhe Nebbiolo and save the bottle of single vineyard 2005 Fratelli Alessandria Barolo Monvigliero to serve with the meal.

First Do No Harm

I know it is a paraphrasing of the Hippocratic oath, but it works for wine, as well. While we aim for Olympian success when we choose a wine to go with food, I'm willing to bet your life does not depend on it. Follow the basic rules above, and you won't err too grievously. As your experience level grows, so will your successes. And that's a good thing! Enjoy!

COOKING WITH THE WINEMAKERS

Winery Visits: What They Cook

Mont Saint=Michel

Rouen

Paris

Tours

Beaune

Lyon

Domaine Weinbach

Nantes

Bordeaux

Marseilles

Corsica

"Tending the Fire in Alsace"
Harvest at Domaine Weinbach
Kaysersberg, France

As I added a log to the blaze in the wood-fired stove in the fall of 2013, it struck me that the path that had taken me away from the wood-fired grill in my kitchen at Buck's Fishing & Camping had brought me more or less full circle to *this* kitchen in a country manse in Alsace. In fact, it was here at Domaine Weinbach that this book really began.

As I stood with Madame Colette Faller in her large, warm kitchen in February 2012, that was the moment that sparked the idea of cooking the harvest with winemakers. It wasn't the first time I had ever been in a kitchen with a winemaker. I had been invited to eat with them and their families many times when visiting their estates—peeking over their shoulders to see what they were cooking, taking notes, or frantically trying to

The kitchen at Domaine Weinbach, Kaysersberg, France

memorize everything so that I could jot it all down as soon as I got back to my room. Likewise, I had hosted many winemakers in my home in Virginia. But that time, in that amazing kitchen, while I listened to her tell about the family cook, Madame Marie, and the meals they shared with their harvest workers at the very table where my camera bag was resting—I wanted to cook in that kitchen at harvest time almost more than I wanted to take my next breath.

Harvest is a busy time. It is also a moving target. Its timing is determined by many factors—most of them weather-related—all with the end objective of perfectly ripe pristine grapes. Since I was cooking for three different wineries on this particular trip, trying to coordinate multiple visits in different regions was challenging. I could try to tell you that the planning was half the fun, but who am I kidding—delicious food, stellar wine, and engaging friends in the charged harvest atmosphere? That was fun on a whole new level—absolutely exhilarating!

Located just outside of Kaysersberg, France, along the Alsatian *Route des Vins*, Domaine Weinbach occupies a special place in the wine world. In an area long known for high quality, Madame Colette and her two famous daughters, Catherine and Laurence, collectively known in Alsatian wine circles as *Les Filles Faller* (the Faller girls), produce world-class wines that are elegant, structured, and true to their region. Established in 1612 by Capuchin monks, the winery is located in the original Clos des Capucins. A label around the neck of the bottles imprinted with the likeness of a Capuchin monk toting a large, traditional wooden cylindrical wine basket pays homage to these origins.

During the French Revolution in the late 1700s, the estate became property of the State. The Faller brothers purchased it in 1898 and eventually bequeathed it to their son and nephew, Théo. Extremely dedicated to quality and improving the standards of Alsatian wine in general (he was instrumental in establishing Alsatian AOC regulations), Théo ran the estate, making improvements and raising the level of his own wines. After his death in 1979, his widow, Colette, took over the estate and elevated its quality even

Madame Colette Faller

further, bringing it to national and international prominence. These improvements continued when Colette's two daughters joined her in the family business, with Catherine in charge of the commercial side and Laurence as the winemaker. Théo Leiber-Faller, Catherine's son, manages the work in the vineyards and represents a third generation actively involved in the Domaine.

Bordered by the Vosges Mountains on the west and the Rhine River on the east, Alsace is the easternmost wine region in France. It is also one of the driest. The Vosges Mountains produce a rain-shadow effect with all of the storm clouds emptying out in the Lorraine region on the western side of the mountain range. Colmar's annual rainfall level is among the lowest in France, and during the summer the warmth of extended sunlit days allows grapes to achieve fuller ripeness levels than in the Loire Valley or northern Burgundy (approximately 275 and 150 miles further south, respectively).

Alsace is divided into two departments, the Haut-Rhin in the south and the Bas-Rhin in the north. The majority of larger producers are located in the Haut-Rhin where wines are generally of better quality. Excellent wines can be found in the Bas-Rhin,

Gewurztraminer Grapes ready for harvest, Clos des Capucins, Domaine Weinbach

although site location is key in attaining adequate levels of ripeness. Vineyards follow a north/south line along the lower slopes of the Vosges Mountains.

Alsace is a region rich in geologic complexity. According to world-renowned wine expert Jancis Robinson (Master of Wine, editor of *The Oxford Companion to Wine*, and author of many extremely important wine books), there are twenty major soil formations in Alsace with vineyards on the higher elevation and steep slopes on the lower sections of the Vosges Mountains made up of thin topsoil with subsoils of gneiss, granite, sandstone, Grès des Vosges (pink sandstone), schist, and volcanic rocks. Lower altitude vineyards on the Rhine-delta bed have thicker topsoil with clay, marl, limestone, and sandstone subsoil.

This varied geological composition results in wide-ranging styles of wines with broader, weightier wines grown on clay/marl vineyards; elegant, finesse-driven wines on limestone and sandstone soils; while oily textured wines with minerally, gunflint, and petrol aromas (especially with Riesling) are more likely found on flint, schist, shale, and slate soils.

Traditional architecture, Riquewihr, France

With almost 38,000 acres of vineyard in 119 villages, Alsace is the only region in France to produce almost all varietally labeled wines. The four Nobel grape varieties are Riesling, Gewurztraminer, Pinot Gris, and Muscat. There are fifty-one individual Grand Cru Appellations in Alsace. With very few exceptions, all Grand Crus are made entirely from one of these four varieties. Almost 90 percent of the wines produced in Alsace are white, with Riesling being both the most planted grape and the last to ripen, and it is in Alsace where Pinot Gris arguably achieves its greatest level of quality. Other white grapes include Pinot Blanc, Auxerrois (a close relative to Pinot Blanc), Chasselas, and Sylanver. Pinot Noir produces delicate light red to rosé-colored wines. Crémant d'Alsace can be either white or rosé and is made predominantly from Pinot Blanc; however, Pinot Noir, Riesling, Pinot Gris, Auxerrois, and Chardonnay are also allowed. Two late harvest sweet wines are produced: *Vendanges Tardives* (VT), which means late harvest, and *Sélection de Grains Nobles* (SGN), which means the selected grapes (*grains*) are infected with the noble rot *botrytis cinerea*. (See Wine Terms, page 472.)

Many of the Weinbach vineyards have been farmed organically for years, and Laurence began converting the property to biodynamics in 1998 (twenty of seventy-four acres). As of the 2005 vintage, all of the Domaine's vineyards have been farmed biodynamically, and in 2010 they received official certification from Ecocert, the French Organic Certification Body. According to Laurence, these biodynamic practices result in extremely healthy soil and vines and combine with drastically low yields to produce high "quality, terroir-driven, and aromatically complex grapes and wines."

In addition to the twelve-acre Clos des Capucins, the Domaine is comprised of four Grand Cru vineyards—Schlossberg, Furstentum, Mambourg, and Marckrain—and one *lieu-dit* (single vineyard parcel), Altenbourg. Soil types vary from vineyard to vineyard, with sandy silt granite in the Clos des Capucins; granitic sandstone and sandy acidic siliceous sand in Grand Cru Schlossberg; marl, limestone, and sandstone with pebbles in Grand Cru Furstentum; clay and marl with magnesium in Grand Cru Mambourg; limestone, marl, and granitic magnesium-enriched sand in Grand Cru Marckrain; and limestone, clay, and sand in the lieu-dit Altenbourg.

Domaine Weinbach produces a range of wines from Riesling, Pinot Gris, Gewurztraminer, Muscat, Pinot Noir, Sylvaner, and Pinot Blanc grapes. Most of the wines from Domaine Weinbach are dry; however, a few Vendanges Tardives, SGN, and extremely rare Quintessences de Grains Nobles wines are produced from select vineyards when ripeness levels warrant it. They also produce the following wines that are not dry but not considered as Vendanges Tardives, either: Riesling Grand Cru Schlossberg Cuvée

Sainte Catherine L'Inédit, Pinot Gris Altenbourg, and many of the Gewurztraminers (Cuvée Laurence Altenbourg, Grand Cru Furstentum, and Grand Cru Mambourg).

Alsace is famous for its picturesque towns with their colorful half-timbered houses decorated with window boxes overflowing with multihued flowers and its delicious and at times rustic cuisine.

I remember playing tennis a few years back with a woman who had just returned from a trip to Alsace. When I inquired about her trip, she could not stop talking about how terrible the food was. I was stunned! Hello? Choucroute? A gazillion Michelin-starred restaurants? I managed to close my dropped jaw and ask her what she meant. "Pig, Pig, Pig," she replied. *Now, hold on there, Betty (not her real name), what on earth is wrong with that?* I didn't actually say that, but my inner monologue screamed it. I knew she wasn't vegetarian, nor did she avoid pork for religious reasons (in which case my inner monologue would need to just shut up), and she wasn't some skinny, workout-crazy chick either, she was an average, middle-aged woman. Okay, I'm not going to try to tell you that the traditional cuisine of Alsace is low-calorie, but the word "terrible" should not even be in the conversation. In fact, the following list of regional specialties reads like a who's who (or a what's what) of deliciousness.

Foods of Alsace

Tarte Flambée: A thin tart topped with heavy cream or crème fraîche, onions, and bacon lardons, then baked or broiled until the cream is golden brown.

Choucroute: Mild sauerkraut, flavored with goose or duck fat, juniper berries, cumin, onions, black pepper, and white wine. *Chou Rouge with Apples* is a version of this made with red cabbage, red vinegar, and apples. It can also include chestnuts.

Choucroute Garnie: Sauerkraut "garnished" with boiled potatoes and various meats: smoked pork belly, sausages (Frankfurt, Montbéliard, Strasbourg), smoked pork chops, and pig knuckles, to name a few (a less common version features fish).

Baeckheoffe: A large, deep ceramic casserole layered with marinated meats (beef, lamb, and pork), white potatoes, leeks, and white wine, its lid sealed tight with luting pastry (a closure made from a strip of pastry dough). Baeckheoffe was traditionally assembled and taken to the village baker on Monday morning to cook all day in the dying embers of his bread oven while the local women were doing laundry . . . by hand, ugh.

Coq au Riesling: Chicken, onions, and sliced white mushrooms braised in Riesling and finished with heavy cream and served over egg noodles. Think Coq au Vin, but with Riesling . . . and cream. *Poisson au Riesling,* a fish version of this same dish often made with *sandre* (a local river fish), is also found.

Foie Gras: Alsace has some of the best foie gras around. A luxury item on charcuterie plates (often served with Gewurztraminer or Riesling jelly), it can also be found stuffed under poultry skin for a decadent holiday dinner.

Wild Game: Wild game is quite popular in Alsace, particularly pheasant, duck, and partridge, as well as deer and wild boar.

Fleishnacka: A cooked beef, egg, and onion mixture rolled jellyroll style in egg dough. When crosscut horizontally, it resembles a snail shape.

Carpe Frite: Alsace's version of fish and chips uses carp instead of cod.

Cervela: Savory pork sausages similar in texture to a frankfurter or bologna. This is one of the main components of the Winemaker's Salad, which, since it consists of eggs, mayonnaise, and thinly sliced Cervela, has very little to do with our idea of a salad.

Knack: A frankfurter traditionally from Strasbourg, the capital of Alsace.

Presskopf and Tête de Veau: Head cheese made from the meat from the head of pork or veal suspended in savory aspic.

Escargots Alsaciens: Snails cooked with parsley, garlic, and onions in a white wine sauce.

Bouchées à la Reine: Individual puff pastry cups with a creamy stew inside. The stew is most frequently made with chicken, mushrooms, leeks, and carrots but can also be made from veal.

White Asparagus: Poached white asparagus, usually eaten with ham and mayonnaise. It appears on every Alsatian restaurant menu in the spring when it is in season.

Spaetzle: Traditional egg pasta.

Bretzel: Soft pretzels. Some lore says they originated in Alsace. I'm not getting involved in that!

Munster: Forget every pre-conceived notion you have about Munster. It is *not* those orange-rimmed cheese slices you find prepackaged in the deli section of your local convenience store. Real Alsatian Munster is a wonder—something to be savored for the truly delicious and somewhat stinky cheese that it is. Serve it with toasted cumin seeds and a late harvest Gewurztraminer and prepare to be wowed.

Kugelhopf: Part cake, part bread, this lightly sweet cake with a dense eggy texture is traditionally made in a special Kugelhopf mold (somewhat similar to a Bundt mold) and can be filled with dried fruits (raisins and currants) and sometimes nuts. It is almost always finished with a dusting of powdered sugar—delicious as a coffee cake.

Pain d'Epices: A dense spice cake made from honey, rye flour, and spices (traditionally aniseed, cinnamon, nutmeg, and clove). It contains no sugar, butter, oil, or eggs.

Tarte au Fruit: A fruit tart made with seasonal fruits. The two most well known are apples and cream, and questche, named after the long blue plums that are in season for a short time in September.

Tarte au Fromage Blanc: A lightly sweet cheesecake made with *fromage blanc* (soft white cheese) and sprinkled with powdered sugar.

Although many of these Alsatian dishes are heavy, the Alsatian people generally are not overweight. Marie Spendler, the Fallers' chef, pointed out that these are special occasion foods, many of which are more suited for winter, and that the Faller ladies augment them with vegetable soups, lots of salad, and seasonal vegetables. In fact, the lunches that I helped cook included vegetable soup for the first course and vegetable side dishes cooked without any added fat. The ladies were health-conscious in their habits, although Théo appeared to be less so. Slender yet muscular, he breezed in from the vineyards and hurriedly helped himself to mammoth portions of *Saucisson Sec* (a French dry sausage

Pot Roast and Pig's Feet, Domaine Weinbach, Kaysersberg

similar to salami), soup, pot roast, pig's feet, carrots, Munster, and a slice of fruit tart before hustling back out to the fields—a perfect example of the metabolism of youth and hard physical labor.

Over the lunch of pot roast and pig's feet that Marie and I had prepared, the Faller ladies explained their Domaine, its wines, and some regional food customs, including many of the foods from the list above, detailing food and wine pairings (in this case a delicate Weinbach Pinot Noir that was superb with the pot roast and pig's feet, its bright cherry fruit and high acidity a perfect foil for the rich unctuousness of the dish) and recommending local restaurants. The welcome was warm, and they seemed amazingly calm given that the harvest—delayed due to a lengthy period of rain—was starting that very afternoon. I made arrangements to come back the next morning to help Marie prepare Choucroute Garnie for the Faller family, their harvest workers, and a group of visiting

Madame Colette starting the fire

clients. On the menu the day after that? Chicken and Riesling for the same crew *and* a group of journalists. Madame Colette, Catherine, and Laurence conferred with Marie about menu choices before moving on to other duties. I took my leave, relishing how delicious the pot roast and pig's feet had been with the Pinot Noir and excited about the next day's cooking.

When I arrived the next morning, I found Madame Colette—perfectly dressed in chic white pants and a blue silk jacket with a matching blue stone necklace—pruning her roses in front of the house. I followed her into the kitchen, where Marie and Madame Andrée, the Fallers' other cook, were unloading the groceries. Colette bustled around, starting the fire in the massive white enamel wood-burning stove—a showpiece with reservoirs for heating water and a French cooktop (a round flat iron cooking surface)—and instructing me on how to maintain the fire. The simple action of stoking the wood fire, so reminiscent of the rhythm of working the wood grill at Buck's, was incredibly relaxing—a familiar pattern 4,000 miles from home.

While we prepared Choucroute Garnie, Vegetable Soup, and a classic Alsatian Apple Tart, Marie continued the discussion of food traditions at Domaine Weinbach, giving me oral recipes of other family favorites like Breaded Pork Chops with Red Cabbage, Onions, and Apples and the Coq au Riesling slated for the next day's lunch.

As lunchtime neared, Madame Colette reappeared and sent me to fetch the wire basket of wines she had set outside to chill in the crisp autumn air.

Luncheon wines. Domaine Weinbach

The cooks at Domaine Weinbach, Marie Spendler and Madame Andrée, setting the table.

We hurriedly finished setting the table with lovely traditional Alsatian plates in preparation for the guests' and harvesters' arrival.

Once everything was finished, the ladies insisted that I stop working and enjoy the dishes Marie, Madame Andrée, and I had cooked and the wines carefully selected to accompany each course beginning with the 2011 Altenbourg Pinot Gris with the Vegetable Soup and continuing with the 2011 Pinot Gris Cuvée Sainte Catherine with the Choucroute Garnie. We finished up with a 2009 Pinot Gris Altenbourg Trie Spéciale Vendanges Tardives. Its sweet acidity was just lovely with the Alsatian Apple Tart, but it was the next-to-last pairing of 2008 Gewurztraminer Grand Cru Mambourg Vendanges Tardives with aged Munster that completely blew me away. I'm loath to admit I am generally not a huge fan of Gewurztraminer, but that combination taught me the error of my ways. The spicy/sweet florality of the wine was fabulous with the savory unctuousness of the cheese and its accompanying toasted cumin. What a revelation!

During the course of the meal, all three Faller ladies took turns sitting down and chatting with me—another example of the warmth of their hospitality. Regretfully, I had to leave immediately after lunch. The extensive rains that had so troubled France in 2013 meant that the first part of my stay in Alsace had been rainy and harvest had been delayed. Consequently, I had been able to spend only three days at Domaine Weinbach. (My first three days in Alsace had been spent sightseeing in the lovely towns and tasting with other winemakers.) Sadly, I had a plane to catch in Paris the next day and would have to miss the Coq au Riesling.

As I was leaving, Catherine asked if I had room for a few "little" bottles of wine—which turned out to be six delicious full-size bottles. Madame Colette hugged me, and Laurence, who had spent so much time discussing her wines and her vision for the Domaine, pressed a hand-drawn map into my hand, illustrating the way to the car rental agency where I was to return my trusty Fiat Panda. As I drove away, I marveled. From the first contact I had with Catherine in 2011 to tasting with Madame Colette at the winery in February 2012 and then to correspondence with Laurence to set up the cooking adventure and the visit itself in the fall of 2013, the Faller ladies of Domaine Weinbach had been wonderful—a group of complex, extremely intelligent, and dedicated women who welcomed me graciously and shared their world with me. Oh, and by the way, Laurence's directions were perfect.

Sadly, the year following my visit was a difficult one at Domaine Weinbach. In May 2014, Laurence passed away after a sudden heart attack at the age of forty-seven. Her mother, Colette, died in February the next year at the age of eighty-five. Their deaths were felt deeply throughout the wine world and, very particularly, in Alsace and by their own family. I met up with Catherine at Vinexpo in Bordeaux in June 2015. She was noticeably quieter, but she assured me that she and Théo continue the family business despite the palpable absence of her mother and sister.

The Winemaker Recommends: Catherine's favorite pairing is foie gras and Gewurztraminer. She also recommends it with Traditional Thanksgiving dinner.

Alsatian Leek, Carrot, and Semolina Soup

Yield: Eight 8-ounce servings │ Ease of Preparation: Moderate │ Ease of Sourcing: Simple
Wine Pairing: Alsatian Pinot Gris or a crisp unoaked white wine

This simple soup makes an easy first course. The ladies at Domaine Weinbach told me they often start a meal with a vegetable soup to counterbalance the richness of their local cuisine.

INGREDIENTS

½ lb. leeks (the tender white and pale
    green parts)

½ lb. carrots

2 qt. water

2 Knorr chicken bouillon cubes
    (see note below)

⅓ cup fine semolina flour

¼ cup heavy cream

Kosher salt

Black pepper, fresh ground

WHAT YOU'LL NEED

Food processor with metal blade
4-quart saucepan

TIMING

Prep Time: 15 minutes
Cook Time: 20 minutes

PROCESS

Slice leeks in half lengthwise. Leeks often can have hidden grit between the layers. To clean, slice the leeks in ½ inch slices and place in a plastic container three times deeper than the volume of the leeks. Fill the container with cool water and swirl the leeks around with your hands to loosen the grit. Let the grit settle. Then, using your hands as a scoop, lift the leeks out without disturbing the grit at the bottom of the container.

Peel the carrots and place the carrots and the cleaned leeks in a food processor with a metal blade. Process the leeks and carrots until they are very finely diced. Marie Spendler at Domaine Weinbach uses a food processor to mince the leeks and carrots. You may choose to mince it by hand, but the key is to get the vegetables very small, approximately twice the size of a cooked grain of rice.

Bring 2 quarts of water to a boil in the saucepan. Add the leeks, carrots, and the bouillon cubes and bring back to a boil before reducing to a simmer. Continue to simmer until the vegetables are just barely al dente. Do not overcook the vegetables—you do not want them to be mushy. You want to be able to feel the texture of the vegetables when you eat them.

Whisk the semolina into the simmering soup. Continue to whisk until the soup thickens slightly. If it becomes too thick, add a small amount of water to adjust the consistency. Right before serving, stir in the heavy cream and heat through without boiling it. Taste the soup for seasoning levels. Add salt as needed.

Serve hot, garnished with a quick grind of black pepper.

Note

Marie used Knorr bouillon cubes. If you prefer not to use bouillon cubes, substitute chicken stock, either store-bought or homemade. You will need to adjust the salt level depending on the type of stock you use.

Beef Roast with Pig's Feet

Yield: Serves 8 (with leftovers) | Ease of Preparation: Moderate | Ease of Sourcing: Difficult
Wine Pairing: Alsatian Pinot Noir or young Red Burgundy

I ate this for the first time at Domaine Weinbach with the Faller family and their wonderful cook, Marie Spendler. It was early October, and they were pausing for a quick lunch before starting the harvest that afternoon. The secret to this simple recipe is time. Take the time to brown the meat well and then cook it until tender. It really cannot be rushed, as both the beef roast and the pig's feet need time to achieve the desired tenderness. The resulting dish is rich with sticky meat juices—gelatinous and shiny from the pig's feet. Feel free to succumb to the urge to lick your fingers.

INGREDIENTS

¼ cup canola oil

Kosher salt

3 lb. beef blade roast (preferably organic or natural)

4 pig's feet (cut in half lengthwise)

2 large onions

3 cloves garlic

3 cups white wine

Bouquet Garni (leek, 4 stalks fresh parsley, 8 stems fresh thyme, and 1 stalk fresh rosemary) tied together with cook's twine

1 Knorr beef bouillon cube (see note #2 below)

2 bay leaves

Fresh ground black pepper

Water

WHAT YOU'LL NEED	TIMING
Large heavy-duty Dutch oven with lid (just large enough to hold the roast and the pig's feet)	Prep Time: 15 minutes
Food processor with a small bowl	Cook Time: Minimum of 2½ hours

PROCESS

Heat oil in the Dutch oven. Rub the roast and feet with kosher salt and add them to the Dutch oven. Brown well on all sides. Take the time to really get everything really brown. This will increase the flavor of the dish.

While the meat is browning, finely mince the onions and garlic in the food processor. Since the onions will be cooking for two or more hours, size is more important than the uniformity of the cut.

When the meat is well browned, remove and cook the onion, garlic, and a good pinch of kosher salt in the pan juices over medium heat until translucent and lightly golden, stirring frequently to keep from burning and to loosen the little pieces of meat stuck to the pan. The onions and garlic should be soft, not crunchy.

Deglaze the pan with the white wine and add the bouquet garni. Return the roast and feet to the dish and add enough water to cover halfway up the roast. Add the bouillon cube, bay leaves, and a couple grinds of black pepper. Bring to a boil, and then reduce heat to medium low, cover, and simmer for at least two hours, turning the meat periodically and adding water as needed to maintain the level until the meat is fork tender.

When the meat is very tender, remove the lid and cook about 15 minutes more on medium heat to reduce the pan juices, turning periodically. The surface of both the roast and the pig's feet should be a little sticky and glazed with the cooking juices. Taste the juices to see if you need to add salt or pepper.

To serve, slice the roast against the grain and serve a few slices of beef and one pig's foot per person with a spoonful of pan juices on top. At Domaine Weinbach, Marie served it with cooked carrots. It is also delicious with boiled, peeled baby potatoes.

Notes

#1. Pig's feet were not a usual item on the table when I was growing up, but I love them now. I buy mine from my friend Beau Ramsburg at Rettland Farm near Gettysburg, Pennsylvania. If you aren't lucky enough to have a pig farmer in your life, ask your local butcher or at an Asian grocery store. They can also be special ordered online from Heritage Foods USA. If you can't find them or don't want a foot in your mouth, substitute a fresh ham hock.

#2. If you prefer not to use bouillon cubes, substitute beef stock. You will need to adjust the salt level depending on the type of stock you use.

Choucroute Garnie

Yield: Serves 6 | Ease of Preparation: Moderate | Ease of Sourcing: Moderately difficult
Wine Pairing: Weinbach Pinot Gris Cuvée Sainte Catherine, dry Alsatian Riesling or Pinot Gris

Alsace's most famous dish, Choucroute Garnie has many variations. This is the version that we made at Domaine Weinbach. They served it with slab bacon and Montbéliard sausages, a smoked pork sausage from nearby Franche-Comté. Marie Spendler, the Faller's cook, explained that they often add uncured pork belly. The silkiness of the meltingly tender slab bacon, the savory tartness of the sauerkraut, and the juicy crunch when you bite through the casing of the smoked pork sausage are fantastic—it's no wonder this dish is such a classic. Different versions also include smoked pork chops, frankfurters, bratwurst, ham hocks, and braised pig's feet. At Domaine Weinbach, they serve it with boiled baby potatoes, and in the neighboring department of Lorraine they serve it with boiled turnips, as well. Less traditional choucroutes may be found with duck confit, and a fish version was popularized in the 1970s in response to the heaviness of the traditional pork "garnish."

INGREDIENTS

2 large yellow onions

⅓ cup duck fat

2 Tbsp. cumin seeds

2 Tbsp. coriander seeds (cracked)

2 tsp. juniper berries

2 qt. sauerkraut, preferably freshly
    fermented

4 bay leaves

Kosher salt

Black pepper, coarsely cracked

1 bottle unoaked white wine (preferably
    Alsatian Pinot Blanc or Pinot Gris)

3 pieces slab bacon cut lengthwise
    in ¾-inch slices (approximately
    1½ lbs.)

6 Montbéliard or other smoked pork
    sausage links

18 small peeled potatoes

Dijon mustard as a condiment

Optional: Choice of one or two of the
    following: bratwurst, smoked pork
    chop, smoked ham hock, frankfurter
    in casing, braised pig's foot, uncured
    pork belly

WHAT YOU'LL NEED

Large heavy-duty Dutch oven

1 stockpot (12 qt. for simmering the
    bacon and sausage)

1 large saucepan (8 qt. for cooking the
    potatoes)

A serving platter large enough to hold the
    sauerkraut, the meats, and the boiled
    potatoes.

TIMING

Prep Time: 20 minutes

Cook Time: 1½ hours

PROCESS

To begin, finely chop the onions. Marie used the food processor, but you may chop them by hand if you wish. Melt the duck fat in the Dutch oven. Add the cumin, coriander, and juniper berries to the fat and cook for a minute to release the flavors of the spices. Add the onions and sauté until translucent. In the meantime, rinse the sauerkraut and drain very well, pressing out the excess moisture. This removes the aggressive vinegar flavor.

Add the sauerkraut to the onion mixture and fluff with a fork to mix well. Add the bay leaves, one teaspoon salt, cracked black pepper, two cups of white wine, and a cup of water. Cover and simmer, stirring periodically, adding additional water and white wine as the liquid quantity reduces.

Heat water in the large stockpot until simmering. Add the slab bacon to the water and simmer over low heat for 30 minutes. In the last 10 minutes add the smoked pork sausage and continue to simmer.

After the meat has been cooking for 15 minutes, place peeled potatoes in cold salted water, bring it to a boil, and cook until fork tender, between 15–20 minutes. (For the potatoes to cook evenly, it is important to start the potatoes in cold salted water and then bring them to a boil.) Once they are tender, strain and return them to their pan. Cover them and keep them warm.

After 45 minutes, taste the sauerkraut mixture. It should be somewhat acidic, but not nearly as acidic as it was before it was rinsed. The flavor should be a complex combination of wine, spices, and fermented cabbage. If it isn't acidic enough for your tastes, add some more wine and reduce again. Check the salt level and adjust if necessary.

In the last 5 minutes, add the drained meats to the sauerkraut mixture and fold gently to coat the meats, being careful not to break them apart.

Once everything is heated through and you are satisfied with the seasoning, mound the sauerkraut on a large serving platter, arrange the meats and boiled potatoes on the sauerkraut, and serve family style with Dijon mustard as an accompaniment.

Notes

#1. I'm quite partial to acidity. Taste the sauerkraut when you open it. If you find it to be on the mild side, you may want to drain off the excess liquid but not rinse it.

#2. Optional garnishes.

If you are adding these optional garnishes, you may want to cut back on the amount of slab bacon and the number of Montbéliard sausages.

Pork belly: Add to the hot water with the slab bacon.

Braised pig's feet: Braise in small casserole dish with duck fat, minced onions, salt, white wine, and water for 2 hours until fork tender.

Frankfurters and Bratwurst: Add to the water with the slab bacon and pork sausage in the final 5 minutes.

Smoked pork chop: Add to the sauerkraut mixture 10 minutes before serving to heat through.

#3. Montbéliard sausages are a coarsely ground smoked pork sausage from the Franche-Comté region of France. I have not found a good source in the United States. I have had good success substituting Stuttgarten Knackwurst or the slightly more peppery Smoked Bratwurst from the German Gourmet Deli in Falls Church, Virginia. Their website is www.germangourmet.com. They have an online store and are a good source for German/Alsatian ingredients. If you cannot find a vendor in your neighborhood, you can source the Stuttgarten Knackwurst, Smoked Bratwurst, and smoked pork chops through them. As a last resort, you could substitute a high-quality kielbasa for the Montbéliard, although I strongly urge you to make the extra effort to find the Montbéliard, Stuttgarten Knackwurst, or Smoked Bratwurst . . . because they are delicious!

Coq au Riesling
Chicken in Riesling

Yield: 4 Portions | Ease of Preparation: Moderate | Ease of Sourcing: Moderate
Wine Pairing: Dry or off-dry Alsatian Riesling

This dish is Alsace's version of Coq au Vin, except they use Riesling and add cream. It is rich and lush and, other than the wine, surprisingly affordable. Marie Spendler, the Faller's cook, explained to me that when feeding a big group—like a harvest crew—affordability is definitely a factor. Taste it. I think you'll be amazed that affordability can taste this luxurious.

INGREDIENTS

For the Chicken:

4 chicken leg quarters or 4 each
    chicken thighs and legs
2 Tbsp. canola oil
¾ cup finely minced onions
2 cups (8 oz.) small white button
    mushrooms sliced ¼-inch thick
2 bay leaves
3 cups dry Alsatian Riesling
⅛ cup heavy cream
1 tsp. cornstarch
Salt
Finely ground black pepper
Finely ground white pepper

For the Noodles:

8 oz. dried spaetzle or thin egg noodles
2 Tbsp. unsalted butter
1 Tbsp. finely minced flat leaf parsley

WHAT YOU'LL NEED

Skillet or frying pan large enough to
    hold four leg quarters
Oven-safe baking dish large enough to
    hold four leg quarters
Wooden spoon or firm plastic or metal
    spatula
Large pot to cook the noodles
Strainer
Instant read meat thermometer
    (optional)

TIMING

Prep Time: 15 minutes
Cook Time: 1 hour

PROCESS

Special Instructions:

This dish has 2 components, the chicken and sauce, and the noodles. You will need to start the water to cook the noodles about halfway through the chicken cooking process.

Preheat the oven to 180° F.

For the Chicken:

Rinse chicken leg quarters and pat them dry. Season all sides of the chicken with salt and black pepper. Heat the skillet over medium-high heat and add enough canola oil to generously film the bottom of the pan.

When the pan is hot, place the chicken pieces in the pan skin side down. If you do not have a skillet large enough to cook all four pieces in one pan, you may need to use two skillets or work in batches. However, since you will be making the sauce in the same pan, one larger skillet is preferable. Brown the chicken well on the skin side before turning it to brown on the other side. (If it sticks when you try to turn it, leave it a little longer on that side. It will release easily when it is ready to turn.) Take the time to brown the chicken to a lovely dark-gold color. This step is important, as it will increase both the flavor and the appearance of the finished dish. When the chicken is browned, but not cooked all the way through, remove it to a baking dish and pour out all but 2 or 3 tablespoons of grease from the bottom of the skillet. You want to make sure there is enough fat to cook the onions and mushrooms, without making the final dish too greasy. (Make sure you are careful to wipe any grease drips from the side of the skillet to prevent a flare-up when you return the pan to the heat.)

Add the minced onions and a dash of salt to the still hot skillet and use a wooden spoon or firm spatula to scrape the pan to loosen all of the yummy brown bits stuck to the bottom of the pan. Because you have salted the onions, they will release a small amount of moisture and help to deglaze (or clean) the pan. Once the onions have begun to soften, add the mushrooms and sauté them until they begin to soften. Do not add salt to the mushrooms, as that will cause them to exude too much liquid and will flood the pan. You are trying to sauté the mushrooms, not boil them. Do not brown either the onions or mushrooms to a caramelized state. They should be partially cooked, not brown and crispy.

Begin the noodle preparation (see instructions below).

Return the chicken to the pan, stirring it so that it mixes with the onions and mushrooms and add the bay leaves and enough white wine to come half way up the sides of the chicken. Scrape the pan to make sure nothing is stuck to the bottom, cover the pan, reduce the heat to medium-low, and simmer for 15 minutes, stirring periodically. If the liquid level gets too low, add the remaining wine or a small amount of water to keep the mixture from cooking dry. Cook the chicken until it is firm but not hard when you press it with your finger or until it has reached an inner temperature of 160° on a meat thermometer, approximately 15–20 minutes. Remove the chicken to the oven-safe dish and place it in the preheated oven to keep warm.

Raise the temperature on the onion-mushroom-wine mixture and reduce the liquid slightly to concentrate the flavors. (This should only take a couple of minutes.)

While you are reducing the cooking liquid, mix the heavy cream and 1 teaspoon of corn starch together.

When the liquid contents of the pan have reduced to about 1 cup, taste the pan sauce for seasoning and add salt and white pepper to taste.

Lower the heat to medium-low and whisk in the cream and starch and stir for a moment until it thickens. Remove the chicken from the warming oven and put it back in the pan. Add any juices from the baking dish to the pan, as well. Gently turn the chicken pieces to coat them with the sauce, cover the pan, and remove it from the heat.

For the Noodles:

Bring a large pot of salted water to a boil.

Following the instructions on the package, cook the spaetzle or egg noodles until they are al dente. Strain the excess liquid and return it to the cooking pot off heat along with 2 table-spooons unsalted butter. Cover and reserve.

When the chicken has finished cooking, place the pot with the warm spaetzle over low heat and stir to make sure all of the butter has melted and the noodles are warm. Taste for seasoning and add salt and white pepper as needed. At the last minute, stir in the finely minced parsley.

This dish looks great either individually plated or family style. Serve with a bed of spaetzle and arrange the chicken on top of it. Spoon a little of the mushroom pan sauce on the chicken and spaetzle and pass the remaining sauce at the table.

Notes

#1. Although the food sourcing for this recipe is easy, I urge you to take the time to find a good source of local chicken from a good purveyor. It doesn't need to be organic. All-natural, kosher, or Amish chickens are also great. Please avoid factory-raised chickens if possible. Happy chickens are delicious chickens!

#2. If you cannot find dry spaetzle (or even better, fresh spaetzle), buy dry, thin egg noodles from the grocery store. You can use standard egg noodles, but I find the thinner ones work better with this dish.

#3. No Alsatian Riesling or off-dry German Riesling at your store? Feel free to use a Pinot Gris, Pinot Grigio, Albariño, or unoaked Chardonnay with this dish. Riesling is delicious and lends a lovely complexity to the dish, but the above wines will be fine substitutes.

Breaded Pork Chops
with Red Cabbage and Apples

Yield: Serves 6 | Ease of Preparation: Moderate | Ease of Sourcing: Simple
Wine Pairing: Alsatian Pinot Noir or young Red Burgundy

Marie Spendler at Domaine Weinbach described this recipe to me while we were cooking lunch one day. It is simple, yet delicious. The golden brown pork chop against the colorful red cabbage is just plain lovely to look at and even better to eat.

INGREDIENTS

For the Cabbage and Apples:

⅓ cup canola oil

2 cups finely sliced yellow onions

Kosher salt

1 tsp. cumin seeds

3 cloves

1 qt. finely shredded red cabbage

2 cups thinly sliced unpeeled apples, core removed

1 cup red wine

½ cup red wine vinegar

2 Tbsp. sugar

2 grinds black pepper

¼ cup chicken stock or water

¼ lb. butter

For the Pork Chops:

1 cup all-purpose flour

2 cups toasted dry breadcrumbs

Kosher salt

1 large egg

¾ cup whole milk

½ tsp. medium grind black pepper

6–8 oz. bone-in pork loin chops (approximately ¾ to 1 inch thick)

½ cup canola oil

⅛ cup unsalted butter

WHAT YOU'LL NEED

1 large sauté pan (approximately 12 in.)

1 large skillet (approximately 15 in.)

3 breading trays large enough to hold a pork chop

1 large oven-safe baking tray

instant read meat thermometer (optional)

TIMING

Prep Time: 45 minutes

Cook Time: 30 minutes

PROCESS

For the Cabbage and Apples:

Preheat the oven to 400° F.

Heat ⅓ cup canola oil in the large sauté pan over medium heat. Add the onions, ½ tsp. salt, and cumin seeds, and sauté, being careful not to brown the onions. After the onions are softened, add the cloves and the red cabbage and sauté until coated in oil and slightly softened. Add the apples and stir again. Add the red wine, vinegar, sugar, black pepper, and chicken stock. Cook on medium-low heat for 25 minutes until softened, adding a slight amount of water as needed if the cabbage mixture gets dry. At the last minute before serving, stir in the butter and swirl around until glossy. Adjust for seasoning.

For the Pork Chops:

Place the flour and breadcrumbs in two separate breading containers. Add 1 tsp. of kosher salt to the breadcrumbs and mix well. Crack the egg into the third breading container. Beat the egg until it is homogenous. Add milk to the egg. When you have been cooking the cabbage for 10 minutes, salt and pepper the chops on each side. Dredge the chops in the flour. Pat the chops to remove the excess flour. Dip the chops in the milk and egg, and then dredge both sides in the breadcrumb mixture. Be careful to coat both sides thoroughly with the breadcrumbs.

Heat the oil and butter on medium-high heat in a skillet just large enough to hold the chops without touching. If your skillet is not large enough to hold all the chops at once, work in two batches.

Lower the heat to medium and brown both sides of the pork chops, taking care not to burn the breadcrumbs. This should take about 4 minutes on each side. Being careful not to disturb the crunchy coating, remove the chops from the frying pan, place them in the baking dish, and put them in the preheated oven. Bake them for about 8 minutes until they spring back to the touch. Remove from the oven and let it rest for 5 minutes. Plate the warm cabbage mixture on each plate and arrange the rested pork chop on top.

> **Note**
>
> Pork temperature. In 2011, the USDA released new temperature guidelines for cooking pork that lowered the recommended cooking temperature by 15° F from 160° F to 145° F. If you prefer to use a meat thermometer to check the temperature of your pork, slide the thermometer in the meaty side of the chop. Do not touch the bone with the thermometer, as this will interfere with a correct temperature reading. Remove the chop from the oven when the temperature reads 140° F and let it rest for 5 minutes. The final temperature will rise to 145° F during the rest time. This is sometimes called carryover cooking.

Alsatian Apple Tart

Yield: 1 large tart　|　Ease of Preparation: Moderate　|　Ease of Sourcing: Easy
Wine Pairing: Domaine Weinbach Pinot Gris Altenbourg Vendanges Tardives or an unoaked dessert wine.

For many years, Alsatian Apple Tartlets were winter staples on my menu at Buck's. When Marie at Domaine Weinbach told me that it was to be our dessert at lunch one day, I was curious to see how my recipe compared. It's a classic for a reason: slightly sweet pie dough filled with tart apples lightly coated with a frothy custard that sets up and caramelizes in the oven—excellent. My recipe differs slightly from Marie's in that I add a little finely grated lemon peel to the custard mixture to provide a contrast for the richness of the custard and the sweetness of the apple.

INGREDIENTS

For the Dough:

11 oz. all-purpose flour
Pinch salt
2 Tbsp. sugar
11 Tbsp. chilled unsalted butter
½ cup extremely cold water

For the Filling:

Peel of one lemon, finely grated
Juice of 1 lemon
3 large crisp pie apples
4 egg yolks
3 Tbsp. sugar
Pinch cinnamon
Pinch salt
¾ cup heavy cream, whipped until
   frothy and slightly thickened

WHAT YOU'LL NEED

Food processor with metal blade
Pastry scraper
Microplane or lemon zester
Rolling pin
11-inch fluted tart pan with removable
   bottom
Pastry brush
Medium-sized kitchen bowl

TIMING

Prep Time: 30 minutes
Rest Time: 30 minutes
Cook Time: 50 minutes

PROCESS

For the Dough:

Place the flour, salt, sugar, and the chilled butter in the food processor and process until it is the texture of grains of sand. With the processor still running, pour in the cold water a couple of drops at a time until it forms a loose ball.

Dump the contents of the food processor out on a floured board and bring it together to form a disk. Wrap tightly in plastic wrap and chill for 30 minutes.

After 30 minutes, roll the dough into a circle on a floured surface until it is about ⅛-inch thick and line the tart shell, being careful not to tear the dough. Roll the rolling pin across the top of the tart to trim away the excess dough.

For the Filling:

Preheat the oven to 425° F.

In a medium-sized bowl, add the juice of one lemon to a couple of cups of cold water.

Peel and core the apples. Slice them in quarters and then cut each quarter lengthwise into four slices. Submerge the slices in the cold lemon water and continue peeling and slicing the remaining apples. When finished, drain the apples and pat dry. Arrange the apples in a circular pattern in the tart shell. There is usually an empty space in the center of the first circle. Arrange a second, smaller circle in the center with the apples facing the other direction. Depending on the size of your apples, you may need to use two layers of apples so that the level of the apples is approximately as high as the side of your tart shell.

Cook the apple-filled pie for 15 minutes.

While the pie is cooking, stir the grated lemon peel, egg yolks, sugar, salt, and cinnamon together. Fold in the whipped heavy cream—working it just until the mixture is homogenous. The frothiness of the mixture lends a nice texture to the caramelized surface of the tart. Pour the egg mixture over the apples in the pie. Use the pastry brush to paint the exposed apple pieces with the cream mixture.

Finish baking the pie until the apples are softened and the cream/egg mixture is golden brown and set.

Cool slightly before cutting. Serve with vanilla ice cream, crème fraîche, or on its own.

Notes

#1. Make sure you use pie apples. They are crisp and hold their shape well. Examples of pie apples are: McIntosh, Jonathan, Jonagold, Pippin, Braeburn, and Honeycrisp. These are just a few suggestions. Ask your local farmer what they recommend.

#2. This also makes great individual tarts. If you decide to go that route, you should pre-bake the empty tart shells for 10 minutes. Also, since the tart will be smaller, apple slices are too large. Cube the apples in ¼-inch cubes. You will only need to bake the apple-filled small tarts for 5 or 10 minutes, until the apples are just barely tender, before adding the egg and cream mixture. As with the larger tarts, cook until the custard has set and the top is golden brown.

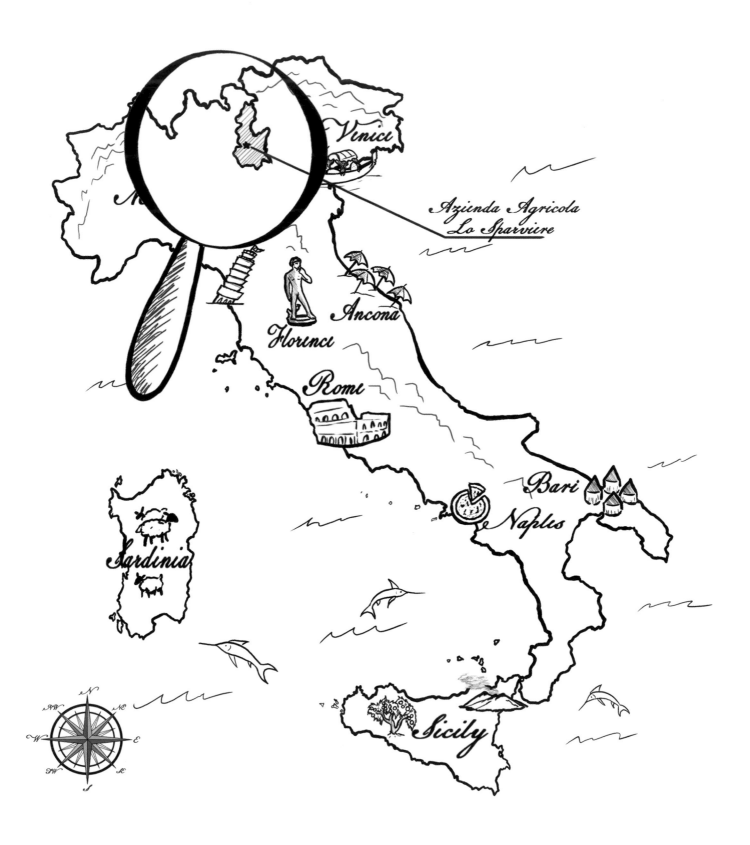

Azienda Agricola
Lo Sparviere

Vinici

Ancona

Florence

Rome

Bari
Naples

Sardinia

Sicily

"The Many Facets of Monique Gussalli Beretta"

A Visit to Lo Sparviere
Monticelli Brusati, Franciacorta, Italy

It was not the first time that I had met Mrs. Monique Poncelet Gussalli Beretta. My husband, Jeff, works for her family, and over the years I have attended company events with him in the United States and in Italy, including a gorgeous summer afternoon spent sipping wine and nibbling hors d'oeuvres amidst the lush greenery on Isola di San Paolo, the family's private island in the center of Lake Iseo. It was, however, the first occasion where she and I had interacted one-on-one for an extended period of time, and I was truly impressed. It wasn't simply that she was charming, because she was. It was her lively intelligence, her kindness, and her dedication that struck me. Owners of a family-owned multinational company specializing in firearms, clothing, accessories, and luxury goods, the Berettas are the world's oldest industrial dynasty, with documentation of a business transaction between Maestro Bartolomeo Beretta and the Arsenal of Venice in 1526. As the matriarch, Mrs. Beretta could have contented herself with her family, charitable work, and social events. Instead, she is very involved in the family's wine business, including at Lo Sparviere, the family winery in Franciacorta, in Northern Italy.

Jeff had mentioned my interest in winemaking families to Mrs. Beretta, and she kindly invited me to have lunch with her at Lo Sparviere, to taste the wines, and to explore her family's food traditions. Mrs. Beretta and her driver, Paolo Rossi, picked me up at my hotel in Sarnico on the northwest side of Lake Iseo for the half-hour car trip to Lo Sparviere, the family winery nestled on the glacier-carved slopes south of Lake Iseo. They are an interesting pair. She is slender and elegant with an engaging smile and an easy laugh. He is tall and lean with a trim mustache and beard—quiet, unobtrusive, yet very alert. Their communication is often unspoken, his devotion to her seemingly boundless. On the way to Lo Sparviere they took me on a tour of the region so I could get a better sense of the area. It was at this point that I discovered that Mrs. Beretta's genteel manners and kind demeanor mask sharp intelligence and unimpeachable logic.

Although I've been to the Beretta Headquarters in Gardone Val Trompia and have stayed in nearby Brescia, somehow I had the mistaken impression that Brescia was closer to Lake Garda than it actually is. (It's kind of amusing because as a general rule I have an excellent sense of direction and have driven by myself around northern Italy

Mrs. Beretta and Paolo Rossi

on multiple occasions.) In reality though, Brescia is almost equidistant between the northern lakes of Garda and Iseo, with the Franciacorta vineyards lying to the west, on the Iseo side of the city. While en route to the winery in Monticelli Brusati, I twice mentioned Lake Garda, on one occasion asking when we would be getting close to it. Mrs. Beretta patted my hand and turned to Paolo and calmly said, "When we get to the winery, we need to get her a map." I almost laughed. She clearly was going to straighten out my confusion in as no-nonsense a fashion as possible.

When we arrived at the winery, Mrs. Beretta's pride was immediately evident. The u-shaped outer courtyard is lovely, with huge vibrant pink hydrangea bushes (hydrangea are a particular weakness of mine), baskets overflowing with red geraniums, and an arbor of vines heavily laden with bunches of grapes. A charming stone water well, antique winery equipment, and a pistachio-colored 1953 Fiat 500G pickup truck rounded out the quaint picture.

View of Lo Sparviere from San Zenone Bell Tower
Photo credit: Agricole Gussalli Beretta

It is a beautiful property with an impressive cellar building that dates to the 16th century. Lo Sparviere owes its name to the hawk that appears on the coat of arms gracing the massive fireplace in the enormous main hall. Adjacent to the main hall, the walls of the comfortable dining room are lined with portraits. Mrs. Beretta drew my attention to a large framed display with a portrait and documents devoted to family ancestor Luigi Gussalli, a pioneer in the aerospace movement and author of three books on space travel. A contemporary of Oberth and Goddard, Luigi's first book, *Can We Attempt a Space Journey to the Moon?*, was written in 1923 and advocated the use of a four-stage rocket that shed its stages until only the final one remained to land on the moon and make the return flight home. His second book, "*Jet Propulsion for Astronautics: Reduction of Fuel Consumption Makes Space Exploration a Reality,* posited the idea of an auxiliary solar engine; and his third book, *Interplanetary Travel Exploiting Solar Radiations: a Fuel-Free Propulsion System is the Key to Interplanetary Travel,* theorized about the use of solar radiation in space travel. It is easy to understand why Mrs. Beretta is so proud of her family's visionary forefather.

The ceilings in the main part of the winery are adorned with ornate wooden beams with decorative painting and carving. A sitting room and a small but modern kitchen finish out the public part of the building, but what really caught my fancy were the private rooms in the adjacent tower.

The slender tower is four stories high with a single room per floor. On the first floor is a cozy family kitchen with a lovely wooden winding staircase leading to the next three floors, first a sitting room, then a bedroom, and finally a study for family patriarch Ugo Gussalli Beretta, Monique's husband. Still in use during part of the year, each room is lovingly decorated with family heirlooms and photos including a very sweet photo of Mr. and Mrs. Beretta on their wedding day. The view from the window in the bedroom overlooks the estate, the vineyards, and the lush rolling hills of Monticelli Brusati.

The most curious detail was in Mr. Beretta's study. Beckoning me forward with a wave of her hand as if sharing a secret, Mrs. Beretta showed me a group of small doors approximately twelve by eight inches that opened to reveal, not a small

cabinet as I had expected, but a bird's nest built into the walls of the building—its nest still occupied—such a charming and unexpected detail!

After the tour of the tower, Mrs. Beretta and I stopped in the kitchen for a lesson in some Beretta family recipes with the family cook, Giulia Pezzali. She was assembling a Pigeon and Penne Pie. It wasn't a pie in the traditional sense of the word, with a thin crust in a shallow and wide pie plate. Rather, a slightly thick cross between bread dough and piecrust carefully lined the sides of a four-inch tall springform pan. Inside the dough were rows of penne pasta coated in a luscious pigeon stew—delicious! Mrs. Pezzali also showed me how to make Fried Sweet Milk, a thick custard allowed to set until firm enough to cut into squares. The squares are then breaded, fried, and dusted with confectioner's sugar.

Wines of Franciacorta

References to Franciacorta date to 1277. The name refers to the *Curtes Francae*—monastic villages founded by Clunaic monks. The commune of Brescia exempted the *Curtes Francae* from paying taxes in exchange for the monks reclaiming and farming local land.

The terrain in Franciacorta is morainic, meaning it was carved out by glaciers, resulting in a soil rich in sand and silt and poor in clay. The undulating hills left by the glaciers, the diverse soil type, and the geographical location—bordered in the north by Lake Iseo and the prealpine hills, and in the south by Mount Orfano on the northern edge of the Po River Valley—provide a moderated continental climate that is warmer in the winter and somewhat cooler in the summer than surrounding regions. (This mitigation of climate—warming in the winter and cooling in the summer caused by large bodies of water—is known as the Lake Effect and is very influential throughout wine growing regions around the world.)

Vegetation in the region is almost Mediterranean, and, in addition to wine, the area surrounding both Lake Iseo and neighboring Lake Garda produces delicious olives and olive oils despite their relatively northern location.

Sparkling Franciacorta DOCG (*Denominazione di Origine Controllata e Garantita)* and still Curtefranca DOC *(Denominazione di Origine Controllata)* and Sebino IGT *(Indicazione Geografica Tipica)* wines are produced in the same geographical area. (See Wine Terms, page 472.)

Sparkling Wines of Franciacorta

There is a relatively short but important history of sparkling wine production in Franciacorta beginning in 1961, when Guido Berlucchi released the first sparkling wine in the region. Since then, the winemakers of the region have modeled their sparkling wine production after Champagne. As my friend Riccardo Ricci Curbastro—a well-respected winemaker in the region and the former President of the Franciacorta Wine Consortium, the Italian Federation of DOCs (FEDERDOC), and the first President of the European Federation of Origin Wines (EFOW)—explained to me, the local Consortium established regulations that were at least as strict as those required in Champagne. Unlike in Champagne, there is no négociant presence (see Burgers, Beer, and Brut Champagne, page 367) in Franciacorta, so all wines are estate bottled. There is also a very strong movement toward ethical and organic winemaking in Franciacorta.

All sparkling wines of Franciacorta are made in the traditional method, meaning they undergo a secondary fermentation in bottle while in contact with the wine yeasts (lees). Because of the heat and favorable weather in the region, wines with low-to-no dosage succeed admirably every year in Franciacorta. (Dosage is the addition of a "dose" of sugar to a finished sparkling wine immediately before the final cork is inserted. This dosage determines the dryness level of the finished wine.)

Nonvintage Franciacorta: Made from Chardonnay, Pinot Nero, and/or Pinot Bianco (maximum 50 percent), Nonvintage wines must spend eighteen months on lees.

Nonvintage Franciacorta Rosé: Made from a minimum of 25 percent Pinot Nero (although 100 percent is allowed) and a maximum of 50 percent Chardonnay or Pinot Bianco, Nonvintage Rosés must spend twenty-four months on lees.

Satèn: These wines are bottled with lower atmosphere (producing less bubbles and a soft "satin" texture). Satèn wines spend twenty-four months on lees. Satèn may be made from Chardonnay or Pinot Bianco (the latter of which may not account for more than 50 percent of the blend).

Millesimato (Vintage Franciacorta): Vintage wines (including Vintage Rosé and Satèn) are produced using the same grapes as the Nonvintage wines and must spend thirty months on lees. At least 85 percent of the wine must be from the vintage noted on the label.

Riserva: Relatively rare, Riserva level wines (including Rosé and Satèn) are produced using the same grapes as the Vintage and Nonvintage counterparts and must spend sixty months on lees.

Curtefranca DOC

Curtefranca DOC is the designation for still wines produced in the same geographic region as Franciacorta sparkling wines.

Curtefranca Bianco DOC: These still white wines are produced from a minimum of 50 percent Chardonnay and a maximum of 50 percent Pinot Nero and Pinot Bianco.

Curtefranca Rosso DOC: Curtefranca Rossos are still red wines that are produced from a blend of the following grapes: Merlot (minimum 25 percent), Cabernet Sauvignon (between 10 percent and 35 percent), Carmenere and/or Cabernet Franc (minimum 20 percent between the latter two).

Sebino IGT

Non-DOC wines from the same geographic region as Franciacorta and Curtefranca, these wines vary greatly in style, with some wines showing friendly easy-drinking qualities, while others are of a more serious bent. White, Red, *Novello* (Young), and *Passito* (Sweet) wines are produced.

Sebino IGT Single Varietal Wines: IGT rules permit single varietal Sebino IGT wines to be produced using the grape name on the label providing the wine contains 85 percent of that grape variety. Permitted varieties under this designation are Chardonnay, Pinot Bianco, Pinot Nero, Cabernet Sauvignon, Cabernet Franc, Merlot, Carmenere, Nebbiolo, and Barbera.

Photo credit: Agricole Gussalli Beretta

Sebino Bianco IGT wines may use all of the white grapes mentioned above for single varietal wines as well as seven others (Friulano, Garganega, Manzoni Bianco, Müller-Thurgau, Pinot Grigio, Riesling, Trebbiano, and Welschriesling), while **Sebino Rosso IGT** wines may use all of the red grapes mentioned above for single varietal wines as well as nine others (Corvina, Croatina, Groppello, Marzemino, Montepulciano, Pinot Nero, Rebo, Sangiovese, and Schiava).

Wines of Lo Sparviere

Lo Sparviere's rather unusual stony clay and limestone soil combines with the winds from Lake Iseo and results in even cooler conditions than much of the region. Costantino Gabardi, brand manager for Agricole Gussalli Beretta (the umbrella company of all Beretta wineries), explained that this enables them to pick their grapes later than the majority of the neighboring wineries while still retaining freshness at a riper maturity level. They produce seven sparkling wines under the Franciacorta DOC with four Nonvintage wines and three *Millesimato* Vintage wines. Other than the Rosé Cuvée Monique, which is 100 percent Pinot Nero, all of the sparkling wines of Lo Sparviere are 100 percent Chardonnay.

Nonvintage Wines

NV Brut Cuvée 7: Recommended as an aperitif, Cuvée 7 is made from 100 percent Chardonnay planted on a slightly sloping southwest-facing vineyard with red soil (limestone, clay, and silt). It is stainless-steel fermented and aged and spends thirty months on the lees.

NV Satèn: Soft and perfect as an aperitif, the Satèn is 100 percent Chardonnay grown on morainic soils in a north-facing vineyard. Per DOC regulations, it is bottled at lower atmosphere than their other wines. It is fermented and aged in a combination of stainless-steel (80 percent) and large wooden barrels (20 percent) before bottling and aging twenty-four months on the lees.

NV Extra Brut: A bit richer and more complex than the previous two wines, the NV Extra Brut works equally well as an aperitif or with lighter dishes. It is grown on south-facing morainic soils. Ten percent of the Cuvée is fermented and aged in two-to-four-year-old

barriques with the other 90 percent in stainless steel. It undergoes thirty-six months lees aging.

NV Franciacorta Rosé Cuvée Monique: Cuvée Monique, a lovely rosé named after Mrs. Beretta, is made from 100 percent Pinot Nero grown on silty clay soils. After a short maceration on the grape skins (eight to twelve hours), the wine is lightly pressed and then fermented in stainless-steel tanks and oak barrels. It spends twenty-four months on the lees.

Millesimato Vintage Wines

Brut Millesimato: All Chardonnay grown in a south-facing vineyard with reddish clay-silt soils. It is fermented for six months in stainless-steel tanks before bottling. Once bottled it spends forty-eight months on the lees.

Extra Brut Millesimato: 100 percent Chardonnay grown in a northeast-facing vineyard with morainic, red clay, and silt soils. The wine is partially fermented and aged in oak barrels and spends sixty months on the fine lees. This wine is intense and rich and can stand up to fuller foods like roasted leg of pork or ripe soft cheeses.

Millesimato Dossaggio Zero Riserva (Zero Dosage): 100 percent Chardonnay grown on east-facing limestone, red clay, and silt soils. The *Dossaggio Zero* is partially fermented and aged in oak barrels and spends seventy-two months in bottle on the lees.

Before lunch, Costantino gave me a tour of the vineyards and the cellar. We returned to the main hall to taste the current vintage of Lo Sparviere wines. As with most wineries in Franciacorta, Lo Sparviere is best known for its sparkling wines, with the 2007, 2008, and 2009 Extra Brut and the 2007 Dossaggio Zero receiving the coveted *Tre Bicchieri* (three glasses award) from *Gambero Rosso* (the premier wine guide in Italy). Lo Sparviere also produces two still wines, Dossello Curtefranca Bianco, from 100 percent Chardonnay; and Il Cacciatore Curtefranca Rosso, a blend of Merlot and Cabernet.

Foods of Franciacorta

As I noted before, the olive oils from Lake Iseo and nearby Lake Garda are delicious. *Olio dei Laghi Lombardi Sebino* (Sebino is another name for Lake Iseo) with its delicate yet fruity flavor profile is produced from Leccino (40 percent) and a combination of Frantoio, Casaliva, Pendoline, and Sbresa olives.

Other important foods and regional dishes include:

Casoncelli alla Bresciana or Bergamasca: What you call this dish depends on whether you live in Brescia or Bergamo. Casoncei (as they are called in the local dialect) are delicious meat-filled pasta. Traditionally sauced quite simply with butter and sage, Casoncelli ranks highly on the list of Jeff's absolute favorite dishes, and with the simplicity of the savory ingredients and the delicacy of the pasta, there is little wonder why. I can usually count on receiving a text photo of Casoncelli whenever he travels to Gardone, just to make me jealous.

Beef with Olive Oil: This dish originates in Rovato in the southern part of Franciacorta. It is a combination of a confit and a braise. Beef shoulder is braised in olive oil from Sebino and a broth flavored with aromatics and anchovies. The broth is then thickened with fine breadcrumbs or corn flour. It is delicious especially when served with polenta or rustic bread to sop up the juices.

Meat

Sausages: Local sausages include: *Luganega,* a fresh pork sausage; *Salami Monte Isola,* a lightly smoked pork sausage from the island of Monte Isola in the center of Lake Iseo; *Salamina Mista,* sausage made from pork, horse, and/or beef—this can be either fresh or aged; and *Soppressata Brescia,* a coarse ground large pork sausage. The granddaddy of them all is the *Ret Denominazione Comunale di Capriolo.* For this, leg meat sourced from pigs raised within thirty kilometers (nineteen miles) of the village of Capriolo is made into coarse ground sausage and put into the bladder of a pig before aging. The resulting sausage is quite large—weighing anywhere from nine to thirty pounds. It is frequently served at celebrations and weddings.

Lardo Flavored with Curtefranca Bianco: Salt-cured pork fat back, this delicacy has a creamy, silky texture. The addition of local white Curtefranca wine compliments its richness.

Horsemeat: Typical of the region, horsemeat is often served braised or as tartar.

Fish

Clusane Baked Tench: Tench is a freshwater fish from Lake Iseo. This recipe from the fishing town of Clusane on the southern shores of Lake Iseo calls for stuffing the fish with a mixture of cheese, breadcrumbs, local olive oil, salt, and parsley before baking it for several hours.

Lake Iseo Dried Sardines: Recognized as a Slow Food Presidium by the Slow Food Foundation, Agone or Shad from Lake Iseo are not sardines at all. Rather, it is their resemblance to sardines—especially when salted and oil-cured—that gives them their name.

Slow Food Presidium

The Slow Food Foundation for Biodiversity recognizes the need to protect our food heritage and biodiversity. It has designated more than 500 products throughout the world as Slow Food Presidia. The Slow Food website states that Presidia "sustain quality production at risk of extinction, protect unique regions and ecosystems, recover traditional processing methods, and safeguard native breeds and local plant varieties." The Presidia involve more than 13,000 small-scale food producers in fifty-six countries and include farmers, fishers, butchers, herders, cheesemakers, bakers, and more. They emphasize recovery of traditional knowledge, respect for the seasons, and animal welfare as well as protection of crafts and safeguarding native breeds of animals, fruits, and vegetables. They also stress saving products that are "good, clean, and fair."

Cheeses

There are also many fine cheeses from the area, the most famous being *Robiola Bresciana*, a soft cow's milk cheese from Brescia. Also of note is the *Fatuli della Val Saviore* (Slow Food Presidium), a very rare small smoked goat cheese, and the *Casolet Nostrano*, another soft cow's milk cheese.

Lunch at Lo Sparviere

After the wine tasting, we sat down in the elegant yet warm dining room at Lo Sparviere to enjoy the fruits of Mrs. Pezzali's labor, beginning with the NV Satèn and *Olive all'Ascolana*, olives stuffed with a ground meat mixture, rolled in breadcrumbs, and fried until crisp. Although *Olive all'Ascolana* are not from Franciacorta (Ascoli Piceno, where the recipe originates, is located far to the south in the region of Le Marche), Mrs. Beretta confided that she serves the olives because she likes them. Seems like a good reason to me. (I have been obsessed

with these olives ever since, making them for special guests and ordering them whenever I see them in a restaurant—which is almost never.)

Our meal continued with the NV Extra Brut and the 2007 Extra Brut with the Pigeon and Penne Pie, and the NV Rosé Cuvée Monique with a savory yet tart Marinated Pheasant in Vinegar Sauce.

For dessert, there was a selection to choose from that included the Fried Sweet Milk, Grandmother Zina's Chocolate Cake (rich and densely chocolaty), Red Wine Tart, and White Wine Donuts.

The food was excellent—the wines a delicious accompaniment—but what struck me was that Mrs. Beretta had invited her whole administrative staff to join us. Costantino Gabardi, who had given me the tour of the vineyards and cellar; Stefano Berger, export manager for Agricole Gussalli Beretta; Silvia Sabotti; and Chiara Pagani of Lo Sparviere were all gathered around the table, enjoying the traditional food and wine. They spoke to Mrs. Beretta with a lovely combination of respect and marked affection—her warmth and infectious laugh putting everyone at ease. Clearly, they were

immensely devoted to her. Mrs. Beretta is Belgian born, and Italian, French, and English mingled seamlessly in the group. All the while, Paolo Rossi, with a quick wardrobe change from his dark-gray driving jacket into a pristine white jacket complete with braided gold epaulets, brass buttons, and white gloves—apparently his responsibilities don't just include driving Mrs. Beretta—brought out plates of food, helped serve us, and poured wine, seeing to Mrs. Beretta's guests, including me, as he periodically gently nudged me, subtly reminding me to take photos of the dishes as each new one was presented. I was having such a good time I almost forgot I needed to take pictures of the food.

After lunch, we took coffee in the salon off the dining room and discussed the Agricole Gussalli Beretta project, which began with Lo Sparviere and has continued to expand (under the guidance of Mrs. Beretta's elder son, Pietro Gussalli Beretta) with the acquisition of three other wineries, Castello di Radda in Chianti, Orlandi Contucci Ponno in Abruzzo, and Forte Masso, a new property in Montforte d'Alba in the prestigious Piemontese Barolo zone. Mrs. Beretta and her staff had made arrangements for Jeff and me to visit Castello di Radda the following week, where we would reconnect with Costantino Gabardi and meet Marina Orlandi Contucci Ponno. Our Tuscan agenda included a tour of the new winery, tasting the wines of Castello di Radda and Orlandi Contucci Ponno (I was very touched that Marina Orlandi Contucci Ponno offered me

Costantino Gabardi and Vickie.

a gift of a vintage cookbook on traditional recipes from Abruzzo), and a lunch with Costantino, Massimo Ferrari of Beretta Holding, and Linda Favilli, our tour guide at Castello di Radda at Antica Trattoria Le Torre in Castellina in Chianti, where the chef prepared a luncheon to showcase the foods of Chianti.

I always bring a little something as a gift when I visit someone, especially someone who has gone to such trouble on my behalf, but I was a bit nervous about choosing a gift for Mrs. Beretta. I didn't want to appear to be currying favor, and yet I didn't want to bring anything paltry, since the plans that had been sent to me in advance were so generous. Jeff told me not to worry, saying he would take care of it because he knew the perfect gift for her. I did choose a gift for her when visiting my friend Jean-François Coquard of Tenuta Mazzolino—a magnum of 2007 Mazzolino Nero Oltrepo Pavese Pinot Nero "Noir"—in the hopes that she would like it. Not only was it a *tre bicchieri* wine like some of her own wines, the label art was designed by

Jeff in Chianti

Jean-Michel Folon, a famous Belgian artist. She was very appreciative, but it was Jeff's gift of three classic Country and Western CDs that made her day. She laughed girlishly and said, "Oh, that Jeff, he knows me so well." Turns out they had listened to Country and Western music together several times before. He really did have the perfect gift for her.

On the way home, Mrs. Beretta had Paolo drive us by her son Pietro's home to introduce me to her daughter-in-law and her new granddaughter. It was yet another side of this complex woman—doting grandmother. After a quick visit, we hopped in the car and sped back to Sarnico, arriving just in time for the massage that she had scheduled for me at the hotel spa. While en route, Mrs. Beretta invited me to use the tower apartment at Lo Sparviere as a base the next time I was in town. She made sure that I had copies of all of the recipes of the food we had eaten and details on the wines we had drunk. The day may have seemed relaxed and unhurried, but it was clear that however charming Mrs. Beretta is, her elegant unflappable demeanor is just one facet of a complex personality that includes an organized, able businesswoman; a loving wife, mother, and grandmother; a country music fan; an outdoorswoman; a dog lover; and an avid ambassador for her company and her region. It is little wonder those who know her hold her in such high esteem.

The Winemaker Recommends: Pigeon and Penne Pie with Lo Sparviere Franciacorta Extra Brut.

Frico

Yield: approximately 32 small fricos | Ease of Preparation: Easy
Ease of Sourcing: Simple if you use Parmigiano Reggiano
Wine Pairing: NV Satèn Franciacorta or Friuli Pinot Grigio

This classic snack from Friuli could not be easier to make. Its simple success relies upon the deliciousness of its main ingredient. Traditionally made from Montasio, a firm cow's milk cheese from Friuli, I use Parmigiano Reggiano in this version. (Even living in a sizeable city, I find it difficult to locate a reliable supply of Montasio.) Mrs. Monique Gussalli Beretta served it at as a whimsical hors d'oeuvre at a garden party on their private island in the middle of Lake Iseo. A circle of cheese was spread over a small skewer prior to baking. Once it cooled, the frico became a frico lollipop.

INGREDIENTS

1 lb. Parmigiano Reggiano or Montasio
   cheese
Fresh cracked black pepper
Optional: Chiffonade of arugula

TIMING

Prep Time: 5 minutes
Cook Time: 4–8 minutes per batch of
   Frico

WHAT YOU'LL NEED

Rotary cheese grater with fine holes
Half sheet tray
Silicone baking mat, half sheet-tray
   sized
Metal, ceramic, or marble tray for cooling
Paper towels
Thin metal spatula

PROCESS

Preheat the oven to 350° F.

Take the Parmigiano Reggiano out of the refrigerator an hour ahead of time (bringing the cheese to room temperature makes it easier to grate). Use the Rotary cheese grater to grate the cheese. One pound of Parmigiano Reggiano should yield eight cups of cheese.

Line the sheet tray with the silicone baking mat. Pile 1½ tablespoons of cheese on the silicone mat in thin round layers about 3½- to 4-inches in diameter. Make sure you spread it out evenly. If you get the wafer too thick, it will be chewy instead of crispy—too thin will make it fragile. Sprinkle a small amount of fresh cracked medium grind black pepper on the cheese.

Place the sheet tray in the preheated oven. Set the timer for 3 minutes but *do not walk away*. Carefully watch the fricos as they change color. After 3 minutes, rotate the cookie sheet and set the timer for 2 more minutes. Again, *do not leave!* You are looking for golden brown, not dark brown. When the frico is bubbling and uniformly golden, remove the tray from the oven. Let the tray sit for a minute or two so the frico will solidify a bit, then carefully slide the spatula under the frico and transfer it to the paper towel-lined cooling plate. Allow it to cool. It will become firm and crispy.

Notes

#1. If you find Montasio, add ½ tsp. of all-purpose flour to the cheese before cooking. This helps to crisp it.

#2. If you do not wish to grate your cheese yourself, make sure you purchase finely shredded cheese, not grated. Grated cheese is too powdery in texture, and the fricos will fall apart.

#3. I sometimes add very thin strips of arugula to the frico before baking for an added visual touch. Arugula adds a little pepperiness, so if you do this, go easy on the cracked pepper. You don't want to overpower the cheese.

#4. If you wish to make frico lollipops, place a short skewer on the silicone sheet and then place the cheese on top and bake following the recipe instructions.

Olive all'Ascolana
Stuffed Olives Ascolana Style

Yield: 60 Olives | Ease of Preparation: Difficult | Ease of Sourcing: Moderate
Wine Pairing: Lo Sparviere Franciacorta or other Franciacorta wine, Orlandi Contucci Ponno Cerasuolo d'Abruzzo "Vermiglio"

Mrs. Monique Beretta served this as an appetizer when I visited her at the Lo Sparviere winery in Franciacorta. A popular appetizer from the Marche region of Italy, Mrs. Beretta confided that she was serving them because she "likes them." Seems like a good reason to me! This is not a recipe to make for a crowd! It is quite time-consuming, and people eat them like popcorn. In Italy, you can buy Olive all'Ascolana prestuffed and already breaded in gourmet stores. Oh Italy . . .

INGREDIENTS

3 10-oz. jars jumbo queen Manzanilla
    olives (pitted)
2 oz. unsalted butter
⅓ cup finely diced carrot
⅓ cup finely diced celery
⅔ cup finely diced onion
1 clove very finely minced garlic
7 oz. ground veal
½ cup unoaked dry white wine (like a
    Pinot Grigio)
2 oz. prosciutto or lardo cut in ¼ inch
    strips
¾ cup chicken, meat, or vegetable
    stock, separated into ½ cup and ¼
    cup
Grated peel of one lemon
Pinch freshly ground nutmeg
4 large eggs
1 Tbsp. minced parsley
3 oz. freshly grated Parmigiano
    Reggiano cheese
Soft inner part of two bread rolls, torn
    in small pieces
Kosher salt
Black pepper, freshly ground
2 cups all-purpose flour
2 cups very fine dry breadcrumbs
Extra-virgin olive oil for frying

WHAT YOU'LL NEED

Large plastic container for soaking the
    olives
12-in. skillet
Food processor with metal blade
    attachment
2 pastry bags with metal tip with a
    ¼-inch round opening
Tall plastic one-quart container (like
    the kind you get at a deli)
Rubber spatula
Two trays large enough to hold
    60 olives in one layer
3 small mixing bowls
Small spider skimmer
Metal skimmer
Electric fryer or high-sided cast iron
    frying pan
Paper towels

TIMING

Olive Soaking Time: At least 4 hours or
    overnight
Prep Time: 2½–3 hours
Frying Time: 30 minutes

PROCESS

For the Olives:

Soak the olives in cold water for 4 hours (or overnight) to remove some of the brininess. Do
not skip this step or the dish will not taste balanced—the olive flavor will overpower the delicate meat filling.

For the Veal:

Melt the butter in the skillet over medium heat. Add the carrots, celery, and onions and sauté
until lightly brown. Add the garlic and cook for 1 minute. Add the veal to the pan and stir to

break up the veal. Cook until nicely browned. Add the white wine, stir, and cook until it evaporates. Stir in the prosciutto or lardo and cook for a minute. Add ½ cup of the stock, lower the heat, and cook covered for 10 minutes or until the veal is softened. Once it is softened, allow it to cool.

For the Stuffing:

Once the veal mixture is cooled, place it in the food processor with the metal blade attachment and process it in pulses until it is the size of a large grain of rice. Add the grated lemon peel, the nutmeg, one egg, the parsley, the grated Parmigiano, the inner parts of two soft rolls, and the remaining ¼ cup of stock, and pulse again a few times until it is mixed together. Do not overprocess. You don't want it to be a homogenous paste. Taste to check for seasoning and add salt and pepper if needed.

Filling the Pastry Bag and Stuffing the Olives:

Drain the olives, shaking vigorously to remove excess water.

There will likely be more stuffing than will fit in one bag, and refilling the bag once it is empty is super messy. You are better off just using two bags. Place the pastry tip into a bag and place the bag into the deli container tip end down. This enables you to fill the pastry bag more easily. Use the rubber spatula to scoop veal mixture into the pastry bag. Try to be as neat as you can. Once it is three-quarters full, twist the top of the bag closed and set it to the side. Repeat with the second bag.

Trim the tip of the pastry bag, twist the top again, and begin piping the veal filling into an olive, pushing firmly to make sure it is filled all the way. Place the olive in the tray and continue piping until all of the olives have been stuffed.

Breading and Frying the Olives:

The three small mixing bowls will serve as your breading station. Normally, I use rectangular flat trays to bread food, but I have found that bowls work better for this recipe. You will be swirling the olives to coat them and the round shape of a bowl works better with the round shape of the olive.

Pour the olive oil in your fryer or frying pan but do not turn it on yet. Breading the olives takes a bit of time. If you are using a tall-sided frying pan, make sure that it is only half full, as the oil will bubble and rise during the frying process, and you do not want it to bubble over.

Place 1 cup all-purpose flour in the first bowl, 3 well-beaten eggs in the second bowl (be sure you beat them until the white of the albumen is completely broken down), and ¾ cup dry breadcrumbs in the third.

Place 5 or 6 stuffed olives in the flour and swirl them around until they are completely coated with the flour. I know the batches seem small, but considering the effort you have put into stuffing the olives, you will want to make sure you do not damage them during the breading process. Use one hand to transfer the flour-covered olives to the egg mixture. (This will be your dry ingredient hand.) Swirl the flour-covered olives in the egg mixture until they are completely coated in egg. Use your other hand (this will be your wet hand) or a small skimmer to lift the olives out of the eggs. Make sure the egg coating does not come off the olives when you lift them out of the eggs. Sometimes it will sheet away from the flour, leaving an eggless spot. If this happens, pop the olive back into the egg and swirl it again until the olive is completely coated.

Transfer the olives to the bowl with the breadcrumbs, being careful not to drip any excess egg to the breadcrumbs. Swirl the breadcrumb bowl until the olives are coated and use your dry hand to transfer the olives to a waiting tray. Repeat the process until all of the olives have been coated in breadcrumbs. You may need to replenish your breading trays when the levels get low.

About halfway through the breading process, begin heating your oil. Heat it to 350° or until the oil sizzles when you sprinkle a small amount of flour in it.

Once you have finished breading all the olives and the oil is hot, fry the olives in the oil. Depending on the size of your fryer, you may have to fry in multiple batches. Fry the olives until the coating is dark golden brown. Use the metal skimmer to remove the olives and drain on a paper-towel covered tray. When all the olives have been cooked, allow them to cool slightly and serve warm.

Notes

#1: The original recipe for Olive all'Ascolana uses Ascolana olives, a large, firm green olive from Ascoli in the Marche.

#2: In the Marche, the preparation for this dish entails peeling the meat of the olive away from the pit in a helical shape as if you are peeling an orange or apple. Once that is done, the recipe instructs you to make a small football-shaped oval of the meat mixture and to reconstruct the peeled olive around the meat. I tried this. It is a pain in the neck and does not result in a better product. In fact, the olives I prepared in this fashion were even more delicate.

#3: Taking Notes #1 and #2 into account, I determined that Queen Manzanilla Olives worked best. They can be found pitted, although sometimes they are stuffed with pimentos. If they are stuffed with pimentos, you will need to remove the pimentos before soaking the olives in water. The important thing is that the olives be as large as you can find. Take my word for it. You do not want to make this dish with small olives.

#4: These olives can be prepared ahead of time and reheated in a 350° oven. Or if you are making them ahead of time, you can freeze them after breading but before frying.

#5: Make sure you use fine breadcrumbs for this recipe. If you purchase breadcrumbs, panko for example, and find they are not fine textured, pulse them in the food processor until they reach a fine consistency. This will aid in the breading process.

Pigeon and Penne Pie

Yield: One medium-sized tart—Serves 8 | Ease of Preparation: Difficult
Wine Pairing: Lo Sparviere NV Extra Brut Franciacorta, Lo Sparviere Millesimato Extra Brut Franciacorta

I had this unusual dish while lunching with Mrs. Monique Gussalli Beretta and her staff at Lo Sparviere, the Beretta winery in Franciacorta. While pigeon is not an easy ingredient to find, all of the other components of this Beretta family favorite are readily available. The flaky crust is a savory Pasta Frolla (Italy's version of short-crust). The tart is filled with penne pasta tossed in a braised pigeon sauce. It's not exactly 4 and 20 blackbirds baked in a pie, but it's still pretty impressive.

INGREDIENTS

For the Pigeon (Squab):

3 pigeons (squab) approximately 1 lb. each (See note #1 below)

Kosher salt

Black pepper

12 thin slices of pancetta

3 Tbsp. plus ½ cup unsalted butter

2 cups plus 1 cup dry white wine

10 juniper berries

Bay leaf

2 cups homemade stock (chicken or veal)

For the Crust:

3¼ cup all-purpose flour, plus ½ cup reserved

½ tsp. kosher salt

2 sticks (8 oz.) unsalted butter, cubed and chilled

2 large eggs, beaten until homogenous

⅓ cup ice cold water

For the Pasta:

4 quarts water

Kosher salt

12 oz. dry penne rigate pasta

¼ cup extra-virgin olive oil

WHAT YOU'LL NEED

Sharp kitchen shears

Nonstick skillet with lid, large enough to hold 6 pigeon halves

Butcher's twine

Aluminum foil

Food processor with a metal blade

Springform pan (8 inches in diameter x 3 inches high)

Rolling pin

Medium saucepan with lid

Large pot for cooking pasta

Colander to strain pasta

Pastry brush

Baking sheet

Pastry tip or small piece of parchment paper rolled into a funnel

TIMING:

Pigeon (squab) Prep Time: 20 minutes

Pigeon (squab) Cooking Time: 1½ hours

Piecrust Prep Time: 20 minutes

Pasta Cooking Time: 15–20 minutes

Assembly: 30 minutes

Baking Time: 1 hour 15 minutes

Resting Time: 30 minutes

PROCESS

For the Pigeon (Squab):

Cut the pigeon in half lengthwise with your kitchen shears. Rinse and pat dry. Lightly salt and pepper the pigeon. Wrap 2 slices of pancetta around each pigeon half, tying them with butcher's twine.

Place your skillet over medium-high heat and melt 3 tablespoons butter. When it is melted and sizzling, place the pigeon in the pan skin side down. Monitor the cooking progress. When the pancetta and skin are browned, turn the pigeon to the other side and brown that side. Add 2 cups of white wine, the juniper berries, bay leaf, and enough stock to come halfway up the pigeon. Take a large sheet of foil and place it directly on the pigeon (you may need to use 2 pieces). Place the pan lid over the pigeon and foil, and reduce the heat to simmer. (The foil and the pan lid create a perfect environment for braising.) Cook for 45 minutes to an hour, adding stock as needed to keep a layer of liquid in the pan.

Remove the pigeon from the pan, reserving the pan juices. Quickly debone the pigeon, discarding bones, gristle, and skin. Keep only the pigeon meat and the crispy pancetta. (This will be pretty hot. If you wish, you can switch over to making the dough while the pigeon cools a bit.) Shred and slice the meat into small pieces. Place the meat and the pan juices in the medium saucepan. Add the remaining cup of wine and enough stock to just cover the pigeon meat. Cut your foil to fit into the saucepan and cover the pigeon with it. Place the lid on the saucepan and simmer the pigeon on low. Stir periodically to make sure it does not stick. If the liquid evaporates, add the rest of the stock or water. Keep cooking until the pigeon is meltingly tender. This will take between 30 minutes to an hour. Once it is ready, raise the heat to reduce the juices slightly and taste for seasoning.

For the Piecrust:

Place 3¼ cups flour and ¼ tsp. salt in the bowl of the food processor. Pulse to mix. Add the cubes of butter and pulse until the butter chunks are the size of a pea. Measure ⅓ cup of beaten egg, add it to the flour/butter mixture, and process quickly. (Keep the remaining egg to use to paint the crust later.) The flour, butter, and egg mixture will have a sandy consistency. Work quickly now. With the processor running quickly, add the ¼ to ⅓ cup ice water. When the dough begins to come together, it's done.

Flour your cutting board and dump the contents of the processor on the board. It will have a moist sand-like texture. Knead the dough until it comes together and has a uniform texture. This should take about one minute. This is not bread—do not overknead it. Divide the dough into 2 disks. Use ¾ of the dough to make the first disk and ¼ to make the second disk.

Roll the first disk into a circle approximately 13 inches in diameter. It is important to make sure your circle stays round. I find that turning my dough frequently on a generously floured board makes this process easier. Roll your dough over the rolling pin and carefully place it into the springform pan, keeping it centered over the pan. Lift and lower the dough until it reaches the bottom of the pan and gently press it against the sides. You will have excess folds of dough along the side. Fold and press it until it is smooth. You should have between ½ to 1 inch of excess dough at the top of the pan. Trim any excess over that amount.

Roll the second disk into a circle the exact size of the top of your tart pan.

For the Pasta:

Fill your large pot with water and bring to a boil. Once it boils, salt generously. Cook your penne following package instructions. When it is almost completely cooked, strain the pasta, reserving a couple of cups of pasta water. The pasta should be somewhat al dente. Toss the pasta with a little olive oil. If you are not using it within the next 15–20 minutes, refrigerate until ready to use.

Assembly:

Preheat the oven to 350° F.

Remove the juniper berries and bay leaves from the pigeon sauce. Place the pigeon sauce and penne pasta in the skillet and heat. Toss to coat the pasta. Add ½ cup of reserved pasta water, stir, and toss. The water and the sauce should form an emulsion. If you need more liquid, add more water. If the sauce is not thick or rich enough, add a couple of pats of the extra ½ cup of butter, swirl, and stir. Taste the pasta and sauce. Add more butter if needed. The sauce should be a thick, shiny glaze and should taste rich and wonderful. You could stop right here and have a really superb pigeon and pasta dish—but, let's not! (Note: Make sure there is excess sauce on the pasta. That will keep the finished dish from being too dry.)

Carefully line the bottom of the tart with a layer of pasta and pigeon. Take the time to arrange the pasta up neatly so that the layer fills the bottom of the tart. Turn the pan and add another layer. Not to sound like an engineer, but the structural integrity of this dish depends on making sure each layer is even and well packed. When you reach the top of the tart, pour any extra juices over the pasta and add a dab or two of butter.

Place the second, smaller disk of dough on top of the pasta. It should fit inside the top of the bottom crust. Press down to compact the pasta even more. Make an egg wash by combining a small amount of water with the remaining egg. Paint the egg wash on the edges of the top crust. Fold the outer crust over and smooth it with your fingers to seal the tart shut, using more egg wash as needed. Try to eliminate any signs of a seam for better presentation. Cut a hole in the center of the crust and insert a small pastry tip or a funnel made of parchment paper into the hole. This "chimney" will allow steam to escape. Paint egg wash on the top of the tart.

Set the tart pan on a baking sheet and place it in the preheated oven. Bake for 1 hour and 15 minutes. Turn the tart twice during the baking process.

Remove the tart from the oven. Carefully run a knife around the inside rim of your tart pan to loosen the tart from the pan and release the removable side of the pan. Let the tart sit for 30 minutes before serving.

Ease of Sourcing: Difficult if you use pigeon (unless you have a hunter in the family). Simple if you use other poultry (See Note #1).

Notes

#1. Pigeon is rarely hunted in the United States. Squab is young domesticated pigeon. Squab is available at some gourmet butchers and online at www.dartagnan.com. (d'Artagnan is a New York-based purveyor of meat and gourmet foods.) Both squab and pigeon have a gamey, rich flavor. You could substitute other fowl—dark meat turkey, pheasant, quail, duck, or even dark meat free-range chicken. If you have a hunter in the family, make sure they keep the skin on the bird when they dress it. If there is no skin on the bird, you will need to increase the amount of butter and pancetta used in the recipe.

#2. Pancetta is Italian dry-cured pork belly—the French call it *ventrèche*. It is available at most gourmet stores, Italian markets, and online through Amazon and d'Artagnan (d'Artagnan calls it ventrèche). If you cannot find it, you may substitute the most neutral-flavored thin-sliced bacon you can find. If your bacon is strongly flavored or smoky, blanch it for a minute or two in boiling water and drain it well.

Marinated Pheasant

Yield: Serves 4 | Ease of Preparation: Moderate | Ease of Sourcing: Difficult
Wine Pairing: Lo Sparviere Brut Rosé Cuvée Monique

At times people are faced with the dilemma that they have an abundance of an ingredient and need to find good recipes for it. At my house it usually seems to be zucchini or tomatoes. Mrs. Beretta told me that with all of the hunters in her family, she sometimes finds herself with quite a bit of pheasant. This recipe from a friend of hers, Mara Caldesi, is one of her dishes to tackle the surplus. The marinated pheasant is slow poached in an olive oil vinegar bath. Depending on whether you have a wild or farm-raised pheasant, the cooking time may vary greatly.

INGREDIENTS

One pheasant, cut in pieces
¾ cup carrots, peeled and sliced in ⅛ inch rounds
½ cup onions, peeled, cut in half and sliced in ¼ inch slices
3 cloves garlic, peeled and left whole
8 sage leaves
6 bay leaves
4 cloves
2 tsp. kosher salt
½ tsp. finely ground black pepper
4 grinds (2 pinches) ground nutmeg
2 cups extra-virgin olive oil
½ cup white vinegar

WHAT YOU'LL NEED

Oven-safe Pyrex casserole dish or enamel-coated casserole dish large enough to hold two layers of pheasant pieces and three layers of vegetables.
Medium bowl
Whisk

TIMING

Prep Time: 30–45 minutes
Baking Time: 3–4 hours for a wild pheasant, 2 hours for a farmed-raised bird.

PROCESS

Preheat the oven to 350° F.

Cut the pheasant in pieces (see Note #2 below). Rinse and dry the pieces.

Layer one third of the carrots and onions, one clove garlic, 3 sage leaves, and 2 bay leaves in the bottom of the casserole dish. Place half the pheasant on top of the vegetable layer. Sprinkle 2 cloves, 1 teaspoon kosher salt, ⅛ teaspoon ground black pepper, and a pinch (2 grinds) of nutmeg on the pheasant. Continue the layers: one-third vegetables including the sage and bay leaves, the other half of the pheasant, and all of the spices, then the final layer of vegetables, sage, and bay leaves.

Whisk the oil and vinegar together and pour it over the pheasant (you may not need to use it all). Place the casserole in the preheated oven and cook at 350° F until the oil begins to lightly bubble (approximately 15 minutes). Lower the heat to 275° F and cook an hour and 45 minutes for a farm-raised bird, at least 3 hours for a wild pheasant. If the oil stops bubbling, raise the heat slightly until it starts lightly bubbling again. The dish is done when the carrots and pheasant are tender and the pheasant skin is light golden.

Notes

#1. If the pheasant is farm raised, the white meat may be lean. In that case, you may want to remove it about 15 minutes early to keep it from getting too dry.

#2. Unless you have a hunter in the family, pheasant is not all that easy to source. Farm-raised pheasant is available at certain periods of the year in gourmet butchers or specialty stores. Whole pheasant can also be ordered online from d'Artagnan and other specialty meat purveyors. If you get it from a butcher, ask them to cut it into serving portions for you. There are also good tutorials online on how to cut a chicken apart. Use the same technique with a pheasant. Save the back, neck, and ribs to make stock.

Fried Sweet Milk
Latte Dolce Fritto

Yield: 12 pieces (2" x 1½") | Ease of Preparation: Moderate, but time-consuming
Ease of Sourcing: Simple
Wine Pairing: Sweet Moscato, either still or sparkling

Mrs. Beretta served this delicious and fun dessert when I joined her for lunch. The inside is creamy lemon-flavored custard and the outside is crispy with a powdered sugar topping. Be careful, it's messy! You may not want to wear black!

INGREDIENTS

For the Custard Mixture:

½ cup all-purpose flour
3 Tbsp. granulated sugar
¼ tsp. kosher salt
4 large eggs
2 cups whole milk
1 tsp. finely grated lemon peel
Pan spray

For Frying:

1 cup all-purpose flour
4 large eggs, beaten
2 cups dried breadcrumbs
Canola oil
1 cup confectioner's sugar as garnish

WHAT YOU'LL NEED

Small mixing bowl
Medium mixing bowl
4-quart saucepan
Fine microplane
Whisk
Rubber spatula
8 x 6 in. rectangular ceramic or glass
    dish
Plastic wrap
Long slender metal spatula
2 soup spoons
3 breading trays
6-quart saucepan for frying, or electric
    fryer
Slotted spoon or spider
Small mesh strainer
Serving platter
Paper towels

TIMING

Prep Time: 15 minutes
Cook Time: 30–40 minutes
Cooling Time: 4 hours or overnight
Breading and Frying Time: 30 minutes

For the Custard:

Mix the ½ cup all-purpose flour, sugar, and kosher salt in the medium mixing bowl until well combined. Break the eggs separately in a small bowl and beat until uniform in texture. Mix ½ cup milk into the dry ingredient mixture to form a paste, making sure there are no lumps. Add the beaten eggs to the flour and milk paste and mix until lump-free. Do the same with the remaining milk. Once it is smooth, add the grated lemon peel.

Spray the rectangular baking dish with pan spray.

Heat the egg and milk mixture in the 4-quart saucepan over low heat while whisking constantly. It should thicken slowly. Frequently scrape the sides and bottom of the pan with the rubber spatula. You want the mixture to thicken but not to scramble. Remove it from the heat if it begins to curdle and stir for a moment before returning it to the heat.

The custard is done when it is the consistency of mashed potatoes (or polenta, as Giulia Pezzali, the Beretta family cook, put it). You should be able to see the bottom of the pan when you drag the whisk through it, and the whisk marks should remain visible in the custard. This takes 30 to 40 minutes but is very important to the finished dish.

Transfer the custard into the rectangular dish. *Do not strain the custard.* Straining keeps it from setting up adequately.

Use pan spray to lightly coat a piece of plastic wrap. Place the plastic wrap directly on the custard to prevent a thick skin from forming. Chill the mixture in the refrigerator for at least four hours or overnight. It should be firm to the touch and should not jiggle when you shake the dish.

Frying Process:

Put the flour, three beaten eggs, and the breadcrumbs in three separate breading trays.

Cut three even lengthwise sections of custard. Turn the pan and cut four even sections along the custard. You will have twelve 2-inch x 1½-inch pieces of custard. Using the long metal spatula, carefully remove the custard pieces from the baking dish. This is a delicate process. The squares may not come out of the pan perfectly, but try not to break the custard apart. Using the two soup spoons, coat the custard squares in the flour, then the eggs, and then the breadcrumbs. Be careful that the custard is completely coated in crumbs. Once the custard is well breaded, gently shape the sides with the spoons or your fingers. You are trying for a rectangle shape.

Pour two inches of canola oil into the 6-quart saucepan and heat to 350° F. If you do not have a thermometer, you will know that the oil is hot enough when a sprinkling of breadcrumbs sizzles when you drop them in the oil.

Fry the coated pieces in batches, being careful not to overcrowd the pan. When they are golden brown, remove them with the slotted spoon to a paper towel-covered plate. Work quickly to finish frying the rest of the custard pieces.

To Garnish:

Put some confectioner's sugar in a small mesh strainer and tap the side of it to dust the fried milk squares with the sugar. Gently turn the squares and dust the other side with sugar, as well.

Notes

#1. When frying, always be sure not to get the level of the oil too high in your pan. It will bubble a little when you fry the food, and you don't want it to bubble over. If in doubt, choose a larger pan.

#2. Although I stated that this recipe is moderately difficult, it is actually not that complex. It just takes patience and a bit of time. Removing the pieces from the pan is a bit tricky, and the breading can be a bit messy. Don't let that discourage you. The result is really delicious.

#3. If you do not want to mess with cutting and removing the custard pieces from the pan, consider using a mini muffin pan instead. Line each muffin hole with a piece of plastic wrap, leaving an extra inch on all sides. Fill the muffin tin with the custard mixture, fold the excess plastic over the custard, and gently press to remove air bubbles. Chill overnight, then bread, and fry according to the recipe above.

Wine Tart "Lo Sparviere"

Yield: one 9-inch cake | Ease of Preparation: Moderate | Ease of Sourcing: Simple
Wine Pairing: Lo Sparviere Il Cacciatore Curtefranca Rosso, Recioto della Valpolicella,
or red Passito Method Wine

I first tasted this lightly sweet cake when lunching with Mrs. Beretta at Lo Sparviere, the Beretta family winery in Franciacorta. People frequently recommend serving chocolate with Cabernet. I generally am not a fan of this because I think the wine should be at least as sweet as the dessert, but Italian desserts are much less sweet than their American counterparts and this dense, moist cake—flavored with red wine and a hint of chocolate—pairs quite well with Il Cacciatore, Lo Sparviere's Cabernet/Merlot based Curtefranca Rosso.

INGREDIENTS

5¼ oz. slightly softened unsalted butter
(1 stick +2½ Tbsp.)
4¼ oz. granulated sugar
4 eggs, with the yolks separated from
the whites
1 tsp. baking powder
2 cups all-purpose flour
½ tsp. kosher salt
½ tsp. powdered cinnamon
3 oz. semisweet chocolate (64 percent
cacao), either morsels or chopped
1 tsp. liquid vanilla extract
¾ cup medium-bodied red wine
(red Curtefranca, Valpolicella, or
unoaked Cabernet or Merlot)
Confectioner's sugar

WHAT YOU'LL NEED

Parchment paper circle cut to fit inside
the 9½-inch cake pan
Pan spray
Electric mixer with whisk and paddle
attachments
Large mixing bowl
Medium size mixing bowl
Double boiler or medium mixing bowl
and medium saucepan
9½-inch cake pan
Metal whisk
Rubber spatula
Fine mesh strainer to sift confectioner's
sugar
Baking rack
Two long spatulas
Decorative platter

TIMING

Prep Time: 25 minutes
Cooking Time: 35 minutes

PROCESS

Preheat the oven to 350° F—preferably on the convection bake setting.

Measure out all of your ingredients ahead of time. Spray the cake pan with pan spray and line the bottom of it with a circle of parchment paper the size of your pan.

For the Egg Whites:

Using the whisk attachment on your electric mixer, whip the egg whites to stiff peaks. If you have two bowls for your mixer, place the bowl with the egg whites in the refrigerator. If you have only one bowl for the mixer, scrape the whites into the medium kitchen bowl and store them in the refrigerator. Wash and dry the electric mixing bowl.

For the Batter:

Using the paddle attachment on the electric mixer, cream the butter and sugar together until it is fluffy, the sugar granules have completely dissolved, and the color has changed to a pale (almost white) hue. Scrape the sides of the bowl periodically. This may take some time. Allow ten minutes to get it to the correct consistency. Do not shortcut this step.

While the butter is creaming, melt the chocolate bits in the double boiler. If you don't have a double boiler, place a small mixing bowl over a small saucepan half filled with hot water and melt the chocolate bits over medium heat. Once it is melted, take the chocolate off the heat.

Mix the dry ingredients (baking powder, flour, kosher salt, and cinnamon) together.

Add the vanilla to the wine.

With the mixer on low, add the egg yolks to the butter and sugar and mix until fluffy. Work in intervals going forward, shutting off the mixer to add new ingredients to avoid splashback. Do not add a new ingredient until the mixture is fluffy. Add one quarter of the dry ingredient mixture and then add the melted chocolate. Continue mixing, alternating dry with liquid until all the ingredients have been added and the batter is homogenous, scraping the bowl as you go along. Scrape the wine batter into the large mixing bowl.

Remove the whipped egg whites from the refrigerator and quickly whisk them to bring them back to their original stiffness if necessary.

It's time to switch to the spatula. Add one quarter of whipped egg whites to the wine batter and gently mix to lighten the batter. Use the spatula to clear a spot in the center of the remaining egg whites. Scoop the batter into the center of the egg whites and fold them together gently. Be careful. Although you want to completely mix the two parts together, you need to keep as much of the fluffy texture of the stiff egg whites as possible. That is will help make your cake fluffy.

Pour the batter into the prepared cake pan. Gently shake it back and forth to fill the pan and smooth it with the spatula. Bake in a 350° F oven for 30 to 35 minutes. Test the cake after 30 minutes by piercing it in several places with a wooden toothpick. If the toothpick comes back clean, you're good. If some crumbs or batter stick to the skewer, bake it a few minutes longer and retest.

When the cake is done, remove it from the oven and allow it to cool on a baking rack in the pan for 30 minutes. At this time, run a knife around the edges of the cake to loosen it from the pan and remove the cake by turning it onto a plate. Slide it back onto the baking rack to finish cooling. Since you lined the cake pan with parchment paper, you should not have any trouble removing the cake from the pan. Remove the parchment paper and discard it.

Once the cake is cool, use the fine mesh strainer to sift confectioner's sugar on the cake. Use the two long spatulas to carefully lift the cake and place it on the cake plate or decorative platter.

Grandma Zina's Chocolate Cake

Yield: One Chocolate Cake | Ease of Sourcing: Simple | Ease of Sourcing: Simple
Wine Pairing: Recioto della Valpolicella, or a red Passito Method Wine

Franco, Mrs. Beretta's younger son, likes to say that he inherited his love of chocolate from his Belgian mother. Mrs. Beretta served this dark chocolate family favorite at our luncheon in Franciacorta. The process of mixing the batter well before adding the next ingredient, and the addition of egg whites whipped to stiff peaks, allow the cake to rise, resulting in a tender, moist cake.

INGREDIENTS

For the Cake:

1–2 Tbsp. softened butter or pan spray

2 Tbsp. all-purpose flour

½ cup plus 2 Tbsp. unsalted blanched almonds

4 large eggs

4.4 oz. bittersweet (70 percent cacao) chocolate broken into small chunks

8½ Tbsp. unsalted butter

Heaping ½ cup granulated sugar

6 Tbsp. cornstarch

½ tsp. kosher salt

For the Chocolate Glaze:

2.9 oz. bittersweet (70 percent cacao) chocolate

¼ cup water

⅓ cup granulated sugar

TIMING

Prep Time: 45 minutes

Baking Time: 30 minutes

Cooling Time: 1 hour

Resting Time: Overnight

WHAT YOU'LL NEED

9½-inch cake pan

Food processor with metal blade attachment

Electric mixer with whisk and paddle attachment

Small kitchen bowl

Medium kitchen bowl

Small saucepan

Double boiler or a medium saucepan and a medium kitchen bowl (large enough to sit in the saucepan without falling into it)

Wooden spoon

Rubber spatula

Whisk

Toothpick or wooden skewer

Butter knife

Pastry cooling rack

Microplane for grating chocolate, box grater, or sharp kitchen knife

Frosting spatula or butter knife

Cake plate or decorative platter

Two large long spatulas

PROCESS

For the Cake:

Prepare the cake pan. Use softened butter or pan spray to cover the inside of the pan, then coat it with flour. Discard excess flour.

Preheat the oven to 350° F—preferably on the convection bake setting.

Rough chop the almonds. Use the food processor to grind the rough chopped almonds to the size of half a grain of rice. Do not overprocess. You do not want to make almond butter. If large chunks of almond remain, use a kitchen knife to finish chopping them by hand, but since you have already rough chopped them beforehand, this should not take too long.

Separate the yolk and white of the eggs. Use the whisk attachment of your electric mixer to whip the egg whites to stiff peaks. If you have two bowls for your mixer, place the bowl with the beaten egg whites in the refrigerator. If you have only one bowl for the mixer, scrape the whites into the medium kitchen bowl and store the beaten egg whites in the refrigerator. Wash and dry the bowl.

Place the clean mixing bowl on the mixer. Use the paddle attachment to beat the egg yolks on medium speed until they are pale yellow and creamy (approximately 5 minutes).

While the eggs yolks are mixing, melt the butter in the small saucepan. Allow to cool slightly.

Place an inch of water in the double boiler (or the medium saucepan). Place the 4.4 oz. of chocolate chunks in the top of the double boiler (or the medium bowl). Place it over the water-filled pan. Heat the water and stir the chocolate with the wooden spoon until the chocolate melts. Remove from the heat.

Mix the granulated sugar into the yolks and beat on medium speed until the sugar dissolves (approximately 3 minutes).

It is very important to mix each ingredient in very well before beginning to add the next ingredient. This will make the batter fluffy and light. With the mixer set to medium, drizzle the cooled but still liquid butter into the egg yolk and sugar mixture. Slowly add the melted chocolate, then the cornstarch, and finally the ground almonds and kosher salt. Mix on low for 5 minutes until incorporated.

Remove the egg whites from the refrigerator. If they have deflated, whisk them lightly by hand until they form stiff peaks again. (Do not overbeat or the egg whites will fall.)

Use the rubber spatula to lightly stir ¼ of the egg white mixture into the cake batter. This will lighten the batter. Use the spatula to clear a spot in the center of the remaining egg whites. Scoop the batter into the center of the egg whites and fold them together gently. Be careful. Although you want to completely mix the two parts together, you need to keep as much of the fluffy texture of the stiff egg whites as possible. This is what will make your cake fluffy.

Pour the cake batter into the prepared cake pan and bake for 30 minutes in the preheated oven. Check to see if the cake is done after 25 minutes by piercing the cake with the toothpick. If the toothpick comes back clean, the cake is done. If not, return it to the oven for 5 more minutes or until the toothpick comes back clean.

Remove the cake from the oven and let it cool for 30 minutes.

After 30 minutes, run a butter knife around the side of the cake and flip the cake onto the pastry cooling rack. Let the cake cool completely. Place the cake on a plate (not the decorative one).

For the Chocolate Glaze:

Grating chocolate is a messy endeavor. If you use a box grater or chocolate microplane, you need to work very quickly lest your chocolate melt in your hands. I find it best to chill the chocolate chunks before grating. My personal preference is to chill the chocolate and use a very sharp knife to thinly shave the chocolate. Place the chocolate shavings in a medium kitchen bowl and set aside.

When the cake is completely cooled, heat ¼ cup water and ⅓ cup granulated sugar in the small saucepan to make a syrup. Once the sugar has dissolved and the syrup is hot, whisk it into the shaved chocolate to melt it. Continue to whisk until it is smooth. Pour the chocolate glaze over the cooled cake and smooth it with a frosting spatula.

Place the cake in a safe place to store overnight.

To Serve:

The following day, use the two long spatulas to carefully lift the cake and place it on the cake plate or decorative platter.

Note

Letting the cake rest overnight allows the frosting to set up, becoming firm to the touch. Giulia Pezzali, Mrs. Beretta's family cook, decorated her cake with whimsical fondant flowers. If you are experienced in working with fondant frosting, the sky is the limit as to how you could decorate this cake. If you prefer your frosting to be soft and gooey, frost the cake as soon as it has cooled and serve immediately.

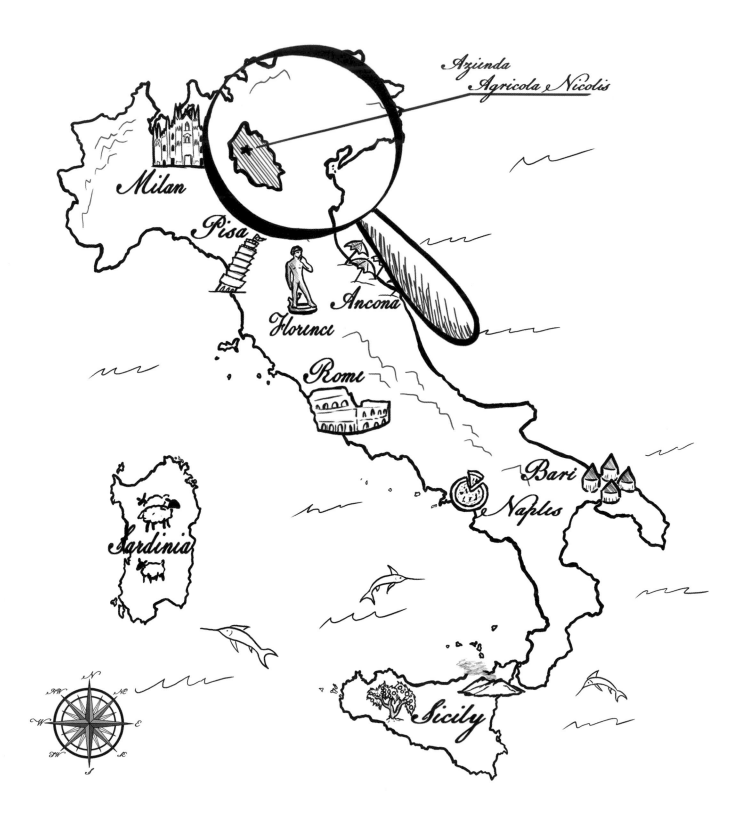

Azienda
Agricola Nicolis

Milan

Pisa

Florence

Ancona

Rome

Sardinia

Bari

Naples

Sicily

"In the Heart of Amarone Country"
A Visit to Azienda Agricola Nicolis e Figli
San Pietro in Cariano, Veneto, Italy

When you sell wine for a living, people ask you a lot of questions. Sometimes the questions are easy, like *What is the main red grape in Burgundy?* (Pinot Noir). Sometimes they are considerably more complex, like, *What is the difference between the Red Burgundies of Volnay and those of Morey-Saint-Denis?* (This requires a long explanation about climate, soil type, sun exposure, and grape clones and continues on into different winemakers, etc.)

Oftentimes, the questions involve a judgment call where your personal opinion influences your answer. Take the following oft-asked question, *What's a good food wine that I can afford to drink during the week on a regular basis?* Obviously some of that depends on what the person can afford. (See the section on "How to Buy Wine" where I explain that one person's inexpensive is another person's splurge.) When the customer wants something affordable and French, I steer them to Beaujolais. When they have a hankering for something Italian, I recommend Valpolicella. I used to recommend Chianti, but Chianti prices have risen to the extent that a value-oriented customer might want

something slightly less expensive. Enter Valpolicella, stage right, or stage left . . . whatever. The structure and flavor profile of Valpolicella make it a really good food wine, and its relatively reasonable price makes it affordable.

Having long been a fan of the wines of the Nicolis Family in Verona Province, I visited their winery on two recent trips to Italy to taste their wines and talk about food. Located in San Pietro in Cariano in the heart of the Valpolicella Classico zone, Azienda Agricola Nicolis Angelo e Figli is a family affair. Established in 1951 by Angelo Nicolis, it is currently run by Natalia, the matriarch, and her sons. Giuseppe is in charge of the winemaking, while Giancarlo manages the vineyards.

Giuseppe and Giancarlo Nicolis
Photo credit: A. A. Nicolis e Figli

Wines of Valpolicella

The Valpolicella wine region is located in the Venetian province of Verona in northeastern Italy. The name is thought to be a combination of Latin and Greek meaning "valley of many cellars." Valpolicella's traditional heart is the Classico region located in the prealpine Monte Lessini hills northwest of Verona on the eastern side of Lake Garda.

Although the region expanded rapidly in the 1960s (resulting in an unfortunate drop in the quality level of some wines), the best wines still come from the Classico region of the Fumane, Marona, and Negrar Valleys, where the hilly terrain, limestone soils, and cool temperatures produce better-quality grapes and, therefore, better wines.

Valpantena is a smaller region to the east of the Classico zone that is producing fine quality wines, as well.

The heavier soils and warmer climate on the flatter lands further to the east, while easier to farm, produce less concentrated grapes. Wines from that part of the region are more affordable, albeit less distinguished.

The main grapes of Valpolicella have historically been Corvina, Rondinella, and Molinara—Corvina with its thick skin is the most important and distinguished of this trio, lending color, body, and firm tannins. It makes up the largest percentage of the traditional blend. Rondinella, with its higher yields, also contributes color. Molinara is a lighter-bodied grape and produces paler, more acidic wines. There is a movement away from the use of Molinara, while Corvinone (a subvariety of Corvina) and Croatina are replacing it in the blend. Additionally, up to 15 percent of other grape varieties can be included in the blend. The following types of wines are produced in the Valpolicella DOC zone: **Valpolicella DOC; Valpolicella Classico DOC,** Valpolicella from the Classico Zone; **Valpolicella Superiore DOC,** Valpolicella with higher alcohol content and increased minimum aging requirements; **Valpolicella Ripasso DOC; Amarone della Valpolicella DOCG;** and **Recioto della Valpolicella DOCG.**

In order to understand the last three wines on that list, it helps to explain them in reverse order.

Recioto della Valpolicella DOCG

Historically a sweet wine made from dried grapes using *apassimento,* the Passito method. (See Wine Terms, page 473.) The grapes are dried (in the olden days on straw mats—nowadays in plastic crates) in a breezy party of the cellar or a fan-equipped drying room (until at least December 1st following the harvest, on average 100–120 days) until they become raisins. The small amount of juice pressed from these raisins is then made into wine. The sugar levels of the juice used to make Recioto (as with all *passito* method wines) are quite high. This produces a very flavorful, concentrated wine with residual sugar and medium to medium-high alcohol levels.

Amarone della Valpolicella DOCG

Also called *Recioto Scapato,* which means it is a Recioto whose fermentation has "escaped" or gotten away from the winemaker and fermented to full dryness. It was the popularity of Amarone (with its first commercial production in the 1960s making it a relative newcomer to the Veronese wine scene) that, in the 1980s, turned the Valpolicella industry away from its path of producing cheap lackluster wines and toward a focus on high quality. Amarones are powerful, rich, and high in alcohol.

Valpolicella Ripasso DOC

Ripasso is produced when a finished Valpolicella wine from the most current vintage is poured (or passed) through the grape skins and yeast from the previous year's Amarone fermentation. This often produces a secondary fermentation. It always increases the color and alcohol content of the wine and adds richness to the flavor profile. These wines are sometimes casually referred to as "Baby Amarone."

Wines produced in the region that do not fall into the standards set by the Valpolicella governing body—generally because of the use of grape varieties not authorized in the Valpolicella blend (either because of the type of grape or the proportions used)—are labeled **IGT Veronese**.

Whenever I see Giuseppe Nicolis, I remember the first time I met him. My friend Alberto Panella, the owner of Grappoli Imports (his representative in Virginia), had brought him to Arrowine, the independent wine store where I worked at the time, to show us his wines. That summer I was deeply immersed in a series of private Italian lessons at a local language school, and I began speaking Italian with Giuseppe. He

Marogne wall. Photo credit: A.A. Nicolis e Figli

seemed to understand me, but I was only getting about one quarter of what he said. The accent from that part of Italy is quite strong, and my ears weren't up to it. Since then, I have learned that there are a myriad of regional accents in Italy, but even on subsequent encounters, I can still aver that Giuseppe's accent is quite a challenge for me. We managed to communicate on that day, and even as recently as April 2016 at Vinitaly, the massive annual wine Trade Show in Verona, Italy, I was able to comprehend his Italian as long as we were speaking about wine and food. I like to say that I speak *italiano di vino, cibo ed alberghi* (wine, food, and hotel Italian).

Giuseppe explained to me that they vinify their wines separately based on the location of the vineyards. Grapes for the Valpolicella Classico are grown in the benchland vineyards (the narrow strip or bench of relatively level land at the foot of the hills). The hill vineyards with their microclimates and traditional *marogne*-lined terraces are dedicated to growing grapes for Amarone and Recioto.

Marogne are ancient stone walls. These walls are used in the vineyards of Valpolicella for several reasons. They mitigate vineyard slope by producing multiple small flat levels that are easier to farm than steeper slopes and manage water drainage by blocking or slowing the speed of water runoff on the hills. Because they are dug into sloping vineyards, Marogne walls may only be installed in vineyards with deep soils.

The Nicolis family produces seven wines:

Valpolicella Classico
Valpolicella Classico Superiore
"Seccal" Valpolicella Classico Superiore
    Ripasso
Amarone Classico
"Ambrosan" Amarone Classico
Recioto Classico
"Testal" Rosso Veronese

Foods of Verona

Valpolicella is located in the Veneto, a large region in Northeastern Italy. The Veneto (which takes its name from Venice) has more food Denominazione di Origine Protetta (DOP) than any other region. (DOP is a designation that certifies the quality and origin of a specific food product.) Its geography is quite diverse, with numerous rivers (the Adige, Po, Piave, Brenta, and Tagliamento), the eastern half of Lake Garda, the Adriatic

Sea, mountains in the North (The Carnic Alps, Venetian Prealps, and the Dolomites), and flatlands in the East. This diversity as well as a relatively warm climate given its northern location (influences from the Adriatic Sea and Lake Garda) enables it to produce vegetation that is much more Mediterranean than the latitude would logically suggest.

Cuisine from the Province of Verona, where the Valpolicella vineyards are found, benefits from meat-oriented dishes from its inland section and the abundance of fish from Lake Garda. The cuisine of the city of Verona itself on the southern border of the Valpolicella zone is very meat-centric, while that of Lake Garda is more fish-oriented. As it was explained to me, when you are at a restaurant in Verona, you order meat. Drive to a restaurant in Bardolino fifteen minutes to the west, and you'll eat fish from Lake Garda.

During my several visits to the Nicolis winery as well as multiple visits to Verona and Lake Garda, a picture of the cuisine of the region emerged.

Meat

Horse Meat:

Let's get this out of the way. While not everyone in Verona or the neighboring towns eats horse, there *is* a culture of eating horse (and, to a lesser extent, donkey). Because of the high iron content, some people find that horsemeat tastes a bit sweet. Others are too fond of horses to eat them. Despite these considerations, the consumption of horses does exist in this and other parts of Italy. The most common equine dishes are:

Carpaccio di Cavallo: Raw, thinly sliced horse.
Sfilacci: Thin strands of horsemeat, either dried or raw.
Pastissada: Horsemeat and red wine stew.
Costata: Horsemeat steak.
Straccotto di Cavallo or Asino: Well-cooked horse or donkey, usually in a meat sauce.

Other meat:

Beef, pork, and duck are very common.

Cured Pork: Salumi plates abound in the region, and meals often start with a tray of local salame and, although it is not local, prosciutto.

Lesso (Bollito Misto) con Pearà: A mixture of boiled meats. This definitely starts with beef but can also include pig's knuckle, chicken, veal head, and sausage. It is served with a Pearà sauce made from bone marrow, bread, and lots of ground black pepper, from which it gets its name. In restaurants, the Lesso is often served *in Carello,* in a cart filled with broth and boiled meats that is rolled through the dining room with the waiter stopping at customer's tables to slice off pieces of the desired meats and garnishing it with the delicious sauce.

Beef Braised in Amarone: Beef Braised in Amarone, especially *Guancia* (beef cheeks) *all'Amarone,* can be found on most menus in the region. Often served with polenta.

Duck Ragu: Duck cooked in red wine until it is falling apart tender. Delicious!

Game and Foraged Foods

There is a long tradition of hunting and foraging in the region, with hare and wild birds being favorite quarry.

Polenta Osei is a local favorite. Martina Fornaser, the Manager of Sales and PR and a long-time employee at Azienda Agricola Nicolis, shared her mother's recipe for this traditional dish. Although *tordi* (thrush) and *fagiano* (pheasant) are traditional in Valpolicella, any small bird will do. Once the birds are deboned, they are stuffed with bread, parmesan, prosciutto, and aromatics before being pan seared in butter and simmered in white wine until tender. They are then served over polenta along with their pan sauces. In September, there is a Festival in nearby Cisano called the *Festa degli Osei*.

Fish

Scoglio: A fish mixture made with fish, *gamberetti* (small prawns), and *calamari*.

Trota Affumicata: Smoked Trout.

Trota Grillata: Grilled Trout.

Polenta di Renga: Polenta with herring. A favorite dish on Ash Wednesday, herring is boiled, salted, grilled, and pickled before being served over warm polenta.

Brodo, Polenta, Risotto, and Pasta

Brodo: They eat lots of *brodo* (an incredibly flavorful broth) in this part of Italy. Whether it is *Tortellini di Valeggio in Brodo* with small meat and cheese filled dumplings from the Valeggio Valley south of Garda, or *Pappardelle in Brodo con fegatini*, pappardelle (actually tagliatelle) in broth with veal liver, the *brodo* is always chicken and it is always homemade.

Polenta: This traditional side dish is served with many regional braised meat dishes, but it can also be eaten at breakfast time, although in that case it is usually sweetened.

Risotto: The best rice from the region is *Vialone Nano IGP* from south of Verona. Although there are many different types of risotto dishes, Valpolicella is best known for *Risotto all'Amarone*. Natalia Nicolis gave me a fabulous recipe for this savory dish flavored with Amarone. Properly prepared risotto has the consistency of a thick soup, and the rice should be slightly al dente.

Pasta:

There are many different types of pasta in the region. The following are some of the most well known.

Bigoli: This is an extruded pasta in the form of a long tube. Although it is served with lots of different sauces, *Bigoli con Sugo di Anatra* (Bigoli in Duck Ragu) is one of my very favorites.

Tagliatelle con Tartuffi: Long pasta with truffles.

Ravioli Tartuffi e Ricotta: Truffle and ricotta stuffed ravioli.

Tortellini di Zucca: I'll admit I don't understand this dish—Tortellini stuffed with pumpkin and Amaretti cookies and served with a butter and sage sauce—but there are those who love it, including some good friends of mine.

Gnocchi di Mais: Cornmeal gnocchi with butter and sage.

Cheese

Local cheeses include: *Asiago* (a firm cow's milk cheese), *Monte Veronese* (Aged cow's milk similar to *Grana Padano*), and *Ubriaco* (cow's milk cheese soaked in grape pomace). *Ubriaco* means "drunk" in Italian, so the name makes complete sense. *Gorgonzola*, the well-known cow's milk blue cheese, is a popular pairing with the local sweet wine, Recioto della Valpolicella.

Desserts

Cherries and Peaches: The most well-known fruits from the region, these are eaten raw or made into fruit tarts.

Shortbread (Pasta Frolla): Quite popular in the region. Variations include: *Tortafrolla di Verona*, plain shortbread often served with Recioto della Valpolicella; *Sbrisolona di Mantova*, shortbread with almonds from the town of Mantova; and *San Vigilini*, shortbread with pine nuts and raisins.

Zabaglione al Recioto con Panna Montata: Recioto-flavored Zabaglione with Whipped Cream.

Pandoro (literally golden bread) is a sweet bread from Verona that is baked in a special tall, star-shaped mold. It is topped with vanilla-flavored powdered sugar, like a mountain with snow on top.

Mealtime with the Nicolis Family

I may not always understand all that Giuseppe says, but with my Italian, his English, and Martina Fornaser's help, I was able to get a clear a picture of the Nicolis family and their food culture.

The winery tasting room has a large kitchen and dining area where guests are welcomed for wine tastings. In April, at the end of Vinitaly, the Nicolis family has a big party, inviting many clients. Even though they have a big kitchen at the winery, they hire a caterer for this event because they do not have a catering license.

Harvest

Because the workers at Nicolis are local, they go home for lunch—even during harvest. At the end of harvest, the Nicolis family celebrates the end of the hard work by hosting a big feast for the harvesters either at the winery or in a local restaurant where they eat and open lots of different wines. Giuseppe is very curious about what other winemakers are doing and frequently tastes the wines of other winemakers.

I asked Martina what she likes to eat. She is very modest and doesn't like to talk about herself a lot, but she opened up when we started talking about food of the area. She is originally from the area and lives only five kilometers away from the winery in the charming lakeside town of Pescheria. She shops at the local fishmonger and the butcher shop for her fish and meat. Otherwise, she shops either at the *chilometro zero* (kilometer zero means food from that very kilometer) organic farmer's market or purchases food directly from local farms, i.e., she goes to the peach farm to buy her peaches. She only goes to a supermarket to buy the staples she cannot purchase elsewhere.

One thing stood out, whether I was speaking with Giuseppe or Martina. The Nicolis family is very proud of the bounty of food of the region, their wines, and their corner of the world in the verdant hills in the heart of Amarone country.

The Winemaker Recommends: Natalia Nicolis Recommends Risotto all'Amarone with Azienda Agricola Nicolis Amarone della Valpolicella Classico.

Quail with Polenta
Polenta Osei

Yield: Serves 4 | Ease of Preparation: Moderately Difficult
Ease of Sourcing: Moderately difficult | Wine Pairing: Valpolicella Classico

This is a traditional family recipe from Martina Fornaser of Azienda Agricola Nicolis. In the Veneto, they use tordi (thrush). I use semiboneless quail from d'Artagnan. This is a fabulous dish for dinner parties. It takes a bit of preparation ahead of time, but since there is very little to do at the last minute, you can enjoy time with your guests. You only have to disappear for a couple of minutes to reheat the quail and sauce when it's time for the main course. Perfect!

INGREDIENTS

For the Stuffing:

One baguette or a firm loaf of unsliced fresh white bread (note: sandwich bread is too soft)

2 Tbsp. unsalted butter

½ cup finely minced shallots

4 oz. finely sliced Prosciutto cut into ⅓ inch strips (be careful not to let them clump together)

½ cup finely shredded Grana Padano

Kosher salt

Black pepper, finely ground

For the Quail:

8 semi-boneless quail

⅓ cup extra-virgin olive oil

1 cup finely diced carrots (⅛-in. dice)

1 cup finely diced celery (⅛-in. dice)

1 cup finely diced onions (⅛-in. dice)

4 Tbsp. unsalted butter, cold and cubed

1 bay leaf

2 large sprigs fresh thyme

1 cup unoaked dry white wine, like a Pinot Grigio

1 cup chicken stock

Kosher salt

Black pepper

WHAT YOU'LL NEED

Food processor

8 pieces of butcher's twine, cut in 5-inch strands

1 small sauté pan (approximately 8 inches)

1 large skillet, (approximately 15 inches)

1 sheet tray with wire baking rack

TIMING

Prep Time: 60 minutes

Cooking Time: 40 minutes

PROCESS

Preheat the oven to 350° F.

For the Stuffing:

Remove the crust from the baguette or loaf of bread. Cut the bread into chunks and process in the food processor until you have soft, fresh breadcrumbs.

In the small pan, sauté finely diced shallots in 2 tablespoons of butter. Remove the pan from the heat and combine the shallots, 2 cups of breadcrumbs, prosciutto, and the Grana Padano. Add a small amount of salt and pepper to taste.

For the Quail:

Preheat the oven to 350° F.

Take the quail out of the package and remove the metal skewers that are inserted in the quail. Pat the quail dry.

Fill the interior cavity of each quail with enough of the breadcrumb mixture to plump the quail and make it look as if it still has bones. Using the strand of butcher's twine, tie the legs shut and fold the wings behind the shoulder blades. (Use a slipknot so that it will be easier to untie once the quail is cooked.) Brush any excess breadcrumb mixture from the outside of the quail.

Sauté the quail breast side down in olive oil in the large skillet. When the skin is golden, turn the quail and continue cooking on the other side (approximately 3 minutes per side). Remove from the pan, placing it on the sheet tray with the baking rack. Put the tray in the 350° F preheated oven. After 5 minutes, remove the quail and let it rest.

In the meantime, cook the finely diced carrots, celery, onions, thyme, bay leaves, and a pinch of kosher salt in the original skillet pan, scraping and using the moisture from the vegetables to deglaze the pan.

While the vegetables are cooking, remove the twine from the quail legs.

When the vegetables are just short of al dente, add the wine and raise the heat to medium high. Cook several minutes until the wine evaporates by about half. Add enough chicken stock to just barely cover the vegetables and continue cooking until the vegetables have softened. Remove the thyme and bay leaves and whisk the cold cubes of butter into the vegetable mixture. Swirl the pan in a circular motion while whisking in the butter. Swirling keeps the sauce from breaking. Add the rested quail back to the pan for a moment and baste it with the sauce to reheat.

Serve with soft polenta (see recipe below) and garnish with the vegetables and sauce.

Notes

#1: Semiboneless quail is fantastic. The wings and legs still have bones, but the cavity is boneless. It makes it super easy to stuff. Ask your local specialty butcher or gourmet store if they can order some for you. Alternately, it is available from d'Artagnan online at www. Dartagnan.com. You could, of course, use whole quail if semiboneless is not available. I like my quail just slightly pink. If you like yours a little better done, leave it in the oven an extra 5 minutes. If you cannot find semiboneless quail and wish to use whole bone-in quail, stuff the quail as you would a turkey. In this case, you will need to cook the quail longer so the stuffing inside the cavity gets warm. If you have a friend who hunts that offers to bring you some quail, make sure he plucks the quail and leaves the skin on. Quail without the skin becomes dry quite quickly. Serve the whole quail by cutting it in half directly through the breastbone and arranging it on the polenta. Cutting it in half will make it easier to eat the stuffing.

#2: Grana Padano is a parmesan-like cheese from the Po River Valley in Northern Italy. In fact, as you drive the A-4 from Verona to Milan, there is a huge statue of a round of Grana Padano on the roadside. If you can't find Grana Padano, you may substitute Parmigiano Reggiano.

#3. If you wish to serve this at a party, you can prepare it ahead of time up until the point of whisking in the butter. At the last minute, reheat the sauce and whisk in the butter and rewarm the quail in the sauce before serving. In this case, however, you should cook the quail for a shorter time in the oven, as it will cook a bit more when you reheat it.

Polenta

Yield: 6 side dish portions | Ease of Preparation: Easy | Ease of Sourcing: Simple

INGREDIENTS

1 cup polenta
6 cups water
2 tsp. kosher salt
4 Tbsp. unsalted butter
½ cup Grana Padano

WHAT YOU'LL NEED

4-quart saucepan
Whisk
Rubber spatula

TIMING

Soaking Time: 30 minutes
Cooking Time: 45 minutes - one hour
    and 15 minutes (depending on the
    coarseness of your polenta)

PROCESS

Place the polenta and 5 cups of water in the saucepan. Stir to loosen and allow the polenta to soak for 30 minutes. Add salt and bring the polenta and water to a boil, whisking until it is smooth. Reduce the heat to low and cook, whisking occasionally. The heat needs to be low—if the polenta bubbles and spits aggressively (not sure how else to describe it!), lower the heat and add a little more water. The mixture should take around an hour to cook fully. Taste to see if it is done. If it is still al dente, continue cooking until all the grains are soft. Continue to add more water if necessary. When it is finished, whisk in the butter and cheese, cover, and keep warm.

Note

Polenta is a dish and an ingredient. Polenta the ingredient is basically Italian cornmeal. Look for medium or coarse ground yellow cornmeal. The coarser the grind of polenta, the longer it will take to cook. The package does not have to say polenta. Some people use instant polenta. Try to avoid this if you can. It is parcooked, and, frankly, it tastes as if you are trying to shortcut not just the prep time, but the flavor, as well.

Risotto all'Amarone

Yield: Serves 4–6 as a first course, 3–4 as a main course | Ease of Preparation: Moderate
Ease of Sourcing: Simple but expensive
Wine Pairing: Azienda Agricola Nicolis Amarone della Valpolicella Classico (See Note #2 below)

There are versions of red-wine risotto throughout Northern Italy. Around the charming historic town of Verona east of Lake Garda, locals use Amarone, the full-bodied dry red wine made from dried grapes for which the region of Valpolicella is so famous. Natalia Nicolis, the matriarch of the Nicolis winemaking family in San Pietro in Cariano, shared her recipe for this classic rice dish with me.

INGREDIENTS

2 quarts beef broth
½ stick unsalted butter, divided in half
¼ cup extra-virgin olive oil
1 medium onion, very finely diced
Kosher salt
1 lb. Carnaroli, Arborio, or Vialone
    Nano rice
1½ cups of Amarone della Valpolicella
2 oz. grated Grana Padano or
    Parmigiano Reggiano cheese

WHAT YOU'LL NEED

Large Dutch oven or pot
3-quart saucepan
Ladle
Wooden spoon

TIMING

Prep Time: 10 minutes
Cooking Time: 30–40 minutes

PROCESS

Warm the stock in the saucepan.

Place half the butter and the extra-virgin olive oil in the Dutch oven and heat over medium heat. When the butter has melted, raise the heat to medium high, add the onions and ½ teaspoon kosher salt, and cook until the onions have softened and are light golden, approximately 5 minutes. Be careful not to burn them. Add the rice and stir for several minutes to toast and coat the rice with oil.

Slowly add 1 cup of the Amarone and stir until it evaporates.

Lower the heat and stir one ladle of stock into the rice. Continue stirring. Once the stock has evaporated, add another ladle and repeat the process, adding stock when it evaporates and stirring. You may not need to use all of the stock.

After 10 to 15 minutes, taste the rice. Finished risotto is meant to be slightly al dente with a fairly loose texture—not brothy like a soup, but not dry—more like a rice stew. Because the rice will continue cooking a bit while you finish the dish, you must stop cooking while it is slightly less well done than your final desired texture. Add one final ¼ ladle of stock. Turn the heat off and add the rest of the Amarone, stirring vigorously. Continuing to stir vigorously, add the rest of the butter and, finally, the grated cheese. Taste the rice and add salt if needed.

Notes

#1: Risotto requires a special type of short-to-intermediate grain rice. The majority of risotto rice is grown in the Po River Valley and is classified by the length and size of the grain with designations ranging from *ordinario* for the shortest grain to *semi fino, fino,* and *superfino* for the longest grain.

The three main Italian risotto rices are:

Arborio, the most common variety, has a large, plump grain.

Carnaroli is a premium-quality rice with soft starch that dissolves well in liquid yet remains relatively firm. Carnaroli is the preferred risotto rice throughout much of Italy.

Vialone Nano, the preferred risotto rice in the Veneto (Verona and Valpolicella country!), also has a very high starch content that allows it to absorb twice its weight in liquid.

#2: Wine for cooking vs. wine for drinking. You always hear the adage to never cook with a wine you won't drink, but what happens when the wine in the recipe is super expensive, as is the case with Amarone della Valpolicella? My preference would be that you go ahead and use the more expensive wine, but if that is not realistic with your budget, substitute a wine of similar weight and flavor profile. In the case of Amarone, if you do not wish to cook with a bottle of wine that costs more than $50, try to find a Valpolicella Ripasso (wine soaked along with the pressed skins of Amarone). It is rich and has some of the ripe, dried fruit characteristics of Amarone. If you cannot find either, substitute a high-quality Zinfandel, preferably one with limited use of oak.

"First, You Must Shoot the Wild Boar . . ."
A Visit with Giorgio Colutta
Manzano, Friuli, Italy

I had to laugh when I opened the email from my friend Giorgio Colutta. An avid hunter, Giorgio is a well-respected winemaker in Friuli in northeast Italy. The opening line of his recipe for Wild Boar Sausage in Balsamic Vinegar was "First you must shoot the wild boar," which perfectly embodies *The Wine Table* concept of sourcing the freshest, most local ingredients possible.

My Italian encounter with Giorgio was delayed by traffic jams, my complete inability to pass trucks on a mountainous Italian road in my little Fiat 500, and finally by darkness. The trip from Cannara in Umbria to Manzano in Friuli that should have, according to my Italian friends, taken me five hours, had taken nine instead, and I still had yet to reach Venice. I called Giorgio, and his genial voice assured me that he would welcome me whenever I arrived. I knew Giorgio from his visits to Washington, DC and had made arrangements to visit his winery and explore the wine and food of the region.

Friuli Colli Orientali

Friuli Venezia Giulia is a diverse geographical region, with the dramatic coastline of the Gulf of Trieste, the lagoons of Grado and Marano, the rolling wooded and stream-crossed hills along the border with Slovenia, Lake Sauris and Barcis, and the Carnic Alps, all within an hour's drive of one another. (That's if I'm not the one driving.) This diversity extends to weather as well, with Trieste exhibiting the smallest temperature ranges in all of Italy, while the mountains in the north, although lovely during the summer, record some of the coldest winter temperatures in the nation every year. This varied geography and climate provides Friuli with an amazing array of food, and the wines of the region are up to the task of pairing with said foods.

Wines of Friuli Colli Orientali

Azienda Agricola Giorgio Colutta is located in Friuli Colli Orientali near Manzano in the province of Udine. The region's name translates literally as the Eastern Hills of Friuli and up until recently was known as Colli Orientali del Friuli. Wine in the region dates back to the Roman Empire, but it has been garnering attention since the 1970s. (It received DOC status in 1970.) Friuli Colli Orientali spreads along the eastern hills of Udine Province close to the border with Slovenia and is divided in three zones: Ramandolo in the north, Cialla in the middle, and Corno di Rosazzo in the south.

The local soil, known as *Flysch di Cormons* or *Ponca*, dates to the Eocene era. It is cool and light-colored, made up of alternating strata of limestone, marl, and sandstone, and has a significant amount of marine fossils. This favorable combination of friable rock and clay shrinks and swells with water, producing cracks that drive the roots deep. Although its breakable structure unfortunately renders it susceptible to landslides, Flysch soils produce fleshy aromatic whites wines that are both high in alcohol and racily acidic from international grape varieties like Sauvignon Blanc, Pinot Grigio, Pinot Bianco, and Chardonnay (with some Chardonnay and Pinot Bianco being aged in barriques). Recently there is a movement away from these international varieties back to the indigenous grape varieties like Friulano and Ribolla Gialla.

The 1980s saw a shift away from light fruity red wines made from local grape varieties toward the use of international grapes for red wines, as well. Many of these red wines were aged in small French barriques (See Wine Terms, page 472) and bottled as Vino di Tavola. Now, as with the white wines, many Friulian winemakers are moving back to producing wines from indigenous grape varieties like Refosco, Schioppettino, and Pignolo.

White Wines of Friuli Colli Orientali DOC

Well known for white wines made from international grapes—crisp Pinot Grigios and racy Sauvignon Blancs—*Fruili Colli Orientali* also produces delicious wines from traditional varieties. Friulano (formerly Tocai Friulano) makes a crowd-pleasing wine that is super fruit-driven with nutty notes. Golden-colored Ribolla Gialla can be elegant with complex nutty, floral, and piney characteristics. Allowed white grape varieties are Chardonnay, Friulano, Gewurztraminer, Malvasia, Pinot Bianco, Pinot Grigio, Ribolla Gialla, Riesling, and Sauvignon Blanc. If the wines are labeled with a single grape variety, they must be 85 percent of that variety. For example, *Friuli Colli Orientali Friulano DOC* must contain at least 85 percent Friulano.

Wines labeled *Friuli Colli Orientali Bianco DOC* may have any proportion of the allowed white grape varieties.

Red Wines of Friuli Colli Orientali DOC

Although the region is not as well known for red wine, some delicious Friulian reds can be found both locally and internationally. Allowed red grape varieties are as follows: Cabernet Franc, Cabernet Sauvignon, Merlot, Pignolo, Pinot Noir, Refosco and Refosco dal Peduncolo Rosso, Schioppettino, and Tazzalenghe.

Refosco dal Peduncolo Rosso produces a full-bodied wine with a combination of strong herbal and wild briary fruit notes. Pignolo, which is also full-bodied, has plum and blackberry notes, and with Schioppettino we find a lighter red—elegant yet spicy. International grapes like Cabernet Sauvignon, Merlot, and Cabernet Franc produce smooth, yet full-bodied wines. As with the white DOC wines, all varietally labeled red *Friuli Colli Orientali DOC* must contain 85 percent of that grape variety, e.g., Friuli Colli Orientali Schioppettino DOC must contain 85 percent Schioppettino. Blends may contain any proportion of the allowed red grapes.

There are four subzones for still wine in Friuli Colli Orientali. These subzones specialize in specific grape varieties:

Rosazzo is a DOCG that produces wines from a minimum 50 percent Friulano blended with Pinot Bianco, Chardonnay, Sauvignon, and Ribolla Gialla.

Faedis: Refosco Nostrano.

Prepotto: Schioppettino.

Cialla: Whites: Ribolla Gialla, Verduzzo Friulano or Bianco (a blend of Picolit, Ribolla Gialla, and/or Verduzzo) and Reds: Refosco or Schioppettino. The Rosso is a blend of the two.

Sweet Wines of Friuli Colli Orientali

Two indigenous grape varieties (Verduzzo and Picolit) produce delicious honeyed dessert wines made from dried grapes.

Ramandolo DOCG: Formerly a subzone of Friuli Colli Orientali, Ramandolo was raised to DOCG status in 2001. It is produced from 100 percent Verduzzo Friulano grown in the hills surrounding the small village of Ramandolo near Udine.

Colli Orientali del Friuli Picolit DOCG: Elevated to DOCG status in 2006, this is a delicious honeyed dessert wine. When from the greater Friuli Colli Orientali region, it must contain at least 85 percent Picolit. However, when labeled from the subzone of Cialla, it must contain 100 percent Picolit.

Sparkling Wines of Friuli Colli Orientali: Sparkling wines from Friuli Colli Orientali can be produced in either the Metodo Classico or Metodo Charmat from either Ribolla Gialla (100 percent) or a blend of Chardonnay, Pinot Bianco, Pinot Grigio, and/or Pinot Nero.

Giorgio Colutta

Giorgio's fifty-acre farm has vineyards in Buttrio, Manzano, and Rosazzo. Vineyard practices combine modern techniques with traditional methods of the region. As with most quality-conscious producers, Giorgio believes that the wine is made in the vineyards, and he employs techniques that respect the environment and exercises the utmost care to obtain the best grapes possible.

The winery is a remodeled farm building that has been completely modernized while still retaining old-world charm with exposed old stone walls and antique ceiling beams. The *Villa Padronale,* the original building, was expanded to include vinification areas, a barrel cellar, bottling line, and an air-conditioned warehouse, all of which are powered using solar energy that allows them to be self-sufficient and to respect the environment. In 2005, Azienda Agricola Giorgio Colutta was the first winery in the region to receive ISO 9001 certification, an international guarantee of the quality control in his products and services.

Attached to the winery, in the old main house, are a lovely tasting room and an agriturismo with well-appointed guest rooms. (I can vouch for the comfort level of the rooms, since that's where I stayed when I visited.)

Giorgio is committed to the movement in the region to refocus attention on the indigenous Friulian grape varieties.

The winery produces an extensive line of wines in four different categories. Almost all of his wines are labeled Friuli Colli Orientali DOC (exceptions to this are noted below).

Traditional Line

Most of the wines in this line-up are single varietal wines from international grapes. White wines include: **Pinot Grigio Friuli Colli Orientali DOC, Sauvignon Friuli Colli Orientali DOC, Chardonnay Friuli Colli Orientali DOC,** and **Friulano Friuli Colli Orientali DOC** (a local variety). Red wines from the traditional line are **Merlot Friuli Colli Orientali DOC, Cabernet Friuli Colli Orientali DOC** (a blend of Cabernet Franc and Cabernet Sauvignon), **Cabernet Sauvignon Friuli Colli Orientali DOC,** and **Refosco dal Peduncolo Rosso Friuli Colli Orientali DOC** (a local variety).

Cru Line

The prevalent use of international grapes in Friuli in the past had threatened the survival of many autochthonous grape varieties. The Cru line (with a few exceptions) highlights these indigenous varieties and showcases the flavors and qualities that are so precious to the region. The line includes: two white wines, **Nojâr Friuli Colli Orientali Uvaggio Bianco DOC** (a blend of Sauvignon, Chardonnay, Ribolla Gialla, and Friulano), **Ribolla Gialla Friuli Colli Orientali DOC,** and three red wines, **Selenard Friuli Colli Orientali Uvaggio Rosso DOC** (a blend of Refosco dal Peduncolo Rosso, Schioppettino, and Pignolo), **Schioppettino Friuli Colli Orientali DOC,** and **Pignolo Friuli Colli Orientali DOC.**

Bubbles and Dessert

One of the top wines of the region, **Picolit Colli Orientali del Friuli DOCG,** is produced using Picolit grapes that dry on the vines. Picolit vines produce very few clusters with few, and therefore, very concentrated grapes, and the wine produced is rich and sweet. Another sweet wine, **Verduzzo Friulano Passito DOC,** is produced using the Passito method, where the grapes are picked and then dried in plastic crates in the winery until they become raisins that are then pressed to make wine. This wine is fermented and aged in oak, resulting in a deep, rich, honeyed wine.

Colutta Sparkling Wines: Giorgio produces three sparkling wines using the Charmat Method: Prosecco DOC (100 percent Glera), Ribolla Gialla Vino Spumante Friuli DOC, and Brut Rosé Spumante VdT made from 100 percent Merlot.

Ecofriendly Line

As farmers, the Coluttas are very concerned with the environment, and they have devised a line of ecofriendly wines that respects the environment in each stage of the production cycle. These considerations include: reuse of rainwater; use of environmentally friendly products; installation of solar panels, making them self-sufficient with regards to energy consumption; use of pruning remains for heating; and utilizing recycled materials for packaging (cork, paper, and cardboard). Additionally, they use lighter-weight bottles to reduce the amount of energy used to produce and ship the bottles.

The three wines in the Ecofriendly line are **Friulano Friuli Colli Orientali DOC, Pinot Grigio Friuli Colli Orientali DOC,** and **Friuli Colli Orientali DOC Refosco dal Peduncolo Rosso.**

In addition to his work to promote local grapes and his ecofriendly line of wines, Giorgio is the cofounder of an emotionally touching project called *Diversamente DOC.*

Diversamente DOC is a joint venture between Giorgio, the local chapter of ANFFAS (the National Association of Families of Disabled People), and a few others. The project began with the 2011 vintage and brought together seven local intellectually disabled people of various ages. They were involved in many aspects of raising a small plot of Friulano on Giorgio's property, including labor in the fields, in the winery, label design, tasting, and bottling. The project's inaugural vintage launched successfully with the presentation of 650 magnums at Vinitaly 2012. On the day I visited Giorgio, the group was having lunch in the main tasting room at the winery after working that morning in the fields. We sat down and chatted with the group while they were enjoying ice cream at the end of the meal, and it was clear from the rapport that Giorgio had with them that both sides were reaping great benefits from the relationship.

Foods of Friuli

Sadly, due to my extended car trip en route to Manzano where I hit three stops in traffic on the autoroute between Florence and Padua (and by stopped I mean, get out of your car and walk around kind of stopped—set up a table and picnic kind of stopped), I missed the opportunity to join Giorgio and his family for dinner at his home in Udine that first evening.

Happily, we were able to have lunch together the next day at Ristorante Elliot nestled in the hills above verdant vineyards to discuss Friulian food and wine and to share delicious regional fare accompanied by some of Giorgio's wines. Our appetizer of local cured meats and Montasio cheese was perfect paired with Giorgio's 2012 Colutta Friulano, but the Pan-Roasted Rabbit with Chanterelles Mushrooms and a glass 2007 Colutta Cabernet (a blend of Cabernet Franc and Cabernet Sauvignon) really stole the show. In fact, it might just be the best rabbit dish I have ever eaten. (I tried unsuccessfully to finagle the recipe from the chef but had to settle for recreating the dish on my own.)

Giorgio is tanned and fit with bright blue eyes, platinum blond hair, and a ready smile. He is extremely proud of his heritage and region, and he explained to me that Friulian gastronomy is quite varied due in large part to the aforementioned geography, but it is also strongly influenced by contact with its Venetian, Slavic, and Austrian neighbors.

Soups

The names of many of the soups in the region mirror some of these influences. Names like:

Fasûj e Uardi: Herb flavored barley, bean, and pork soup.

Bòbici: Ham, bean, and potato soup from Istria.

Jota: A sauerkraut, bean, sausage, and potato soup from Trieste.

Paparot: A cornmeal, spinach, and garlic soup from Pordenone.

Boreto alla Graisana: This white fish chowder from Grado is served in two courses (similarly to Bouillabaisse). The first course is a bowl of fish soup, and the second course is a bowl of fish with a small amount of soup as a sauce.

Grains

Wheat, rye, barley, and corn grow well in the plains of the region, and many local dishes incorporate these grains.

Polenta: Cornmeal ground into polenta takes many forms in Friuli, as a base for stewed meats, baked into bread, and as a thickener for soups like **Paparot** (mentioned above).

Pan de Sorc: is a corn-based sweet bread from Gemona near Udine that has received a Slow Food Presidium.

Pasta

Lasagne ai Semi di Papavero: A specialty of Trieste, this dish is made from lasagne noodles that are sprinkled with butter, sugar, and poppy seeds.

Cjarsons: Although some recipes for this ravioli dish from the town of Carnia near Udine are said to include as many as forty ingredients, all of the recipes call for stuffing the pasta with potatoes, raisins, and *fines herbes*.

Bauletti: Hand-folded packets of pasta filled with ham and cheese.

Offelle: Pasta stuffed with spinach, pork, and veal.

Dumplings and Gnocchi

Canederli: Bread dumplings commonly found in northeastern Italy and surrounding countries, they can be served in a soup, in a butter sauce as a first course, or as an accompaniment to roasted meats.

Gnocchi: While the most common recipes for gnocchi stick to standard base ingredients like potatoes or bread, Friuli also specializes in gnocchi made from pumpkins and unusual sweet ingredients like prunes or plums (The latter two are served with a sauce of butter, cinnamon, and sugar, and topped with grated bread.)

Meats

Friuli is famous for its pork and pork products, especially the area around Carnia.

Prosciutto di San Daniele DOP: Sweet, delicate, and moist Prosciutto di San Daniele is my favorite of the big name prosciutto/jamòn/jambon foursome—which is not to say that I don't love the others, it's just in this case, I do have a favorite child—sorry. Prosciutto di San Daniele is produced in the hills around the small town of San Daniele fifteen miles north of Udine.

Other less well-known (but delicious) prosciuttos from the region are **Prosciutto di Sauris IGP**, from nearby Carnia (a well-respected pork producing region to the north of Udine and San Daniele), **Prosciutto Carso**, and **Prosciutto di Cormons.**

Other Regional Salumi

Pitina: Recognized as a Slow Food Presidium, this cured meat from Pordenone is made from finely minced deer or goat meat, seasoned with salt, garlic, and black pepper before being rolled into balls, breaded in cornmeal, and smoked in a fireplace.

Salame di Sauris: Smoked and natural versions of this salame are made in the hills near Sauris.

Pindulis: This jerky-like meat is made from dried, smoked strips of mutton or goat.

Fine examples of **Prosciutto di Oca** and **Salami di Oca** (goose) are also quite appreciated in the area.

Fagagna Pestàt: This Slow Food Presidium is a local butcher specialty produced by only two butchers from the town of Fagagna near Udine. Lard from locally raised, GMO-free pigs is ground with carrots, onions, leeks, rosemary, garlic, and parsley. The lard mixture is then stuffed into casing and aged for a period of several weeks to a full year. Fagagna Pestàt is not eaten on its own, but rather is meant to be used as an ingredient in cooking.

Muset e Brovada: A dish featuring a sausage made from pork shin, snout, and skin that is cooked and served over a warm slaw of pickled turnips.

Cèvapcici: Slavic in origin, Cèvapcici are meat patties made from a combination of beef, pork, and lamb.

Rambasici: Cabbage stuffed with beef, pork, salami, and vegetables.

Hunting, Fishing, and Foraging

There is an abundance of game in Friuli, from rabbit to wild boar. In season, stewed and roasted game graces local tables. The mountains near Lake Sauris are dotted with smokehouses that produce wonderful smoked speck and silky smoked trout (*Trota Affumicata di San Daniele*), and the forests and fields yield a bounty of lovely seasonal mushrooms.

Vegetables

Asparagus of Tavagnacco: In a region famous for its asparagus (Friuli is said to have the finest asparagus in Italy), Tavagnacco, with its annual asparagus festival, is recognized as *the* asparagus capital.

Sculpit (Silena inflate): This little-known green has thin spiked leaves and balloon-like bulbs topped by small white flowers. The plants are found growing wild in the springtime. Their leaves are finely chopped and used in risotto and frittatas.

Additionally, four vegetables from Friuli have caught the attention of the Slow Food Foundation and have been awarded Slow Food Presidia.

Cavasso and Valcosa Onions: Traditionally, the women of the region used long reeds to weave together these bright red onions from Pordenone Province to carry to market.

Gorizia Rosa: Beautiful bright red-and-pink-tinged radicchio (named because they look like a rosebud about to open) flourish in the alluvial soils around Gorizia.

Aglio di Resia is a very aromatic garlic with pinkish red skins from the Resia Valley in Udine Province. They have small bulbs with five to eight cloves and no cloves in the center of the cluster.

Ladric di Mont, Radic di Mont, Radic dal Glaz: Also known as mountain radicchio or mountain radish, Radic di Mont is a wild chicory with distinctive purple shoots that appears in the Carnic Alps for fifteen to twenty days in early May at altitudes of more than 3,000 feet. The melting snow and cool temperatures make the Radic very tender, and it is quite sought after by local foragers. Each forager is limited to one kilogram (2.2 pounds) of Radic per day. While it is not unusual to find Radic di Mont in other parts of the Alps, the Slow Food Foundation recognizes the particular Carnic practice of preserving Radic in oil in jars so that it can be enjoyed year-round.

Cheese

Cheeses are mostly made from cow's milk, with no real history of sheep or goat cheese in the region.

Montasio DOP: The most famous cheese of Friuli is a medium-soft yet grateable unpasteurized cheese with delicate fruity and nutty flavors. While good on its own, it shines as frico, a crispy baked cheese appetizer—delicious served with a chilled glass of Friulano. (See Frico recipe, page 76.)

Formadi Sot la Trape: This Ubriaco-style cow's milk cheese is soaked in the must (see Wine Terms, page 473) of Pignolo or Schioppettino. The name literally means cheese under the grape must.

Latteria Turnaria Cheese: *Latterie* are creameries that make cheese. *Latteria Turnaria* are cooperative creameries that function by a *turnaria* system. This system was established in 1880 and involved co-op members taking turns making cheese in the co-op facilities from the milk from their own cows. This system is disappearing, and the Slow Food Foundation has designated Latteria Turnaria Cheese as a Slow Food Presidium to protect this practice. The name of the cheese is actually *Latteria*, and it is produced predominantly from milk from Pezzata Rossa cows that are raised on small farms around the town of Buja in Udine Province.

Formadi Frant: Another Slow Food Presidium, *Formadi Frant* was established as a method to use broken or misshapened mountain cheeses. The defective cheeses are chopped up and mixed first with milk, then with cream. The mixture is placed in wooden molds and aged forty days before it is sold.

Desserts

As with many other dishes in Friuli, many of the desserts of the region exhibit influences from the neighbors to the north and east.

Apple Strudel: Stuffed with apples, pine nuts, and raisins.

Gubana: A yeast-raised dough that is rolled jellyroll style around a filling of apples, cinnamon, dried candied fruit, and nuts.

Presnitz: From Trieste, this sweetened dough is filled with nuts, spices, and chocolate, rolled in a long thin dowel shape, and then coiled in a spiral.

Castignoli: Chestnut cookies

Frituli: Pumpkin fritters

Panettone, Pandoro, and Colomba

Panettone and **Pandoro** are traditional Italian cakes served at Christmas time.

Panettone is a sweet yeast cake studded with candied fruit. It is originally from Milan but can now be found throughout Italy.

Pandoro (literally golden bread) is a sweet bread from Verona that is baked in a special tall, star-shaped mold. It is topped with vanilla-flavored powdered sugar, like a mountain with snow on top.

Colomba di Pasqua is a traditional Italian Easter yeast bread. The cake is shaped like a dove, the symbol of peace and resurrection. (*Colomba* means dove in Italian.) Soft and fragrant, Colomba is rich with butter and eggs, and filled with raisins and candied orange peel. The sweet crisp crust is baked-on almond icing that is applied before baking.

Giorgio is a big proponent of Friulian wine and food. He owns a wine bar in Udine that specializes in local products. Like me, Giorgio loves talking about food and wine, and his food and wine pairing recommendations were quite extensive. He recommends

Friulano with salty foods like Prosciutto di San Daniele, Soppressa (Salame), Montasio Cheese, and Frico. For game dishes, especially wild boar, he likes Refosco, and he loves the combination of pizza and sparkling Refosco.

He described customs for special occasions like at Easter when Friulano is served with eggs made in many different preparations, Pignolo accompanies roast lamb; and the traditional Easter cake, *Colomba di Pasqua*, is paired with Verduzzo.

At Christmas, they serve Tortellini in Brodo with Pinot Grigio or Schioppettino, Wild Boar with Pignolo or Refosco, and Panettone or Pandoro cake with Picolit.

During wild boar hunting season, if they are lucky enough to shoot a wild boar, he throws a big party and serves lots of Refosco.

Giorgio is extremely curious about other people's wines, and unless he is with a client or guest, he drinks wines from other winemakers—sometimes those of local friends or competitors.

At harvest time, the winery staff eats together, while the harvesters generally eat on their own. The exceptions are in difficult situations like a rush situation, on extremely hot days, or at the end of a particularly hard task when they have a dessert and a drink at the end.

At the end of harvest, the winery staff and harvesters celebrate with a special dessert and a special celebration wine on the day harvest ends. Then two weeks after harvest, Giorgio throws a big harvest party at the winery to fete the occasion.

Giorgio shared that harvest is a time of extreme importance and great joy, the culmination of an entire year's worth of work, an anxious time "depending on the progression of the season, where hail or rain can ruin the fruits of our hard work in a few seconds but this is the beauty of having a 'factory' built of stars, sun, and grapevines!" So, not only is Giorgio intelligent, compassionate, and proud of his winery and his region, he has a way with words, as well.

The Winemaker Recommends: Wild Boar with Refosco!

Pan-Roasted Rabbit
with Chanterelle Mushrooms

Yield: Serves 4 | Ease of Preparation: Moderate | Ease of Sourcing: Difficult
Wine Pairing: Colutta Cabernet, or another medium-bodied red Italian wine

I had this dish while lunching with Giorgio Colutta on the outdoor veranda at Ristorante Elliott in Manzano. The setting was so beautiful overlooking the green rolling hills of Friuli, and this was one of the most delicious rabbit dishes I have ever eaten—tender rabbit lightly dressed in a rabbit glaze and delicately sautéed chanterelles—the sepia tones of the rabbit glaze and the ochre hue of the chanterelles making it a feast for the eyes, as well. Despite my cajoling, I could not convince the chef to give me the recipe. This is my version. Rabbit is tricky. Similar in flavor to chicken, it can be chewy and lacks skin to add fat to the dish. Marinating it ahead of time adds both moisture and flavor complexity to the dish. Unfortunately, rabbit can also be a bit expensive and difficult to find. To make matters more complicated, it can be challenging to portion, so my version uses only leg quarters. Why bother, you ask? Because it is exceedingly delicious!

INGREDIENTS

For the Marinade:

½ cup diced carrots

1 cup diced onions

½ cup diced celery

2 cloves garlic, crushed

2 bay leaves

4 sprigs thyme

2 sprigs rosemary

1 sprig sage

1½ Tbsp. kosher salt

10 black peppercorns

2 cups crisp unoaked white wine

For the Rabbit and Mushrooms:

4 rabbit hind legs

1 Tbsp. extra-virgin olive oil

2 Tbsp. + 1 Tbsp. + 4 Tbsp. unsalted
    butter, divided

1 lb. chanterelle mushrooms, carefully
    cleaned

2 Tbsp. finely minced shallots

2 Tbsp. lemon juice

Kosher salt

black pepper, freshly ground

3 cups rabbit stock or chicken stock,
    preferably homemade

WHAT YOU'LL NEED

Nonreactive container to marinate the rabbit

One large skillet—big enough to hold the
    4 rabbit legs

Medium roasting pan

One skillet for the mushrooms

4-quart saucepan

Skewer to poke the rabbit

Instant read meat thermometer (optional)

TIMING

Marinade Prep: 30 minutes

Marinating Time: 6 hours to overnight

Cooking Time: 45 minutes to one hour

PROCESS

For the Marinade:

Combine all of the ingredients for the marinade.

Marinate the rabbit for at least 6 hours, preferably overnight, turning the container periodically to make sure all parts of the rabbit get exposed to the marinade.

For the Rabbit and Mushrooms:

Preheat oven to 400° F.

Over moderately high heat, melt 1 tablespoon olive oil and 2 tablespoons butter together in the skillet. Remove the rabbit from the marinade and wipe it dry, making sure there are no pieces of vegetables from the marinade. (Strain the marinade reserving 1 cup for later use.) Add the rabbit pieces to the skillet and begin browning it. You want to develop a nice brown color. When you have developed good color on both sides, transfer to the roasting pan and roast for 20–30 minutes.

When they are just firm to the touch, remove the roasting pan from the oven. Pierce the thickest part of the rabbit thigh with a skewer. If the juices run clear, your rabbit is done. If it is still pink, cook for several more minutes.

While the rabbit is cooking, deglaze the skillet with the cup of reserved marinade, scraping to get all the brown bits off the bottom of the pan. Pour this mixture and 3 cups of stock into the saucepan and boil to reduce to make a glaze. This should take 20–30 minutes.

If your rabbit finishes cooking before your stock is reduced, remove it from the oven and continue reducing the stock. Keep the rabbit in a warm place so that it stays warm but does not continue cooking. To check that the glaze is done, dip a spoon into it and draw your finger along the back of the spoon. If it leaves a distinct line, the glaze is done; if not, continue reducing. When the glaze is nice and thick, whisk in the 1 tablespoon of cold butter. Return the rabbit to the skillet and pour the glaze over it, turning the individual legs to coat them in the glaze. If the rabbit has cooled off, reheat it on low heat.

In the meantime, melt 4 tablespoons butter in a skillet large enough to hold the mushrooms. When the butter starts to foam, add the mushrooms and toss until coated. Add the minced shallots and swirl until coated. Cook for several minutes until the mushrooms start to soften and add lemon juice, salt, and finely ground black pepper to taste. Keep warm.

Arrange a portion of chanterelles on each plate and place the rabbit leg on it. Spoon the reduced rabbit sauce over the rabbit and mushrooms and around the plate.

Notes

#1. If you are experienced with rabbit butchery or are lucky enough to have an artisan butcher in your area, you may make this dish with a whole rabbit cut into pieces. Portion your rabbit (or have the butcher do it for you) including separating the rack from the saddle. You should have two tiny racks of rabbit, two hind legs, two forelegs, and the saddle. Save the leftover bones and meat scraps to make rabbit stock. The presentation is much nicer if you take this option, but remember that the smaller pieces will cook more quickly than the large hind legs. Both whole rabbit and rabbit hind legs are available at gourmet butcher shops or through d'Artagnan online, where the rabbit hind legs come conveniently packaged four to a package.

#2. If you are not comfortable gauging the temperature by pressing with your finger or the skewer method, you may use a meat thermometer, but be careful not to touch the tip of the thermometer to the bone of the rabbit. The USDA suggests an internal temperature of 160° F for rabbit. Pull your rabbit at about 155° F. Carryover cooking will bring it up to 160° F while you finish making the sauce.

#3. Chanterelle mushrooms can be found in spring and fall at most gourmet stores and farmer's markets. If you cannot find them, substitute beech or shiitake mushrooms. The flavor will be different, but it will still be delicious.

Balsamic Glazed Wild Boar Sausages

Yield: 4 portions | Ease of Preparation: Simple
Ease of Sourcing: Moderately difficult if you use wild boar sausage.
Wine Pairing: Giorgio Colutta Refosco or Pignolo, or Northern Rhône Syrah

Giorgio Colutta is an avid hunter. Every fall, he and his son hunt for wild boar. If their hunt is successful, friends and family gather to celebrate and feast. A couple of years ago, he invited me to join them. Sadly, I was unable to attend, so he sent me this recipe. The email begins, "First you must shoot the wild boar." He goes on to say, "prepare sausage from it," but notes that the recipe works well with pork sausage in case you don't have wild boar sausage just lying around. I've made it with wild boar as well as pork sausage. Wild boar sausage is darker, gamier, and leaner. Pork has lighter flavors and a higher fat content. Both are delicious!

INGREDIENTS

8 links wild boar sausages
2 cups balsamic vinegar (no more
    than two years old. Aged balsamic
    vinegar is too thick.)
Optional: 1 Tbsp. olive oil

WHAT YOU'LL NEED

Skillet large enough to hold 8 sausages
Tongs

TIMING

20 minutes

PROCESS

Preheat your skillet over medium heat. Add sausages to the skillet and press to keep them as flat as possible. Brown one side at a time. If the sausages are very lean, use a bit of the optional oil so they don't char.

Once browned on all sides, add half the balsamic vinegar to the pan, lower the heat to medium-low, and cook covered for 10 to 15 minutes, turning the sausages every 5 minutes. If the vinegar begins to thicken, add a little more. Be very careful not to let the vinegar reduce too much, or it will turn into a syrup and burn. The sausages are cooked when they are firm to the touch.

Serve with polenta (recipe on Page 114) or roasted potatoes.

Notes

#1. Wild Boar sausages are not available on every grocer's shelf, but d'Artagnan sells packages of 4 links each online. Should you wish to substitute pork sausage, use thick links, not thin breakfast links. Thin links will cook too quickly before you have time to develop the balsamic glaze.

#2. Refosco are Pignolo are not household grape names. If you cannot find them, I would substitute a Northern Rhône Syrah.

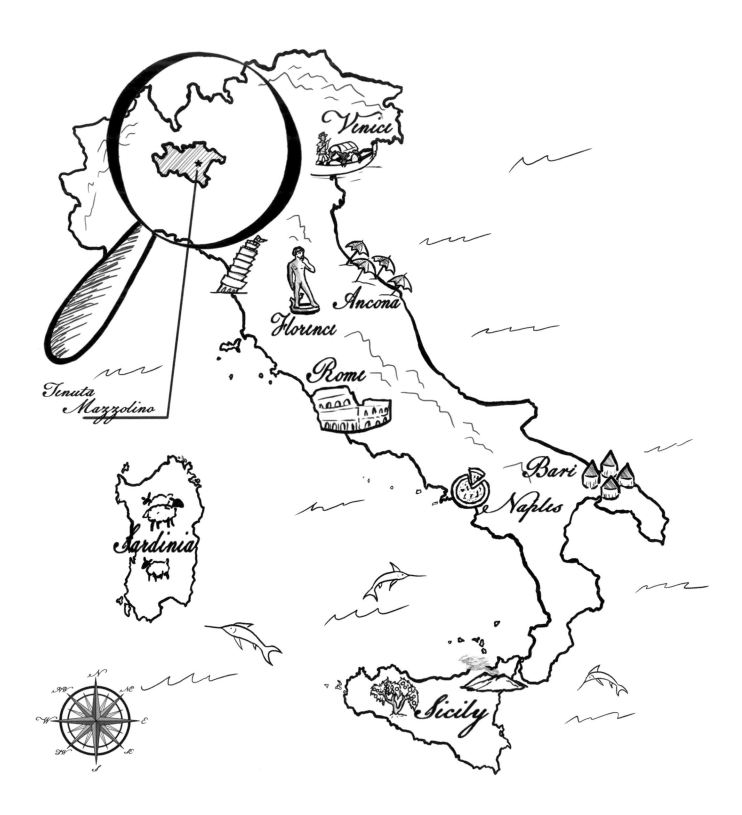

Tenuta
Mazzolino

Vinici

Florinci

Ancona

Romi

Sardinia

Bari

Naplis

Sicily

"Franco-Italian Reality"
A Visit with Jean-François Coquard
Tenuta Mazzolino, Oltrepò Pavese, Italy

One of the reasons people travel is to experience new things—"to expand their horizons." Each time we do so, we add a layer to our character. If the experience is positive, that layer adds a favorable texture to our essence. Even if the experience is negative, it changes us somehow, informs our thinking and the way we look at our own world.

As an adult, most of my traveling has been to Europe, and the things I have seen while traveling have refined my view of the world. I was born in Kansas, the middle child of a career Air Force family. As with most military families, we moved a lot, returning to Kansas when my Dad was stationed places where we could not follow and for vacation every summer. I ended up back in Kansas for high school and college. Since college, after time spent as an exchange student in France, I have lived in Northern Virginia across the Potomac River from Washington, DC. So, do I feel like a Kansan? Frankly, no. I love going home to visit my family, but it is clear to me that living in a city has changed me. I like the proximity to cultural opportunities and to shopping, particularly great wine and food shops. At the same time, I value farms and farmers, partly because as a chef I find these people and their work important, but also because my mother was

The Coquard family
Photo credit: Jean-François Coquard

raised on a farm in Kansas and I was exposed at a young age to farm life and values and to the bounty of my grandmother's garden. Both where I am from and where I live now have shaped who I am.

I think this is how Jean-François Coquard and his family must feel. Jean-François is originally from Beaujolais in east central France, but after graduating with an oenology degree, a *Diplôme National d'Oenologue* (DNO) from the Université de Bourgogne in Dijon, he spent fifteen years as the oenologist at Tenuta Mazzolino (a fifty-five-acre estate owned by the Braggiotti family since 1980) in Corvino San Quirico in Italy's Oltrepò Pavese region.

Oltrepò Pavese is in Lombardy in northern Italy. It is named after the famed Po River and literally means "on the other side of the Po, in the region of Pavia" because of its location south of the Po River where the hills begin their rise to the Ligurian Apennines. The Po is Italy's longest river, originating in the Cottian Alps on the border of France and Western Italy and emptying 405 miles away into the Adriatic Sea between Venice and Ravenna. The Po River Valley is Italy's widest and most fertile valley. Wine from Oltrepò Pavese accounts for half of the wine production in the region of Lombardy.

Wine Laws of Oltrepò Pavese

Sparkling Wines of Oltrepò Pavese

Oltrepò Pavese Metodo Classico DOGC: Oltrepò Pavese's most important wine is Oltrepò Pavese Metodo Classico DOCG, a sparkling white wine made from 70 percent Pinot Nero and 30 percent of either Chardonnay or Pinot Grigio. The rosé version must contain 85 percent Pinot Nero. Oltrepò Pavese Metodo Classico DOCG must spend fifteen months on the lees and vintage-dated wines must age twenty-four months before bottling. The local wine consortium has designated the name *Cruasé* for this rosé traditional method sparkling wine. Only members of the Consortium may use the name *Cruasé*, a combination of the words Cru and rosé. Blanc de Blancs traditional method sparkling wines from Chardonnay are also produced but are not entitled to the DOCG designation.

Sangue di Giuda dell'Oltrepò Pavese DOC: *Sangue di Giuda* (Judas's blood) is a lightly sparkling semisweet red wine made from Croatina. It is delicious with salami—the sweet fizziness cutting through the fat and saltiness of the salami.

Still Wines of Oltrepò Pavese

Oltrepò Pavese's history of selling bulk wine to Milan, small property size, and a large co-op presence make it a region with relatively lower quality levels when compared to its neighbors to the north (Piedmont and Franciacorta).

Oltrepò Pavese DOC is a large DOC that covers most of the region. The rules of this DOC are extremely broad and allow white, red, still, sparkling, and sweet wines. Certain single-variety wines may attach the grape name to the end of the wine name, e.g., Oltrepò Pavese Chardonnay DOC and Oltrepò Pavese Pinot Grigio DOC.

Oltrepò Pavese Rosso DOC from Barbera, Croatina, Uva Rara, and Vespolina can be quite good. The allowed white grapes for Oltrepò Pavese Bianco DOC are Riesling Renano, Riesling Italico, Chardonnay, Cortese, Malvasia, and Moscato. Pinot Nero is used for rosé still wines.

There are four other DOCs for still wine in Oltrepò Pavese—all for red wine: Casteggio DOC, Buttafuoco dell'Oltrepò Pavese DOC, Bonarda dell'Oltrepò Pavese DOC, and Pinot Nero dell'Oltrepò Pavese DOC, of which the latter two are of considerably higher quality.

Tenuta Mazzolino

Bonarda dell'Oltrepò Pavese DOC: This still red wine is made from a minimum of 85 percent Bonarda (a.k.a. Croatina) and a maximum of 15 percent Barbera, Vespolina, and/or Uva Rara.

Pinot Nero dell'Oltrepò Pavese DOC: The best still red wines of Oltrepò are Pinot Nero dell'Oltrepò Pavese DOC—Burgundian-style, oak-aged Pinot Nero with a small but qualitatively significant presence.

This region of Italy (once part of the Piedmont) has strong historical links to France as is evidenced by the important role of Pinot Nero in their wines. Oltrepò Pavese is the third largest producer of Pinot Nero/Noir in Europe after Burgundy and Champagne (much of this Pinot Nero is used in production of Oltrepò Pavese Metodo Classico DOGC). The local consortium notes that the Romans had early genotypes of Pinot Nero in Oltrepò Pavese. They posit the possibility that it was this Pinot Nero that the Romans brought to Southern France. Either way, the Pinot Nero currently found in

Mazzolino Cruasé aging on riddling racks.

Oltrepò Pavese was brought from France in the mid-19th century after the onset of Phylloxera. (See Wine Terms, page 474.)

As noted, the most well-known wines of Oltrepò Pavese are sparkling, but the region's DOC still Pinot Neros are receiving accolades among the world's wine press. With his background in Burgundy, Jean-François was well suited to make that happen, and his single varietal premium cuvée called simply "Noir" is a stellar blend of Burgundian grape and winemaker with the soil and sun of Oltrepò Pavese. Every year of his tenure at Tenuta Mazzolino, Jean-François's Noir received at least *due bicchieri* (two glasses) out of the three possible in the *Gambero Rosso Guida dei Vini d'Italia*, Italy's top wine guide. For three years, it received two "red" *bicchieri* (red indicates the wine was nominated for *tre bicchieri* but fell slightly short), and for six years, Jean-François's Noir received *tre bicchieri* (three glasses), the highest award.

Tenuta Mazzolino

Tenuta Mazzolino produces a wide range of wines:

Pinot Nero: Mazzolino makes three wines from Pinot Nero: **Noir,** their flagship Gambero Rosso-awarded red, is rich and complex, suitable for aging; **Terrazze,** a softer lighter version, is meant for early consumption; and **Cruasé Brut Metodo Classico,** their sparkling rosé.

Bonarda: the local name for Croatina.

Corvino: 100 percent Cabernet Sauvignon.

Val di Pra: a blend of Croatina, Cabernet Sauvignon, Merlot, and Barbera.

Vivace: a lightly sparkling wine made from Croatina (Bonarda).

Chardonnay: Mazzolino makes three Chardonnays: **Blanc** is oak fermented and aged with the aim of producing a Burgundian-style wine; **Camarà** is a fresher, brighter wine with fermentation and aging in stainless steel; and their **Blanc de Blancs,** a Brut Traditional Method Sparkling wine.

Foods of Oltrepò Pavese

Given the incredibly fertile soils of the Po River valley, agriculture is of paramount importance, and as is true throughout Italy, the food culture is rich with local products.

Rice is the primary crop, and *risotto*, not pasta, has a starring role in the local cuisine (which is not to say there aren't some really fine pasta dishes to be had there as well, including various types of *agnolotti, ravioli,* and *malfatti*). *Risotto con pepperoni* (bell pepper risotto), *Risotto con fiore di zucca* (squash blossom risotto), and *risotto con funghi* (mushroom risotto) are some of the best-known rice dishes in Oltrepò Pavese.

Corn, another common crop, is ground for polenta and used in *Polenta di Mosto* (Polenta flavored with Grape Must).

Pork

As with much of Italy, cured pork products are extremely popular.

Salame di Varzi DOP is the most famous pork product in Oltrepò Pavese. In 1989, this coarse ground dried salame was the first salame to receive the DOP designation (Protected Designated Origin). The designation asserts that Salame di Varzi is distinguished from other dried Italian sausages by the favorable weather conditions produced by the combination of sea breezes from the Ligurian coast and currents of cooler air flowing down from the mountains through the Staffora Valley. These winds allow for the use of less salt in the curing process. The curing mixture is comprised of salt, whole black peppercorn, red wine infused with garlic, and potassium or sodium nitrate. Additionally, Salame di Varzi is produced using the leg, shoulder, and neck, prime cuts of meat that are traditionally used to make prosciutto and coppa in other regions of Italy. In accordance with tradition, the aging process takes place in traditional aging cellars with a temperature range between 50 and 54° F and 95 percent humidity. The history of Salame di Varzi dates back to the 13th century, when the Marchesi di Malaspina used to offer it to guests as a special treat.

Other regional pork products include: **Pancetta Pavese**, salt-cured pork belly; **Cotechino Pavese**, a pork sausage similar in preparation to salami that must be cooked prior to eating; **Coppa**, ham (similar to prosciutto) made from the shoulder and neck of the pig; and **Lardo**, salt-cured fat back, traditionally flavored with rosemary and black peppercorns. (Lardo comes from the fattier back portion of the pig, where there is almost no meat, while pancetta comes from the belly, where, as with bacon, there are strips of meat running through the fat.)

Cheese

The most famous cheeses of the Oltrepò Pavese are **Caprini** goat cheeses of various ages; **Formaggella di Menconico**, a soft raw cow's milk cheese from near Pavia; and **Nisso dell'Oltrepò**, a creamy, intensely flavored cheese made from cow and goat milk.

Honey: While acacia honey is especially appreciated, delicious woodland, blackberry, and chestnut honeys can also be found.

It was in his capacity as Tenuta Mazzolino's winemaker that I first met Jean-François. He was on a ride along with his Washington, DC, distributor Michael Downey Selections and popped into Arrowine and Cheese, where I was working at the time.

On another occasion several years later, when I was the Executive Chef of Buck's Fishing & Camping, I was standing in the dining room at Buck's in the middle of the afternoon. We weren't open for dinner yet, but I heard a pounding on the front window. I could see someone peering inside and waving. It was Jean-François. He had been driving by with a salesperson from Michael Downey Selections

Tasting Room, Tenuta Mazzolino

and spotted Buck's (where he had eaten on several occasions) and insisted they stop just to say hi. After quick hugs, they went on their way but returned to dinner later that evening. Jean-François is a total carnivore, and he loves Buck's signature Wood-Grilled Prime Strip Steak.

I liked his wines from the first time I tasted them, and since I'm a total Francophile, we have always had involved discussions about his native Beaujolais region and Lyon, the "gastronomic capital of France." One of the things that first drew me to Jean-François was that he is almost as food-obsessed as I am. This mutual food craziness made him the perfect guide to take me on a food tour of Oltrepò Pavese.

I *could* tell you that planning my visit to Jean-François was half the fun, but that would be a blatant lie. I enjoyed the emails back and forth hammering out the details, but the trip itself was a total blast!

After a tour of the Mazzolino winery where we tasted current vintages of their wines, we headed out for a fantastic lunch at Ristorante Leon d'Oro in nearby Casteggio. Open weekdays at lunchtime only, Leon d'Oro is geared toward the wine industry—its clientele is made up of winemakers and the vendors who sell to them. Not surprisingly, it was a predominantly male crowd. We were joined at lunch by another friend, Claudio Giorgi, the agronomist at Tenuta Mazzolino.

The food was fantastic—exactly what I like—simple, traditional, and local. The owner and his son spent the first several minutes arguing rather loudly (okay, they were shouting) over whether or not to seat us. It seems they had both taken a reservation for the last table, but hey—we were there first! We grabbed that last table before they could change their minds. Once we sat down, they could not have been nicer. We clinked chilled glasses of sparkling Mazzolino Cruasé Brut Rosé and waited for our food. I was surprised when Jean-François mentioned that it is not customary to drink at lunchtime at the local "workers" restaurants in the area, but given the professions of all of the restaurant patrons, wine at lunch is the norm at Leon d'Oro.

The meal began with multiple plates of appetizers: a cured meat platter with Salame di Varzi, Prosciutto, and Pancetta; small colorful sweet peppers stuffed with tuna; marinated roasted red and yellow sweet bell peppers; and huge slices of fried fresh Porcini drizzled with delicious olive oil (sinfully extravagant to me, since Porcini are so hard to come by in the US). But the best dish was simple yet so delicious—thin slices of zucchini breaded and fried in olive oil. The chef told me the secret to the breading was the combination of extremely fine dried breadcrumbs and double 00 pasta flour. All I know is the zucchini was hot and succulent, and the breading was fine, yet crunchy, lightly flavored by the pristine olive oil and the perfect amount of salt.

The leitmotif of simplicity continued throughout the subsequent courses: *risotto con funghi,* mushroom risotto—creamy and redolent with umami from the mushrooms and the Parmigiano Reggiano; and *agnolotti con Brasato,* ravioli filled with braised beef and lightly sauced with a thin coating of meat broth, minuscule shreds of braised beef, and Parmigiano Reggiano. I was so pleased with the delicacy of the flavors of this dish, not at all what I was expecting from beef ravioli. The chef's hand at dressing the pasta was a perfect example of the supreme importance of not oversaucing pasta—a habit to which many American cooks fall prey. To quote Mario Batali, "The pasta is the game—the sauce is the condiment." Dessert was *gelato affogato al caffè,* vanilla gelato with espresso poured over it—again, very simple and completely satisfying.

With no menu, service that's familiar without being fawning, and a chef dedicated to local high-quality ingredients and culinary restraint, Leon d'Oro is the type of restaurant I wish would open up near my house. This is a restaurant I would return to again and again, assuming I'm ever in Casteggio for lunch on a weekday—and that I remember to make reservations!

After lunch, Jean-François and I hopped in his car and headed out for an afternoon visiting artisanal food producers. First we stopped at Fattoria I Gratèr, a local goat cheese producer who sells at Jean-François's Saturday farmer's market. Marco and Giovanna

Buzzi produce six cheeses on their farm in the quiet hills of the Val Schizzola. With only 50 goats, the herd is fairly small and they only use milk from their own goats for their cheeses. *Camosciata delle Alpi,* a heritage breed of goats known for their chamois-colored coats with black stripes down the back and on their faces, is valued for the high quality of their milk. Marco is completely dedicated to sustainable and humane practices. His goats are happy and the cheese is delicious. They also produce ricotta and yoghurt from goat milk. Additionally, they sell fruit and fruit juices grown in a small greenhouse on their property.

Our second stop of the day was at Salumificio Magrotti, an artisanal producer of Salame di Varzi. Owner Piero Magrotti took us on a tour of the facility. Piero and his family are one of thirteen producers approved to produce Salame di Varzi. Piero took us on a tour of the Salumificio beginning in the shop where finished Salame is offered for sale to the public and then took us to the aging rooms, some of which were several floors below ground level. Because of the humidity, beneficial mold occurs on the sausages while they age. The sausages are brushed periodically to remove the mold and

expose the skin to air to encourage aging. That part of the tour was a bit uncomfortable. I am not usually sensitive to mold, but the tight underground quarters and presence of such an extreme amount of mold and high humidity were oppressive and made it difficult to breathe. I was not unhappy when we mounted the stairs and emerged in the butcher room, where slabs of pork were hung to age before being broken down into manageable portions for grinding.

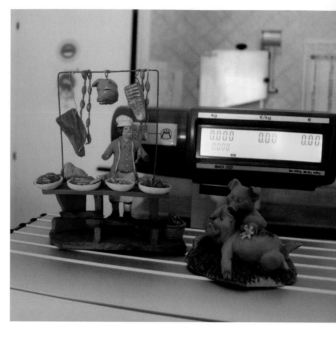

Despite the old adage about not wanting to see your sausage being made, the Magrotti facility was pristinely clean, and the product is so delicious I can definitely recommend the experience. Salame di Varzi comes in seven sizes, with the largest being the *Cucito* so named because two pig casings are sewn together before stuffing (*cucire* means to sew in Italian). Piero explained that this larger size allows for longer aging and adds to the complexity of the finished *Cucito*. Not surprisingly, the Cucito was my favorite of the Magrotti Sausages.

Our final stop of the day was at Albergo Ristorante Selvatico in Rivanazzano Terme, where Piera Spalla Selvatico and her daughter Michela run the kitchen, while Piera's

Piero Magrotti, Salumificio Magrotti

other daughter Francesca charmingly manages the front of the house of this elegant yet comfortable family-owned inn and restaurant. Jean-François, Claudio, and I were on a mission. We were going to learn to make risotto from a master. Piera is a local celebrity chef specializing in recipes from Oltrepò Pavese and Lombardy. Piera and Michela had a full cooking schedule planned complete with appetizers, a main course, desserts, and, of course, risotto.

Piera and Michela's kitchen is staffed primarily by women, the atmosphere quiet and friendly. I felt very comfortable putting on my apron and jumping in to help. We made Fried Eggplant and Tomato Stacks with Melted Mozzarella, Bonèt di Cioccolato with Stewed Peaches, Baked Peaches with Amaretti Cookies, and I prepped for Squash Blossom Risotto. When dinner rolled around, I joined Jean-François and Claudio on the flower-bedecked patio for the first couple of courses: a platter of local meats including a silky Lardo and, of course, Salame di Varzi, followed by the Eggplant Tomato stack. Then it was time to make the risotto. Now, I don't want to throw Jean-François or Claudio under the bus, but when the time came to make the risotto, it became clear that they were more interested in eating it than cooking it. I'll give Jean-François credit for coming into the kitchen to take photos of *me* cooking the risotto with my camera!

Texture is very important when making risotto, and it is paramount to avoid overcooking the rice and letting the dish get too dry. Think al dente rice stew, and you'll be on the right track. I have cooked risotto often over the years, and I was happy to see that my technique was correct. Approval from someone of Piera's stature was a validation.

Still, the most surprising part of the evening was the large black truffle sitting with my mise en place for the risotto. When Piera told me we were making squash blossom risotto, I expected the diced zucchini, minced shallots, and grated cheese (plus I had diced, minced, and grated all the ingredients earlier in the day). When she handed me a truffle at the end of the cooking process and instructed me to grate a good half of the truffle into the risotto "to add complexity and flavor," I had to laugh. She had buried the lead. No restaurant in the United States would make a risotto with a significant quantity of truffle in it and not list truffle as the first ingredient in the name of the dish. Such is the dignified, understated aspect of Piera's personality.

Jean-François and Claudio approved the risotto, and I have to thank Jean-François for raiding his wine cellar and bringing some fantastic wines to dinner. That in turn spurred Francesca to go deep into the Selvatico cellar to share some gems of her own. Thank goodness I was staying the night in one of the rooms above the restaurant—driving home afterwards might have been challenging.

The next morning, I was up, maybe not bright but definitely early, for another cooking session with Piera and Michela. We were going to be making malfatti. *Malfatti* literally means "poorly made" and refers to the uneven shape of this hand-rolled pasta. There are many variations of malfatti. The version we made that morning featured zucchini. They have such an abundance of zucchini in the summer, they are constantly searching for ways to use it (anyone who has ever grown zucchini is familiar with that dilemma), although Michela also recommends making it with spinach. The batch we made used thirty eggs, since we were featuring it on the lunch menu that day at the restaurant. That's a lot of eggs!

After we made the malfatti, Piera and I met Jean-François, his wife Isabelle, and his children at a local hydroponic strawberry farm. It was amusing listening to Jean-François, Isabelle, and the kids switching back and forth between French and Italian. All four of his children were born in Oltrepò Pavese, and they are all fluent in Italian and French and quite conversant in English and Spanish.

Piera making malfatti

Since that visit to Italy, I've seen Jean-François several times in Virginia for a trade show with Michael Downey Selections. Jean-François is a popular regular in that group. It always makes me laugh, the Italian guys say he's French, the French guys say he's Italian.

A couple of years ago, Jean-François and his family moved back to France, settling down in his hometown of Chessy in the Pierres Dorées part of southern Beaujolais where his family has lived for thirteen generations. Isabelle is from there as well, and they decided it was time to move closer to their families. He has started his own wine business, JF Coquard Vins, growing grapes and making wine on his family property, buying other grapes to produce wine in Beaujolais, France, and Lombardy, Italy, buying wine to blend his own cuvées, and working as a consulting winemaker. They have renovated a 200-year-old stone house built by one of his ancestors and are settling well into their life in France. Their time in Italy is over for now, but their lives benefitted so much from the experience. As Jean-François explained, "when my kids were in Italy, they were cool because in Italy they were 'Frenchy' and now it is fun for them to be 'Italiano.'"

Isabelle shared her family recipe for Blanquette de Veau with me and recommends serving it with hand-cut tagliatelle pasta. In verifying certain details of the recipe, I asked Jean-François if she really meant pasta like in Italy or did she mean *pâtes* or *nouilles*, the French words for pasta or noodles. I could almost hear the horror in his response. "Definitely not *nouilles*," he said. "That's only good for the French or Americans." His comment reminded me of a conversation I had with his kids at the strawberry patch in Oltrepò Pavese. I asked them in French if they liked *nouilles*. They looked at me puzzled. Jean-François said, "She wants to know if you like pasta." They understood that immediately and let me know they definitely liked pasta.

Back in Beaujolais, the family grows a lot of their own vegetables in a garden they share with Jean-François's dad. They have a local butcher, baker, and cheesemonger in Chessy. There is a huge outdoor market in Villefranche, and the Halles of Lyon (named after Paul Bocuse) is world-famous. His frequent travels to Italy allow him to keep the family supplied with Parmigiano Reggiano, excellent olive oil, and good ripe tomatoes to make pasta sauce. Clearly, although they have moved back to Beaujolais, their link with Italy is still strong. As I said, our travel experiences shape who we are and what we become. It doesn't matter if they feel Italian or French; Jean-François, Isabelle, and their kids have the right idea—celebrating both sides of their cultural upbringing and enjoying every minute of it.

The Winemaker Recommends: With Blanquette de Veau he advises JF Coquard Vins Beaujolais Blanc "Les Pierres Dorées"; or if you prefer red, he recommends JF Coquard Vins Morgon "Les Charmes."

Fried Zucchini

Yield: Serves 4 as a first course or 8 as appetizers | Ease of Preparation: Moderate | Ease of Sourcing: Simple
Wine Pairing: Oltrepò Pavese white or young unoaked Mâcon

I had this dish as an appetizer during lunch at Ristorante Leon d'Oro in Casteggio in Oltrepò Pavese with Jean-François Coquard and Claudio Giorgi of Tenuta Mazzolino. It was perfect—crunchy outside and meltingly soft inside—delicious with Tenuta Mazzolino Camarà Blanc, an unoaked Chardonnay. Make sure you use young zucchini, less than 1½ inches in diameter: the skin is tender and large seeds have yet to develop.

INGREDIENTS

4 medium zucchini (6–8 inches long)
1 large egg
1 cup half-and-half
1 cup homemade dry breadcrumbs or
    panko crumbs
1 cup flour
Kosher salt
Extra-virgin olive oil
Maldon salt for garnishing

WHAT YOU'LL NEED

Food processor
Two shallow pans for breading
Deep frying pan or electric fryer
Slotted spoon or spider for lifting
    squash out of oil
Paper towel-lined platter

TIMING

Prep Time: 15 minutes
Frying Time: 15 minutes

PROCESS

Cut the ends off the zucchini and cut them in half. You will have 8 log shapes approximately 3 inches long. Cut them in 3 slices lengthwise.

Beat the egg well. Whip in the half-and-half, being careful to mix it very well so that the whites of the egg are completely blended in. Put the flour, breadcrumbs, and 1 teaspoon of kosher salt in the food processor and process for 30 seconds. Put the egg mixture in one breading pan and the breadcrumb mixture in the other.

If you do not have an electric fryer, place 1 inch of olive oil in your frying pan, making sure the level is 1½ to 2 inches below the top of the pan. You do not want the oil to boil over during the cooking process. Heat the olive oil to 350° F degrees. If you don't have a thermometer, test the heat of the oil by sprinkling a pinch of flour in the oil. If it sizzles, the oil is ready.

Working quickly in small batches, dip the zucchini in the egg mixture and lift out with a fork, shaking off excess liquid. Coat the egg-moistened zucchini in the flour. Shake off the excess flour and drop in the oil. (Do not over coat the zucchini. Thin but complete breading is key to the delicate crunch of this dish.) Fry the zucchini in the hot oil. Do not crowd the pan. You will need to cook in several batches. Fry until lightly golden, remove before it browns. Place the fried zucchini on the paper towel-lined platter and sprinkle with a small amount of Maldon salt. Repeat with the remainder of zucchini and serve immediately.

Squash Blossom Risotto (with Truffles)

Yield: Serves 8 as an appetizer, 6 as an entrée | Ease of Preparation: Moderate
Ease of Sourcing: Moderate to difficult depending on the season.
Wine Pairing: Tenuta Mazzolino Blanc or other Oltrepò Pavese Bianco

While visiting Jean-François Coquard in Oltrepò Pavese, I had the opportunity to join Chefs Piera Spalla Selvatico and Michela Selvatico in the kitchen of Albergo Ristorante Selvatico, their restaurant in Rivanazzano Terme. Piera is a local celebrity chef and an expert at making risotto. Piera had told me we were making squash blossom risotto, so I was quite surprised to see the large black truffle sitting next to the diced zucchini, minced shallots, and grated cheese "to add complexity and flavor," she said. I had to laugh. She had buried the lead. No restaurant in the United States would make risotto with truffle in it and not list truffle as the first ingredient in the name of the dish. Adding truffle is optional, but I think it adds a lush, earthy note to the dish.

INGREDIENTS

¾ cup squash blossoms cut in ⅓-inch
    strips
⅓ cup olive oil
⅔ cup unsalted butter, divided
1½ cups finely diced yellow onions
Kosher salt
1 clove minced garlic
2 cups risotto rice (Carnaroli, Arborio, or
    Vialone Nano)
½ cup crisp unoaked white wine
    (e.g., Pinot Grigio)

2 quarts heated homemade chicken stock
    (or vegetable stock)
3 cups zucchini cut in ¼ inch dices
    (approximately two medium zucchini)
¾ cup grated Parmigiano Reggiano +
    1 cup for garnishing
Finely ground black pepper
Optional: one small black truffle or one
    3 oz. container of d'Artagnan Black
    Truffle Butter

WHAT YOU'LL NEED

Paper towels
Small paring knife
4-quart saucepan
Dutch oven
Wooden spoon
Ladle
Optional: Microplane grater to grate the
    truffle

TIMING

Prep Time: 30 minutes
Cooking Time: 30–40 minutes

PROCESS

If you are using the optional truffle, grate the truffle (approximately ½ cup) with a microplane grater.

To clean the squash blossoms, use your paring knife to gently open them up. Remove the stamen and the stem and lightly rinse the blossoms under cool water. There may be insects inside the blossoms. Place them on paper towels to dry. Once they are dry, cut them in ⅓-inch strips and set them aside. If you are not using them right away, it is best to refrigerator them.

Warm the stock in the saucepan.

Place ⅓ cup butter and ⅓ cup extra-virgin olive oil in the Dutch oven and heat over medium heat. When the butter has melted, raise the heat to medium high, add the onions and ½ teaspoon kosher salt, and cook until the onions have softened and are translucent and light golden, approximately 3 minutes. Add garlic and stir for 10 seconds. Be careful not to burn the onions and garlic. Add the rice and stir to toast and coat the rice with oil, approximately 2 minutes.

Add white wine and stir until almost completely evaporated.

Lower the heat to medium and stir 1 ladle of stock into the rice. Continue stirring. Once the stock has evaporated, add another ladle and repeat the process, adding stock when it evaporates and stirring continuously. You may not need to use all of the stock.

After about 10 minutes, add the diced zucchini, stir for a moment, and then add another ladle of stock. When the liquid reduces, stir in the optional grated truffles or just continue adding liquid. At this point, you should start checking the doneness level of the rice. If the rice is still completely opaque, continue to add liquid. As the rice turns from opaque to more translucent, you are approaching doneness. Test the texture of the rice. It should be just under al dente. If it is still very firm, add more stock. Once it is just short of al dente, stir in the squash blossoms. Add another ladle of stock and stir.

Finished risotto is meant to be slightly al dente with a fairly loose texture—not brothy like a soup, but not dry and more like a rice stew. Because the rice will continue cooking a bit while you finish the dish, you must stop cooking while it is slightly less well done than your final desired texture. Add one final ¼ ladle of stock. Turn the heat off and stir in the rest of the butter. Add the grated Parmigiano Reggiano cheese. Taste the rice and add salt and black pepper to suit your taste. The risotto should have a loose consistency. If it is tight, add a little extra stock.

Serve immediately with Parmigiano Reggiano to garnish.

Notes

#1. Truffles are seasonal and extremely expensive. I find them periodically at the mushroom stand at my farmer's market, and they are available at gourmet specialty stores. Additionally, d'Artagnan sells fresh truffles in season and canned truffles year-round. If the cost of truffles is prohibitive, one alternative is to substitute d'Artagnan's Black Truffle Butter for the final ⅓ cup of butter at the end of the recipe. Some people find the taste and aroma of truffle to be overpowering. If you are one of those people, definitely leave it out.

#2. Squash blossoms are one of my favorite summer ingredients. Bright yellow and extremely delicate, the blossoms add color and a delicate zucchini flavor to dishes.

#3. Risotto requires a special type of short-to-intermediate grain rice. (See "In the Heart of Amarone Country," page 101.)

Spinach Malfatti

Yield: 4 portions | Ease of Preparation: Moderate | Ease of Sourcing: Simple
Wine Pairing: Oltrepò Pavese Chardonnay or Soave Classico

Mother/daughter chef team of Piera and Michela Selvatico taught me to make this traditional recipe early one morning on my visit to Oltrepò Pavese. Their charming restaurant Albergo Ristorante Selvatico in Rivanazzano Terme is a local family-run gem. Piera's other daughter Francesca and her husband, Sergio, run the elegant dining room and oversee the extensive wine list. The original recipe calls for 30 eggs. I scaled it down to more manageable proportions.

INGREDIENTS

8 oz. fresh spinach with the stems
   removed
2 oz. unsalted butter + ½ cup
1 medium onion, cut in quarters
2 sprigs thyme
4 oz. dried breadcrumbs
4 oz. 00 pasta flour + ½ cup
4 oz. ricotta cheese
2 oz. Grana Padano + ½ cup extra
2 large eggs
Kosher salt
Nutmeg
4 sage leaves, chiffonaded (cut in strips)

WHAT YOU'LL NEED

Large saucepan (4½ quarts or larger)
Large sauté pan
Pastry board
Large pot for cooking the pasta

TIMING

Prep Time: 30–45 minutes
Cooking Time: 20 minutes

PROCESS

Wash the spinach very carefully to remove grit. Boil 2½ quarts salted water in the large saucepan and add the spinach. Cook it until it is softened. Carefully drain the spinach to remove the excess water and finely chop it. It should resemble a spinach purée.

Melt 2 tablespoons of butter in the large sauté pan and add the onion pieces and the thyme sprig and cook it for several minutes to flavor the butter. Remove the onion and thyme and put the breadcrumbs in the butter, stirring it until they become golden. Once they are browned, add the spinach and stir the mixture well.

Scrape the spinach and breadcrumb mixture on to the pastry board. Add the flour, ricotta, and Grana Padano and form a well in the center. Place the eggs, kosher salt, and a pinch of fresh ground nutmeg in the center of the well. With your hands, gently bring the mixture together to form a dough that is homogenous but delicate.

Divide the pasta dough in pieces approximately ¾ cup in size. Flour the pastry board and roll the dough between your hands and the board to form a pasta log approximately ¾ inch in diameter. Cut the logs into 1½ inch pieces. Gently roll the pieces, using your fingers to round the edges a bit.

Bring a large amount of water to boil in the large pasta pot. Once it boils, add kosher salt. The water should taste salty.

Cook the pasta in the boiling water. The pasta will rise to the top of the boiling water as it cooks, but you may want to sacrifice one or two malfatti to test if they are done. They should be soft and taste cooked all the way through. If it tastes of raw flour, the pasta is not done. This takes between 15 and 17 minutes.

While the pasta is cooking, clean out the sauté pan and heat the remaining ½ cup of unsalted butter in the pan. Add the sprigs of sage and kosher salt to the butter. Taste the melted butter to make sure it is adequately salted. Remove the pan from the heat.

Once the pasta is cooked, drain it and add it to the sage butter. Toss it to coat. Portion it out in bowls and dust it with Grana Padano.

Notes

#1. 00 flour is what the Italians use to make pasta. It is available at most Italian specialty markets. It is also available online through Amazon. I like the Antica Caputo brand.

#2. Although Piera and Michela suggest using Grana Padano, feel free to substitute Parmigiano Reggiano if you cannot find Grana.

#3. I can usually find spinach at my local farmer's market year-round, so if I make this in the winter, I use spinach, but the first time I ate this dish, Piera made it with zucchini. As anyone who has ever grown zucchini knows, it is quite abundant during the summer. Piera said they are constantly looking for ways to use it. To make it with zucchini, bake one pound green zucchini with butter, a small red onion, and a sprig each of marjoram and thyme until the zucchini is meltingly soft and then purée it in a food processor or with a stick blender. Once it is puréed, proceed with the recipe above.

#4. Both the spinach and zucchini versions are delicious in the summer sauced with a fresh tomato sauce made by sautéing a little garlic, tomatoes, and basil in olive oil until they are completely softened and homogenous.

Blanquette de Veau
with Hand-Cut Tagliatelle

Yield: 6 portions | Ease of Preparation: Moderate | Ease of Sourcing: Moderate

Wine Pairing: JF Coquard Vins Beaujolais Blanc "Les Pierres Dorées"

or if you prefer red JF Coquard Vins Morgon "Les Charmes"

Blanquette de Veau differs from most braised meat dishes in that every effort is made not to brown the meat and vegetables. In fact, blanquette actually means "white stew." Although further to the north in the Côte d'Or, Blanquette is often made with pearl onions and white button mushrooms, Isabelle Coquard's recipe from Beaujolais eschews the use of pearl onions and does not include mushrooms. Carrots and leeks add color to the dish, but the concept of a white stew is still the same. The sauce is a white stock-based béchamel further thickened with an egg yolk and crème fraîche.

INGREDIENTS

2 lbs. veal shoulder cut in 1½-in. cubes

4 Tbsp. + 2 Tbsp. unsalted butter

1 large onion, medium dice

1 cup dry white wine (preferably an
　　unoaked Chardonnay)

Water

3 carrots cut in ¼-in. rounds

2 leeks, cut in 1-in. lengths

Bouquet garni made of 1 stalk celery,
　　1 bay leaf, 3 thyme sprigs, 1 oregano
　　sprig, and 3 parsley sprigs

Kosher salt

White pepper

2 Tbsp. all-purpose flour

1 egg yolk

½ cup crème fraîche

6 portions hand-rolled and cut
　　tagliatelle (see recipe below)

WHAT YOU'LL NEED

Heavy-duty Dutch oven with cover

4 quart saucepan

Strainer

Large pot for cooking pasta

Paper towels

Small sauté pan

Medium whisk

Small bowl

TIMING

Prep Time: ½ hour

Cook Time: 1½ hours

PROCESS

Carefully dry the pieces of veal with paper towels. Melt 4 tablespoons butter in the Dutch oven over medium-high heat and place the veal in a single layer in the pan. Do not crowd the pan. It may be necessary to cook the veal in 2 batches. Cook the veal until it just begins to get gold. Sometimes the veal will exude some liquid. Continue cooking the veal until the liquid evaporates, being careful not to brown it. If it begins to brown, lower the heat. This is important because you do not want the dish to take on a brown color. The bottom of the pan should be moist but not full of liquid. At this point, add the diced onions and cook them on medium heat until they begin to soften, again being very careful not to brown them.

When the onions begin to soften, add 1 cup of white wine, stirring the bottom of the pan to make sure the onions are not sticking. Add the carrots, leek pieces, bouquet garni, 1 tablespoon kosher salt, and ½ teaspoon white pepper. Add enough water to almost cover the meat. Bring to a simmer and cover. Continue to cook for at least an hour until the veal is meltingly tender.

Making a roux! While the veal is cooking, melt the remaining 2 tablespoons unsalted butter over medium heat in the small sauté pan. Once the butter is melted, whisk in the 2 tablespoons flour and cook for a minute, whisking the whole time to keep it from browning. Remove it from the heat for use when the veal is finished cooking.

To make the sauce, strain the veal broth into a 4-quart saucepan. Discard the bouquet garni, keeping the veal mixture on the side. Rinse the Dutch oven and return it to the stove. Scrape the roux into the Dutch oven—do not turn the heat on yet. Heat the reserved veal broth. When it is simmering, turn the heat under the Dutch oven to medium and whisk the stock in to the roux to make a thickened sauce. In a separate bowl, whisk the egg yolk and crème fraîche together.

Temper! Stir half a cup of the hot veal sauce into the bowl with the egg yolk and crème fraîche mixture to temper it. This will keep the egg from curdling. Reduce the heat to low and whisk the egg yolk, crème fraîche, and veal sauce mixture into the contents of the Dutch oven. Once this is all incorporated, return the veal and vegetables to the pan and taste for seasoning and reheat the Blanquette, being careful not to boil the sauce.

Serve with homemade tagliatelle.

Notes

 # 1. If you cannot find veal shoulder, you might consider substituting pork shoulder, although the flavor will not be as delicate.

 # 2. The last time I made this dish, I found some white carrots and used only the white part of the leeks—making it a truly white dish.

 # 3. If you do not wish to make your own homemade tagliatelle, feel free to use a high-quality tagliatelle or egg noodle. (Just don't tell Jean-François!) Steamed rice would also be a delicious option.

Fresh Pasta Dough

Yield: 4 portions | Ease of Preparation: Moderate | Ease of Sourcing: Simple

The following pasta recipe can be used as the basis for all sorts of pasta. Although dried pasta saves time—and in certain regions of Italy is traditional—good homemade pasta is delicious and, since with planning it doesn't take that much time, is well worth it. If you do not have time to make it fresh, and there are no stores carrying locally made fresh pasta, use high-quality dried pasta. DO NOT USE the national-brand "fresh" pasta in the deli section of your local grocery store. It is full of preservatives and has an odd, unappealing texture. This recipe employs a ratio and can be expanded to produce a larger batch by doubling or tripling the recipe. As with any recipe where there are very few ingredients, the quality of the egg is key.

INGREDIENTS

2 cups flour + ½ cup reserved,
    preferably 00 pasta flour
3 large eggs, preferably free range from
    a farmer you know
1 Tbsp. extra-virgin olive oil
1 tsp. kosher salt
1 Tbsp. unsalted butter, very chilled
    and shaved into slivers

WHAT YOU'LL NEED

Pastry scraper
Pasta rolling machine or Rolling pin
Pastry board
Plastic wrap

TIMING

Mixing time: 15 minutes
Resting time: at least 30 minutes
Rolling and Cutting Time: This
    depends on what type of pasta you
    are making and the size of your
    batch.

PROCESS

Place 2 cups flour on the cutting board and make a clearing in the center. You should be able to see your cutting board in the center of the flour. This is called the well method of making dough. Put the eggs, the oil, and the salt in the center of the well. Use a fork to mix the eggs and pull a little flour at a time from the inside of the well wall into the center and mix the eggs and flour together. Once it is just barely combined, use your hands to bring it together and sprinkle the slivers of ice-cold butter on the dough. Scrape everything together with the pastry scraper and form the dough into a ball.

Knead the dough for 5 or 6 minutes. If the dough is too dry during the kneading process, sprinkle a tiny amount of water on the dough and continue working. If it is too wet, sprinkle some of the reserved flour on the dough. Once you are satisfied with the texture of your dough (it should be medium firm, supple, and a little tacky to the touch), place it in a plastic bag or wrap it in plastic. Let it rest for at least 30 minutes if you are going to use it right way. If you do not use it within the hour, you may wish to chill it, but you will need to take it out of the refrigerator a bit early to allow it to come back to room temperature before rolling it.

Cut a 2 oz. piece of dough (approximately 2 inches around). Roll it to the desired thickness either using a pasta machine or by hand with a rolling pin on a generously floured board. If using a machine, begin on the widest setting. Fold the dough over and run it through the widest setting again. Repeat this six times. Turn the setting to the next smallest level and run the dough through. Continue rolling the dough, choosing a smaller setting each time. Depending on the calibration of your machine, you may wish to stop at the next to the last setting or you may need to use all seven settings. Cut it into the appropriate shape for your intended pasta.

Notes

#1. 00 flour is what the Italians use to make pasta. It is available at most Italian specialty markets and gourmet stores. It is also available online through Amazon. I like the Antica Caputo brand. If you cannot find it, use all-purpose flour.

#2. Pasta machines are readily available at kitchen specialty stores and online and range from $25 for a sturdy no-frills hand-crank model to a $150 attachment for a Kitchen Aid stand mixer. Professional large machines can cost as much as $6,000. Most of the less expensive models come with a roller to sheet the pasta and two sizes of cutting rollers for long pasta—Spaghetti (Tagliolini) and Fettuccine are standard. Following are sizes of common pastas:

Fettuccine—¼ inch wide

Tagliatelle—¼ to ⅓ inch wide

Pappardelle—¾ to 1 inch wide

Gelato Affogato
Gelato with Coffee

Yield: Serves 4 | Ease of Preparation: Simple | Ease of Sourcing: Simple

Lunch at Il Ristorante Leon d'Oro in Casteggio was capped off with a simple two-ingredient dessert. Gelato Affogato, "drowned" sweet icy vanilla gelato in the dark heat of rich strong espresso, is a perfect contrast of temperature and flavor!

INGREDIENTS

8 scoops vanilla gelato

4 shots hot espresso

TIMING

Chilling Time: 30 minutes

Assembly Time: 5 minutes

WHAT YOU'LL NEED

4 wide-mouthed wine glasses or
   decorative bowls

Ice cream scoop

Espresso machine

Espresso cup or small pitcher

PROCESS

Chill 4 glasses or bowls for 30 minutes.

Place 2 scoops of gelato in each glass/bowl and return to the refrigerator.

Make 4 shots of espresso.

Remove the glasses/bowls from the refrigerator and quickly pour 1 shot of espresso into each glass/bowl.

Serve immediately before the gelato melts.

Notes

#1. Since there are only two ingredients in this dish, use the best gelato and espresso you can find. If you do not have an espresso machine, substitute the strongest, darkest cup of coffee you can.

#2. What's the difference between ice cream and gelato? The short explanation is that ice cream is made with cream, milk, sugar, and egg yolks. It is aggressively whipped to incorporate a lot of air and is served very cold. Gelato (the Italian word for ice cream) is made using more milk, less cream, and rarely includes egg yolks. Gelato is churned more slowly, incorporating less air into the mixture and is served at a higher temperature than ice cream. For my money, my friends Rob Duncan and Violetta Edelman, founders of Dolcezza Gelato, make the best gelato around. If you are lucky enough to be in the DC area, stop by one of their storefront locations. I know you'll be glad you did. If you cannot find gelato, substitute a high-quality ice cream.

Mont Saint=Michel

Rouen

Paris

Tours

Beaune

Lyon

Nantes

Bordeaux

Marseilles

Corsica

Domaine
Larredya

"A Picnic in the Clouds . . . with Shepherds, of Course"
An Afternoon Hike in the Pyrénées with Jean-Marc Grussaute of Camin Larredya Jurançon, France

I'm going to be honest. Sometimes people, and by "people" I mean me, complain when they are on extended wine trips. You're in a car for long stretches at a time (longer than necessary if you get lost) racing between winery visits—sometimes four or five a day. You are tired, staying in sometimes sketchy hotels, forced into close proximity with other people, and frankly, there is a huge amount of sensory overload. (It's what my daughter-in-law Milena calls a first-world problem.) Don't get me wrong, the good definitely outweighs the bad—meeting amazingly talented and dedicated people, the array of flavors, smells, and colors—and I absolutely recognize how much better it is than cleaning toilets or slaving over a hot grill in a restaurant, for example, but it is exhausting.

Every once in a while, though, you are lucky enough to travel with people with a saner outlook on life—people who plan a little exercise into the day to clear the cellar-induced cobwebs out of your head. My great friends Ed Addiss and Barbara Selig of Wine Traditions are two such people, and traveling with them is an absolute delight. By the time the opportunity to travel with them arose, I had pretty much sworn off importer-organized wine trips—certainly if I was going to a country where I spoke the language. Still, when Ed and Barbara gave my former boss Doug Rosen and me an opportunity to accompany them on a trip to Southwest France, I happily accepted.

The Wine Traditions portfolio is made up of small family-owned wineries with a strong focus in southwestern France—Bordeaux, the Basque Country, Jurançon, and regions from the southern foothills of the Massif Central—regions with names like Gaillac and Marcillac and grapes like Len de L'El and Fer Servadou growing in the fields. Although somewhat more common now, these are still obscure grapes from obscure regions, and Wine Traditions seeks out the best producers from these regions—

Shepherd's cabin from afar

producers making wine, well, traditionally.

Their trips are planned at a more civilized pace with one or two winery visits per day, nice hotels, breaks for lunch and dinner, and, in the case of our visit with Jean-Marc Grussaute of Camin Larredya in Jurançon, a very special treat. Instead of their normal break day in the Pyrénées where Barbara and Ed organize a hike from the picture-perfect town of St.-Etienne-de-Baigorry across the border into Spain, Jean-Marc invited us on a picnic in the Pyrénées Mountains to visit his friend Stéphane Chetrit. Stéphane is one of the few remaining shepherds who stay every summer up in the mountains with his flock—a

Ed Addiss carrying our lunch

practice almost abandoned since the advent of four-wheel-drive vehicles. Stéphane even makes Ossau-Iraty cheese in his *cuyala* (the local name for the small shepherd's cabins) on the mountain.

I should note that it is highly possible that ten days of drinking wine, riding in a car, and sitting down for two long meals a day may not have prepared me for the trek to our picnic spot. Our journey involved a car ride to a mountain lake in the Vallon du Soussouéou, where we parked the car in the shadow of the Pic du Midi Ossau and took a 15-minute funicular cable car ride up the mountain, *and then* we walked for an hour to reach the *Cabane de Seous,* Stéphane's *cuyala.* And, since I had not been planning on hiking in the mountains, I may not have been wearing the best shoes possible. Still, I loved every minute of it (especially since I was only responsible for carrying my own bottle of water). Jean-Marc and Ed were charged with carrying our picnic up the mountain in their backpacks. It was so beautiful, sunny and clear with few clouds in the sky, the tinkling bells around the sheeps' necks serving as an audio beacon to the *cuyala.* I was fascinated to see the pristinely clean room where Stéphane makes his delicious cheese inside that picturesque mountain cabin.

The backdrop of craggy mountain peaks and boulder-strewn Pyrenean pastures, where massive Great Pyrénées dogs performed the tasks for which they were bred, herding Stéphane's flock, only enhanced the experience. Our picnic was comprised of Stéphane's cheese, ripe fragrant slices of melon, Jambon de Bayonne, salad in a tasty vinaigrette (some of which unfortunately leaked from its container in Jean-Marc's backpack and ran down his legs on the hike up the mountain), and the hugest loaf of rustic bread I've ever seen paired with Jean-Marc's wine chilled by the cold water of a nearby stream. It could not have tasted better had it been an elegant meal in a fancy restaurant. In fact, from my point of view, our picnic was superior. It was simple and perfect—exactly in keeping with the philosophy of this book—Eat What the Winemaker Eats.

Stéphane Chetrit, Doug Rosen, and Jean-Marc Grussaute

One of the traditional provinces of France, Béarn is part of Gascony in Southwestern France and along with the Basque Country makes up the department of Pyrénées-Atlantique. The Béarn is located in the foothills, plateaux, and peaks of the Pyrénées Mountains and is bordered by the Basque country to the west, Spain to the south, Gascony to the north, and Bigorre to the east. Pau, the capital of the Béarn region, is home to petroleum giant Total S.A. (originally Elf Aquitaine). Also significant are the aerospace industry, tourism, and agriculture, with seed corn being the most important crop.

Food from this part of the Pyrénées may not be flashy, but as with many of my favorite regions, it lives and dies on the quality and freshness of its ingredients.

Foods of the Béarn

Cheese

Béarn High Pasture Cheese: The practice of making summer, high mountain pasture cheeses (as Stéphane does in his mountain cabin) in the Béarn Valleys of Ossau, Aspe, and Baretous has been awarded a Slow Food Presidium in an effort to preserve the tradition.

All of the milk of these raw-milk tomme-style cheeses comes from the native *Basque-Béarn* breed of sheep, a breed that is particularly well adapted to its high-altitude living conditions. The shepherd/cheesemakers spend three months each summer living in small stone huts, tending their sheep, and making their cheese. The sunny pastures located between 3,000 to 7,000 feet have colorful flowers, alpine cover plants, and wild mountain thyme. The sheeps' diet, the slow aging (at least four months, although Stéphane aged his longer), and the limited production that ensures careful attention to each cheese produce a semifirm cheese with delicate nutty flavors and aromas of nuts and mushrooms. Equally important, each dairy's cheese is unique with the nonrefrigerated milk preserving each pasture's microbial flora and producing a distinctive taste.

Ossau-Iraty AOC Cheese: Ossau-Iraty is my favorite cheese in the world. It is firm without being hard with nutty, fruity, grassy flavors—delicate yet not bland. Who knows why something becomes a favorite? All I can say is that as much as I love all sorts of cheeses, Ossau-Iraty is my favorite.

Ossau-Iraty is traditionally made from unpasteurized sheep's milk cheese (although there is a movement in the EU to require pasteurization in cheesemaking) from two regions in the Pyrénées, the Valley of Ossau in the Béarn and the beech forests of Iraty in the Pays Basque. Ossau-Iraty is the appellation under which Stéphane makes his cheese. It received its AOC status in 1980 and must be made from raw milk from only two breeds of sheep, Basque-Béarn and Manech.

Soups

Garbure: Of the many soups of the Béarn, Garbure is perhaps the most well known, and there are as many recipes for it as there are cooks making it. Originally from the vast region of Gascony, there are regional as well as seasonal variations, with fall versions sporting cabbage and chestnuts, while spring versions might feature favas, tarbais beans, and baby vegetables like cabbage, carrots, and new potatoes. Some authorities insist that there must be a ham bone with a bit of meat attached (*trébuc*), others insist that there must be duck or goose confit, while still others insist there must be beans and goose fat.

Everyone does agree on three things: 1) It must be cooked for a very long time and the flavor continues to improve after a few days in the fridge; 2) It should be served in a large communal tureen and needs to be thick enough that a serving spoon plunged into the soup tureen can stand up on its own; and 3) after all the meat and vegetables have been consumed, the final step is the *chabrot* or *goudale,* where a small amount of red wine is swirled into the last bit of broth in the bottom of the bowl and sipped directly from the bowl. Use a spoon if you must, but definitely do not skip this last step!

Soupe à l'ail: Garlic soup is quite basic, made from garlic, bread, and vegetable stock. At the last moment, it is customary to poach an egg in the broth. While *Tourin* from the Dordogne is basically garlic egg soup, the Béarnaise version incorporates garlic, onions, and tomatoes.

Cousinette: An herb-based soup featuring sorrel, chard, mallow, chicory, and cream.

Nettle soup: This delicate yet hearty soup requires a special-handling label, as the nettles themselves are dangerous to touch bare-handed. Once cooked, however, the combination of nettles, leeks, potatoes, and garlic make for a delicate yet filling bowl of soup.

Eggs and Mushrooms

Oeufs Béarnaise: Eggs cooked sunny side up and served with olive oil-stewed red and green bell peppers, Jambon de Bayonne, and garlic.

Mushrooms: My favorite mushroom, *Cèpes* (a.k.a. porcini), are found throughout this part of France and can be used in a variety of ways from sautéing to grilling or as an ingredient in an omelet. However they are cooked, they are delicious. Also, available in spring, morels can be made into an omelet or served as an accompaniment to roast chicken.

Meat, Fish, and Poultry

Meat:

Jambon de Bayonne IGP: Even though its name comes from Bayonne, a well-known Basque town, Jambon de Bayonne can be produced anywhere in the Adour River Basin. It was first developed in Salies-de-Béarn by curing ham in salt from the town's famed mineral springs. The town owes its name to the salty springs whose water is said to be seven times saltier than the ocean. The Consortium of Jambon de Bayonne is located in Pau, and the ham must be produced with pigs from the southwestern regions of Pyrénées-Atlantique, Landes, Gers, and Hautes-Pyrénées, using only salt from Les Salies-de-Béarn.

Fish:

Poisson du Gave: *Gave* is the local name for the rushing rivers coming down from the Pyrénées. They are particularly prized for their trout and salmon. *Truite du Gave* calls for cooking river trout in dry Jurançon wine and serving it with an egg, cream, and mushroom sauce. Local smoked salmon is also popular.

Poultry:

This is poultry country, especially duck and goose, but turkey and corn-fed chicken are also popular.

Confit of Duck or Goose: Possibly my favorite dish in the whole world! I love making it even more than I love eating it, and that's saying a lot. Originally conceived as a way to preserve duck and goose, the method of salting, seasoning, and then slow-cooking the duck pieces in rendered fat until is falling-off-the-bone tender has remained in vogue because it removes a large amount of the actual fat from the dish and it is incredibly luscious. An essential component of many traditional Southwestern recipes like Garbure or Cassoulet, Confit is delicious on its own, its skin crisped and served with lovely potatoes fried in duck or goose fat.

Daube of Goose in Madiran: Goose stewed with root vegetables and Tannat-based red wine from Madiran.

Grilled Magret of Duck: *Magret de Canard* is the boneless breast of a foie gras duck—which means a duck raised to produce foie gras. André Daguin, the famed chef of L'Hôtel de France, a two-star Michelin restaurant in Auch, was the first to sear this cut of duck like a steak. André Daguin's daughter, Ariane, the founder of luxury food purveyor d'Artagnan, has done much to make *Magret* available in the United States.

Duck à la Béarnaise: Duck braised in Jurançon wine and tarragon vinegar.

Foie Gras with Grapes: Seared foie gras with a sauce of grapes and veal stock.

Roast Quail: Quail roasted with butter and white wine. Served over toasted bread.

Alycot: Wings (ailes), neck (cot), and giblets of goose stewed with vegetables and Jurançon wine.

Poule au Pot: This traditional dish was made famous by Henri IV, who is said to have stated, "If God keeps me, I will make sure that no peasant in my realm will lack the means to have a chicken in the pot on Sunday!" The idea must have seemed fairly populist at the time. *Poule au Pot*—literally Chicken in the Pot—is a chicken stuffed with milk-soaked bread, Jambon de Bayonne, and either sausage meat or chicken giblets, sometimes both. It is poached in water or chicken stock with potatoes, carrots, and leeks until tender and served hot with cornichons on the side.

We can also credit Henri IV for **Béarnaise Sauce,** although he personally had nothing to do with it. One of the classics of French cooking, Béarnaise sauce is said to have been invented in Henri's honor by Jules Colette, a chef at the restaurant Le Pavillon Henri IV, during the 19th century. He named it Béarnaise because Henri, a noted gourmand, was from Béarn. It is an emulsion of butter, eggs, vinegar, shallots, tarragon, and black pepper, and is a frequent accompaniment to steak and shellfish.

Okay. Here is the Cliff Notes version. The Béarn region was historically protestant. Henri's mother, Jeanne d'Albret Queen of Navarre, was a staunch Calvinist. Upon her death in 1572, Henri became Henri III King of Navarre. In 1589, at the death of his cousin Henri III King of France, Henri III of Navarre became Henri IV King of France. (Confusing, I know.) Despite much battling back and forth, he was never able to take Paris because of his Protestant faith and the resulting Catholic resistance. Finally in 1593, he converted to Catholicism, stating, "Paris is worth a Mass." Although not terribly popular during his lifetime, he became known as "Good King Henri" after his death because of his good works for his subjects and their standard of life.

Desserts

Merveilles: Fried sweet dough frequently dusted with powdered sugar.

Pastis Bourrit: A traditional flour cake made drunk ("*bourrit*") with the addition of Armagnac. Frequently served at weddings.

Croustade: This apple tart can be made with a variety of crusts—puff pastry, sweet pie dough, or phyllo dough.

Wines of the Béarn

Jurançon is one of the oldest wine appellations in France, having received its AOC status in 1936. It was planted some 2,000 years ago by the Romans, and at the baptism of Henri IV of France in 1553, it was Jurançon wine that was used (along with a clove of garlic) to anoint the future king's lips. During the 16th century, the Princes of Béarn and the *Parlement* of Navarre introduced the notion of a cru system to rank vineyards according to the value of their parcels. This is said to be the first tentative effort at a vineyard classification system in France.

The appellation of Jurançon covers approximately 2,000 acres planted on steep slopes in twenty-five communes of the Pyrénées. Gros Manseng and Petit Manseng are the most common grape varieties, making up 65 percent and 30 percent, respectively, with Petit Courbu, Courbu, Lauzet, and Camaralet combining for the final 5 percent. These varieties achieve excellent ripeness levels while retaining high acidity. Because of the extreme slopes, vineyards are either planted in terraces or in amphitheater-shaped formations, sometimes both. Soils are a combination of ancient seabeds dating to before the formation of the Pyrénées in the south and in the north, *terrein* soils that consist of

Vineyard at Camin Larredya

Jurançon pudding stones, large limestone and clay galets (large pebbles), and siliceous gravel deposited during the actual formation of the mountains.

There are two appellations for white wine in Jurançon: Jurançon and Jurançon Sec.

Jurançon: Wines with this appellation designation are *moelleux* or sweet wines with required potential alcohol by volume (ABV) levels of 12 percent or above with a required sugar level of at least 212 grams/liter in the grape juice at harvest. Generally, this sweetness level is achieved by harvesting grapes at *surmaturité* (technically over-ripe). Sugar concentration levels can be achieved by drying the grapes on the vines in a method called *passerillage* rather than through the noble rot *botrytis cinerea*. (See Wine Terms, page 472.) These wines are rich yet high in acidity with flavors of peaches, confit of citrus, tropical fruit, honey, and nuts.

Jurançon Sec: Wines with this appellation designation (which received its AOC status in 1975) are vinified dry and must have ABV levels between 11 and 14 percent with residual sugar levels below 4 grams/liter.

Jean Grussaute planted the vineyards at Camin Larredya in Chapelle de Rousse over 40 years ago on lovely steeply terraced vineyards, their slopes curving to follow the amphitheater shape of the hillside. His son Jean-Marc, the current owner along with his mother, Jany, have been estate-bottling wines from the estate since 1988. They began farming organically in 2007 and received organic certification in 2010.

Jean-Marc produces two Jurançon Secs, La Part Davant and La Virada, both of which are wines that while quite pleasant in their youth can definitely be aged for extended periods.

He also produces two Jurançons: Costat Darrer and Au Capceu—delicious sweet wines capable of aging for 20-plus years.

After our visit to Stéphane, the shepherd in the mountains, we drove to Jean-Marc's winery for a quick tour and wine tasting before heading to his house for a meal prepared for us by his wife, Christelle. Again, delicious simplicity was the watchword. Thin slices of ham that Jean-Marc had cured himself, a zucchini gratin, green salad, and a croustade—an apple tart that Christelle calmly whipped up while we stood and watched—amazing!

It was fantastic to sit on their patio overlooking their amphitheater of vineyards and discuss his philosophy of winemaking and the way that food and wine figures into their lifestyle from the organics of their vineyards to the ham that he cures himself. From the time we met him in the little village at the foothill of Stéphane's mountain until our al fresco dinner in the rainbow hues of the setting sun, the whole day communicated in actions better than words how important food, wine, and the basics tenets of the two combine to inform Jean-Marc and Christelle's lifestyle, and I was quite honored to have been invited to experience it along with them—if only for a day.

The Winemaker Recommends: Jambon de Bayonne and Melon with Camin Larredya Jurançon Sec La Part Davant.

Jambon de Bayonne
with Summer Melon

Yield: Serves four | Ease of Preparation: Simple | Ease of Sourcing: Simple to Moderate
Wine Pairing: Camin Larredya Jurançon Sec La Part Davant

Cured ham and melon is a summer classic on par with tomatoes and mozzarella or corn on the cob. With only two components, it is imperative to pick the best ingredients you can. Although many people associate this dish with Italy, it will be forever linked in my memory with the day I spent in the Pyrénées with Jean-Marc Grussaute of Camin Larredya, shepherd Stéphane Chetrit, and my friends Ed Addiss, Barbara Selig, and Doug Rosen. The sweet, clean, melon flavors accented by the salty, porky, dry-cured Jambon that Jean-Marc had cured himself combined for something refreshing and sublime—perfect on a hot summer day. This dish is so simple, it hardly needs a recipe.

INGREDIENTS

12 paper-thin slices Jambon de
    Bayonne
Two small or one large ripe cantaloupe

TIMING

Prep Time: 15 minutes

WHAT YOU'LL NEED

Cutting board
Chef's knife
Decorative platter (optional)

PROCESS

Slice the melon in half lengthwise. Discard the seeds.

If the melon is small, cut it into eight spears. If it is large, cut it into twelve spears. Peel the melon slices.

Wrap a slice of Jambon around each spear of melon.

Serve chilled either on a decorative platter or individual plate with three slices per person.

Notes

#1. Jean-Marc's Jambon Sec was house-cured, but since none of us will be able to get any of that, Jambon de Bayonne IGP (see note, page 170) is the closest thing to it. If you are unable to find Jambon de Bayonne, substitute Jamón Serrano or Prosciutto di San Daniele or Prosciutto di Parma.

#2. Melons. The French produce delicious melons. I prefer the Charentais variety. Farmer Bob Jochum, from Leedstown Farm in Leedstown, Virginia, produces my favorite melons—a small, sweet, and juicy variety of Charentais called Sugar Cube Melons. These melons are small, less than two pounds each, with a high sugar content. Bob picks them at peak ripeness—never bringing them to market unless they are perfect. If you do not have someone like Bob in your life, look for melons that are firm (but not rock hard) with no bruises. Smell them. If they are sweetly fragrant, you are good.

Zucchini Gratin

Yield: one large gratin or 12 to 14 small individual gratins. | Ease of Preparation: Simple | Ease of Sourcing: Simple
Wine Pairing: Camin Larredya Jurançon Sec or another soft unoaked white wine

Christelle Grussaute served a delicious Zucchini Gratin for dinner at Camin Larredya. The simple combination of shredded zucchini and garlicky cream is fantastic, and because it can be made ahead of time and reheated, it is a great dish for no-fuss, stress-free entertaining.

INGREDIENTS

For the Zucchini:

2 lbs. medium to small zucchini
2 tsp. kosher salt

Optional: 15 to 20 squash blossoms

For the Gratin Cream:

2 cups heavy cream
4 garlic cloves, peeled and lightly crushed
1 sprig rosemary
4 sprigs thyme
1¼ tsp. kosher salt
¼ tsp. finely ground white pepper

WHAT YOU'LL NEED	TIMING
Box grater or food processor with grating attachment	Active Prep Time: 20 minutes
Large kitchen bowl	Resting Time: 1½ hours
Medium saucepan with lid	Cooking Time: 20 to 35 minutes for small gratin, 45 minutes to 1¼ hour for large gratin
Fine mesh strainer	Resting Time: 20 minutes
1½-quart oven-safe gratin dish or 12 to 14 four-oz. ramekins	

PROCESS

For the Zucchini:

Use the box grater or food processor to grate the zucchini. Place in the kitchen bowl and stir in 1 teaspoon kosher salt. Put the salted zucchini in the strainer and place over the bowl. Let this sit for one hour. The salt will cause the zucchini to exude excess moisture. It also tenderizes and flavors the zucchini.

For the Gratin Cream:

Place all ingredients in the saucepan. Heat over medium heat until it begins to simmer and then turn off the heat. (Be careful, the cream will boil over at the drop of a hat, so don't step away while you are heating it.) Cover and let the cream and garlic mixture steep for 30 minutes before straining.

Assembling the Gratin:

At the end of one hour, preheat the oven to 375° F. Press all the excess liquid from the zucchini. Rinse the bowl and return the zucchini.

At this point, if you have squash blossoms, rinse them, remove the stem and stamen, and tear into strips. Add the blossoms to the zucchini and place into your gratin dish, dividing equally if making individual gratins. Add enough of the gratin cream mixture to almost cover the zucchini. Press down to coat the top layer of zucchini, but do not cover it with the cream. You should definitely be able to see the zucchini above the level of the cream.

Bake for 20 minutes if you are making small gratin (45 minutes to 1¼ hour for a large gratin). The gratin is done when the top is golden brown and the zucchini cream mixture is firm. Check it at 20 minutes (45 minutes for a large gratin). If it is not browned or is still loose, continuing cooking until it colors and becomes firm.

Remove from the oven and let it rest for 10 to 20 minutes. Serve warm. This dish can be made ahead of time and reheated prior to serving.

Ossau-Iraty with Black Cherry Jam

Yield: 2 cups | Ease of Preparation: Simple | Ease of Sourcing: Moderate
Wine Pairing: Camin Larredya Jurançon Costat Darrer or Au Capceu

Our picnic lunch with winemaker Jean-Marc Grussaute in the high pasture outside Stéphane Chetrit's mountain cabin stands clearly in my memory as a sparkling moment (and not just because of the bright sunlight!). The slices of local ham, crunchy bread, and crisp Jurançon Sec chilled in a nearby mountain stream satisfied our appetites— piqued by the mountain air and the brisk hike up the mountain—but for me, the star of the day was Stéphane's cheese. Ossau-Iraty is my favorite cheese in the world. It is firm without being hard, with nutty, fruity, and grassy flavors—delicate yet not bland. Who knows why something becomes a favorite? All I can say is that as much as I love all sorts of cheeses, Ossau-Iraty is my favorite. Black Cherry jam is a classic accompaniment to Ossau-Iraty.

INGREDIENTS

1½ lbs. dark cherries (pits removed),
　　approximately 2 lbs. before
　　removing the pits
1 cup granulated sugar
½ cinnamon stick
1 two-inch sprig rosemary
2 cloves
½ tsp. lemon zest
2 Tbsp. lemon juice
¼ tsp. kosher salt
1 lb. Ossau-Iraty

WHAT YOU'LL NEED

Cherry pitter
Microplane lemon zester
6-quart saucepan

TIMING

Prep Time: 30 minutes
Cook Time: one hour

PROCESS

Remove the pits. Rough chop two-thirds of the cherries. Keep one third whole.

Place the cherries, granulated sugar, cinnamon stick, rosemary, cloves, lemon zest, lemon juice, and kosher salt into the saucepan. Stir everything together. Bring to a boil, then reduce to a simmer and continue cooking over medium-low or low heat for 45 minutes to an hour, stirring periodically. The jam is finished when the cherries have softened and melted somewhat into the juices.

Cool the jam and serve with slices of Ossau-Iraty Cheese.

Notes

#1. Ossau-Iraty cheese is a sheep's milk cheese from two Pyrénées regions: Ossau in the Béarn Valley and the Iraty Forest of the Pays Basque. If Ossau-Iraty is not available at your local cheese shop, substitute P'tit Basque, Idiazabal, or Young Manchego. I recommend taking the cheese out of the refrigerator one hour before serving.

#2. A cherry pitter is one of the kitchen gadgets that I really cannot do without. Not only is it quite time-consuming to pit cherries without one, but it works to pit olives, too!

Mont
Saint=Michel

Rouen

Paris

Tours

Beaune

Lyon

Nantes

Bordeaux

Domaine du Cros

Marseilles

Corsica

N
NW   NE
W   E
SW   SE
S

"Vickie Dreams of Aligot"
A Visit with Denise and Philippe Teulier
Domaine du Cros, Marcillac, France

I'm not sure "dreams" is the correct term. "Fantasizes" might be a better choice. I mean, it doesn't wake me up at night or anything, but thinking about the combination of mashed potatoes, garlic, crème fraîche, and cheese has certainly occupied a good bit of my time.

The first time I had Aligot, I was dining at a restaurant in Montpellier, France. The waiters served it in a showy fashion, holding two spoons high, rotating them in a quick circular motion so the cheesy potato

mixture rose and fell like taffy being pulled before landing in a pool of melted starchy lactic goodness on my plate. It was delicious, and I really wanted to eat it again. The second time I had it, it afforded me the opportunity not just to eat it, but to learn to make it, as well. And you know what they say about giving a girl a plate of Aligot vs. teaching her to make Aligot. If you teach her how to make it, she can feed it to herself (and all of her friends) for the rest of her life.

About a week into our trip with Ed Addiss and Barbara Selig of Wine Traditions, our itinerary took Doug Rosen and me to the rather obscure region of Marcillac in the department of Aveyron on the southwestern edge of the Massif Central. (The Massif Central is a large elevated region in the center of France made up of mountains and plateaux. Generally speaking, when you hear the phrase *La France Profonde*, Deep France, this is the area to which they are referring.) Geographically, four main rivers influence the Aveyron: the Lot, the Truyère, the Tarn, and the Aveyron, for which it is named. These rivers flow through high rocky mountainous plateaux called Causses (from the *Occitan* language meaning carved out by rivers), leaving deep gorges in their wake. Also significant are the Rougier areas with red-colored iron oxide soils, the most famous of which is the Rougier of Camarès.

Not everyone is familiar with the wines of the Aveyron. Marcillac is its most famous appellation, and it isn't exactly a household name. (Although I think it should be. I considered becoming the appellation's unofficial booster at one time but thought, "Why limit myself when there are so many geeky appellations that need my help?")

Wine has been made in Marcillac for almost 1,000 years. Originally under the control of the Abbey of Conques, Marcillac was consumed locally by clergy, gentry, miners, and agricultural workers. Through a series of events over the course of many years (World Wars, Phylloxera, you know, minor stuff), wine production declined until it reached its nadir in 1965, at which time a group of determined local producers banded together to save their wine industry from extinction, improving landscaping techniques with the use of terraces to allow mechanization and applying for VDQS status (the level below AOC). They continued to work to improve the quality of the wines and in 1990 received the AOC designation. Centered around the Vallon de Marcillac, a narrow deep valley, the AOC of Marcillac covers 500 acres with 400 acres of vineyards planted at middle elevations on *rougier*, the region's red iron-rich limestone and clay soils and the remaining vineyards on higher elevation limestone, scree, and schist soils. The vineyards are steeply terraced at altitudes of 1,100 to 1,650 feet, an optimal altitude for ripening that when combined with predominantly southern exposure helps avoid risk of frost.

The principal grape is Fer Servadou (90 percent), locally known as Mansois. (Although when you consider that Marcillac is arguably the most well-known wine region in the world for Fer Servadou, I am perplexed as to why it isn't known universally as Mansois.) Cabernet Franc, Cabernet Sauvignon, and Merlot make up the remaining 10 percent of plantings. Ninety percent of wine production is red, with the balance being rosé. White wines of the region are bottled with a Vin de Pays designation.

Historically, the Aveyron is an agricultural region lacking any real industrial economy. Up until the twentieth century, most of the farmers were subsistence farmers feeding their families and producing rye, chestnuts, and, with their arrival in the mid-19th century, potatoes. Ninety percent of agricultural goods in the Aveyron are livestock or livestock output, i.e., cheese or dairy products. Currently the Aveyron is the most important producer of sheep in France, with the majority of the sheep being raised for the milk they provide to the Roquefort cheese cartel, the region's largest employer. Most farms are small family-owned operations, and although 40 percent of production is beef and dairy products, an important segment of these farms specializes in labor-intensive crops like gherkins, strawberries, and tobacco.

Given the fact that beef and sheep make up such a large percentage of the agricultural output, it seems rather contradictory that the home diet is quite heavy in poultry and pork. To be sure, there are standout products—Beef from Aubrac, Veal from Ségala, and Lamb Lou Paillol and Aveyron—but there do seem to be a surfeit of recipes for all sorts of poultry from duck and geese to chicken, thrush etc., and, of course, lots of pork.

Regional Food Products

Cheese of the Aveyron

Roquefort: I do not think it can be stressed enough how important a role Roquefort has played in food culture—particularly in the fight that the producers of Roquefort have waged to protect their name. It is a battle that dates back to a Parlementary Decree granted by King Charles IV in 1411 stating that the producers of Roquefort had a monopoly to produce cheese in Roquefort-sur-Soulzon. Roquefort was the first product to receive AOC status in France in 1925, and regulations state that the cheese must be produced from raw milk from Lacaune Sheep raised in the Aveyron and a few neighboring regions. Roquefort must be aged and processed in natural caves under Mont Combalon. It is the bacteria Penicillium Roquefort found within these caves that gives Roquefort its "Blue." Other cheeses produced by the same method but not aged in Roquefort-sur-Soulzon cannot be called Roquefort. (Just as sparkling wines not produced in the Champagne region cannot be called Champagne.) There are seven producers of Roquefort of which Société des Caves de Roquefort is the largest, producing 60 percent. The cheese is best eaten between the months of April and October.

Laguiole: One of my very favorite cheeses, Laguiole is made from raw cow's milk. This firm cylindrical cheese named for the village of Laguiole located on the plateau de l'Aubrac received its AOC in 1961 and is produced from the milk of two breeds of cattle, Aubrac and Simmental, grazing at altitudes of between 2,600 to 4,500 feet. A large wheel of Laguiole can weigh as much as 110 pounds. Young fresh Tome de Laguiole is a key ingredient in Aligot.

Le Pérail: A soft sheep's milk cheese.

Bleu des Causses: Raw cow's milk blue from the Causses mountain plateaux.

Therondels: A firm cheese with a rough parchment-colored skin made from raw cow's milk.

Meats and Charcuteries

Aubrac Beef: A traditional pure race from Aubrac, this tan-colored breed has long, lyre-type horns. Historically highly regarded for its milk (often used to produce Laguiole cheese), the influx of cheaper dairy breeds transferred the emphasis from milk production to meat production. Beef of Aubrac is prized in Parisian steakhouses and butcher shops throughout France.

Veal from Aveyron and Ségala: Valued for its rosy flesh, this veal must be from either Limousin or Blonde d'Aquitaine breeds of cattle. It is traditionally reared within spacious stables in the presence of its mother, its milk diet augmented with grains.

Lamb: Delicious and delicate, the most famous are the Agneau Lou Paillol and Agneau d'Aveyron.

Charcuterie: The Aveyronnais love charcuterie. It can be pork: dried sausages like Saucisse and Saucisson Secs or dried and smoked hams (of which the Jambon de Najac is reputed since the middle ages, when Rabelais immortalized it *The Life of Gargantua and Pantagruel,* stating, "There is no good ham but from Najac.") Duck and goose are also extremely popular with confit, rillettes, smoked magret, duck or goose neck stuffed with pâté, and fritons (thin strips of crispy duck or goose skin, known as grattons in other parts of the country).

Regional Dishes

These products along with other regional specialties are frequently featured on the Aveyronnais table.

Aligot: A combination of mashed potatoes, garlic, fresh Tomme de Laguiole, crème fraîche, and white pepper.

Soufflé au Roquefort: Fluffy and eggy with the tang of Roquefort and crème fraîche.

Tarte au Roquefort: Similar flavor notes to the aforementioned soufflé, but the buttery tart shell mellows the tanginess of the cheese somewhat.

Soupe au Fromage: Not a soup at all, rather, this is a hot casserole with cabbage, potatoes, and Laguiole cheese.

Cabbage Soup: A filling and comforting winter dish made richer with the addition of lard and potatoes.

Potato Fricassée: A potato and sorrel omelette.

Omelettes de Cèpes: Not just an Aveyronnais recipe, this luscious omelette can be found throughout France whenever this treasured mushroom (a.k.a. porcini) is in season.

Cèpes à la Combrétoise: The local name for a dish of cèpes sautéed simply in oil with a little *persillade* of parsley, garlic, and a dash of salt and pepper. Combret is a lovely little Aveyronnais village.

Salade de Gésiers: Again, while not specific to the Aveyron, this salad is decadently luscious. The meltingly tender duck or goose gizzards are balanced by the slight bitterness of the frisée lettuce and the tart tangy mustard vinaigrette.

Farçous: Forgotten for years, this simple yet delicious egg and chard pancake happily has come back in fashion. Farçous calls for a thick crêpe batter to which you add a mixture of sautéed chopped chard, onions, garlic, shallots, chives, and parsley. Some variations call for the addition of raisins or prunes. Add the chard and onion combination to the crêpe batter and fry small pancakes until golden brown and just firm. This makes a lovely lunch with a green salad or a creative side dish for dinner. I also like them on the diminutive side as a vegetarian hors d'oeuvre at a cocktail party with a dollop of crème fraîche and a sprinkling of chives.

Pascade: A savory Yorkshire pudding-type pancake made from egg, flour, milk, and parsley.

Estofinado or Estofi: Although far from the ocean, the miners of Decazeville had a tradition of cooking with stockfish. Boatmen on the Lot River brought stockfish to the Aveyron from Bordeaux and the Atlantic. The boatmen hung the dried fillets from the bow of their boats, and by the time they docked in Bouquiès, the fish was rehydrated. Made from rehydrated stockfish, potatoes, garlic, parsley, and walnut oil, Estofinado is similar to the Provençale dish Brandade. Some Estofinado recipes call for eggs, some for crème fraîche. The 200-member organization *The Confrerie of Estofi* in Decazeville regulates its preparation. (Of course it does.)

Saupiquet of Lapin: Rabbit in a rabbit liver stew.

Hare Stew: Hare stewed in red wine.

Chou Farci: Cabbage stuffed with a mixture of ground meat (pork or beef), parsley, garlic, milk-soaked bread, and eggs.

Fricandoux: This is basically a pâté wrapped in caulfat. The meat farce is made from pork belly, pork meat, and pork liver that is seasoned and formed into a ball before being wrapped in the caulfat and fried. Fricandoux are generally eaten cold on a charcuterie plate.

Poule Farcie: An old chicken stuffed with a mixture of ham, spinach, milk-soaked bread, egg, garlic, and parsley. The chicken is trussed and roasted before being served with rice and its pan juices.

L'Astet Najacois: An herb-stuffed pork roast wrapped in caulfat, this savory delicacy is named for Najac, the lovely hill town known for its amazing pork products, specifically, as I noted above, Rabelais's favorite Jambon de Najac.

Daube de Sanglier: Wild Boar stewed in red wine. This is a dish that seems to span borders. I have eaten it throughout France as well as in many regions of Italy—basically wherever wild boar roam. (See recipe for Braised Wild Boar, page 272.)

Tripous: Tripe stew in which lamb or veal tripe is stuffed with a mixture of garlic, minced ham, tripe, and cloves. The belly is sewn up or folded into a package before being tied to hold its shape. It is then simmered in an aromatic broth made from ham, bacon, a beef bone, a veal foot, celery, leeks, parsley, onions, and chives for at least three hours. Once it is tender, juniper, thyme, bay leaves, and saffron are added, and the liquid is reduced until it thickens somewhat. A bit of cognac is added to the pot just before serving. **Trenel Millavois:** This is the version of Tripous from the region around Millau. Tripous is frequently served with Aligot.

Desserts

Desserts in the Aveyron are not fancy, relying heavily on local products rather than involved techniques. Meals frequently end with **Apple Walnut Tarts; Walnut Cakes; Croquant aux Amandes,** Biscotti-like almond cookies; **Conquises,** an orange hazelnut, carob, or chocolate candy; or **Flone,** a delicious sheep milk ricotta cheesecake. Breakfasts and afternoon tea or coffee feature **Fouace,** a ring-shaped coffee cake made from flour, yeast, butter, eggs, sugar, and orange blossom water. Consider yourself lucky if **Gâteau à la Broche** is on your plate. This time-consuming cake is reserved for special occasions like holidays and weddings. The cake is made by turning a conical mold on a spit called a *broche*. As the *broche* spins slowly in front of a hot fire, very thick crêpe batter is meticulously ladled over the cone. The layer of batter cooks, and after quite a bit of time, a lacy thick cake is formed. After it is carefully removed from the cone mold, the resulting cake resembles a golden-brown Christmas tree and is served standing upright on a plate.

Liqueurs, Eaux de Vie, and Wine: Dinners are often finished with Liqueurs or Eaux de Vie made from walnuts, quince, or prunes.

Wines of the Aveyron

Marcillac is the most significant wine region of the Aveyron, although some interesting AOC wines are also currently being made in the **Gorges et Côtes de Millau,** as well as the **Vins d'Entraygues-Le-Fel et d'Estaing** appellations.

Julien and Philippe Teulier
Photo credit: Domaine du Cros

Domaine du Cros is the largest producer in Marcillac. Up until 1982, the four-genera-tion property had only two-and-a-half acres of vines. Since 1982, they have studiously increased their holdings by buying and renting older vineyards until they have reached their current size of 74 acres. Incorporated in 1984, the property is currently run by fa-ther and son team Philippe and Julien Teulier. (Philippe is the President of the *Syndicat des Vignerons de l'AOC de Marcillac*, the local wine bureau.) Although machine harvest-ing was made possible in the appellation with terracing and slope redesign in the 1960s, all of the Teuliers' grapes are hand harvested. Du Cros produces three red Marcillacs, all from Fer Servadou. The vineyards extend over both the moderate elevation rougier soils and limestone scree deposits on the higher slopes. The grapes are macerated in temperature-controlled stainless-steel tanks. The only things that differ between the three cuvées are the age of the vines and the aging treatment.

Lo Sang del Païs (The Blood of the Countryside) comes from 25-year-old vines. It un-dergoes a 21-day maceration and is aged in stainless steel and very old oak and chestnut barrels for 8–12 months before being bottled. Super quaffable with spicy red fruit and soft tannins, this has long been one of my go-to house wines.

Cuvée Vieilles Vignes and Les Rougiers are both from a selection of vines between 50 and 80 years of age. They undergo a 35-day maceration. The Vieilles Vignes (old vines) ages 18 months in old large oak and chestnut barrels ranging in age from 30 to 200 years old before being bottled, while Les Rougiers is aged in new and used small oak barriques, which layers a vanilla patina over the dark fruit and spiciness found in the Vieilles Vignes.

Domaine du Cros also makes a **Marcillac Rosé** from Fer Servadou in the *saignée* method and a floral **Vin de Pays Blanc de Blancs** from Muscat à Petits Grains and Issal (a local variety).

Although it is possible to find the Domaine du Cros Rosé and Blanc de Blancs in a few shops in Paris, I can attest that many of the steakhouses and meat-centric bistros in Paris pour Marcillac Rouge, specifically Domaine du Cros Marcillac. One of my favorite restaurants, Maison d'Aubrac in Paris, has both the Vieilles Vignes and Les Rougiers on their list. I enjoy the steak at Maison d'Aubrac (from Aubrac Beef, of course), but the real reason I go is for the Aligot!

SAIGNEE METHOD. In the *saignée* method, winemakers "bleed" off some juice after between six-to-twelve hours of maceration to produce a rosé wine. This serves two purposes. The obvious first one is it gives them a rosé wine and second, because a smaller volume of liquid is left in the tank to macerate with the original amount of skins, the remaining wine is concentrated.

Photo credit: Domaine du Cros

I was quite happy when I realized that my trip to the Southwest with Ed and Barbara was going to include a stop at Domaine du Cros. It's not exactly on the beaten path, but Du Cros Marcillac was probably one of my most recommended country French wines when I worked at Arrowine in response to a customer asking for something "different and affordable" to go with grilled meat.

As we got closer to the winery, driving through the slightly mist-covered rolling verdant hills winding through the countryside near Rodez, Barbara mentioned that Denise Teulier, Philippe's wife, was a fabulous cook and predicted that we were in for a real treat. What an understatement! Not only did Philippe give us a great tour of the steeply terraced vineyards, their winery and cellar with its huge chestnut vats—some of which were more than 200 years old—but he opened bottle after bottle, vintage after vintage of his wines, a move designed to show us their ageability. As we tasted wine in their farmhouse kitchen, I began to realize that Denise was pulling out all the stops cooking for us. Slender and tanned, with a slightly raspy voice, she laughed and talked, all the while pulling together a fantastic meal. Hors d'oeuvres with Domaine du Cros Blanc de Blancs were followed by a truly delicious platter of house-cured salmon with a dill and boiled potato salad and chilled Marcillac Rosé. I remember Doug nudging me with his elbow, acknowledging how great the salmon was.

When Denise unwrapped two enormous *Côtes de Boeuf*, bone-in rib steaks (Aubrac beef, of course), I knew we were in for something special. Although I knew I technically was supposed to be taking notes on the wines, I simultaneously began tracking her with my eyes. When she grabbed an umbrella to go outside in the drizzling rain, I followed and discovered a grill set up in the lee of the house, large embers of wood logs glowing. I watched as Denise added grape vine cuttings to the fire—very exciting! The huge steaks that came off of that grill made standing outside in the rain totally worth it, but the real heart-stopping moment for me was when I saw her begin to beat grated cheese into steaming potatoes that she had just passed through a food mill. "Holy Shit!" I whispered to Doug. "She's making Aligot!" He gave me one of his typical looks, a bit of a puzzled glare—after all, I was interrupting his wine tasting to gush about some food event. (For those of you who don't know us, this was a long-standing pattern in our relationship. Doug meticulously taking notes, very serious about the technical aspects of wine—me very interested in wine, but from the standpoint of what food goes with it. All I can say is it was a dynamic that worked for us!)

We already know that I love Aligot. I mean what's not to love? The combination of smooth garlicky mashed potatoes, buttery cheese, and tangy crème fraîche is a subtle but heartwarming showstopper. And that's before you see evidence of its elasticity when served by an experienced showperson.

Denise assured me that along with diligence in really beating the cheese into the potatoes until the amalgamation forms elastic ribbons, there are a few other important rules, the most important of which we cannot achieve in the United States at this time. Denise insisted that fresh Tomme de Laguiole cheese is a must—the problem being that due to FDA regulations, fresh Laguiole is not available in the United States. I have had good success substituting aged Laguiole or Cantal cheese. I can only imagine how good it would be if I had the correct cheese. (Actually, I don't have to imagine it. I have had it at her house.) She also insisted that in addition to cooking some garlic in with the potatoes, at the last minute one clove of fresh garlic must be grated into the potato before adding the crème fraîche and cheese to the mixture so that there is a fresh garlic component to the dish. This dish is comfort food at its most satisfying. No wonder it is nicknamed *Le Ruban d'amitié*, the ribbon of friendship, with local Aligot societies (yes, there is more than one local Aligot Society), declaring that it reinforces conviviality and unleashes cordiality.

Our meal at Domaine du Cros was fabulous. Philippe and Denise paired the wines and food together in a perfect example of how they should be served. The Marcillac Rosé with the salmon salad, Lo Sang del Païs and the Vieilles Vignes with the amazingly rich, wood-grilled Côtes de Boeuf d'Aubrac and Aligot. Even though it was gray and drizzling outside, the atmosphere around the Teuliers' farmhouse table was warm and cozy. We laughed, ate, and drank those hearty country wines—some quaffable, some more serious—all intended, like the Aligot, the ribbon of friendship, to engender a feeling of conviviality and welcome. It's no wonder I still dream about it.

Note: Unfortunately, Denise passed away a few years ago. I'm glad to have met her—she, and the experience of watching her that day, are things I would not like to have missed.

The Winemaker Recommends: Côte de Boeuf with Domaine du Cros Marcillac Rouge "Vieilles Vignes."

Aligot

Yield: 6 to 8 generous portions | Ease of Preparation: Moderate
Ease of Sourcing: Moderate to difficult. It's all about the cheese.
Wine Pairing: A rustic red like Domaine Du Cros Marcillac "Lo Sang del Païs" or Cahors

This elastic, cheese-laden dish is a paean to all that is good in the world. Fluffy mashed potatoes, cheese, melted gooeyness—it is comfort food at its most basic. This dish is from the Auvergne in the Massif Central of France—a specialty of home chefs and classic restaurants alike. Although less well known than the ubiquitous (and also delicious) Frites (French Fries), Aligot figures prominently on menus in steakhouses throughout Paris—many of which are Auvergnat owned. You can even find it in to-go containers at local farmer's markets throughout Central France. One of the first times I ate this was at Domaine du Cros in Marcillac. I almost wept when I realized that was what Denise Teulier was making. Not only were we going to get to eat it, I was going to learn to make it! What a treat!

INGREDIENTS

1½ lbs. Russet potatoes

2 large cloves peeled garlic, 1 whole, the other sliced as thin as you can get it

2 oz. unsalted butter

1 lb. Laguiole or Cantal cheese

3 oz. crème fraîche

Kosher salt

White pepper, finely ground

WHAT YOU'LL NEED

6-quart pot to cook the potatoes

Food mill or potato masher

Strainer

Large spoon

Box grater

TIMING

Prep Time: 30 minutes

Cooking Time: 30 minutes

PROCESS

Peel the potatoes and cut them in one-inch cubes. Cover them in cold water if you are not using them right away.

Place the potatoes and the whole clove of garlic in cold water in the 6-quart pot and cook until extremely soft (approximately 20 minutes).

While the potatoes are cooking, grate the cheese on a box grater.

Strain the potatoes and pass them through a potato ricer or a food mill back into your pot. If you do not have a ricer or food mill, return the potatoes to the pan and use a potato masher to mash them extremely well. Make sure there are no lumps!

Turn the heat to low, stir the potatoes for a minute to make sure all excess liquid is evaporated. With your spoon, beat in the butter until it is completely melted and mixed in. Stir in the crème fraîche. Add the clove of sliced fresh garlic to the potato mixture. Continue stirring and beat in the cheese. You may want to add it in three batches to give it a chance to melt more easily. Continue stirring and beating for approximately 5 minutes. You need to develop an elastic texture. When it is completely incorporated, you should be able to lift your spoon, and the cheese and potato mixture will form an elastic ribbon.

Add kosher salt and white pepper to taste. Serve warm.

Notes

#1. Denise Teulier assured me that I would never be able to make Aligot in the United States because it can only be made with fresh cheese, Tomme d'Auvergne or Tomme d'Aubrac, neither of which is available in the US due to government regulations regarding importation of fresh cheese. I have seen recipes and spoken to chefs in France who make it with aged Cantal, Laguiole, or Tomme d'Auvergne. Here's the rub: depending on where you live, even those may not be easy to find. I can find Cantal quite easily and Laguiole with a bit more difficulty at Arrowine in Virginia. I would imagine those with well-stocked local cheese shops could do the same. Unfortunately, this isn't true everywhere. They can be purchased online through certain specialty cheese shops, and my sister Lori found Cantal through Amazon.

#2. If you do not have a potato ricer or food mill, you could mash your potatoes in a mixer, but be careful not to overbeat them at this stage—you want to remove the lumps but not turn them into glue. For some reason, once you start adding the butter, crème fraîche, and cheese, this does not seem to be a problem.

Côte de Boeuf

Yield: 6 portions | Ease of Preparation: Moderate
Ease of Sourcing: Moderate. If you know a good butcher you should be able to order a bone-in rib steak fairly easily. Make sure you tell them you want it nice and thick! Prepare to pay a premium price for this cut of meat.
Wine Pairing: Domaine du Cros Marcillac Rouge "Vieilles Vignes," Cahors, or another rustic red

Indelibly etched in my memory is the image of Denise Teulier of Domaine du Cros in the Marcillac region of the Auvergne, umbrella in hand to guard against the rain, cooking two huge bone-in rib steaks over a fire made from wood and grapevine cuttings. The meat and fat juices sizzled. The raindrops, slipping under awning and umbrella, hissed. I stood with her while she cooked—listening to her pronounced accent and tracking her deft juggling of umbrella, meat fork, and cigarette, all the more impressive given the expressive hand movements that accompanied her rapid speech. The Auvergnats or Aveyronnais are known for their beef (in fact, they showcase it in the many cafés and restaurants they own in Paris) from the Aubrac breed of cattle, and Côte de Boeuf is the king of all cuts.

INGREDIENTS

Two large bone-in rib steaks
    (approximately 2 to 2½ lbs. each)
Kosher salt
Fresh cracked black pepper

TIMING

Grill Time: 10–15 minutes
Baking Time: 10–15 minutes
Resting Time: 20 minutes

WHAT YOU'LL NEED

Grill, preferably wood or charcoal for
    better flavor
Long tongs
Roasting pan large enough to hold
    both steaks
Cutting board
Instant read meat thermometer
    (optional)

PROCESS

Take the steaks out of the refrigerator an hour before you plan to cook them to take the chill off.

Preheat the oven to 450° F.

Make sure that the grill grates are extremely hot. Salt and pepper your steaks right before placing them on the grill. (Some people swear that you should not salt your meat before cooking. I'm not a fan of that. I think you need to salt it before cooking to develop flavors and to make sure the meat is seasoned through and through. Otherwise, you are just salting the outer layer of the steak.)

Place the steaks on the hot grill and leave them for three-to-four minutes before checking them. Once they have nice grill marks, keep them on the same side, but rotate them 90 degrees for the next set of marks. Once those marks have developed, flip the steaks and repeat this process. Transfer the marked steaks to the roasting pan and put it in the oven to finish cooking, flipping them after a couple of minutes for even cooking. If you like your steak extremely rare, you may not need to cook them in the oven at all. (See Note #2 below regarding meat temperature.)

Take them out on the rare side of doneness for your taste. Experienced grillers can check this by pressing on the meat. However, steaks like this are not cheap. (Two steaks will run you around $100 conservatively.) If in doubt, use a meat thermometer to check the temperature and remember that the steaks will continue to cook while they rest on your cutting board. I like my steaks medium rare, so I pull them when they are very rare, and the carryover cooking brings them to medium rare while they rest. Because grill heat varies, exact cooking time is difficult to pinpoint. You may want to start checking the temperature of the steaks after they have been in the oven for five minutes.

To serve, slice away the bone and then slice the steak against the grain. Feel free to fight over the bone.

Cooking Côtes de Boeuf

Notes

#1. You could cook the steak completely on the grill, but it would require that you make your fire on one half of the grill so there are two discrete heat zones—the one over the coals providing extremely hot direct heat and the other providing indirect heat and functioning more like an oven. First you would mark the steak on the direct heat side of the grill (marking means developing those cool crisscross grill marks on your meat) before transferring the steaks to the indirect heat side of the grill to finish cooking. I don't recommend this unless you don't have access to an oven. You will have better success if you mark the steaks on the grill and finish it in the oven.

#2. Meat Temperatures. Following are general guidelines for beef cooking temperatures:

Rare: 120–125° F

Medium Rare: 130–135° F

Medium: 140–145° F

Medium Well: 150–155° F

Well: Above 160° F

I should mention that the USDA does not recommend eating meat cooked to less than 145° F, meaning nothing less well done than medium.

At Buck's we found that if we pulled the steaks at temperatures at least fifteen degrees lower than the desired final temperature, by the time the steaks rested, they were perfectly done. Our steaks were prime dry aged strip steaks that we rested for 10–15 minutes before serving. We taped a yellow sticky note on the ticket holder of the line as a cooking guide. Obviously, some cooks do this by feel, but since we charged $40 for a steak and they took 30 minutes to cook and rest, I "encouraged" my cooks to use a thermometer until they were very experienced at hitting temperatures. To take the temperature of the steak, slide an instant-read meat thermometer horizontally into the side of the steak being careful not to touch the bone.

#3. Cowboy Cuts, Tomahawk, bone-in rib steaks, and ribeyes. These are all variations of the same cut of meat, the rib steak. A *bone-in rib steak* is exactly what the name indicates, a steak cut from the rib portion of the cow. Cowboy and Tomahawk steaks are bone-in rib steaks with frenched bones; in the case of the Cowboy cut, the frenched bone is short—approximately 2 inches. For the Tomahawk, the bone is longer—between 4–5 inches. Ribeyes are the rib steak with the bone removed. Rib steaks are rich, juicy, and flavorful with considerable marbling.

"Magical Vineyard Tour"
A Visit with Jean-Pierre Charlot, Domaine Joseph Voillot
Volnay, France

From the moment you meet Jean Pierre Charlot of Domaine Joseph Voillot, you see the twinkle in his eye, the ready smile. He is a bit of a dichotomy. A large man with a deep voice and correspondingly throaty chuckle, he could easily be mistaken for a French character actor perpetually cast in the role of the local French denizen. In reality, Jean Pierre is a deft winemaker, thoughtful and committed to his land, his village, and the wines he produces.

A former professor of Oenology at the Wine School in Beaune, Jean Pierre's origins are deeply rooted in Burgundy. His father worked for well-known wine négociant Bouchard Père et Fils, and Jean Pierre studied Oenology and worked as a wine broker upon graduation. Affairs of the heart provided him the opportunity to become even more directly immersed in wine when he married one of the daughters of respected Volnaysien winemaker Joseph Voillot, whose family has been making wine in Volnay for five generations. Jean Pierre stepped into the family business as Joseph's right-hand man, and the pair worked together for 15 years until Joseph retired.

Every time I would run across Jean Pierre in Washington, DC (usually at his importer Vintage 59's annual portfolio tasting), our conversations would center on two topics, his wine (of course) and food. Since I'm obviously interested in what winemakers eat, I asked him if he cooked. He laughed and told me, "No, I eat." And then he proceeded to recommend his favorite restaurants in Burgundy and to describe traditional dishes.

Wines of Burgundy

Located to the southeast of Paris, Burgundy is one of the best-known wine regions in France and is comprised of five subregions of which the Côte d'Or is arguably the most famous. The Côte d'Or with its prestigious Premier and Grand Cru vineyards stretches from just south of Dijon to the town of Chagny and is further divided into the Côte de Nuits and the Côte de Beaune (where Domaine Joseph Voillot is located.) The Côte Chalonnaise, the Mâconnais, and Beaujolais subregions extend south from the Côte d'Or, while Chablis in the Yonne department to the north and west is separated from the other four subregions both geographically (some 70 miles away) and geologically— its mother lode of Kimmeridgian soils enabling it to produce the raciest Chardonnays in the world. Red wines of Burgundy are produced predominantly from Pinot Noir (the exceptions being Bourgogne Passetoutgrains, which incorporates Gamay into its blend; and Beaujolais, which is 100 percent Gamay). Whites wines from Burgundy are produced from Chardonnay, the quaffable Aligoté, and tiny amounts of Pinot Blanc and Sauvignon Blanc. With the exception of the aforementioned Passetoutgrains, wines of Burgundy are all monovarietal.

Burgundy has a continental climate with cold winters, spring and fall rains, and relatively mild short summers. Because of the coolness of the climate, the early ripening varieties of Pinot Noir and Chardonnay perform best here. Geologically, Burgundy is dominated by limestone soils from the Jurassic period, although the soils of the Côte de Beaune have slightly higher sand content than the Côte de Nuits.

The Côte de Beaune begins in Ladoix-Serrigny, stretches south to Santenay (near Chagny), and accounts for arguably the greatest white wines of Burgundy as well as some very fine red wines. From north to south, the principal appellations of the Côte de Beaune are Corton, Corton-Charlemagne, Beaune, Pommard, Volnay, Meursault, Puligny-Montrachet, and Chassagne-Montrachet.

Unlike the large châteaux in Bordeaux, wine estates in Burgundy tend to be small and family-owned. Because the inheritance laws of the Napoleonic Code require that each heir inherit equally, many vineyards or *climats,* as they are called in Burgundy, have extremely divided ownership with some winemakers owning a single row or two of a cherished vineyard. The wines of Burgundy are for the most part delicate and extremely complex wines—lighter in body than their counterparts from Bordeaux, Italy, Spain, or the New World. These are wines for food, and luckily the region produces some amazing cuisine to accompany them.

Foods of Burgundy

Although there are Michelin-starred restaurants in Burgundy to be sure, the cuisine is one of tradition, emphasizing the bounty of local ingredients and wine-based sauces.

Charolais Beef, Bresse Chicken, Burgundy Snails, Burgundy Black Truffles, and, of course, Dijon mustard are marquee names whose rock star status befits their presence at the table with the legendary wines of the region. Standout local dishes use these and other ingredients with one aim, to nourish while at the same time engendering a feeling of warmth and bonhomie. There are no foams or crazy molecular gastronomic techniques. When you start with such perfection, none are needed, which in my opinion (and isn't this whole book about my opinion?) renders the food soulful and more delicious. I like sitting down to a table where I feel comfortable laughing, tearing bread with my hands, and leaning forward, elbows on the table, to share a story or joke. That is how I feel when I'm in Burgundy.

Although the following list is by no means exhaustive, it highlights the most famous Burgundian dishes.

Gougères: Classic as an aperitif, these cheese-flavored puffs are made with a traditional *pâte à choux* (choux pastry) and are sold at almost every pastry shop in Burgundy. Delicious with a glass of White Burgundy (or Champagne), one of their charms is that they can be made ahead of time, frozen, and recrisped in the oven. Good to have on hand when you have a champagne noshing emergency. (C'mon. I *cannot* be the only one who has those on a regular basis.)

Jambon Persillé: Made from ham, shallots, garlic, and parsley in aspic, this is a great picnic dish. Buy it at the local charcuterie, grab a baguette, some radishes, salted butter, and a bottle of wine, and you are all set.

Oeufs en Meurette: I cannot stress enough how delicious this dish is. Take a red-wine poached egg (preferably from a farmer you know), place it on a crispy crouton, and garnish it with pearl onions, button mushrooms, and crispy bacon lardons that have been sautéed and then stewed in a veal stock, red wine, and butter reduction. Cripes, that's good.

Oeufs Brouillés with Black Truffles: Sinfully rich—how could it be otherwise? It's basically the French version of lightly scrambled eggs with a ton of truffles folded inside and shaved on top. It's a little more complex than that, but only barely. And, you guessed it. It relies on perfect ingredients and a delicate hand while cooking it. One second too long in the pan, and your creamy eggs turn to rubber, which is kind of a waste of good eggs and truffles, if you ask me. Another caveat: when offered this as an off-menu special at a restaurant, you should probably ask how much it costs or you might receive a rather expensive surprise when the bill comes. Yes, that is the voice of experience speaking, but it was totally worth it.

Escargots à la Bourguignonne: Snails in their shell stuffed with parsley, garlic, and shallot butter. Honestly, even if the thought of eating snails turns you off, dipping bread in that oozy flavored butter is enough to make ordering this dish worthwhile.

Frog's Legs: As with the aforementioned snails, I'm not really interested in squeamish reactions. You must try this! People say it tastes like chicken. I don't know about that. I tend to think it tastes like a really delicate white firm-fleshed fish. The traditional recipe calls for soaking the frog's legs in salted milk before breading them in flour (I use superfine flour) and sautéing them quickly in butter until golden brown. At the last minute they are tossed with minced parsley, garlic, lemon zest, and a little lemon juice.

Coq au Vin: Purists will tell you that you must use an old rooster to make this dish. Good luck finding one. This dish historically *was* made with a rooster cooked in red wine (preferably Burgundy) for a long time to break down the toughness of the bird. Nowadays, it is generally made with a large stewing chicken. As with the Oeufs en Meurette, it is garnished with pearl onions, button mushrooms, and crispy bacon lardons that have been sautéed and then stewed in a chicken stock, red wine, and butter reduction. Wiping the sauce from the plate with a crust of bread is almost mandatory.

Boeuf Bourgignon: Beef braised in Red Burgundy garnished with pearl onions, button mushrooms braised in a (you guessed it) red wine and stock (in this case beef) reduction. For this recipe, the lardons are braised with the beef rather than in the garnish.

Foraged Bounty: In addition to all of the fabulous products farmed in the region, there is a long tradition of fishing, hunting, and foraging for the ingredients in dishes like:

Crawfish in Nantua Sauce: Crawfish in a creamy butter sauce flavored with crawfish shells.

Rabbit à la Moutarde: Rabbit braised in a creamy Dijon mustard sauce.

Wild Boar Ragout: Wild Boar braised in Red Burgundy.

Pocheuse: Traditional freshwater fish stew made with eel, pike, perch, and tench in a white wine broth.

Sautéed Mushrooms: Sautéed in butter with garlic and parsley. To gild the lily, some people stir an egg yolk into the mixture once it has been removed from the pan. This gives the mushrooms an even glossier texture and added richness.

Cheeses: Fantastic cheeses like Epoisses, Soumaintrain, Abbaye la Pierre qui Vire, Abbaye de Citeaux, and the adorably named Bouton de Culotte (pants button) grace cheese shop windows and eventually cheese plates both in restaurants and on the family dinner table.

Desserts: invariably feature seasonal fruits (pears, peaches, cherries) and the ever-present black currant Cassis.

When discussing some of these dishes and where to find them, Jean Pierre raved about the restaurant across the street from his winery, Le Cellier Volnaysien. Because I am obsessive, I immediately looked it up online. With its cozy, long brick rooms, capped by low vaulted ceilings, and decorated with wine barrels and winemaking paraphernalia, it looked exactly

like the kind of restaurant I love. Likewise, the menu was right up my alley with an emphasis on traditional Burgundian dishes like Escargots à la Bourgignonne and Oeufs en Meurette, dishes unchanged by innovation or "twists." Jean Pierre raved about it, and not to put to fine a point on it (or to cast the first stone), but he didn't seem to be wasting away. In fact, a bon vivant, gourmand characteristic figures prominently in his persona.

Looking at the restaurant's website and talking with Jean Pierre, I knew there would be a meal in my future at Le Cellier Volnaysien. Having enjoyed Joseph Voillot wines many times over the years, a visit to the winery (right across the street) seemed a necessity, as well.

The opportunity to accomplish these two agenda items presented itself in the summer of 2014. When I emailed Jean Pierre to tell him I was coming to Burgundy with my husband, aunt, and uncle and asked him if he was free to see us at the winery, he immediately wrote back. "Yes. Come see me that Saturday. You'll stay for lunch of course.

We're having a big luncheon with a bunch of folks who organize horse-drawn carriage tours through the vineyards of Burgundy. It'll be fun!" Seriously, carriage tours of Burgundian vineyards? Lunch with the winemaker? Where do I sign up?

We arrived at the winery completely unaware that our luncheon and proposed wine tour were all part of a much larger celebration—in my opinion, never a bad problem to have. The producers of Volnay are very proud of the finesse and elegance of their wines and have established an organization called the *Association Élégance des Volnay*. Since 2005, they have celebrated their wines on the last Saturday in June with carriage rides, wine tastings and competitions, and special meals. How lucky we were that our visit coincided with the event! We could have been discouraged that it was raining, but hey, a little rain never hurt anyone.

We each grabbed a glass, hopped into a carriage with its redshirted driver holding the reins of two massive Auxois horses, and were on our way to the vineyards and the tent-covered tasting tables stationed throughout them. Of course, since this was a Burgundian tasting, each table was amply stocked with something to eat, in this case one of my favorite delicacies—Gougères, the savory cheese pastry. We munched and sipped our way around the vineyards (I even took some notes) before arriving back at the winery located in the center of Volnay across from the 13th-century village church, its stout bell tower the tallest edifice in the village.

So far it was a morning well spent. Jean Pierre waved us in and sent us to taste wine in the ancient cellars with Gilles Mathieu, one of Jean Pierre's colleagues (a total Keenan Wynn look-alike). We tasted current and back vintages of wines from Volnay and its neighboring villages of Pommard, Beaune, and Meursault. These appellations are characterized as follows:

Volnay: Stretching from Pommard in the north to Meursault in the south, over half the wines of Volnay are designated Premier Cru. Made from Pinot Noir, wines from Volnay are distinguished by their delicate, elegant qualities.

Pommard: Located just to the north of Volnay, Pommards are the deepest, darkest, and most tannic of the Pinot Noir-based red wines of the Côte de Beaune.

Meursault: South of Volnay, Meursault is an appellation focused almost solely on white wines from Chardonnay. (Red wines from Meursault are generally labeled Volnay or Blagny.) Due to the relatively low water tables, allowing for large underground cellars, prolonged barrel maturation has been the historical norm in Meursault, resulting in increased richness, depth, and aging potential.

Beaune: From the vineyards surrounding the lovely town of Beaune—the historic wine capital of Burgundy—these predominately red wines are lighter than those of Pom-

mard and lack the elegance and finesse of Volnay. Their tendency to medium body, bright cherry fruit, and relatively early drinkability as young wines generally make them a more affordable choice than other red wines from the Côte d'Or.

Many of the wines we tasted at Domaine Voillot were in very small quantities due to the hailstorms that had ravaged the villages in 2012 and 2013. This part of the Côte de Beaune seems to be particularly susceptible to hail and frost especially in recent years.

Domaine Joseph Voillot produces fifteen wines: two whites from Meursault, **Les Chevaliers** and **Les Cras Premier Cru**; and thirteen reds: **Bourgogne Vieilles Vignes**; **Pommard Vieilles Vignes**; four Pommard Premier Crus: **Les Rugiens, Clos Micault, Les Epenots,** and **Les Pézerolles**; **Volnay Vieilles Vignes**; five Volnay Premier Crus: **Les Taillepieds, En Caillerets, Les Champans, Les Fremiets,** and **Les Carelles Sous La Chapelle**; and **Beaune Les Coucherias Premier Cru**.

Emerging from the cellar, we were handed glasses of champagne and offered more gougères as we stood watching Jean Pierre and his friends, all clad in red shirts indicating that they were members of *Les Traits de Merceuil*, the horse-drawn carriage association, jury-rig a canvas rain cover over the food table by attaching it to the winery on three sides with a forklift serving as the fourth tent pole.

Also on the table of appetizers? Saucisson sec and the *best* version of *jambon persillé* that I have ever had. I have long had a love/hate affair with *jambon persillé*. On the one hand, it looks delicious—pink chunks of moist ham with pale green parsley and garlic aspic serving as mortar to hold it together. Frequently, though, the ham is a little tough and the aspic mixture tastes so strongly of raw garlic that it overwhelms the salty porkiness of the ham. This version dispelled my apprehension. It was delicious. The aspic was a delicate blend of the bright green flavor of parsley with subtle hints of garlic, and the ham was moist and tender. When I commented to Jean Pierre how good it was, he assured me that his friends at Charcuterie Moron in Pommard made the best *jambon persillé* around—had won awards for it, in fact. Of course, Jean Pierre would know where to buy the best food and, of course, he would be friends with the people who make it.

We moved inside and feasted on chicken in a delicate cream sauce and another of my all-time favorites, *potatoes fondants*. *Potatoes fondants* are peeled potatoes that are browned in a sauté pan with duck fat and then simmered in chicken stock until they are tender and golden brown. If you want to be fancy you can turn (or trim) the potatoes into uniform football shapes, but these were cut in thick semicircles and they were awesome. I asked Jean Pierre for the recipe, and he told me that with all the details of organizing the tasting event and the carriage rides, he had outsourced the lunch to—you guessed it—Le Cellier Volnaysien. Another winemaker had told me somewhat tongue in cheek that Le Cellier was Jean Pierre's personal lunchroom. Kind of like an executive dining room, except the proprietor is a friend of his, serves outstanding food, and has a kick-ass wine cellar.

I knew that Isabelle, Jean Pierre's wife, made the fruit tarts and I had a hard time deciding between the apricot and the cherry, so I had small bites of both. Jean Pierre wandered around at the event making sure everyone had ample wine—serving Prévoteau-Perrier Champagne, 2012 Schäfer-Fröhlich Schiefergestein Bockenauer Riesling, and his own 2011 Pommard Vieilles Vignes. He was a full-service host, pouring coffee at the end of the meal—jovially making sure that everyone was completely happy. We definitely were. What a wonderful way to spend an afternoon!

N.B. Later that day while out walking in Beaune ten miles away, I was caught in one of two vicious hailstorms that struck about twenty minutes apart. The hail curse had hit the towns of the Côtes de Beaune again, with the northern villages of Pommard and, in particular, Volnay taking the brunt of it. For the third year in a row, Jean Pierre Charlot's vineyards at Domaine Joseph Voillot had suffered catastrophic losses. It was a tragedy for them—almost too much to bear, I am sure, and a starkly heartbreaking contrast to the lighthearted conviviality from earlier in the day. So, although I remember fondly the carriage

Photo credit: Domaine Joseph Voillot

ride, the lovely meal with the delicious wines, and the wonderful *jambon persillé* and *potatoes fondants*, I am particularly struck by the difficult nature of a winemaker's work and mostly marvel at the resilience of these folks and their commitment to their fickle craft.

Note: I had the honor to sit beside Monsieur Joseph Voillot during lunch the day of our visit. Although his health was waning, his smile was charming—his pride in the wines of his Domaine still markedly evident. I was saddened to hear that he passed away shortly thereafter.

The Winemaker Recommends: Favorite pairing Coq au Vin with Joseph Voillot Pommard or Volnay!

Gougères

Yield: 4 dozen quarter-sized gougères | Ease of Preparation: Moderate but messy | Ease of Sourcing: Simple
Wine Pairing: Champagne, Chablis, or Young White or Red Burgundy

Gougères are a huge favorite of mine! They are the perfect accompaniment to Champagne or Burgundy. Bite-sized versions graced the tasting tables in the vineyards of Volnay during the Elégance de Volnay celebration and at Domaine Joseph Voillot, but I've seen larger gougères throughout Burgundy—especially in Chablis. There aren't that many ingredients in the recipe, so the quality of the eggs, butter, and Gruyère are of paramount importance.

INGREDIENTS

1 cup water

3 oz. unsalted butter (¾ of a stick)

1 tsp. kosher salt

1 cup all-purpose flour

4–5 best-quality eggs (1 cup) + 1 extra
   egg beaten for an egg wash

1 cup very finely shredded Gruyère
   cheese + ½ cup for garnish

TIMING

Prep Time: 45 minutes

Cook Time: 20–25 minutes

WHAT YOU'LL NEED

4-quart saucepan

Wooden kitchen spoon

Large kitchen bowl

Rubber spatula

Tall plastic container (quart size like
   you get at a deli)

Piping bags

Pastry tips with round medium
   openings

Paring knife

Two baking sheets lined with silicone
   mats or parchment paper

Pastry brush

Metal spatula

Pastry cooling rack

PROCESS

Preheat oven to 425° F preferably on convection bake setting.

For the Dough:

Heat the water, butter, and kosher salt in the saucepan until the butter melts and the mixture boils. Remove the saucepan from the heat and stir in the flour. It will be lumpy at first. Continue stirring to remove the lumps. Once there are no more lumps, put the pan back on the stove and heat over medium heat, stirring constantly. This will evaporate the liquid from your dough. Don't skip this step. Drying the dough means it can absorb more eggs later. Continue stirring until it forms a loose ball and leaves a film on the bottom of the saucepan—approximately 3–4 minutes.

At this point, put the dough into the kitchen bowl and stir for a minute to cool it slightly.

Quickly beat the eggs to combine the yolks and whites.

Add the approximate equivalent of one egg to the flour mixture. Begin beating the egg into the mixture. At first, it will seem as if the dough and egg will not

blend, but keep at it. The egg will begin to incorporate into the dough. Once it is mixed, add another bit of egg. Continue, beating and adding egg to the dough until all the eggs have been incorporated. The dough will be the consistency of rich mashed potatoes. When you lift your spoon, it will slowly plop back into the bowl.

Mix one cup of very finely shredded Gruyère into the dough.

Filling the Pastry Bags:

I recommend having more than one pastry bag. There is too much dough for one bag, but re-filling the bag is super messy. Plus it is important to work quickly at this point. Place the pastry tip into a bag and place the bag into the deli container tip end down. This enables you to fill the pastry bag more easily. Use the rubber spatula to scoop gougère dough into the pastry bag. Try to be as neat as you can. Once it is three-quarters full, twist the top of the bag closed and set it to the side. Repeat with the other pastry tips and bags until you have used all the dough.

Trim the tip of the pastry bag, twist the top again, and begin piping individual gougères onto the parchment or silicone mat. I like small gougères. I try to start with a quarter-shaped round and pipe two smaller circles above it (for a total of three circles). There will be a curlicue at the top (kind of like a soft-serve ice cream cone). Continue piping gougères, making sure to leave at least an inch between each gougère. (I usually do six rows of four, but if you have small baking sheets, you may need to put less per baking sheet. In this case, you may need more than two baking sheets or you will have to work in batches.)

Once you have piped the gougères, use your pastry brush to gently brush a dab of egg wash on top of the curlicue to smooth it out and sprinkle a little of the reserved Gruyère on top.

Place the baking sheets in the oven and bake for 18–22 minutes, rotating the baking sheets twice during the baking process. If the heat is uneven in your oven, you may need to switch trays from one rack to another in the oven to ensure even heating.

When the gougères are golden brown all over, remove them from the oven. They should resemble little turbans and be light but firm. Use the metal spatula to move them to the pastry cooling rack and then pierce the side of each gougère with the tip of your paring knife to allow steam to escape. Cool them on the pastry cooling rack.

Serve warm or room temperature.

Notes

#1. I've been making gougères for years. They are the perfect accompaniment to a glass of Champagne or Chablis. One of the best things about them is that they freeze very well— allowing you to store a container of them in the freezer for Champagne emergencies. To reheat, preheat the oven to 350° F and bake 5–10 minutes until lightly crispy. This also works if you have leftover gougères from the day before, as they can lose their crunchy texture the next day.

#2. I have always used Julia Child's recipe from *The Way to Cook.* When my friend James Rexroad started working with me at Buck's Fishing & Camping, he showed me a trick for making a large number of gougères for parties. (His single recipe is double the size of mine, and he often doubles even that.) James uses an electric mixer to mix in his eggs. If I'm just making a single batch, I don't do this, because frankly, it annoys me more to get my mixer out and to wash it afterwards than to beat it by hand, but the mixer works well for large quantities. Rather than piping the dough with a pastry bag, James also uses a small #100 scoop (.375 oz.). It enables him to get exactly 95 small round gougères per batch. I like the looks of the hand-piped gougères with their turban shape, but I can't argue with his method when you've got a big crowd. He also recommends adding half a tablespoon of sugar to the 1 cup of Gruyère to help brown the gougères.

Jambon Persillé

Yield: One terrine | Ease of Preparation: Moderate | Ease of Sourcing: Moderate
Wine Pairing: Champagne, Crémant de Bourgogne, Young White Burgundy

This dish is all about balance. The ham should be moist, tender, and light pink. The stock for the aspic must be light and clear but full of flavor, and the aromatic vegetables must be fresh without tasting rawly of their separate components. Although for years I have loved the idea of this dish, it wasn't until visiting Jean Pierre Charlot at Domaine Joseph Voillot in Volnay that the reality satisfied my expectations!

INGREDIENTS

For the Bone Broth:

6-to-7 lb. bone-in fully cooked ham

1 jumbo yellow onion, quartered

2 large peeled carrots, cut into 2-inch chunks

2 large stalks of celery, cut into 2-inch chunks

1 clove garlic

Bouquet garni of: 3 bay leaves, 12 sprigs parsley, and 6 sprigs thyme (tied together or in a cheesecloth wrapping)

1½ cups dry white wine

15 black peppercorns

Water

For the Terrine:

2 packets of gelatin (¼ oz. each)

⅓ cup water

1½ cups bone broth

2 lb. piece of ham removed from the bone-in ham

1 medium garlic clove, minced

¾ firmly packed cup flat-leaf parsley leaves

½ tsp. finely ground white pepper

WHAT YOU'LL NEED

Large stockpot

Kitchen scale

Fine mesh strainer

Whisk

2 Medium bowls

Standard 1½ quart terrine (mine is Le Creuset with a number 32 on the bottom) or large loaf pan

Pan spray

Plastic wrap

Cardboard

Aluminum foil

Meat mallet (or a heavy skillet)

Food processor with metal blade attachment

Kitchen tongs

Sheet tray

One brick or equivalent weight

TIMING

For the Broth: 3 hours

For the Terrine:

Prep and Assembly Time: one hour

Chilling Time: twelve hours or overnight

PROCESS

For the Bone Broth:

Remove the skin from the ham. Cut the majority of the meat off the bone. Reserve two pounds of ham for the terrine and save the rest for later use. Place the bone in the stockpot with onion, carrots, celery, garlic, bouquet garni, and black pepper. Add the white wine and enough water to cover the ingredients by one inch. Bring to a boil and then reduce to a simmer. Skim off any foam and continue simmering for two-and-a-half hours. Discard the ham bone, strain the broth, and let it cool.

Preparing the Terrine:

Prepare the terrine by spraying it with pan spray and then lining the terrine with a layer of plastic wrap, leaving a couple of inches of extra plastic wrap on the edges. You may need to use two pieces of plastic wrap. Make sure there are no bubbles under the plastic.

Cut a piece of cardboard slightly smaller than the top opening of your terrine. Wrap the cardboard in aluminum foil, then in plastic wrap, and set aside.

For the Terrine:

Measure out two pounds of ham and reserve ⅓ lb. for later use.

Some recipes call for cubing or cutting the ham into strips. I have found that tearing the ham into uneven pieces makes the finished terrine more tender. Think of it as if you were building a wall and using natural stone (long torn pieces) instead of uniform bricks (the cubes or strips).

Separate the ham pieces by running your fingers along the seams between the sections of the ham. Remove the silver membrane and excess fat from each piece. Tear the ham into long strips 1½ in. in diameter. Use the meat mallet (or the heavy skillet) to gently pound each strip two or three times. This will slightly flatten the strip and will break it up it a bit, causing it to soften.

In a medium bowl, whisk the gelatin with ⅓ cup cold water.

Heat 1½ cups of bone broth.

While the gelatin is dissolving and the broth is heating, cube the reserved ⅓ lb. of ham and put it in the food processor with the garlic clove, the flat leaf parsley, and the white pepper. Pulse the mixture until it is finely minced but not a paste. The meat should be the size of a small grain of rice.

Whisk the heated broth into the dissolved gelatin, making sure there are no lumps. Measure out 1½ cups of gelatin broth. Reserve the other third-cup gelatin broth for later use. Pour the 1½ cups of the gelatin broth back into the medium bowl and stir the minced meat and parsley into it. This is the "mortar" that will seal your ham "wall."

Place the long pieces of pounded ham into the second bowl. Add one-half cup of gelatin/ minced ham mixture at a time and stir to coat the pieces thoroughly. You are trying to dress the ham, not to drown it. It should look like ham chunks with a loose sauce on them, not ham soup or ham stew. If it looks dry, add another ½ cup of gelatin/minced ham mixture and reassess. You may not need to use the final ½ cup of gelatin/minced ham mixture.

Pour a layer of ham and gelatin into the lined terrine and press down until the layer is relatively level. Use tongs to move the pieces around to make your "wall" stable. Continue using tongs to add more layers—pressing down and arranging the pieces. When you have layered in all of the pieces, press down and rearrange to make the top relatively flat. There will

be gelatin/ham broth in the bottom of the bowl. Pour it over the ham layers, smoothing it out. The level should cover the ham. There should be enough room to add the reserved ½ cup gelatin broth on top of the contents of the terrine. Fold the excess plastic wrap over the terrine. Place the terrine on a sheet tray and refrigerate for 2 hours.

After 2 hours, check to see if the gelatin has begun to set. If it has, place the foil and plastic-wrapped cardboard on top of the plastic-wrapped terrine and put the weight on it. Refrigerate until firmly set, preferably overnight.

To unmold, remove the weight, discard the cardboard piece, unfold the plastic wrap, and using the edges as handles, lift the Jambon Persillé out of the terrine. Unwrap it and slice in ⅓-inch slices. Serve with a sliced baguette, Dijon mustard, and cornichons.

Notes

#1. Use a bone-in cooked ham for this recipe. You need the bone to make the stock, and the meat from a bone-in ham is softer and more tender than a pressed boneless ham. Do not use a country-style ham for this recipe. Country hams are too salty, the texture is too firm, and the color of the meat is too dark.

#2. If you prefer to use gelatin sheets rather than powder, follow the instructions on the package. David Lebovitz has a really good explanation on the differences between powder and sheet gelatin on his website.

Potatoes Fondants

Yield: Serves 4–6 as a side dish | Ease of Preparation: Moderate | Ease of Sourcing: Moderate
Wine Pairing: White or Red Burgundy, depending on the main course it accompanies

Comfort food at its finest, this dish combines potatoes, duck fat, good chicken stock, and a sprinkling of salt. Although the preparation can at times be a bit tedious with the potatoes meticulously knife-turned into minizeppelins—almost an imitation of potatoes themselves—the version at Le Cellier Volnaysien in Volnay right across from Domaine Joseph Voillot is simpler, with each morsel cut into half-inch-thick semicircles before being browned in duck fat and braised in chicken stock until there is a gooey coating of glistening juices surrounding the meltingly tender potato. Take the time to get a light golden color on the potatoes when browning them. It makes all the difference in the final outcome of the dish.

INGREDIENTS

1½ lbs. Russet potatoes

3 Tbsp. duck fat

Kosher salt to taste

1 cup homemade light chicken stock
(light in color, not in calories)

TIMING

Prep Time: 20 minutes

Cooking Time: 30 minutes

WHAT YOU'LL NEED

Potato peeler

Saucepan

Large skillet (with lid) big enough to
hold the potatoes in one layer (or
two medium skillets)

Ladle

Metal spatula

Fork

PROCESS

Peel the potatoes and slice in two lengthwise. Slice each half in ½-inch slices.

Heat the stock in the saucepan. Keep warm.

Melt duck fat in the skillet over medium heat. Once the fat is melted, add one layer of potatoes to the pan. Sprinkle with kosher salt. Keeping the heat on medium, cook the potatoes in the duck fat until they are a light golden color. Flip the potatoes over and color on the other side. When both sides are light gold, ladle in enough stock to come ¼ of the way up the potatoes (approximately ⅓ cup). Cover with the lid and simmer.

After 3 minutes, slide the spatula under the potatoes to flip them. Try not to leave any of the potato stuck to the pan. Add a bit more stock if needed, cover, and cook for three more minutes. (This method reminds me of cooking pot stickers, where you brown the dumplings and then add liquid and cook them covered until done.) Pierce the potatoes to test if they are done. Continue cooking if they are not done. If they are tender, remove the lid and raise the heat to quickly reduce the liquid until it is thick and there is only about ¼ cup left in the bottom of the pan. Do not overcook the potatoes. They should have a glossy coating outside but still be fluffy inside. Taste for seasoning and add kosher salt if you wish.

Can be made ahead of time and kept warm for use within an hour or so. To reheat, add a bit more stock to the bottom of the pan and warm gently.

Note

The most difficult thing about this dish is finding duck fat. Most specialty butchers and gourmet stores carry duck fat, and d'Artagnan sells it online. If you cannot find it, use butter. I would not substitute bacon fat, as the flavor will overpower the dish.

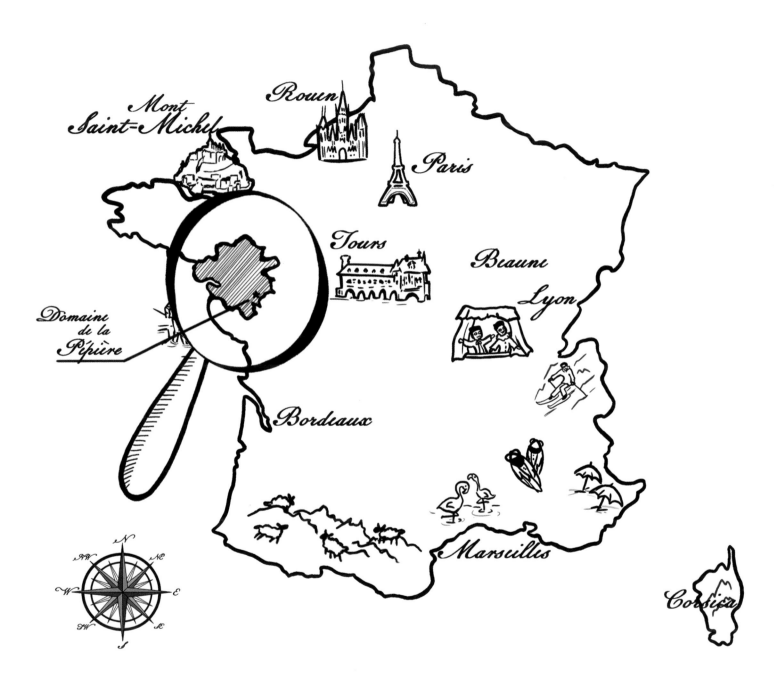

Mont
Saint-Michel

Rouen

Paris

Tours

Beaune

Lyon

Domaine
de la
Pépière

Bordeaux

Marseilles

Corsica

"Oysterfest—Muscadet Style"
A Visit with Marc and Geneviève Ollivier
Domaine de la Pépière, Maisdon-sur-Sèvre, France

Even before my first trip to the *Salon des Vins de Loire*, the annual Loire Valley Wine Fair in Angers, France, with the late Joe Dressner and Kevin McKenna of Louis/Dressner Selections, I knew that one of the highlights of the annual trip was the Oysterfest at Domaine de la Pépière in the little hamlet of La Pépière in Maisdon-sur-Sèvre. How could I not? It seemed as if that was all anyone in the group could talk about! Once I experienced it, I was completely sold as well, and repetition did not make the heart grow less fond. Indeed, my second time was just as wonderful.

Marc Ollivier
Photo credit: Domaine de la Pépière

Muscadet

Located in the department of the Loire-Atlantique, a region that was originally part of Brittany (there is a faction of the population that still campaigns to reintegrate the region into Brittany), Muscadet is one of the westernmost wine regions in France's Loire Valley. Wines from Muscadet are produced from the Melon de Bourgogne grape variety. They are dry, light to medium bodied with high acidity, and have a tangy, rather salty flavor profile. Located at the mouth of the Loire River, Muscadet has a rich and varied geological composition with clay, gravel, and sand soils over gneiss, schist, granite, and volcanic subsoils. This complex array of soils and subsoils with their well-draining qualities add complex diverse flavors and aid with moisture management in the cool, maritime climate.

Muscadet is a region populated for the most part with family-held wineries. Historically, although there were some standouts, Muscadet produced wines of moderate quality destined for supermarket shelves and casual café consumption. Over the last twenty years, the region is experiencing an upheaval in terms of quality, region delineation, and regulations.

Muscadet is broken down into the following subregions:

Muscadet Sèvre et Maine: This largely monocultural region, named for the Sèvre and Maine, the two small rivers than run through it, is located south of the Loire River to the east and southeast of Nantes. Muscadet Sèvre et Maine produces 80 percent of the wine in the area—more than any other Loire Valley wine region. It also contains the highest quality-level vineyards in the Muscadet.

Muscadet-Côteaux de la Loire: This subregion is located east and northeast of Nantes and Muscadet Sèvre et Maine on both sides of the Loire River.

Muscadet-Côtes de Grandlieu: Located to the south and southwest of Nantes and Muscadet Sèvre et Maine in the area surrounding the Lac of Grand-Lieu.

Muscadet: This basic designation is used for sites outside of the three aforementioned regions and is generally of lesser quality.

Wines from the three region-specific appellations may have the notation *Sur Lie* on the label (while wines from the basic designation may not). *Sur Lie* means the wine ages in tank on the residue of dead yeast cells.

Photo credit: Domaine de la Pépière

(See Wine Terms, page 473.) *Sur Lie* regulations for Muscadet were established in 1990 and indicate that the wines have been aged on *lies* (yeast) and require that the wines be bottled between March and November of the year following harvest. *Sur Lie* aging adds flavor and freshness to the wines.

Marc and Geneviève Ollivier live in a modest home adjacent to their winery, its wind-worn limestone a patchwork quilt of colors ranging from rich cream to ochre. Marc's appearance, that of a jovial, young Santa Claus, belies a keen winemaker's intellect and a determined work ethic. His wines show it.

In the past several decades, there has been a movement in Muscadet to harvest and vinify different plots and vineyards separately with the selection determined by soil type, vine age, and location. Marc Ollivier is one of the strongest proponents of this movement. Along with his partners, Rémi Branger and Gwénaëlle Croix, Marc and other like-minded producers are raising the bar for Muscadet and have pushed for the

Marc Ollivier
Photo credit: Bonnie Crocker

implementation of a Crus Communaux system in the region to further define the quality improvements and distinguish the complex and varied terroirs of the region.

Crus Communaux

In 2011, a system of *Crus Communaux* or Communal Crus was established within the boundaries of Muscadet Sèvre et Maine. Comparable to the village-based Crus of Burgundy like Meursault or Puligny-Montrachet, these Crus Communaux were established to denote age-worthy wines from similar terroirs with low yield requirements (45 hl/ha versus 55 hl/ha for the other Muscadet appellations; see Wine Terms, page 472) and twenty-four months of aging on the lees—such a length that they exceed the deadline requiring that wines be bottled by November of the year following harvest as outlined in the *Sur Lie* regulations for the non-Cru appellations and, therefore, are barred from using the words *Sur Lie* on the label. The three Crus Communaux that were recognized in 2011 are:

Clisson: Named after the village of Clisson with the impressive ruins of Château Clisson overlooking the Sèvre River, this Cru Communal is a three-mile-by-seven-mile strip of vineyards located on one of the best hillsides in the heart of Muscadet. Clisson is situated in the southern part of the Amoricain Massif, a two-billion-year-old mountain range (classified as a mountain range not because of its height but rather because of its soil and rugged landscape). The soils consist of well-drained pebbles, sand, and gravel over a subsoil of Granite de Clisson. There are eighteen producers of Clisson Cru Communal, and the wine must age twenty-four months on lees before bottling. Wine from Clisson tends to be rich, fat, and long-lived.

Gorges: Located just north of Clisson, the Gorges Cru Communal straddles the Sèvre River. The soils in Gorges are clay and quartz over a subsoil of gabbro, a dark-colored, coarse-grained intrusive igneous rock. There are sixteen producers of Gorges Cru Communal. Wines must age twenty-four months on lees before bottling. Gorges wines are smoky, rich, and elegant.

Le Pallet: Just to the north of Gorges lies the Le Pallet Cru Communal. Located on the north side of the Sèvre River, Le Pallet is characterized by warm weather and shallow, stony soil on granite, gneiss, and gabbro bedrock. There are currently ten producers of Le Pallet Cru Communal, and wines from Le Pallet must age seventeen months on the lees. According to Richard Hemming, MW, in an article on Jancis Robinson's webpage, the warm weather and particular soil composition in Le Pallet produces wines that have an "elegant aromatic profile which features floral, fruity flavours."

At the time of this writing, there are four other Crus Communaux under consideration by the INAO (*Institut National de l'Origine et de la Qualité*, the organization charged with protecting the quality levels of French National products with Protected Designations), all in the Sèvre et Maine delimited area. These prospective Crus are Mouzillon-Tillières (gabbro subsoil), Château-Thébaud (granite subsoil), Monnières Saint-Fiacre (schist subsoil), and Goulaine (gneiss).

Domaine de la Pépière

Marc Ollivier started Domaine de la Pépière in 1984. *Pépie* is slang for thirst in French, and a stroll through the vineyards with their dry stony terrain makes it quite plain that the name is apt. Over the years Marc has carefully acquired not only vineyards—looking for old vines and high-quality sites with unusual terroir—but partners as well, partners with new perspectives and interests. Because Marc's intent has always been to express the terroir of his land and wines, good viticultural practices were imperative, beginning with hand harvesting in a region where machine harvesting was the norm, the use of wild yeasts—which Marc considers to be part of the terroir itself (see Wine Terms, page 474)—and implementing more natural methods in the vineyards.

Rémi Branger joined in 2007 and helped move the Domaine to organic production. When Gwénaëlle Croix came on in 2013, she encouraged a further move toward biodynamics (see Wine Terms, page 472). Above all, the three of them are adamant that their first concern is the quality of the grapes, and they are convinced these steps have made that amelioration possible.

Marc's aim all along has been to "express Muscadet's terroir in all its different guises." This emphasis on single vineyards began over twenty years ago with Marc's realization that wines from a certain plot of vineyard with granitic soils tasted distinctly different from his other wines from the same vintage with similar vinification techniques. This vineyard plot was Clos de Briord and became Marc's first single vineyard wine. In all, Domaine de la Pépière produces nine wines, six whites and three reds.

White Wines

Muscadet Sèvre et Maine Sur Lie: This is the basic wine from the Domaine. It is sourced from a 30-acre plot of 25-year-old vines on stony, gravel soils over subsoils of Granite de Clisson and Granite de Château-Thébaud. The soils of this vineyard allow for early ripening—a plus for a wine meant for early release. The grapes for the wine are pressed and rest in tank after fermentation *sur lie* until the spring of the following year.

Clos de Briord, Muscadet Sèvre et Maine Sur Lie is a seven-and-a-half-acre vineyard with sixty-year-old vines planted on sandy clay soil over a subsoil of Granite de Château-Thébaud. The uncrushed grapes are put into tank for fermentation with no added yeasts or sugar. After fermentation, the wine spends seven months *sur lie* before bottling.

Les Gras Moutons, Muscadet Sèvre et Maine Sur Lie is from a south-facing vineyard overlooking the River Maine in the village of Saint-Fiacre. Soils of the vineyard are deep siliceous clay over a subsoil of gneiss and foliated rock. This combination is good for encouraging deep roots. As with Clos de Briord, Les Gras Moutons grapes are uncrushed and put into tank with no added yeasts or sugar for fermentation. After fermentation, Les Gras Mouton spends nine months *sur lie* before bottling.

Crus Communaux

Clisson: La Pépière's vineyard in Clisson is grown on gravel, sand, and clay soils associated with river pebbles over Granite de Clisson subsoils. These soils encourage deep rooting and provide excellent drainage. For their Cru Communal Clisson, Marc and his associates gently press the grapes and practice *bâtonnage* (lees stirring) to add aromatic complexity and richness on the palate. The Clisson is aged a minimum of two years on lees before being bottled.

Château-Thébaud: Although still not technically approved as a Cru Communal at the time of this writing, the expectations are clear that Château-Thébaud will attain this designation in 2017. The soils for the La Pépière Château-Thébaud vineyard are a combination of filtering sand and clay over Granite de Château-Thébaud. This soil drives the roots deep between the rocks. The grapes for Domaine de la Pépière Château-Thébaud are not crushed, and as with the Clisson, after fermentation the wines undergo *bâtonnage* to add complexity and richness. The wine is then aged thirty months on lees before being bottled.

Monnières-Saint-Fiacre: As with the Château-Thébaud, Monnières-Saint-Fiacre has yet to be approved as a Cru Communal at the time of this writing, but it too is expected to attain this designation in 2017. The subsoils in Monnières-Saint-Fiacre are schist.

Red Wines

Although this area is not famous for red wines, Domaine de la Pépière produces three red wines:

La Pépie Cabernet, Vin de Pays du Val de Loire: This quaffable red is made from Cabernet Franc (a.k.a. Breton in the Loire dialect) grapes grown on the southwest-oriented Granite de Clisson hills of the village of La Pépière. The grapes are hand harvested, destemmed, and left to macerate four days in tanks. The free-run juices are fermented and then aged five months in stainless-steel tanks.

La Pépie Côt, Vin de Pays du Val de Loire: The sibling of the Cabernet above, La Pépie Côt is made from Côt (another name for Malbec) grapes grown on the same southwest-oriented Granite de Clisson hills of the village of La Pépière. Historically a very common grape in the region, Côt died out in the 1920s and 1930s. The grapes for this wine were replanted with plants given to Marc Ollivier by the respected vigneronne Catherine Roussel from her Clos Roche Blanche vineyards in the Touraine. As with the Cabernet, the grapes are hand harvested, destemmed, and left to macerate four days in tanks. The free-run juices are fermented and then aged five months in stainless-steel tanks.

Cuvée Granit, Vin de Pays de Loire-Atlantique: Although Domaine de la Pépière and the Muscadet region as a whole specialize in white wines, the Cuvée Granit is Marc's flagship red. This cuvée is made from Cabernet Franc, Côt, Merlot, and Cabernet Sauvignon grapes grown on the southwest-oriented Granite de Clisson hills of the village of

La Pépière. Marc and his team use a selection of the oldest vine Cabernet Franc. They also thin leaves to improve sun exposure and green harvest to remove excess bunches of grapes for this cuvée in order to produce riper fruit and lower yields (approximately 50 hl/ha.), thereby adding structure and richness to the wine.

Foods of the Loire-Atlantique

Seafood and Fish

With its proximity to the Atlantic Ocean, the Loire-Atlantique is known for spectacular seafood:

Oysters: The Atlantic coastline of France is justifiably famous for their oysters. Oysters are cultivated in the Bay of Aiguillon in the Vendée and on the Quiberon Peninsula in Brittany. Still further north in Riec-sur-Belon, the famous Belon oysters are world renowned.

Mussels: Buchot mussels (grown following tradition on wooden posts) from the Aiguillon Bay.

Photo Credit: Bonnie Crocker

Sardines de la Turballe: Prized Atlantic sardines as well as anchovies are brought ashore in the fishing village of La Turballe.

Scallops du Croisic: Fresh in the shell sea scallops from the small port of Le Croisic.

Assiette de Fruits de Mer (Seafood Platters): Some people order platters, some go all out and order seafood towers. The selection of heaping chilled seafood ranges from langoustines, crabs, oysters, mussels, clams, whelks, cockles, and more. (Your choice is only limited by the size of your appetite and the thickness of your wallet.)

Beurre Nantais: Inland from the coast, rivers abound with **frog's legs** and **fresh fish** waiting to be sauced with Beurre Nantais (a.k.a. Beurre Blanc), the winey butter-based classic sauce said to have been invented in the region.

Cheese

Le Curé Nantais is a washed rind cow's milk cheese that is aged for a month on spruce boards and periodically washed with salt water. It is said to have been created by a priest (*curé*) escaping from the French Revolution and was originally made in the town of Saint-Julien-de-Concelles on the banks of the Loire River. Production has since moved to the ancient port town of Pornic (now a fashionable resort location). The outside of the cheese is light orange and the inside is smooth and soft. Although the cheese smells quite strong, its flavor is milder than its aroma.

Other Foods

Canard de Challans: Ducks from nearby Vendée are prized for their flavorful red flesh and destined for **Canard au Muscadet**—roast duck with a sauce made by deglazing the pan with Muscadet.

Salicorne de Vendée: Sea beans from the coastal waters of the Vendée.

Sea Salt de Guérande: Along with the Camargue in Provence and Noirmoutier in the Vendée, the medieval town of Guérande, just north of the mouth of the Loire River with its colorful salt ponds, produces wonderfully flavorful sea salt of which Fleur de Sel is the finest grade.

Named for the lovely medieval walled town of Guérande, the salt ponds of Guérande have been in production since the Iron Age. Currently there are five salt works that date to the Carolingian era (780 to 900 A.D.). *Le Guérlandais*, the cooperative of salt producers from Guérande, operates 15,000 *oeillets* (crystallization ponds) arrayed like multi-hued patchwork quilts along the coastline. Le Guérlandais uses natural forces—

ocean, sun, and wind—to produce its salts. The *Paludiers* (salt workers) hand harvest the salt that collects on top of the *oeillets*. The salts are not washed, and no chemical treatments or additives are permitted. The only processing is to sort and sieve the salt for consistent quality. Sea Salt of Guérande received the Label Rouge in 1991 (the only salt producers to receive this designation). Additionally, Guérande Salt and its Fleur de Sel were the first salts to get a PGI (Protected Product Designation). Fleur de Sel de Guérande is less salty than its Mediterranean cousin from the Camargue, and it is considered by some to be of higher quality.

Desserts

Gâteau Nantais: A specialty of Nantes, this soft round pound cake is topped with a white rum or lemon glaze.

Fouace Nantaise: Historically produced between September and November and traditionally served when the new wine was released in October, Fouace Nantaise is a six-pointed, star-shaped, sweet brioche bread. It is sometimes flavored with rum or orange blossom water.

Le Petit-Beurre Cookies: Famous rectangular, scalloped-edge butter cookies from Nantes. Originally made by the famous LU Cookie Company named after the initials of the founders, husband and wife Jean-Romain Lefèvre and Pauline-Isabelle Utile. **Le Petit Ecolier** is a chocolate-topped version of Le Petit-Beurre with the image of a *petit écolier* (little schoolboy) stamped into the chocolate.

Berlingots and Rigolettes de Nantes: These small hard fruit candies often have a soft fruit filling.

Oysterfest

What better way to showcase the variety of wines that Domaine de la Pépière produces than with an oyster extravaganza? Muscadet and oysters are a classic for a reason—the brininess of the oysters is perfectly complimented by the saltiness of the wine. Remember, what floats in the air surrounding the grapes affects their taste. In this case, the salty sea air blown from the nearby Atlantic Ocean is a dominant flavor in the wine.

Some parts of the trip to Domaine La Pépière's Oysterfest were not so pleasant—the freezing cold and the annual tradition of getting lost on the way to the winery, with one car following another along winding country roads that seemed to, and in fact sometimes did, lead to nowhere (although I would imagine the sight of a caravan of Americans in small rental cars backing up along a rutted country lane was probably quite amusing to the locals). Still, the majority of the day trip from Angers was a joy that definitely outweighed the detractions.

Geneviève Ollivier, Marc's wife, is a schoolteacher and the mastermind behind the gastronomic portion of the Oysterfest. Large tables in the front room of the winery groan under the weight of the spread she prepares each year with savory pâtés vying for table space with colorful bowls of slender white and red radishes, crisp crudités, baskets of sliced baguettes, dark rye bread, and bowls of salted butter. But it is the seafood that wins the day. Long platters filled with fresh-as-can-be raw oysters with lemon wedges

Photo credit: Susie Curnutte

Photo credit: Bonnie Crocker

crowd trays of out-of-this-world, house-cured wild Atlantic salmon. The flesh of Geneviève's salmon is sweet and salty, silky in texture, and melt-in-your-mouth delicious. She was kind enough to share her salmon recipe, and it has become a staple for me. The recipe is foolproof—the resulting salmon delectable. I must emphasize, all of the food on that plentiful table always shined brighter when accompanied with the selection of old vintages of various Domaine de la Pépière Muscadet that Marc brought forth from his cellar to accompany the feast.

The Oysterfest is a time of celebration and relaxation before diving into the grind that occurs at the Salon the three following days. It is an opportunity to enjoy wines as they are meant to be drunk, with tasty, simple, pristine local food in the company of friends old and new. It is a true example of *The Wine Table* philosophy and Eating What the Winemaker Eats.

The Winemaker Recommends: Raw oysters with lemon and Domaine de la Pépière Clos de Briord, Muscadet Sèvre et Maine Sur Lie.

Cured Salmon

Yield: 2–3 lbs. | Ease of Preparation: Simple | Ease of Sourcing: Simple
Wine Pairing: Domaine de la Pépière Clisson Cru Communal

I had a version of this salmon at Domaine la Pépière in Muscadet. Every year they host an annual Oysterfest in conjunction with the annual wine show, the Salon de Loire in Angers. In addition to an amazing selection of raw oysters, a whole side of cured salmon is one of the stars. Geneviève Ollivier was kind enough to share her recipe with me. I've tweaked it a little bit over the years, but it remains a dish that relies on impeccably fresh fish and a few other well-sourced ingredients. Geneviève uses fresh dill in hers. I'm not a huge fan of dill, so I sometimes use fresh parsley in mine. Both work well.

INGREDIENTS

1 cup sugar

1 cup kosher salt

2 tsp. freshly ground cumin

2 tsp. finely ground white pepper

2–3 lb. fresh salmon filet (preferably wild salmon), skin-on, pin-bones removed—either one large piece or 2 pieces of equal shape and size

Zest of two lemons, peeled in ½-inch-wide strips

Bunch of fresh dill or Italian flat leaf parsley (whichever you prefer)

Optional garnishes: Lemon wedges, crème fraîche, capers, minced shallots

WHAT YOU'LL NEED

Dish large enough to hold the salmon

Fish tweezers, if necessary

Plastic wrap

Salmon slicing knife or a thin fillet knife

TIMING

Prep Time: 15 minutes

Curing Time: 24 hours

PROCESS

Mix sugar, salt, cumin, and white pepper well. The curing mixture-to-fish ratio is key when curing the fish. I use a scant ¾ cup curing mixture per pound of fish.

Place ¼ cup curing mixture on the bottom of the dish approximately the length and width of your fish. If you are using two fillets, make two strips of curing mixture.

Lay the fish skin side down on the curing mixture. Completely cover the fish in a layer of the curing mixture. (This is more salt than you would use if you were just salting a fish before cooking it. It should be almost completely white.) Don't forget to put the curing mixture on the sides and ends of the fish. Place a layer of herbs and then the strips of lemon rind on the fish.

Tightly wrap the dish containing the salmon in plastic wrap and refrigerate for 24 hours.

After 24 hours, remove the salmon from the refrigerator. Discard the herbs, lemon rinds, and salt mixture. Rinse the fish well and pat dry.

Use your salmon knife or a long thin fillet knife to cut the salmon on the diagonal, keeping the slices as long and thin as possible. Serve with your choice of garnishes.

Note

Ask your fishmonger to remove the pin bones from the salmon fillet. Just to make sure, run your hand along the flesh side of the fillet and use fish tweezers to remove any remaining bones. I think that skin-on salmon fillets make for easier slicing, but if you cannot find skin-on salmon fillets, skinless are fine.

Mignonette Sauce

Yield: 1¼ cup Mignonette Sauce | Ease of Preparation: Simple | Ease of Sourcing: Simple
Wine Pairing: When paired with raw oysters—Muscadet, Chablis, Sancerre, or Blanc de Blancs Champagne

Marc and Geneviève Ollivier prefer to eat their oysters "nature" with a simple squeeze of lemon juice. In my opinion, that is the optimal way to eat raw oysters, but if you want something a little different, I recommend Mignonette Sauce—the classic French accompaniment for oysters on the half shell. The name mignonette traditionally referred to a pouch containing peppercorns, cloves, and spices that was used to flavor liquids. Over the years, it has come to mean cracked black pepper. The tartness of red wine vinegar combines with the shallots and cracked black pepper to add a little zing to the oysters. There are a lot of variations on Mignonette Sauce. Some people use jalapeños, some add fennel or cilantro. I saw a recipe recently that uses cucumber. For my money, the basic recipe is the best—simple and delicious.

INGREDIENTS

¼ cup finely minced shallots

1½ Tbsp. coarse ground black pepper,
    freshly ground

1 cup good quality red wine vinegar

½ tsp. kosher salt

WHAT YOU'LL NEED

Medium nonreactive bowl

Pepper grinder with adjustable settings

Sharp kitchen knife

Cutting board

TIMING

Prep Time: 15 minutes

Rest Time: 30 minutes

PROCESS

Add the shallots, coarse ground black pepper, red wine vinegar, and kosher salt together in the nonreactive bowl and stir. Set aside for 30 minutes to allow the flavors to blend together.

Serve with oysters on the half shell.

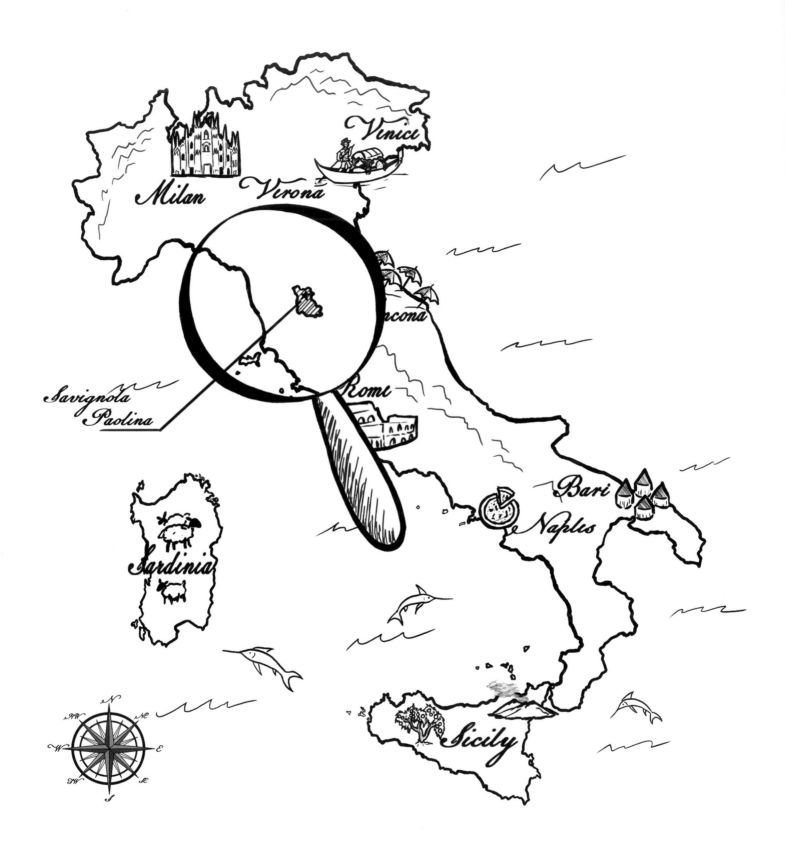

Milan

Virona

Vinici

Savignola
Paolina

ncona

Romi

Sardinia

Bari

Naples

Sicily

"I Think I May Have Invited Them to Dinner"
A Festa "Under the Tuscan Moon"
with Ludovica Fabbri and Friends
Savignola Paolina, Greve in Chianti, Italy

Savignola Paolina, my friend Ludovica Fabbri's winery, is located near Greve in Chianti, Italy. The region of Tuscany hardly needs an introduction. Covering 23,000 square kilometers (8,800 square miles), with some 3.2 million Tuscans privileged to call the hilly mountain-crossed landscape their home, it is sometimes called a nation within a nation. An important region during the Renaissance, Tuscany is steeped in the traditions of art, literature, and science. With seven UNESCO World Heritage Sites, quaint hill towns, and stunning landscapes, this central Italian region is the subject of numerous books and movies and is the destination for large numbers of international tourists.

Agriculturally, although other crops are grown, it is for olives and grapes that the region is justly famous, with rows of grape vines and olive trees alternating on the sun-drenched hillsides. Tuscan olive oils are world acclaimed and delicious, with the most common olive types being Fantoio, Leccino, Pandolio, Maurino, Maraiolo, and Taggiasca, but it is wine for which Tuscany is best known. Winemaking in the region dates back to the Etruscans in the 2nd century BC.

Wines of Tuscany

With thirty-three *Denominazioni di Origine Controllata* (DOC) and eight *Denominazioni di Origine Controllata e Garantita* (DOCG) (see Wine Terms, page 472), the red wines of Tuscany—Chianti (with its seven subregions), Brunello di Montalcino, Vino Nobile di Montepulciano, and Morellino di Scansano—are predominantly produced from Sangiovese or one of its clones. Vernaccia di San Gimignano, Tuscany's most famous white wine, is made from the grape of the same name and was the first Italian wine to receive DOC status in 1966. (It was upgraded to DOCG in 1994.)

The region of Chianti was originally delineated in 1716 by the Medici Grand Duke Cosimo III and included the Central Tuscan townships of Radda in Chianti, Gaiole in Chianti, Castellina in Chianti, and Greve in Chianti. The wines were based on native grape varieties: Sangiovese for its fine bouquet and vigor and Canaiolo for its softening qualities. During the 1960s, in an effort to increase the prosperity of the region, wine practices encouraged the use of high-yielding Sangiovese clones and the mandatory addition of the white grape varieties Malvasia and Trebbiano to increase quantity. Unfortunately, this resulted in a lack of quality. Winemakers wishing to produce higher-quality wines,

Savignola Paolina

either by using 100 percent Sangiovese (usually low-yielding clones) or international grape varieties (for example, Cabernet Sauvignon or Merlot) often with the addition of new French oak were barred by government regulations from calling their wines Chianti. Although originally labeled *Vino di Tavola (VDT),* or table wines, these rule-breaking, sought-after wines like Sassicaia and Tignanello were better known by the famous Super Tuscan moniker. In 1992, the *Indicazione Geografica Tipica (IGT)* designation was established to delineate these wines that were not DOCs and yet not simple table wines.

In the 1980s, the *Consorzio Vino Chianti Classico* (founded under a slightly different name in 1924 and made up of producers from the core original zone) determined the necessity of raising the quality level of Chianti, a region that had expanded greatly over the years. The Consorzio worked to improve the wines of the region with studies of clones, vineyard elevation, and soil types. Better information, increased investment, and the use of consulting oenologists helped to improve the wines.

In 1996, the Chianti Classico DOCG was established. Symbolized by a black rooster, this wine region includes the original four communes of Radda in Chianti, Gaiole in Chianti, Castellina in Chianti, and Greve in Chianti as well as Barberino Val d'Elsa, Castelnuovo Berardenga, Poggibonsi, San Casciano Val di Pesa, and Tavarnelle Val di Pesa. The area encompasses 177,500 acres with 17,290 acres under vine on typical galestro (friable marl) or albarese (marl limestone with high concentrations of calcium carbonate) soils. Wines must include a minimum of 80 percent Sangiovese (although 100 percent is common), with 20 percent of other red grapes allowed—either one of 49(!!!) red autochthonous grape varieties (the most common being Canaiolo or Colorino) or international varieties like Cabernet Sauvignon or Merlot.

Photo credit: Consorzio Vino Chianti

Black Rooster: Wines of Chianti Classico are easily distinguished from other Chiantis by the Black Rooster tag ringing the neck of the bottle. The legend of the Black Rooster and its origin as the symbol of Chianti Classico dates to the medieval times when Florence and Siena—the two powerful republics on each end of the already prized wine region—were fighting for possession of the prosperous vineyards of Chianti. It was determined that a knight would be chosen to represent each republic. Rather than fight it out on the battlefield, it was decided that each knight would depart from their respective city at daybreak and their meeting point would demarcate the boundary point. While Siena concentrated on choosing the fastest horse and the very best rider, Florence took another tack—rooster selection—choosing a black rooster that they kept in a cramped, dark coop and underfed almost to the point of starvation.

The morning of the task, the poor tortured black rooster began to crow the second it was released from the coop, and the Florentine knight set off immediately. The Sienese knight, with his faster horse and his well-fed beautiful white rooster had to wait until daybreak for the cock to crow. With a massive head start, the Florentine knight made it all the way to Fonterutoli, a scant twelve kilometers from Siena, before encountering his foe—putting almost all of Chianti under the domain of the Republic of Florence.

In 2013, Chianti Classico wine designations were expanded to include Gran Selezione, a premium category. The winemakers of the region are working to further improve their wines and boost their already well-respected global reputation, including the possibility of other regulation changes in the future. Currently, three wine designations are permitted in the zone: Chianti Classico, Chianti Classico Riserva (twenty-four months aging, three months of which must be in bottle), and Gran Selezione (thirty months aging, three months of which must be in bottle).

Although individual winery styles vary, the Chianti region as a whole eschews the use of large amounts of new oak, preferring large traditional used-oak casks to allow the typical tart, dark cherry, and terroir-driven flavors of Sangiovese with its extremely high tannins to prevail. In my opinion, this also makes Chianti stellar when it comes to pairing with the world-famous food of the region.

Foods of Tuscany

Simple, with origins in peasant culture, Tuscan cuisine emphasizes (as does most Italian food) the necessity of few but good-quality ingredients. The cuisine is strong in legumes, bread, cheese, vegetables, mushrooms, and fresh fruits.

Ribollita (literally reboiled), the ubiquitous Tuscan soup made from yesterday's minestrone with some beans and day-old bread added, is peasant food at its most delicious. A copious amount of crunchy curly kale is tossed in the pot at the last minute before serving—just long enough to soften it. Top it with grated Parmigiano Reggiano and

Crostini plate, Antica Trattoria Le Torre, Castellina in Chianti

a drizzle of high-quality local olive oil, and you'll have a hard time believing you are eating leftovers.

Panzanella: As with Ribollita, Panzanella transforms day-old bread into something delicious. Panzanella is a bright salad made with stale bread soaked in water, bright juicy tomatoes, basil, olive oil, salt, and vinegar.

Certaldo Onions: The famous red onions from the town of Certaldo near Florence come in both sweet and pungent versions. They are recognized as a Slow Food Presidium.

Sorana Beans: Another Slow Food Presidium has been awarded to these small, flat white beans from Pistoia.

Beef and Poultry

Crostini di Fegatini di Pollo: Tuscan Liver Paté on Crostini is the quintessential Tuscan appetizer. This smooth-textured liver paste served on crunchy bread is again a perfect example of poverty-driven cuisine. Why throw the livers away when you can make a delicious dish with it!

Bistecca alla Fiorentina: This huge slab of bone-in steak—similar to a T-bone or Porterhouse—is sourced from the enormous white *Chianina* breed of cattle (although I have heard rumors that not all of the *Bistecca* served in Tuscan restaurants is actually *Chianina*).

Pork

Along with *Chianina* beef, the other famous domesticated meat in Tuscany is pork from the *Cinta Senese* breed of pig. Smaller in size than many domesticated pigs, *Cinta Senese* are named for the white belt (*cinta*) marking that adorns their otherwise black hide.

Salumi

Cured meat is most frequently made from pork, with the most sought-after being made from *Cinta Senese*. Although there are many different types of salumi, the most famous are:

Finocchiona: Finely ground dried pork sausage flavored with fennel seeds.

Salame: More coarsely ground than Finocchiona, Salame is aged longer, resulting in a dryer, darker sausage.

Salamino: Uses smaller casings resulting in a sausage of thinner diameter.

Affettati Misti, Antica Trattoria Le Torre, Castellina in Chianti

Salamino Piccante: A spicy version of Salamino and is what we think of as Pepperoni in the United States.

Soppressata: A coarsely ground dried pork sausage that is larger in diameter than Salame.

Prosciutto: Prosciutto Crudo is locally made ham.

> **Bazzone Prosciutto** and **Casentino Prosciutto:** Two extremely small production artisanal prosciuttos from Tuscany that are both recognized as Slow Food Presidia.

Lardo di Colannata: Rounding out the selection is this much sought-after delicious, cured pork fat from the small mountain village of Colannata near Carrara, some six miles from the Tyrrhenian Sea.

Antipasto Toscano or Affettati Misti: A traditional Tuscan first course, *Affettati Misti* generally includes finely sliced Prosciutto Crudo, round slices of Finocchiona, Salame, Soppressata, and silky white ribbons of Lardo di Colonnata.

Wild Game

Game like wild boar, hare, deer, and pheasant frequently appear on the table braised as sauces for pastas: silky pappardelle and chewy pici, a local specialty of hand-rolled thick spaghetti-like pasta. (Pici is also available as a dried pasta.)

Cheese

Tuscany is one of the largest producers of sheep in Italy, and those sheep are raised almost exclusively to produce milk for cheese. *Pecora* means sheep in Italian, and Pecorino from Tuscany is world famous.

Pecorino Toscano DOP: Available in both fresh and aged versions. *Pecorino Stagionato,* the aged version, must be aged at least 120 days.

Il Grande Vecchio di Montefollonico (Grand Old Man) is a large strong Pecorino from the area around Siena.

Pecorino delle Balze Volterrane DOP: An artisanal cheese from near Volterra made with raw sheep's milk. It is produced with vegetable rennet from cardoon flowers. It can be fresh, semi-aged, or matured.

Pecorino di Pienza Stagionato in Barriques: A sheep milk cheese from Pienza that is aged at least 90 days in an oak barrel. Pienza is renown for its Pecorino cheese because the town is located in an area rich with clay soils where the sheep pastures are characterized by a series of particular aromatic herbs that make the milk extremely tasty and fragrant.

Pistoia Mountain Pecorinos: These family-produced mountain cheeses are made traditionally from raw sheep's milk from Black Massese sheep that live with the shepherds in the meadows in the mountains above Pistoia. **Pecorino della Garfagnana** is a specific type of this mountain cheese. Pistoia Mountain Cheeses have been awarded a Slow Food Presidium.

Marzolino Cheeses: These sheep cheeses are called *Marzolinos* because production begins in the month of March. They include **Marzolino del Chianti:** a dried, aged strong cheese and **Marzolino del Lucardo:** a fresh milder version.

White Truffles of San Miniato grace the fall Tuscan tables in October and November.

Tuscan Bread: Famous for its thick chewy texture and its lack of salt. Legend has it that the Tuscans, a frugal group, eschewed the use of salt in their bread in reaction to the high price of salt in the Middle Ages. Many others believe that the lack of salt is actually due to the highly spiced and flavored Tuscan food and that Salame, Soppressatas, Finocchiona, and Tuscan Prosciutto Crudo (which is much saltier than northern Prosciuttos) pair better with the salt-free bread. Whatever the reason, your bread will likely taste better with a little salty snack than on its own.

Desserts

Desserts are simple: **Panforte** (bread sweetened with candied fruits and honey), **Crostatas** (fruit tarts), simple cookies, and biscuits.

Savignola Paolina

History

The Savignola Paolina estate has been in the Fabbri family since the 1700s, and they have been producing wine since the late 1800s. It was Ludovica's great aunt Paolina (by all accounts an amazing woman) who put the winery on the map. A gifted raconteuse, she was a nurse, a hunter, a singer, and a poet. Ludo's admiration for her was palpable. She reminisced about sitting at the breakfast table in the very kitchen where Ludo and I were going to cook dinner, having a morning cup of tea and salami panino while Paolina recounted stories of World War II and its effect on the region and their family.

Ludo's grandfather, Uberto Fabbri, had been a soldier during WWI and was a captain in King Victor Emmanuel III's army after the ouster of Mussolini in 1943. During WWII, the King controlled southern Italy, and Germany controlled northern Italy. Uberto was still in northern Italy at the time and as a loyal monarchist did not want to join the German forces. When his men were taken hostage, he offered himself in exchange. The trade accomplished, he was imprisoned in Nuremberg, where he later died from a tongue infection.

While Uberto was off soldiering, Paolina and her mother (Ludo's great-grandmother) worked the winery. They continued the work after Uberto's death, improving the quality and achieving local acclaim.

In 1988, upon Paolina's death at the age of ninety, Ludo's father, Carlo, took over. Ludo joined her father, and in 1998 she took over management of the winery. Currently, Ludo and her two sons, Diego and Pietro, live on the property and operate it with the help of Ludo's new partner. Ludo's wines are characterized by an elegance and finesse that I really enjoy.

The estate is located in a small hamlet. Ludo's parents split their time between their home above the winery and Bologna, where Ludo grew up. She attended the University there, studying English and graduating with a Doctorate in Philosophy. Jeff and I were lucky enough to stay in Ludo's parents' house during our visit. The view from their ochre-colored, brick-lined balcony terrace overlooking the vineyards was spectacular.

The 20-acre estate is planted with 15 acres of vines and two-and-a-half acres of olive trees.

Wines of Savignola Paolina

Rosso di Savignola IGT: This wine is intended for easy drinking, and as such it is aged in stainless steel. It is bottled the spring after harvest and released with no additional bottle aging.

Chianti Classico DOCG: This wine is a combination of 85 percent Sangiovese, with the remaining 15 percent a combination of Colorino and Malvasia Nero. It is aged for twelve months in used barriques and stainless-steel tanks.

Chianti Classico Riserva DOCG: The Riserva is a combination of 90 percent Sangiovese and a mixture of Canaiolo and Malvasia Nera. It is a selection of the best grapes and is vinified separately by grape variety and vineyard site. It ages for twelve months in a 20-hectolitre French oak barrel and twelve months in bottle.

Chianti Classico Gran Selezione DOCG: The Gran Selezione is made from 85 percent Sangiovese and 15 percent Colorino from two vineyards, Vigna del Pozzo and Vigna Grande. It is aged eighteen months in French barriques (of which 40 percent are new) before spending one year in bottle.

Chianti Classico Gran Selezione Vigna del Pozzo Cru: This single vineyard wine from Vigna del Pozzo is a new wine for Ludo. The first year of production was from the 2015 harvest. It is made from very rigorously selected Sangiovese grapes. The vines for this Cru wine are pruned, leaving only three bunches of grapes per vine to increase intensity and structure in the final wine. The aging regimen for this wine is eighteen months in a French oak *botte* barrel (10 hl.) and one year in bottle.

Il Granaio IGT: Il Granaio (Granary in Italian) is Ludo's Super Tuscan, a wine she only makes in really excellent years. It is made from 70 percent Sangiovese and 30 percent Merlot (her only nonindigenous grape variety) and is aged for twelve months in French barriques and large tonneaux (900 liter casks) and bottle aged for six months before release. Il Granaio is rounder and less austere than the Savignola Paolina Chianti Classico Riserva.

Olive Oil

In addition to her four wines, Ludo produces a well-respected olive oil from the estate. The olives are hand harvested in the first couple of weeks in November. Savignola Paolina Extra Virgin Olive Oil is low in acid and high in antioxidants, but more important, it is extremely delicious!

Ludo has vegetables and herbs in her garden and purchases the rest of her produce from a local farmer friend. Although Ludo lives in Tuscany, her heritage is Bolognese, and a good part of her food style evidences this. Ludo's ex-husband, Antonio, was an avid surfer, and she and the boys often visited surfing locations with him. Ludo's cooking is influenced by visits to these coastal regions, as well.

Dinner in Tuscany—Ludo-style

Returning to the kitchen in her parents' home, Ludo acknowledged the slight change in our dinner plans with a smile and a shrug. We were in the process of preparing chicken liver crostini for the *festa* or party that she was throwing for my husband, Jeff, and me. She had invited two other Tuscan winemakers, Gabriele Buondonno and Stefano Grandi, and a group of her friends to come and cook with us. The original objective was to introduce me to family recipes from all three winemakers. But, as I came quickly to understand, Ludo's hospitality turns even a small event into a heartwarming party.

That afternoon as we were cooking together, Ludo was sharing familial recipes and describing the group of friends who were to soon descend upon us with their own recipes and food lore. It suddenly occurred to her that we might want to take a small precaution to ensure a smooth end to our evening. A trio of Indian tourists was renting the apartment on the top floor of Ludo's parents' home. Ludo decided it might not be a bad idea to invite the three visitors to join us for drinks after dinner.

That girl is a genius!

Remember when you were in college and inviting the people who lived in the apartment next door to your keg party only made good sense? Let's be candid, it's harder for the neighbors to call the police because your music is too loud when they are the ones choosing the songs—or to use the current vernacular, when it's their iTunes playlist blaring through the speakers. Clearly, this was not Ludo's first *festa*. I continued carefully stirring the chicken liver purée for crostini and rolling eggplant involtini while Ludo ran upstairs to invite them to join us for after-dinner drinks on the balcony patio.

"I think I may have invited them to dinner . . .," she said as she came back.

My head popped up. "Why?"

"Because they accepted my invitation and then mentioned that two of them were vegetarians. People don't tell you they are vegetarians if they are just invited for drinks, do they?"

I had to agree with her assessment. Unless you are eating at one of the bacon-centric restaurants that seem to be everywhere in the US currently, meat does not figure heavily into drinks.

Ludo seemed completely unfazed at the prospect of having three extra dinner guests (a quality that I have come to understand is totally her personality). We rolled with it, making extra of some of the vegetarian appetizers and adjusting a few other recipes. Ludo took it in stride, as did all of her friends who began to arrive with bags of groceries filled with pasta, house-cured olives, leeks, and *baccalà* (salt cod). Bottles of sparkling wine were opened, and we got down to the business of cooking.

I was in heaven darting from dish to dish. Poor Jeff! Having just finished up a couple of meeting-filled days in Northern Italy, his plan had been to watch, enjoy a glass or two of wine, some good music, and lively conversation. Instead, he was quickly pressed into service as the scribe of the event. As I stirred, sliced, sautéed, and rolled *polpette* (balls) of different types, Jeff was flipping pages back and forth, taking notes on all of the recipes we were preparing. We're lucky he didn't accidentally turn to the wrong page.

The menu was amazing:

Chicken Liver Crostini
Salami di Varzi Magrotti (brought from my visit to Salumificio Magrotti in Oltrepò Pavese)
Fried Anchovies
Eggplant Polpette
Salt Cod Polpette
Eggplant Involtini with Cherry Tomatoes and Sheep Milk Ricotta
Penne Lisce with Leeks and Oil-Cured Black Olives
Stuffed Zucchini
Ludo's Apricot Jam Crostata

We opened many bottles of wine, including some I had brought from my visits to other winemakers, and wines from all three winemakers present that evening: Vernaccia de San Gimignano from Canneta, Chianti Classico from Buondonno, and of course, Ludo's Chianti Classico from Savignola Paolina.

It turned out that Ludo had indeed invited the upstairs neighbors to dinner. The trio arrived with lovely gifts of chocolate and flowers that they had somehow miraculously managed to procure early on a Friday evening in the small nearby town of Panzano.

Glasses of wine were pressed upon them, and they blended right in with the noisy group. Relieved of his duties as recording secretary, Jeff accepted the job of DJ, a role he shared with Ludo. They bonded over philosophy and The Rolling Stones. That seems reasonable to me.

Ludo and Serena

The guest list was charming and varied. The ever-elegant Gabriele Buondonno and the delightfully zen Stefano Grandi represented Ludo's winemaker friends. In charge of making *polpette* (balls) of salt cod and eggplant, recently widowed Franco Filieri was accompanied by his quiet son, Giovanni, a friend of Ludo's youngest boy Pietro, 10. Ludo's oldest son Diego, 12 (already a chef at heart), amused me by quoting from the American television show *The Big Bang Theory* in Italian-accented English. Wickedly funny Serena, calm and lovely Simona, efficient Angela, and quiet Carla rounded out the group. There were lively arguments about all sorts of things, most of them food-related, including a midnight raucous debate about the correct way to make *brodo* (chicken broth) led by Ludo's mother-in-law, Carla, who arrived from Bologna late that evening. It goes without saying that each cook in the group championed their own special recipe.

Although there had been some fear of rain earlier in the evening, the weather held, and we went long into the night and early morning on that lovely balcony overlooking the Sangiovese vines and olive trees. The Indian tourists cried uncle around midnight, but, as they were sated with good food and wine, I doubt they had much trouble sleeping.

As for Jeff and me, we awoke midmorning to the bright and friendly Tuscan sun, made marginally tolerable by good sunglasses and even better memories. Our threesome, Ludo, Jeff, and I, were somewhat subdued during the winery tour, but it was good to see where she, with the help of one full-time employee, accomplishes so much. At the end of the tour, she waved us off with recommendations for a lunch spot on the way to Florence and the promise of seeing us on her next trip to Washington—planned for the following spring.

My path has crossed Ludo's quite a bit the last couple of years—sometimes in Washington and once in Verona at Vinitaly—Italy's massive wine fair. Whether we are cracking crabs in my backyard late into the night, slurping ramen at a noodle shop in DC's

Chinatown, or drinking Champagne under a peach-colored stucco portico in Verona, each time we meet, there is a common thread of food, wine, and friendship. The thread may have started at wine tastings over the years, but the friendship was cemented that evening and into the early hours of the next morning on her balcony overlooking her vineyards—under the Tuscan Moon, as it were.

The Winemaker Recommends: Caprino (goat) or Pecorino (Sheep) Cheese with Savignola Paolina Chianti Classico Riserva.

Salt Cod Fritters
Polpette di Baccalà

Yield: 24 ping pong ball-sized fritters | Ease of Preparation: Moderate but time-consuming
Ease of Sourcing: Moderately difficult
Wine Pairing: Crisp White Wine (at Ludo's house, we paired them
with Podere Canneta Vernaccia di San Gimignano)

One of the many dishes I prepared with the party crowd at Savignola Paolina, Polpette di Baccalà (Salt Cod Fritters) are surprisingly easy to make, albeit rather time-consuming. The hard part is finding the salt cod. Once you've found it, and soaked the fish in water for several days, it is as easy as making meatballs! Despite current relatively low availability levels caused by overfishing, salt cod has a long history as a staple—once by necessity and now by cultural preference—in many of the world's best cuisines. I've eaten Salt Cod Fritters in San Sebastian, Spain, with a glass of Txakoli; in Cascais, Portugal, with a glass of Vinho Verde; in Taormina, Sicily, with Mt. Etna Bianco; and in Rome with a local Frascati. I would say it's ubiquitous if it weren't also so delicious!

INGREDIENTS

To Rehydrate the Salt Cod:

1 lb. dried salt cod
3 quarts water

For the Fritters:

3 oz. dried baguette or other
   firm bread, crusts removed
   (approximately 8 inches of baguette)
¾ cup whole milk
Salt cod, rehydrated and cut in ½-in.
   cubes
¼ cup flat leaf parsley, finely chopped
1 medium garlic clove, finely minced
1 Tbsp. lemon zest, finely chopped
¼ cup extra-virgin olive oil
½ tsp. kosher salt
¼ tsp. coarse ground black pepper
2 cups very fine dry breadcrumbs
Olive oil for frying
Lemon wedges
Optional: Fine sea salt

WHAT YOU'LL NEED

One-gallon container in which to soak
   the salt cod
Plastic container with lid (large enough
   to hold the bread)
Electric mixer with paddle attachment
Rubber spatula
Breading tray or plastic container for
   breading
3-inch-deep cast iron pan or electric
   fryer
Instant read thermometer
Spider or slotted spoon
Paper towel-covered plate

TIMING

Soaking Time: 24 to 48 hours
Prep Time: 1½ hours
Frying Time: 20 minutes

PROCESS

To Rehydrate the Salt Cod:

Place the pieces of salt cod in the one-gallon container and cover with water. Place in the re-frigerator for 24 to 48 hours. Rinse and change the water frequently (several times per day). Drain the water when ready for use.

For the Fritters:

Soak the bread with milk in the plastic container with lid, turning the container several times to make sure all sides of the bread are exposed to the milk. Once it is soft (but not dissolving in the milk), drain it and squeeze out the excess milk.

Place the bread and salt cod in the electric mixer with paddle attachment and mix it until the pieces of bread and cod are completely broken down. Depending on the cod, this may take as long as 15 minutes. The cod should have a fine fibrous texture. Scrape down the side of the mixer and add parsley, garlic, lemon zest, ¼ cup olive oil, ½ teaspoon kosher salt, and black pepper.

Place the dry breadcrumbs in the breading tray. Roll the salt cod mixture into uniform balls the size of a ping pong ball, making sure you compress them so that they are firm. This helps prevent the fritter from breaking apart when fried. Carefully roll each ball in the dry breadcrumbs, making sure to coat it thoroughly.

Add ¾ of an inch of olive oil in your fry pan. Make sure to keep 2½ inches of space above the level of the oil. The process of frying will cause the oil to bubble, and you must be careful not to let the oil bubble over. If using an electric fryer, follow the fryer's filling instructions.

Heat the oil to 350° F. Fry the polpette until they are dark golden brown, being careful not to crowd the pan. You may have to work in batches. To test for doneness, sacrifice one polpetta to see if it is hot all the way through.

Transfer the cooked fritters to your paper towel-covered tray and finish frying the rest.

Serve hot with lemon wedges.

Optional: Sprinkle with fine sea salt after frying.

Notes

#1. Salt Cod (short for Salted and Dried Cod) occurred from a method of preserving fish, often during or for sea voyages. The fish is dried with the addition of salt until it resembles hard planks of fish. Cod, salt cod in particular, is a historically important fish. It is said to have fueled the explorations of Erik the Red, and the Medieval Basques established a salt cod trade that spanned centuries. Many books have been written about the subject including the excellent *Cod: A Biography of the Fish that Changed the World* by Mark Kurlansky. Despite its presence in many cultures globally, Salt cod is not an ingredient that is easily found in parts of the United States. It is available in Italian and gourmet specialty markets. It is also available online through Amazon.

#2. Although the process for rehydrating the salt cod requires rinsing and soaking the fish, it still retains a degree of saltiness. Consequently, I have used very little salt in this recipe. You can always add a sprinkle of fine sea salt once the polpette are fried if you think they need it.

Fried Anchovies
Acciughe Fritte

Yield: 6 appetizer portions | Ease of Preparation: Simple
Ease of Sourcing: Difficult (depending on your access to a good fishmonger)
Wine Pairing: Crisp Italian White Wine (Vernaccia di San Gimignano, Trebbiano d'Abruzzo,
Verdicchio dei Castelli di Jesi, or Falanghina)

The boisterous crowd that Ludovica Fabbri assembled for a festa at her Tuscan home was varied—with winemakers and other friends from all parts of Italy showcasing their family recipes. Ludo herself is originally born in Bologna and her winery is located in Greve in Chianti, but this dish of fried anchovies became a family favorite during annual surfing vacations, and it's a recipe she loves pulling out when she entertains.

INGREDIENTS

30 fresh anchovy fillets (approximately
    1 oz. each), cleaned, gutted, head,
    fins, and bones removed
2 cups all-purpose flour
4 whole eggs, beaten extremely well
2–3 cups fine dried breadcrumbs
1 tsp. kosher salt
3–4 cups extra-virgin oil
2 lemons, quartered

WHAT YOU'LL NEED

Dish large enough to hold the
    anchovies in a single or double layer
2 medium paper or gallon plastic bags
Wok, 3-inch deep frying pan, or
    electric fryer
Spider or slotted spoon
Paper towel-lined platter

TIMING

Prep Time: 15 minutes
Frying Time: 15 minutes

PROCESS

Ask your fishmonger to clean your anchovies for you. Rinse the anchovies and dry them well.

Place the flour in one of your bags. Put the anchovies in the bag and shake them well to coat them.

Place the well-beaten eggs in the dish.

Remove the anchovies from the flour and pat them to remove excess flour before putting them in with the eggs. Turn them to coat. Let them sit in the egg mixture for a couple of minutes.

Add enough olive oil to your frying vessel until the level is 1½ inches deep. You may not need to use all of your oil. Make sure you leave at least a 1½ inch space at the top of your pan so that the oil does not bubble over during the frying process.

Begin heating the oil over medium-high heat. If you have an electric fryer, set the temperature to 350° F. If you don't have a fryer, drop a bit of flour in the oil to test the temperature. (When the flour sizzles but does not immediately burn, it is perfect for frying. If it doesn't sizzle, keep heating. If it burns the flour, turn the heat down a bit.)

Fill the second bag with the fine dried breadcrumbs and salt.

Remove the anchovies from the eggs, shaking off any excess egg. Add the anchovies to the bag with the breadcrumbs and salt. Shake well to coat the anchovies.

When the oil has reached the correct temperature, remove the anchovies from the bag. Pat them to remove any excess breadcrumbs and place them in the heated oil. Do not crowd your pan to the extent that the oil is in danger of bubbling over. You may need to fry in several batches. Use your spider to turn the anchovies over. Fry until golden brown (approximately 2 to 3 minutes). Remove the cooked anchovies to the paper towel-covered platter.

Serve with lemon wedges.

Notes

Ideally, we would all live within a couple of hours of a sea teeming with anchovies. That way, fresh anchovies would be readily available. Unfortunately, that is not the case for most of us. If you live in an area with a good fish market, you will likely be able to get fresh anchovies. In Washington DC, we have access to a large variety of seafood. I checked with Blacksalt, my local fishmonger, and they have fresh anchovies from Spain available pretty much year-round. Call ahead to make sure your purveyor has them, as they sell out quickly. Ask your fishmonger to clean, gut, and debone them for you. They may charge you a fee, but believe me, it is totally worth it. As a last resort, if there is a good fish/seafood restaurant in your town, ask them if they can get fresh anchovies and see if they will order some for you, preferably already cleaned. You would be surprised how many restaurants are willing to do this. Of course, it helps if you are already a regular customer.

Eggplant Involtini
Involtini di Melanzane

Yield: Serves 4 as a side dish, 2–3 as a main dish, or 12 as an appetizer | Ease of Preparation: Moderate
Ease of Sourcing: Simple if you use cow's milk ricotta, Moderate with sheep's milk ricotta
Wine Pairing: Chianti Classico or medium-bodied unoaked red wine

I like to make this dish as a side dish at dinnertime or as a vegetarian main dish for lunch, but I've discovered it works as an hors d'oeuvre, as well. Serve it on a decorative platter with a little cup of toothpicks so guests can just help themselves!

INGREDIENTS

2 Tbsp. salt-cured capers
1 lb. medium-sized Italian eggplants
2 Tbsp. extra-virgin olive oil
6 oz. ricotta (preferably sheep milk, although cow's milk will suffice)
1 cup small grape or cherry tomatoes
2 Tbsp. unsalted butter
½ cup grated Parmigiano Reggiano
optional: 2 oil cured anchovy fillets

WHAT YOU'LL NEED

Small bowl
Electric slicer, food processor with fine slicing attachment, mandolin, or very sharp knife
Nonstick grill pan
Paper towel
Kitchen tongs
Large nonstick baking dish
Small teaspoon
Serrated knife

TIMING

Prep Time: 30–45 minutes
Cooking Time: 18–20 minutes

PROCESS

Soak the salted capers in warm water in the small bowl.

Wash the eggplants. Slice them very thin—approximately ⅛-inch slices. Ludo had an electric meat slicer in her kitchen. How very Italian of her. I was totally jealous. I use the thinnest blade attachment on my food processor, but you could also use a mandolin or a slice it thin with a knife.

Use a paper towel to wipe a thin layer of oil on the grill pan. Lightly grill the thin slices of eggplant on medium heat, turning them once. You are not trying to color the eggplant; rather, you are trying to soften it so that it is malleable enough to roll around the cheese. Work in batches until you have grilled all the eggplant.

Preheat the oven to 400° F. Coat the baking dish with 1 tablespoon olive oil.

Use a small spoon to scoop a small amount of ricotta onto each slice of eggplant. Roll the eggplant around the cheese and place it in the baking dish. Continue until all the slices have been filled and rolled.

Drain the capers and scatter them over the eggplant. Slice the tomatoes in half and scatter them around the baking dish. Add small dabs of butter around the baking dish. Sprinkle with a thin layer of Parmigiano Reggiano.

Bake until the eggplant is lightly brown, the tomatoes have softened, and the cheese has melted (approximately 18 to 20 minutes).

Notes

#1. I am a salt fiend, but I generally do not add salt to this dish. The capers and Parmigiano Reggiano add plenty of salt to the finished dish, but you may want to sprinkle a little salt on the eggplant while you are grilling them.

#2. Sometimes I like to finely mince a couple of oil-cured anchovy fillets and scatter them in the bottom of the baking dish. This adds richness and another note of flavor. If you do add anchovies, you will definitely not need additional salt.

Penne Lisce with Leeks and Oil-Cured Olives
Penne con Porri e Olive

Yield: Serves 6 as a first course or 4 as a main course | Ease of Preparation: Simple | Ease of Sourcing: Easy
Wine Pairing: Buondonno Chianti Classico

Gabriele Buondonno's contribution to our al fresco dinner at Savignola Paolina, Penne Lisce with Leeks and Oil-Cured Olives sounds basic, but the flavors were a complex blend of sweet caramelized leeks and onions, briny oil-cured Maremmano olives from his own olive trees, and umami from Parmigiano Reggiano cheese and a dash of tamari. Although there is very little sauce in this dish, the time you spend stirring the al dente penne with the leek and olive mixture pays dividends, infusing the pasta with the flavors of the dish rather than simply coating it.

INGREDIENTS

4 cups of leeks, dark green tops removed, sliced in half lengthwise and cut in ¼-inch slices (approximately 6 large leeks)

2 cups yellow onions, quartered and cut in ⅛-inch slices (approximately 2 medium onions)

⅓ cup extra-virgin olive oil + ½ cup extra

⅓ cup oil-cured olives, pit removed and sliced in half

1 tsp. tamari

¾ cup water

⅓ cup Parmigiano Reggiano, shredded or grated

1 lb. box penne lisce pasta

1½ Tbsp. kosher salt

WHAT YOU'LL NEED

Cutting board
Sharp kitchen knife
Gallon plastic container
Fine mesh strainer
Wok or 12-inch deep sauté pan
Large pot to cook the pasta
Tongs

TIMING

Prep Time: 30 minutes
Cooking Time: 1 hour

PROCESS

This is a two-part recipe: the sauce and the pasta. Start cooking the pasta after sauce has been cooking about 20 minutes.

For the Leek Mixture:

Place the leek slices in the gallon plastic container. Fill the container with water and swirl the leeks around. Allow the leeks to soak for several minutes. Using your hand like a claw, remove the leeks from the water, being careful not to disturb any dirt that has settled in the bottom of the container. Rinse the container, return the leeks to the container, and fill with water again. Repeat until no more dirt remains in the bottom of the container. Strain the leeks in the fine mesh strainer.

Heat ⅓ cup olive oil in the wok over medium-low heat. Place the leeks and onions on the skillet and cook very slowly, stirring occasionally.

Do not brown or crisp the leek mixture. You want to lightly caramelize the mixture, not to crisp it. After 20 minutes, add the olives and ½ cup of water. Stir and continue cooking until the contents of the wok have completely softened and have turned a light antique gold color. This takes about 30 minutes. Add 1 teaspoon tamari and the remaining ¼ cup of water to loosen the mixture. Set aside until the pasta is cooked.

For the Penne Lisce:

Prepare the pasta according to the instructions on the package. A good ratio for cooking pasta is to use 4 quarts of water to 1½ tablespoons kosher salt to cook one pound of pasta. Cook the pasta to the point right before al dente. Undercooking it at this stage ensures that the pasta in the finished dish will be perfectly done, since you cook it again to combine all of the ingredients in the final step. Reserve 1 cup pasta cooking water and drain the pasta.

To Assemble the Dish:

Place the sauce-filled skillet over medium heat. Add the pasta and stir. Check the liquid level: you will need to add pasta water to the mixture to loosen the mixture although you may not need to use all of the pasta water. Stir the mixture to blend. You may need to add a little extra olive oil and more water as you go along. Stir for several minutes to coat and then add the Parmigiano Reggiano. Stir until the pasta is thoroughly coated with the leek and olive sauce. The pasta should be just barely al dente and glistening with the sauce.

Serve immediately. Offer additional Parmigiano Reggiano tableside.

Notes

#1. Penne is short tubular pasta. It comes in two forms: *Rigate* (with ridges) or *Lisce* (smooth). Although Penne Rigate is the more common of the two, Gabriele likes serving this with Penne Lisce. I have had no difficulty finding Penne Lisce, but if you cannot find it, substitute Penne Rigate.

#2. Oil-cured olives are black olives that are cured in oil rather than in brine. They are available at most grocery stores. I think it is important to make the effort to find them, as brine-cured black olives do not have the same flavor or texture as those cured in oil. However, if you cannot find them and choose to substitute brine-cured olives, try to use Kalamata olives and make sure you drain them very well. I do not recommend using canned black California olives.

Chicken Liver Crostini
Crostini di Fegatini di Pollo

Yield: 2 cups of liver pâté | Ease of Preparation: Moderate | Ease of Sourcing: Moderate
Wine Pairing: Savignola Paolina Chianti Classico

Chicken Liver Crostini is a classic Tuscan dish. As with many Tuscan dishes that are born out of poverty (think Ribollita and Panzanella, both of which incorporate day-old bread), this chicken liver spread enables local cooks to use every part of the chicken. Some versions use chicken hearts, and Ludo says her mother's recipe uses the spleen of the chicken.

INGREDIENTS

1 lb. chicken livers
2 Tbsp. salted capers
¼ cup extra-virgin olive oil
½ cup finely diced onions
½ cup finely diced celery
Kosher salt
½ cup chicken stock
3 oil-cured anchovies
⅓ cup Vin Santo
Baguette sliced in ⅓ inch slices and
    toasted

WHAT YOU'LL NEED

Cutting board
Paring knife
Paper towels
Small bowl
2-quart saucepan
Wooden spoon
Fork or potato masher

TIMING

Prep Time: 30 minutes
Cooking Time: 1 hour

PROCESS

Remove the veins and sinews from the chicken livers. Pat the livers dry with a paper towel and then chop them in quarters. Soak the capers in a small bowl, changing the water once to help remove the salt.

Heat oil over medium heat. Add the onions, celery, and ¼ teaspoon salt; sauté until soft. Raise the heat to medium high and add the liver and another ¼ teaspoon salt. Brown the liver lightly and then lower the heat to low. Cook for 30 minutes, stirring periodically. If it becomes dry, add a little chicken stock to loosen it.

Rinse and drain the capers. Finely mince the capers and the anchovies. Add along with remaining chicken stock and Vin Santo. Cook for 5 to 10 minutes more until the excess liquid evaporates. Taste and add salt if needed.

Mash the liver mixture and mix it until it looks like a paste. The finished mixture has a somewhat grainy texture.

Serve at room temperature or slightly warm with toasted baguette slices.

Notes

#1. Capers. If you cannot find salted capers, you may use capers in vinegar. I would still soak them to remove some of the vinegar flavor.

#2. Vin Santo. A sweet Italian white wine. If you cannot find it, substitute any unoaked white wine.

Stuffed Zucchini
Zucchini Ripieni

Yield: Serves 4 | Ease of Preparation: Moderate | Ease of Sourcing: Simple
Wine Pairing: Podere Canneta Fiore Rosso or young Chianti

One of the many dishes on the table at Savignola Paolina was Stefano Grandi's Zucchini Ripieni (Stuffed Zucchini). Stefano is the winemaker of Podere Canneta, an organic winery near the lovely Tuscan hill town of San Gimignano. Although this version is stuffed with a mixture of ground beef, aromatic vegetables, and Parmigiano Reggiano, Stefano mentioned that one could easily substitute lamb, sausage, ricotta cheese, rice, or vegetables for the ground beef.

INGREDIENTS

Extra-virgin olive oil
½ cup finely diced onions
¼ cup finely diced celery
¼ cup finely diced carrot
½ lb. ground beef
1½ tsp. kosher salt
¼ tsp. ground black pepper
½ cup + 2 Tbsp. water, separated
4 zucchini (8 inches long and 2 inches in diameter)
2 Tbsp. finely chopped flat leaf parsley
1 large egg
2 grinds nutmeg
¼ cup finely grated Parmigiano Reggiano
½ cup fine dry breadcrumbs

WHAT YOU'LL NEED

12-inch sauté pan
Wooden spoon or spatula
Kitchen tongs
Apple corer (to core the zucchini)
Cutting board
Small spoon
Oven-safe pan large enough to hold the zucchini with lid
Aluminum foil

TIMING

Prep Time: 45 minutes
Cooking Time: 40 minutes

PROCESS

Film the sauté pan with 2 tablespoons olive oil. Cook the onions, celery, and carrots over medium heat until they soften. Raise the heat to medium high and brown the ground beef, breaking it up into very small pieces. Once it is browned, add 1 teaspoon salt, ¼ teaspoon black pepper, and ½ cup of water, and simmer on low for 12 minutes.

While the meat mixture is simmering, cut then ends off the zucchini and cut it crosswise in three pieces. Use the apple corer to hollow out the zucchini.

When the meat mixture is done cooking, let it cool and then mix in the parsley, egg, Parmigiano Reggiano, and nutmeg.

Preheat oven to 350° F.

Place each zucchini tube on the cutting board and spoon some of the meat mixture into the zucchini. Press the meat filling firmly into the zucchini. Turn the zucchini over and check to make sure it is completely filled. You may need to add more stuffing.

Once all of the zucchini have been stuffed, place them in the baking dish. Add 2 tablespoons of water in the bottom dish. Drizzle each zucchini with a little olive oil and sprinkle a dash of salt and an even coating of breadcrumbs over them, using all the breadcrumbs. Cover the baking dish with aluminum foil and simmer for 40 minutes.

Serve warm.

Ludo's Apricot Crostata
Crostata di Albicocche di Ludo

Yield: One large crostata | Ease of Preparation: Moderate | Ease of Sourcing: Simple
Wine Pairing: Vin Santo or White Dessert Wine

Ludo's Crostata begins with a pasta frolla crust. Pasta frolla is a short crust that is used throughout Italy in all sorts of regional desserts. Although we used homemade apricot jam that Ludo's mom had made, she also recommends making it with fresh seasonal fruit, noting it is especially delicious with strawberries. I have since made it with rhubarb compote, and that was incredibly good, too!

INGREDIENTS

2 cups all-purpose flour + extra for rolling
the dough

10 Tbsp. unsalted butter, lightly chilled
and cut in small pieces (1¼ stick)

⅔ cup granulated sugar

1 large egg + 1 extra yolk

1½ cups apricot jam or preserves

1 Tbsp. lemon juice (optional)

1 Tbsp. granulated sugar

WHAT YOU'LL NEED

Fork

Pastry scraper (or metal spatula)

Plastic wrap

Parchment paper

Rolling pin

10-inch fluted tart pan with removable
bottom

Paring knife

Large soup spoon

Medium kitchen bowl

Fluted pastry wheel (optional)

Pastry cooling rack

TIMING

Dough Prep Time: 10 minutes

Dough Resting Time: 1 hour minimum
(or overnight)

Assembling the Crostata: 30 minutes

Baking Time: 55 minutes

Cooling Time: 30 minutes

PROCESS

Remove the butter from the refrigerator and allow it to come to room temperature. Mound the flour on a clean flat surface.

Place the butter on the flour and using a fork (or your fingers) break up the pieces of butter into the flour. The finished flour/butter mixture should have a sandy texture.

Add the sugar to the flour/butter mixture and mix until it is well combined.

Make a well in the center of the flour/sugar mixture. Place the egg and yolk in the center of the well. Use a fork to break the egg and yolk, mix them together, and then begin pulling the flour into the center of the well to mix the ingredients and knead the dough until it comes together. Use the pastry scraper to help form the dough into a single ball. Knead quickly for a maximum of 1–2 minutes until the dough is homogenous and smooth. (This is not bread. You do not want to knead it a long time. The finished dough should have the consistency of playdough.) Divide the dough in 2 uneven pieces (the larger piece should be twice as large as the smaller). Wrap in plastic wrap and refrigerate for at least an hour (or overnight). If you chill the dough for more than an hour, you will need to let it warm up for at least 30 minutes before rolling it out.

Preheat the oven to 350° F. Remove the dough from the refrigerator.

Cut a circle of parchment paper that is two inches larger than your tart pan.

Pasta frolla is somewhat delicate. It tears easily—even if you are very careful. Ludo solved this issue by rolling the dough out on a piece of parchment paper. Place the large circle of parchment on the flat surface, flour the parchment lightly, and roll the larger piece of dough into a circle one inch larger than the bottom of the tart pan. Use the edges of the parchment paper to lift the dough into the tart pan, centering it on the pan. Press down gently to make sure the dough fills the bottom of the pan. There should be approximately one inch of dough reaching up the side of the tart pan. Use a paring knife to cut the sides to make them even. The parchment paper will peek out above the edges of your dough. That's what you want. If the dough tears during this process, press the torn pieces together to patch it, smoothing the seam.

Put the apricot jam in a bowl and stir it until it is very smooth. Taste the jam. If it is very sweet, you may wish to add one tablespoon of lemon juice. Use the back of the spoon to smooth a ¼-inch layer of jam around the bottom of the tart shell. (You may not need to use all of the jam.) Do not get jam on the dough on the side of the crostata.

Cut a 12-inch square of parchment paper. Flour it lightly.

Roll the smaller piece of dough into a square. This doesn't have to be perfectly square. Make sure that part of the square is at least 10 inches long. Sprinkle a thin layer of granulated sugar over the dough. Use the fluted pastry wheel (or a knife if you don't have a pastry wheel) to cut ten ½-inch strips. These strips will form the lattice top for your crostata. Lay the strips along the top of the crostata, inside the dough along the sides of the tart pan. (Though I love an alternating latticework top crust as much as the next person, the delicate nature of the dough can make this a bit tricky. Feel free to do the five strips in one direction and then turn the tart pan 90° and lay the other five strips in the other direction.)

Fold the excess dough on the side of the crostata down to make a border on the crostata.

Bake for 35–50 minutes, checking periodically. When it is done, the dough should be golden and the jam should be bubbling. At that point, remove the crostata from the oven and allow it to cool on a pastry rack.

The crostata may be served warm or at room temperature.

In addition to dessert, I can also highly recommend this with afternoon coffee or at breakfast time if you prefer sweet to savory.

Notes

#1. Ludo and I made this on a rectangular baking sheet, but I think the measurements are easier using a round tart pan.

#2. The name is different. The dough is the same. *Pasta frolla* is the same dough as *Pâte Sablée* in French—makes sense since "sable" means "sand" and that is the texture of the flour and butter mixture.

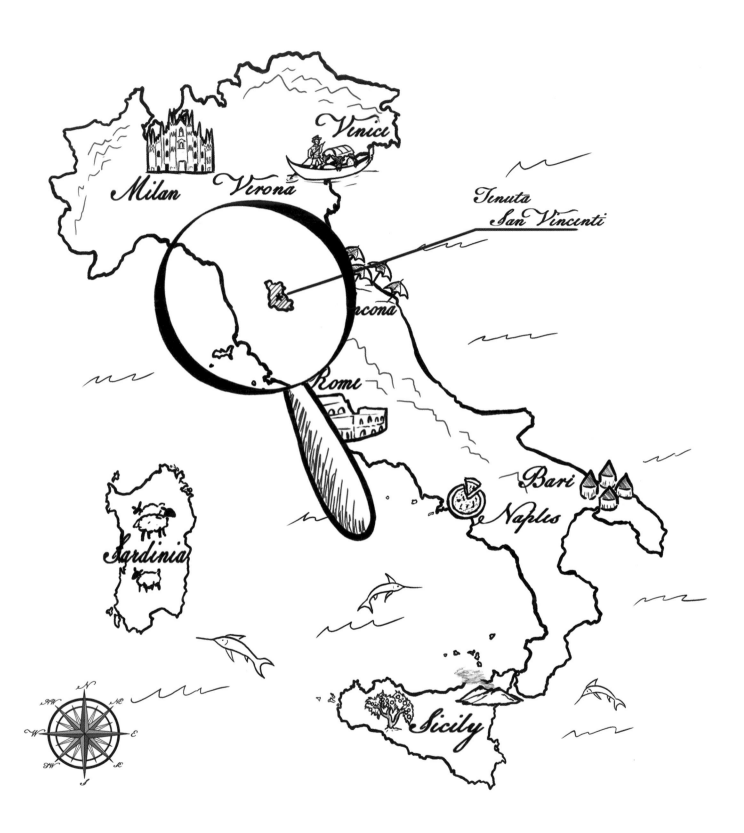

Milan

Verona

Vinici

Tinuta
San Vincinti

Ancona

Rome

Bari

Naples

Sardinia

Sicily

"Amidst the Rosemary in the Hills of Chianti"
A Visit to Tenuta San Vincenti
Gaiole in Chianti, Italy

Although I have read articles written by wine experts downplaying the theory of matching wines with foods from the same region, I find it one of the most important pairing considerations. The idea that a region's food and wine develop based on the same climate, soil, and historical culture seems undeniable. Consequently, it seems logical that they would go well together.

My visit to Tenuta San Vincenti in Gaiole in Chianti is a perfect example of the kind of experience that helped solidify this in my mind. Early in my wine career, I was traveling with a group of wine professionals on a wine tasting tour to Italy with the late David Bryant, and he had chosen San Vincenti for our home base while in Chianti. Roberto Pucci and his lovely wife, Marilena, hosted us at the hilltop agritur-

Photo credit: Tenuta San Vincenti

ismo attached to their winery, and although I remember the comfortable rooms and the scenic veranda, it is the rows of rosemary bushes towering over me—some of them well over six feet tall—that stand out most prominently in my mind. I love the smell of rosemary, and there was no escaping the pungent piney, green aroma permeating the air.

Located on a wooded hilltop in the oldest part of Gaiole, San Vincenti is named for Saint Vincent, patron saint of wine, vineyards, and winemakers, and covers 150 acres of land with the vineyards planted on sand and marl soils. The nearby woods are filled with wild boar, necessitating special electric fencing to protect the grapes from hungry boar.

Roberto's brother-in-law, Francesco Muzzi, has joined Roberto as co-owner at San Vincenti. The winery produces four wines: a Chianti Classico and a Chianti Classico Riserva, both of which are 100 percent Sangiovese; a Chianti Classico Gran Selezione (a relatively new Italian wine classification), which is 85 percent Sangiovese and 15 percent Merlot; and Stignano, an IGT made from 100 percent Merlot.

While I appreciated Roberto's guidance when tasting the wines of the property, I must admit that I was most fascinated with the incredible meals that Marilena was preparing for us every evening. One night, she cooked a huge *Bistecca Fiorentina* over a grate in the fireplace—the thick slab of bone-in steak sizzling as its juices dripped on the coals. It was pretty surreal watching this tiny, elegantly dressed, perfectly coiffed

Photo credit: Tenuta San Vincenti

blonde Italian woman reaching into the fireplace with a long-pronged fork to turn that big piece of meat.

The real revelation for me, however, was the *Cinghiale in Umido*, or Braised Wild Boar, that she cooked for dinner the following evening. This is a perfect definition of using local products in cooking. Marinated in San Vincenti Chianti Classico with aromatics and tons of fresh rosemary from the bushes right outside her kitchen door, that wild boar was delicious, and given the lengths to which Roberto had to go to keep the wild boar out of his vineyards, there's no denying the meal was sourced locally. I offered to help Marilena in the kitchen. To my great disappointment, she wouldn't hear of it. She did allow me to watch while she made the boar, and you can rest assured that I immediately wrote down everything I saw when I returned to my room after dinner. That occasion gave rise to many wonderful meals for me, my family, and my friends ever since, providing both the first course of long pasta (preferably pici, although pappardelle will do as a substitute) dressed with the meat sauce from the bottom of the heavy cooking vessel and a main course, the meltingly tender meat itself, generally accompanied with a green vegetable.

Photo credit: Tenuta San Vincenti

I recognize that there are other ways to pair food and wine, but for me, this memory and the meals it inspired validate my pairing method of serving food with the wine from the same region and is a classic example of the winemaker's family knowing what food goes best with their wines. It's the basis for this book and my favorite motto: *Eat What the Winemaker Eats.*

The Winemaker Recommends: Pici Pasta with Wild Boar Sauce paired with San Vincenti Chianti Classico.

Braised Wild Boar
Cinghiale in Umido

Yield: 6 servings of meat + 6 servings of pasta sauce | Ease of Preparation: Moderate to difficult
Ease of Sourcing: Difficult | Wine Pairing: Chianti or Brunello di Montalcino

I learned to make this dish from Marilena Pucci of San Vincenti in Chianti. Rather, she told me she was going to make it and I stood next to her and watched—frantically trying to memorize every step and ingredient. After dinner, I ran back to my room and carefully noted down the details. Upon returning home, I made it several times for friends and family to refine the recipe. This is a two-part recipe (just as it was at Marilena's home in Chianti). The first part is pasta with wild boar sauce. The second part is the main course of big moist chunks of boar glistening with sticky braising juices.

INGREDIENTS

1 wild boar shoulder cut in 1½-in.
    cubes, or wild boar stew meat
    (approximately 5 lbs.)
2 medium yellow onions, cut in
    medium dice
6 cloves of garlic, peeled and smashed
2 large carrots, peeled and cut in ¼-in.
    slices
2 ripe tomatoes, cut in quarters
Bouquet garni of fresh Italian herbs
    (2 each large sprigs rosemary,
    oregano, parsley, bay leaves)
1 bottle Sangiovese-based red wine:
    Chianti, Rosso di Montalcino,
    Rosso di Toscana
Kosher salt
Freshly ground black pepper
¼ cup extra-virgin olive oil
1 lb. dried Pici or Pappardelle pasta
2 cups freshly grated Parmigiano
    Reggiano
High quality extra-virgin olive oil for
    finishing

WHAT YOU'LL NEED

Plastic or glass container with lid,
    large enough to marinate the boar,
    vegetables, and red wine (if possible,
    it should be watertight so that you
    can flip it and its contents for good
    distribution of the wine)
Large Dutch oven
Aluminum foil
Large pasta pot
13- to 15-inch skillet

TIMING

Prep Time: 45 minutes
Marinating Time: At least 4 hours,
    preferably overnight
Cook Time: 4–5 hours

PROCESS

For the Wild Boar:

Combine the cubes of wild boar shoulder, onions, garlic, carrots, tomatoes, bouquet garni, and enough red wine to cover the meat half way, 1 teaspoon kosher salt, and ½ teaspoon pepper.

Marinate in the refrigerator at least 4 hours, preferably overnight. Reserve any excess wine that does not fit into the marinating container.

Before cooking, strain the wild boar, reserving the marinating liquid. Separate out the vegetables and bouquet garni, putting them aside for later use. Dry each piece of meat with a paper towel to remove excess moisture.

Place a large Dutch oven on the stove and heat over medium-high heat. Add the ¼ cup olive oil. The next two steps are very important. First, when the oil is heated and begins to shimmer, add some of the wild boar to the pan, being careful not to crowd the pan. Crowding the pan impedes your ability to brown the meat. (Unless you have a very large pan, you will have to brown the meat in batches.) Second, really brown all sides of the meat. This takes a good amount of time, especially if you do not have a large pan, but do not shortcut this! These two steps will make all the difference in the world with regards to the depth of flavor achieved later.

Once the meat is browned, remove it from the pan and set it aside. Quickly sauté the vegetables and bouquet garni in the same pan, scraping to remove all caramelized traces from the bottom of the pan. Add the meat back into the pan and pour in some of the reserved marinating liquid. The liquid should come about half of the way up the meat. If there is not enough marinating liquid, add enough reserved wine or water to raise the level of the liquid the required height.

Place a sheet of aluminum foil directly on top of the contents of the pan to create a braising environment. Cover and braise over low to medium-low heat for between 2 to 3 hours, being careful not to boil the mixture, as boiling causes the juice from the meat that mingled with the wine during the marinating process to coagulate and renders the finished sauce cloudy. You are looking for an active simmer. If foam rises to the top, skim it off and lower the heat a bit. During this simmering period, gently stir the contents of the pan every 15 minutes or so, carefully scraping the bottom of the pan to make sure nothing is sticking. Try not to break up the pieces of meat with overly aggressive stirring. You might need to add a little water during the course of the cooking period, but the foil cover should protect from too much loss of liquid. After one and a half hours, remove the foil and continue cooking, covered only by the lid. When the meat is tender but not falling apart, remove the lid. Raise the heat and cook until the sauce thickens, gently stirring periodically. The sauce will become sticky and coat the meat.

When the meat is sticky and tender, remove the chunks of meat and place them with ½ cup sauce in an oven-safe covered dish in a warm oven. There will be sauce, small pieces of meat, and vegetables left over in the bottom of the Dutch oven.

For the Pasta Course:

The vegetables should have softened and melted into the sauce. Mash any remaining chunks of vegetables into the sauce. Discard the bouquet garni. Add ½ cup water and cook the sauce down until it thickens slightly—about 3 minutes on medium heat. When thickened, taste the sauce and add salt and pepper as needed, then place several large spoonfuls in your skillet.

Cook the pasta according to the package directions. Remove the pasta from the cooking water while it is still quite al dente—reserving a cup or so of pasta cooking water. Place the al dente pasta in the skillet with the sauce, turn the heat to medium, and stir or toss to coat the pasta, adding more sauce and some of the reserved pasta cooking water until the pasta is nicely dressed but not drowning in the sauce. Add ½ cup Parmigiano Reggiano and a couple of splashes of olive oil and toss again.

Serve dressed pasta in shallow bowls and offer Parmigiano Reggiano and high-quality extra-virgin olive oil as garnish.

For the Meat Course:

To finish the large pieces of wild boar that you have been keeping warm in the oven, add ¼ cup extra-virgin olive oil to the chunks of meat and stir to coat. Serve with a mixed salad or seasonal vegetable and crusty warm bread. Offer high-quality extra-virgin olive oil as a garnish.

Notes

#1: Wild Boar is not as readily available as some other types of meat. Check with your local butcher or specialty store. (I get mine from the guys at Arrowine and Cheese in Arlington, Virginia.) Wild Boar Shoulder (average weight between 3 and 5 pounds) and 5 lb. packages of Wild Boar Stew Meat are available online from d'Artagnan.

#2: In Tuscany, this is served with Pici, thick, spaghetti-like pasta. In the US, Pici is hard to find, although I can now find it at The Italian Store in Arlington, Virginia. Check with your local Italian gourmet market or specialty store. I have also purchased it online. Pappardelle is a different but delicious substitute.

#3: Italians do not serve their pasta swimming in sauce. It should have a coating of sauce but no extra pool of sauce in the bottom of the bowl. Think of it like a dressing on a salad.

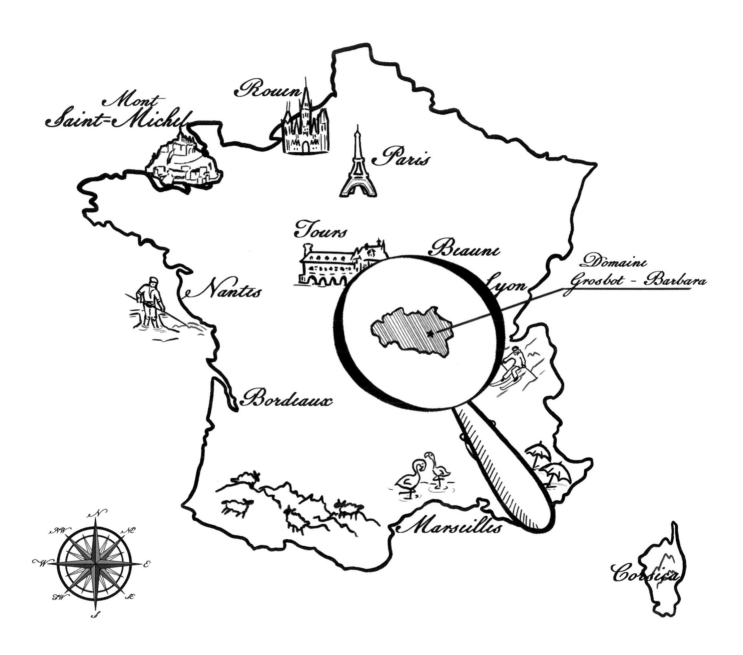

Mont
Saint-Michel

Rouen

Paris

Tours

Nantes

Beaune

Lyon

Domaine
Grosbot - Barbara

Bordeaux

Marseilles

Corsica

N
NW · NE
W · E
SW · SE
S

"The Kindness of Strangers"
A Visit to Monique and Denis Barbara, Domaine Grosbot-Barbara, Saint-Pourçain, France

Much of this book is based on the concept of the kindness of strangers. None have been more kind than the small, tightly knit Barbara family from Saint-Pourçain, France. Located in the central French department of Allier, Domaine Grosbot-Barbara is a modest family winery in the relatively obscure Bourbonnais wine region of Saint-Pourçain. Comprised of the Allier and part of the department of the Cher, the Bourbonnais, one of France's historic provinces, was the birthplace of one of the most important dynasties of European royalty. Beginning with Henri IV and ending in 1848 with the death of Louis-Philippe, eight Bourbon Kings ruled France for over 250 years.

The Allier is defined geographically by the Allier River to the east, The Loire Valley to the north, the highlands of the Massif Central to the south, and the department of the Creuse to the west. Two main rivers, the Allier and the Sioule, run through the region. The Allier River Valley is an important center for cereal production and cattle farming.

Credit: Domaine Grosbot-Barbara

Historically, this was a region of sharecroppers, but land reform regulations in the early 20th century and low population density have resulted in a relatively recent tradition of large family-owned farms.

The famed Tronçais Forest with its 27,000 acres of oak trees (some of which can be traced back to 1580) is located in the northwest corner of the Allier. The forest was planted at the behest of Louis XIV to provide wood for his navy, but its predominant claim to fame is as a prized source of extremely tight-grained oak for barrels for France's cooperage industry.

Located to the west of the small market town of Saint-Pourçain-sur-Sioule, the vineyards of Saint-Pourçain attained AOC status in 2009. Vineyards cover 1,358 acres of land planted on limestone, granite, and gravel soil. Saint-Pourçain vineyards are planted with Chardonnay, Tressallier (Sacy), a traditional Loire Valley variety, and, to a lesser extent, Sauvignon Blanc for white wine; and Gamay and Pinot Noir for red wine. Rosés from Gamay are also produced. During medieval times, the white wines of Saint-Pourçain were among the most respected wines of France. Having since been overtaken in popularity by their cousins from Burgundy and the Loire Valley to the north, Saint-Pourçain is now virtually unknown but can produce delightful, dry, light-bodied wines with moderately high acidity levels. Although Tressallier historically was the most widely planted variety, Chardonnay currently is most prevalent with AOC regulations requiring that it must make up

Investors helping in the vineyards

between 50–80 percent of the blend, while Tressallier accounts for the remaining 20–50 percent.

In 1996, Denis Barbara became partners with established local vigneron Elié Grosbot (now retired). Denis now runs the 16-acre estate located in the tiny hamlet of Montjournal in the commune of Cesset (although some of the Domaine's vineyards are located in nearby communes). Although Denis runs Grosbot-Barbara by himself, he has investors in certain vineyards to help defray costs. The investors contribute financially, but additionally, they arrive several times each year during periods of high labor requirements—such as pruning and harvest time. Domaine Grosbot-Barbara produces approximately 3,000 cases of wine per year. With the exception of La Chambre d'Edouard, which is sourced from three different vineyard sites, the wines of Grosbot-Barbara are all single vineyard wines.

Red Wines

Red wines from Grosbot-Barbara macerate between 15–24 days (depending on the wine) in thermo-regulated tanks at low temperatures. Denis looks for fresh aromas and elegant structure in his red wines.

Chambre d'Edouard: This cuvée is produced from 90 percent Pinot Noir and 10 percent Gamay grown on clay/limestone soils. In 2001, a Pinot Noir-loving family friend named Edouard slept the night away in one of the empty tanks. Afterwards they nicknamed the tank *La Chambre d'Edouard,* Edouard's bedroom, and that is how the Pinot Noir cuvée from Grosbot-Barbara got its name.

Les Ferneaux: 100 percent Gamay from granite soils of the Les Ferneaux vineyard (a soil type where Gamay does well).

Domaine GROSBOT-BARBARA

Les Ferneaux
2015

Photo credit: Domaine Grosbot-Barbara

White Wines

White wines from Grosbot-Barbara are a blend of Chardonnay, Tressallier, and Sauvignon Blanc.

Domaine GROSBOT-BARBARA

Le vin d'Alon
2015

Photo credit: Domaine Grosbot-Barbara

La Vreladière: A cuvée from a 2.2-acre clay/limestone single vineyard producing white wine from 90 percent Chardonnay and 10 percent Tressallier.

Le Quarteron: A cuvée from a less-than-one-acre vineyard on granitic soils planted with Chardonnay (80 percent), Tressallier (15 percent), and Sauvignon Blanc (5 percent), this vineyard is a joint partnership between Denis and a group of local and international wine lovers (including Prince Charles-Henri de Lobkowicz and my friends Ed Addiss and Barbara Selig of Wine Traditions, the importers of Grosbot-Barbara in the United States).

Le Clos Jacques Chevallier: This wine is from a vineyard right next to the Barbaras' house. It is made from Chardonnay and Tressallier grapes grown on granite soils and is a joint venture between Denis and a group of doctors.

Le Vin d'Alon: is a single vineyard that produces both Chardonnay (70 percent) and Tressallier (30 percent). The wine of the same name is made from Chardonnay and Tressallier in the same proportions as the vineyard and is aged in tank.

S.A.S. Le Prince Charles-Henri de Lobkowicz: This white wine is named for Prince Charles-Henri de Lobkowicz. It is a select cuvée from Chardonnay and Tressallier from *Le Vin d'Alon* and is fermented and aged in barrels from the local forests of Tronçais and Jaligny-sur-Bèsbre.

S.A.S. Prince Charles-Henri de Lobkowicz is a direct descendant of the Bourbon Kings. (S.A.S. is the abbreviation for His Royal Highness in French.) Since it is from his ancestors that the Bourbonnais region took its name, Prince Charles-Henri is a strong supporter of the region, as is Denis Barbara. Denis and the Prince met at a preview of a documentary about the Bourbonnais, and they bonded over their mutual love of the region. At the time, Denis proffered the idea of naming a wine in honor of the Prince. Pleased with the notion, the Prince accepted, choosing the design for the label himself. The first vintage of S.A.S. Le Prince Charles-Henri de Lobkowicz was 2007.

On September 9, 2015, Denis and Monique were invited to attend a large celebration that Prince Charles-Henri de Lobkowicz hosted on the occasion of the 11th centenary of the Bourbon family at the Basilica of Saint Denis in Souvigny and featuring the Cuvée S.A.S. Le Prince Charles-Henri de Lobkowicz. Denis and Monique were completely thrilled to have been in attendance at such an important event.

Sparkling Wine

Brut "0": Domaine Grosbot-Barbara produces one traditional method sparkling wine. One hundred percent Gamay from the *Les Ferneaux* vineyard, this dry wine spends four years on the fine lees and as the name indicates, is bottled with zero added dosage.

The distinctive labels for most of the Grosbot-Barbara wines are the work of Benoit-Basset, a local artist from Vichy. She and her husband (a doctor) are part of the group that owns Le Clos Jacques Chevallier with Denis. Le Quarteron is the only wine label that is not painted by Benoit-Basset. The labels for Le Quarteron are painted by local amateur artists and change every year. For 2014, the artist was the 16-year-old son of one of the investors in Le Quarteron.

In addition to the wines from his own Domaine, Denis is the winemaker for the local *Conservatoire des Anciens Cépages,* The Conservatory of Ancient Grape Varieties. Located on the property of the Château de Chareil-Cintrat approximately six miles from Grosbot-Barbara, the Conservatory was established to protect erstwhile local grape varieties—Saint Pierre Doré, Meslier Saint François, Romorantin, Melon, Aligoté, Tressallier, Sauvignon, Pinot Gris, and Pinot Blanc. The vineyard has clay/limestone soil and abuts the Château itself. Each year Denis makes the *Cuvée du Conservatoire,* a hand-harvested blend of the abovementioned grapes. The cuvée is sold at the Conservatory to raise money for research projects.

I had long been familiar with Domaine Grosbot-Barbara when I first met Denis Barbara and his son, Brian. I had been working with their wines for years, delighted at the value offered by the reds and whites. Denis and Brian popped into Buck's Fishing & Camping for dinner one Friday evening, and over a glass of wine, they mentioned *Pompe aux Grattons,* an Auvergnat dish that was a particular specialty of Monique Barbara, Denis's wife. Their description of a brioche-like bread studded with duck or pork cracklings intrigued me, and I really wanted to learn to make it. (At the time, I was serving a cornbread at the restaurant in which I substituted duck fat for butter or shortening.) The more I thought about it, the more the idea of learning to make regional specialties from winemakers took hold until I finally realized that it would make an interesting book, and *that* is how *The Wine Table* was born.

Photo credit: Domaine Grosbot-Barbara

After leaving my position at Buck's, one of the first trips I took was to visit Monique and Denis at their home in the central part of France. So remote was their winery that they insisted upon hosting me at their home. I've stayed at wineries before—larger concerns with rooms or housing dedicated to guests or seasonal workers—but the Barbaras' winery is small and developing. He is the only full-time employee working their small estate, and at the time Monique was an elementary school teacher in a nearby town.

The family and their surroundings are uniquely eccentric. Denis has long flowing silvery brown hair, a regal profile, and dresses in a dapper fashion even when working in the vineyard. Monique is quietly attractive with a lovely smile. Their son, Brian, a student at the wine school in Beaune, is trendy in his skinny jeans and leather jacket.

Upon my arrival at the property, I drove past the small winery buildings, keeping my eye peeled for an office before parking in front of a single-level building with a lovingly tended bower of purple wisteria and pots overflowing with blue flowers of all types. I knocked on the front door, and although there was no answer, it was ajar, so I stepped inside. The first things I saw were two

large postcard racks filled with colorful postcards. I assumed I had stumbled upon the winery office. Further inspection showed that I was in a kitchen decorated in a blue-and-white beach motif with seashells and lighthouses adorning every possible surface. Thinking I had made a mistake, I started to back out, when Monique came in to the room and greeted me warmly. It seemed I had indeed found the correct spot.

A further tour of the house revealed more of Monique's passions with the dining room decorated in an Italian theme with opera references and Venetian masks on the walls. In the living room, low couches with ornately carved wooden armrests draped with silk scarves and an impressive collection of exotic plants evoked a more Arabian mood. I discovered later that although Monique loves the beach and traveling, reinvestment in the small wine Domaine consumes their income, and she travels vicariously through books, cooking, home décor, and postcards received from friends. Whimsical touches were everywhere and combined to produce an exotic, quirky, yet super-charming haven in the middle of *La France Profonde*—Deep France.

The Barbaras welcomed me as if I were an honored guest—almost family—and I cannot stress enough how much their warmth touched me. Brian gave me his room, sleeping instead on one of the silk draped couches in the living room. Meals were involved, high-level affairs with everyone dressing up for dinners that began with a sparkling wine with appetizers and continued through

multiple courses designed to showcase their wines. Monique is an accomplished cook and interspersed our meals with local specialties like Potato Tart (a delicious tart filled with potatoes, onions, and crème fraîche), Duck à la Vigneronne (in the style of the winemaker's wife), Bourbonnais Chicken (roasted chicken finished at the last minute with a Cantal gratin), as well as dishes from other parts of France like Veal Marengo with local Mousseron mushrooms, Scallops with Cream, and a dish she called Spirit of Oysters—oysters served in their shell with lemon and thyme. However, the shining star was, of course, Monique's *Pompe aux Grattons*. Making it with her was the highlight of my visit.

Monique and Denis had prepared a list of local villages and châteaux to visit, and they encouraged me to spend some time at the Saturday morning market in Saint-Pourçain-sur-Sioule, where a flea market shared space with fruit and vegetable stands teeming with brightly colored radishes and strawberries.

Cheese and fishmongers, butchers, bakers, and prepared food vendors exhibited their goods, encouraging customers to sample local delicacies. The *rôtisseur*, a perennial favorite of mine with chicken, ducks, rabbits, and pork roasts turning on a rotisserie spit over a pan of baby potatoes (those delicious potato nuggets glazed with savory meat juices make for a perfect snack while strolling through the market), featured a real

treat—to-go containers of Aligot, mashed potatoes whipped with Laguiole cheese and crème fraîche—fantastic!

Local Food Products

Pompe aux Grattons: This is the dish that started it all for me—crunchy salty bits of duck or pork cracklings baked into a chewy yeast dough. Some versions call for brioche dough, but I find the eggy butteriness of brioche to be a bit too rich—ironic considering the dough contains duck fat and fatty duck cracklings. My quest to learn to make *Pompe aux Grattons* was what sent me to Monique Barbara's kitchen and started out my search for Wine Table foods. Pair it with sparkling wine for a perfect beginning to a good meal.

Pâté de Pommes de Terre (Potato Tart): Historically, the Bourbonnais peasants and sharecroppers lived with a fairly meager larder since much of the more luxurious local bounty was reserved for the gentry. *Pâté de Pommes de Terre*—its flaky short crust filled with potatoes, shallots, and crème fraîche—was a delicious remedy to this dilemma. The nickname for this dish, *Pâté de Tartouffes* (truffle pie), is a tongue-in-cheek reference to the lack of truffles in the local soil, with potatoes playing the role of their truffle—the richest thing to come out of their soil.

Meat and Poultry

Charolais: Perhaps the best-known meat product of the region and famed throughout France, in 1974 Charolais cattle were the recipients of the first Label Rouge (a quality designation). Additionally, Charolais have been awarded their own IGP (Protected Product Designation). These all-white cattle are grass-fed, ranging free in wooded meadows from April to November, at which time cold winter weather forces them inside.

Poulet Bourbonnais: A cross between local white chicken and Brahma (an Asian variety), Poulets Bourbonnais emerged on sharecropper farms at the end of the 19th century. Poulets Bourbonnais are free-range and are prized for their firm, flavorful meat.

Dinde de Jaligny (Jaligny Turkey): Free-range, grain-fed turkeys that are particularly treasured at Christmastime on French holiday tables.

Andouillette de Saint-Pourçain: Traditional sausages made from pork tripe and pork stomach. Similar versions can be found in Troyes and Lyon.

Cheeses

Chambérat: Large, pressed cow's milk cheese made from whole, raw milk. Treasured for flavors of hazelnuts and sweet hay.

Comtesse de Vichy: A soft cheese wrapped in spruce bark, Comtesse de Vichy is similar in texture to Brie or Coulommiers.

Cérilly: Fresh cow's milk cheese made in the "ladle method," meaning they were traditionally formed with a ladle, Cérilly can be eaten very young and fresh or, with a little age, in a drier form.

Desserts

Piquenchâgne: A pear, apple, or quince tart so named because the fruits are placed whole upright in the dough, like an oak planted into the earth.

Pastilles de Vichy: Small mint-, lemon-, or anise-flavored lozenges from the nearby spa town of Vichy. Said to have medicinal qualities because of the use of mineral waters in the recipe.

Other Foods of the Region

Moutarde de Charroux: Production of this flavorful mustard dates back to the 18th century in the medieval village of Charroux.

Vichy Water: A naturally effervescent mineral water from the springs in Vichy, France.

A Bourbonnais Barbecue

One afternoon, a group of engineers from Paris came to help prune one of the vineyards. To help defray the costs of running the winery, these engineers invested in the vineyard Les Maltotes (one of the sources of the Chambre d'Edouard Cuvée). Multiple times each year, the group descends on the Domaine and helps with labor-intensive tasks like pruning, etc. On this occasion, they organized a traditional cookout in the winery courtyard, grilling chipolata pork sausages and pork ribs over vine clippings and charcoal. They were a boisterous crowd who obviously knew one another and the Barbara family very well. The mood was loud and chaotic—I still shudder when I remember watching the engineers squirting lighter fluid directly onto the fire. The atmosphere was a lot of fun but diametrically different from the elegant family affairs Monique had been hosting.

Since returning to the United States, I have received many lengthy letters and emails from Monique filled with information about the dishes we cooked (augmenting the magazines and books she gave me at the time of the visit), her thoughts on a biography of Abraham Lincoln she had recently read, news of Denis and Brian, details of the weather, and how the harvest was progressing. The art of genteel correspondence is alive and well in Monique Barbara's small corner of France. In return, I have emailed her photos of my many *Pompes aux Grattons*.

I have since visited Beaune in Burgundy and dined with Brian—tasting the wines of Domaine Michel Bouzereau, the winery in Meursault where Brian works during the school year. It seemed natural to take him to dinner, as if he were a favored nephew. The emails and letters from Monique continue to arrive, and I never fail to send a postcard to her from my travels to brighten her day and hopefully find a valued place on the postcard rack in her lovely warm kitchen amidst the vineyards of Saint Pourçain. Each time I mail a card, I remember time spent with Monique among her lovely hydrangea, sipping Grosbot-Barbara Brut "0" and nibbling on *Pompe aux Grattons*. A few postcards seem such a small effort to repay the sort of kindness that turns strangers into dear friends.

The Winemaker Recommends: *Pompe aux Grattons* with Grosbot-Barbara Brut "0" Sparkling Wine.

Pompe aux Grattons

Yield: One 9-inch loaf | Ease of Preparation: Moderately Difficult | Ease of Sourcing: Difficult
Wine Pairing: Grosbot-Barbara Brut "0," Crémant de Bourgogne, or Blanc de Noirs Champagne

I love this recipe for a lot of reasons. To begin with, it was this recipe that triggered the idea of traveling to wineries to learn to make regional specialties. When I heard about Monique Barbara's Pompe aux Grattons, I knew I had to learn to make it! It is showy and yet homey at the same time. The combination of the yeastiness of the bread and the rich, savory crunch of the grattons (duck cracklings) is so enticing it's hard to resist. Pretty much you had me at "duck cracklings."

INGREDIENTS

For the Duck Cracklings (crispy cooked duck skin):

3 lbs. of duck skin

For the Pompe:

¼ cup lukewarm water

11 grams baker's yeast (1 Tbsp. + 1 tsp.)

1 cup warm skim milk

2 oz. duck fat (a scant ⅓ cup)

2 Tbsp. white wine

1 extra large egg + 1 for egg wash

1 Tbsp. kosher salt

4½ to 5 cups bread flour

1½ cup duck cracklings, cut in ⅓ x 1 inch strips, plus ¼ cup (prepared in the first step)

WHAT YOU'LL NEED:

Cutting board

Sharp knife

Two hotel pans or large baking dishes

Kitchen tongs

Small saucepan

Instant read thermometer

Electric mixer with paddle or dough hook attachment

9-inch springform pan

Pastry brush

Baking sheet

Large kitchen bowl

Dry clean kitchen towel

TIMING

For the Duck Cracklings:

Prep Time: 30 minutes

Cooking Time: 30 minutes

For the Pompe Dough:

Rise Time: Two sessions: First 1½ hours and second 30 minutes

Cook Time: 1 hour 10 minutes

Cooling Time: at least one hour

PROCESS

For the Duck Cracklings:

Preheat the oven to 400° F.

Slice the duck skin in ½-inch-wide strips. (Duck skin isn't uniformly shaped, so the length of the strips will vary.) Spread the strips in one even layer in the baking dishes and bake, stirring periodically. After 10 minutes, some of the smaller strips may be done. Remove them. You may need to drain the duck fat from the pan periodically. Keep the duck fat! You will need some of it for the dough and other cooking uses. (It is always great to have a jar of duck fat in the fridge for frying potatoes, etc.) Continue rendering the duck skin until the all the strips are dark golden brown. This will take between 15 and 30 minutes. Remove them from the oven, strain off the fat, and allow them to cool. They will crisp up as they cool. Once they are cool, cut them into 1 inch by ⅓ inch strips. Note: Three pounds of raw duck skin will render out to approximately 2 cups of duck cracklings and 1 quart of duck fat.

For the Pompe Dough:

Mix lukewarm water into the baker's yeast. Heat skim milk to approximately 85° F. Add duck fat and white wine to the warm milk. When the yeast starts to bubble, add the yeast, egg, kosher salt, and milk mixture to the mixer. Mix on low speed until incorporated. With the mixer on the low/medium-low setting, add the flour one cup at a time and mix until incorporated. Continue mixing until the dough forms a ball and pulls away from side of the bowl. (The dough itself will basically clean the sides of the bowl.) You may not need to use all of the flour.

Turn the dough out onto a lightly floured board and knead for 5 minutes, adding more flour as needed. When finished, the ball of dough should be elastic and smooth. At this point, begin kneading in 1½ cup of duck cracklings. Knead it very thoroughly to mix the cracklings evenly throughout the dough. This takes several minutes. Form the dough into a ball. Place it in a lightly greased kitchen bowl (feel free to use some of your duck fat!). Cover with a clean, dry kitchen towel and let rise until doubled in size (an hour to an hour and half). Punch the dough down and shape the dough into a round loaf almost as large as your pan, and put it in the springform pan. Let the loaf rise for 30 minutes while preheating the oven to 325° F.

Finely chop the remaining ¼ cup of duck cracklings. Add a pinch of salt. Paint the risen loaf with the egg wash and sprinkle the duck cracklings on the top of the loaf. Place the filled springform pan on the baking sheet and put the loaf into the preheated over. Bake for 1 hour and 10 minutes.

Let the pompe cool for 15 minutes, then open the springform and remove the outer rim. Cool the pompe completely before slicing.

Note

Duck skin is rather difficult to find. Ask your local butcher to order some for you. Alternately, you may purchase a duck and remove the skin, but this seems kind of like the tail wagging the dog. Pork cracklings are frequently used in France to make Pompe aux Grattons, but they aren't exactly household items and rendering them is more difficult than rendering duck skin. If you cannot find duck skin, you may substitute bacon, but I would advise getting one that is only mildly smoked. If you do use bacon, you will need to reduce the amount of salt in the recipe.

Potato Tart
Pâté de Pommes de Terre

Yield: 6 portions as a main course, 8 to 12 portions as a side dish | Ease of Preparation: Moderate
Ease of Sourcing: Difficult (If you use leaf lard), easy if you use vegetable shortening
Wine Pairing: White: Saint Pourçain Blanc or Mâcon Blanc; Red: Saint Pourçain Rouge,
Beaujolais, or Bourgogne Rouge

Although potatoes were not prevalent in the Bourbonnais until the late 1800s, their use quickly spread during this period. The predominantly Catholic population, forbidden from eating meat on Fridays and confronted with the fact that the lakes and their abundant fish belonged to the landed gentry and were therefore off limits, turned to the lowly potato to satisfy their hunger—both physical and gastronomical. The resulting combination of wheat, egg, cream, butter, and potatoes could have yielded something so quotidian. Instead, it created a warming tart—delicious and luxurious despite its humble ingredients. This tart is sometimes called Pâté aux Tartouffes *or truffle pâté. Since the Allier region did not have any truffles, potatoes dug from the ground were the truffles of the poor.*

INGREDIENTS

For the Dough:

1½ cups all-purpose flour
½ cup cake flour
1 tsp. kosher salt
1 egg
4 oz. (1 stick) chilled unsalted butter, cut in medium sized cubes
4 oz. (½ cup) ice-cold leaf lard (or ¼ cup vegetable shortening and 6 oz. butter) (See note #1 below)
⅓ cup ice water

For the Filling:

2 lbs. waxy potatoes
2 Tbsp. shallots, finely minced
2 tsp. kosher salt
1 tsp. finely ground white pepper
1 Tbsp. unsalted butter
¾ cup crème fraîche
One egg beaten well for an egg wash

WHAT YOU'LL NEED	TIMING
Food processor	For the dough: 20 minutes
Pastry scraper	Dough Resting time: 2 hours
Rolling pin	Preparation and Assembly: 45 minutes
8-inch springform tart pan (3 inches tall)	(some of this can be done while dough
Cookie sheet	rests)
Colander	Baking and Resting: 1 hour and 45
Paper towel	minutes to 2 hours
Pastry brush	
One metal pastry tip (to serve as chimney for the tart)	
Plastic squeeze bottle or a piping bag with a pastry tip	

PROCESS

Place the flours and kosher salt in the bowl of a food processor with the metal blade attachment. Pulse to blend. Add the egg and process for 10 to 15 seconds. Add the cold butter cubes and pulse the processor 5 or 6 times. Add the ice-cold leaf lard (or shortening) and pulse 2 times. With the processor running, quickly pour in ¼ cup (of the ⅓ cup) of ice water, reserving the small remaining amount. Shut the processor off immediately.

Pour the dough onto a clean surface. If it is really moist, add ¼ to ½ cup of flour on top of the dough and onto your board. Use your hands and the pastry scraper to bring the mass together and knead the dough until it is smooth and forms a ball. If the dough is too dry, you may need to add an extra small amount of water drop by drop to pull the dough together. (Do not overknead. You are just trying to get the dough to adhere together smoothly.) Divide the dough into two portions: one about ⅔ of the dough and the other about ⅓ of the dough. Form the dough portions into round flat disks, wrap them in plastic, and refrigerate them for two hours or more.

Peel the potatoes and cut them in ⅛-inch slices. Soak in cold water while the dough is resting.

Drain the potatoes in a colander.

Place the springform pan on the cookie sheet.

Remove the dough from the refrigerator and roll the larger disk to a 13-inch circle on a floured pastry board (or countertop). Carefully place it inside the springform pan. Make sure the dough is evenly centered in the pan. Because of the depth of the pan, there will be thick folds of dough. Do your best to evenly smooth out the folds. Trim the excess dough so there is only an extra half-inch of dough sticking above the side of the pan. It may flop over the side of the pan. That's okay.

Roll the smaller dough to form a circle the size of the opening of your springform pan.

By now, the potatoes should be well drained. Lay them out on a towel and pat them dry to make sure there is no excess water. Do not skip this step! Wet potatoes will make the tart soggy.

Arrange a layer of potatoes in the bottom of your tart. Sprinkle the first layer of potatoes with a small amount of the minced shallots, salt, and white pepper. Repeat a second layer of potatoes, more of the minced shallots, salt, and white pepper. Continue layering the potatoes, shallots, salt, and white pepper. Stop when the level of potatoes reaches an inch below the rim of the pan. There will be approximately 6 layers. Scatter the remaining shallots, salt, and white pepper on the top layer. Adjust the top two layers of potatoes so that there is an opening in the center of the potatoes. (You will need this later to insert a steam chimney.) Dot the potatoes with 1-tablespoon dabs of butter.

Spoon ¼ cup of crème fraîche over the potatoes. Place the smaller disk of dough on top of the potatoes. Paint the edge of the small disk with the egg wash. Fold the sides of the bottom dough over the top of the smaller disk. Smooth the edge of the top dough well to close the tart. If necessary, use a little extra egg wash to moisten the edge to help smooth the seam. Ideally there should be no evidence of a seam.

With a sharp knife, make a hole in the center of the dough, wiggling the knife to make sure there are no potatoes directly under the hole. Insert the metal pastry tip into the upper crust of the tart. This will serve as a chimney to let steam escape.

Brush the top of the tart with the egg wash.

Bake in a 350° F oven for one hour and 15 minutes, turning once.

Fill the small plastic squeeze bottle or the piping bag with plain pastry tip with the remaining crème fraîche.

After one hour and 15 minutes, remove the tart from the oven. Remove the metal tip from the top of the tart and use a metal skewer to poke the potatoes to see if they are fully cooked. If the are not done, put the tart back in the oven for 15 more minutes. If they are tender, squeeze as much of the remaining ½ cup of crème fraîche as will fit into the tart.

Bake for 10 minutes more.

Remove the tart and let it sit for 15 minutes before unmolding. Cut in wedges and serve as a first course, as a main course with a salad at lunch, or as a side dish for dinner.

Notes

#1. Rendered Leaf Lard is the highest grade of rendered pork fat, a.k.a. lard. Leaf lard comes from the visceral (soft) fat from around the kidneys and loin of a pig. Rendered leaf lard is lard that has been rendered from this visceral fat. It can be kept for a short amount of time at room temperature, for six months under refrigeration, and considerably longer in a freezer. It is snowy white and has a soft, delicately spreadable consistency at room temperature. I'll admit that leaf lard is not always readily available. I am incredibly lucky to have my great friends Will Morrow and Kent Ozkum from Whitmore Farm who sell rendered Leaf Lard at my local Farmer's Market.

I have found Smoking Goose brand leaf lard at Arrowine in Arlington, and Smoking Goose also sells leaf lard online at www.smokinggoose.com. In a pinch, I have also seen it on Amazon. If you buy lard at your local farmer's market or butcher, you need to verify that it is indeed leaf lard. If it isn't, it is lard rendered from all over the pig and it may taste piggy. If you cannot find leaf lard, use ¼ cup ice-cold vegetable shortening and ¾ cup chilled unsalted butter. (Be careful! The lard sold in blocks on grocery store shelves is treated—often with hydrogenation—to make it shelf stable, deodorize it, and keep it solid at room temperature.)

#2. Piecrust or Puff Pastry? Monique Barbara recommends using a traditional Piecrust (Pâte Brisée) if you want a more rustic look and Puff Pastry (Pâte Feuilletée) if you want something fancier. I prefer a flaky Pâte Brisée. **Important Cheat Note**: *Do not panic about the crust!* If you want to make it with Puff Pastry but do not want to make it yourself, do not worry. There are many frozen options. Believe me, reputable restaurants all over the world buy premade puff pastry. I recommend the excellent Dufour Brand or Pepperidge Farm. While not as good as Dufour, Pepperidge Farm is perfectly satisfactory and more readily available. *As for regular Piecrust, if you don't want to make it, don't sweat it.* Go to the store and buy the premade piecrust in the red box. It's not as good as homemade *pâte brisée*, but it is reasonably good.

#3. Waxy potatoes hold their shape better than starchy potatoes during the cooking process, which in this case is a nice visual, allowing you to see the layers of potatoes when you cut into the tart. Good choices for waxy potatoes are Red Bliss, Inca Gold, or any type of new potato. If you cannot find those, your next best bet is Yukon Gold (an all-purpose potato). Finally, even if you only have standard Russets (a starchy potato), your tart will still taste delicious, you just won't be able to see the layer of potatoes quite as well. For added visual effect, use blue or pink-fleshed waxy potatoes.

#4. If you don't have a pastry-decorating tip to insert into the tart, roll parchment paper into a funnel and use that instead.

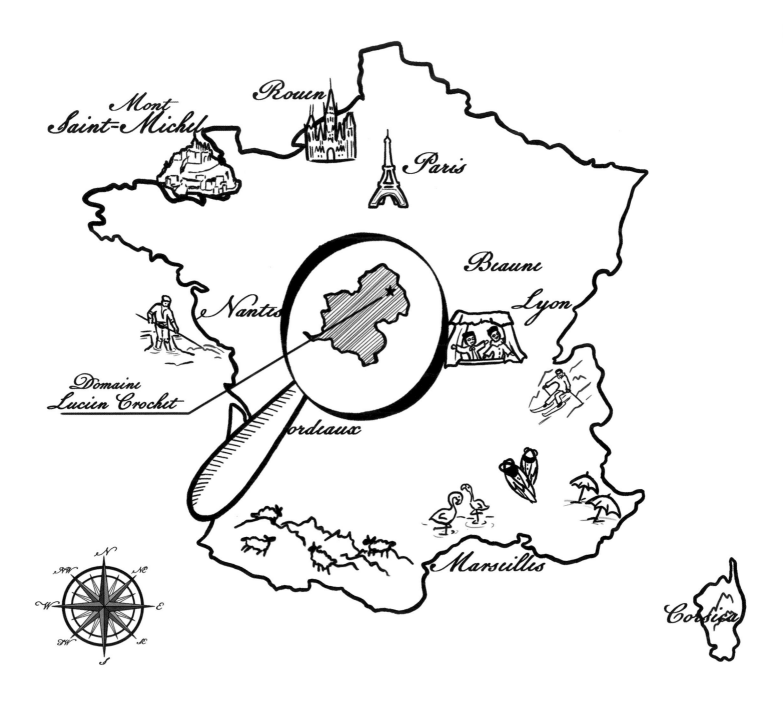

"The Accents May be Different, but Family Doesn't Change"
A Visit with Laurence Crochet, Domaine Lucien Crochet
Sancerre, France

Sometimes when planning a winery visit, you know what you are going to find. When visiting Château d'Yquem, you expect a fancy château. A tour of a Grande Marque Champagne House will invariably include a foray into white chalk caves carved deeply into the hillside adjacent to or below the winery. Still other times, you are completely surprised because either the winemaker or winery itself is so unique, you can't help but be caught unawares. In the case of visiting Laurence Crochet in her home in Bué, France, my surprise was solely based on a feeling of having been there before, having heard the same tones, having been involved in the same conversation—the sense of normalcy and typical family life that could have happened anywhere in the United States—except the house was a zen-like haven nestled in the hills above Bué, and the back-and-forth exchange between mother and college-aged daughter was carried on in lilting French.

Photo credit: Domaine Lucien Crochet

Located in the Sancerrois commune of Bué, Domaine Lucien Crochet has long been a favorite of mine. I have put one or more of their wines on every restaurant wine list I have ever written, and it is an automatic go-to recommendation for me when a retail customer is looking for Sancerre. The wines are clean, refined, and delicious—vibrant, with elegant acidity and the marked minerality that one expects from high-quality Loire Valley Sauvignon Blanc. In 2009, I embarked on a meandering tour following the vein of Kimmeridgian marl (see box below) that runs from the Aube in Southern Champagne through Chablis to Sancerre in the Loire Valley. Domaine Lucien Crochet was my last stop before heading home.

Sancerrois Soil Types:

Terres Blanches: Located in the western part of the region, the chalk on Kimmeridgian marl, known locally as *Terres Blanches*, is studded with ancient sea fossils. (To further understand Kimmeridgian Soil, see the box on page 433.) These soils account for 40 percent of the acreage in Sancerre. Wines from *Terre Blanches* have excellent structure and complex flavors, and although they take a bit of time to come around, they have good aging potential. The village of Chavignol and the vineyard of Les Monts Damnés are the most famous locations of *Terres Blanches* in the Loire Valley. Other important Kimmeridgian outcroppings can be found in Chablis and the Southern Champagne region of France. The Kimmeridgian soils of Southern England and the Franken in Germany bookend the three French wine regions.

Les Caillottes: *Les Caillottes* are seashell-studded fine-grained limestone soils covered in stone and pebbles. Dating to the Portlandian and Oxfordian geological periods, these soils that make up 40 percent of the soil in the appellation are found in the vineyards on low hills surrounding the town of Sancerre itself as well as in Bué, Verdigny, and Sury-en-Vaux. Wines from *Caillottes* soils are bright, racy, and elegant. They are wines that can be drunk and enjoyed immediately after bottling.

Silex: Flinty clay famously found in Pouilly-Fumé, *Silex* comprises 20 percent of the area in Sancerre with vineyards in the communes of Ménétréol and Saint-Satur as well as along the north-south fault line running through the village of Sancerre itself. Wines from *Silex* soils are complex and fuller-bodied, while maintaining the precise acidity necessary for ageworthiness.

Marl: Lime-rich mud or mudstone that contains variable amounts of clays and silt.

Domaine Lucien Crochet

Domaine Lucien Crochet was established when the vineyards of André Crochet (Lucien Crochet's father) and Lucien Picard (Lucien Crochet's father-in-law) merged into one estate. Gilles Crochet (Lucien's son) is in charge the winery now (although I did run into Lucien on my first visit there). Gilles studied Oenology at the wine school in Dijon and uses that expertise to manage the 89-acre estate. Sauvignon Blanc accounts for the lion's share of the estate, with 64 acres planted mostly on the *Caillottes* soils that dominate around Bué. The remaining 22 acres (also on *Caillottes)* are planted to Pinot

Noir used in the estate's red and rosé Sancerres. A small amount of grapes is purchased from a long-term relationship with a neighbor whose vineyards Gilles manages. Gilles also farms a small parcel of the Cul du Beaujeu vineyard in Chavignol that is owned by members of the family of Gilles's wife, Laurence. The vineyards are east-, south-, and west-facing at altitudes between 790 and 918 feet. Altogether, the property produces ten wines: seven whites from Sauvignon Blanc—**Sancerre Blanc, Le Chêne, Le Chêne Marchand, La Croix du Roy, Le Cul du Beaujeu, LC Cuvée Prestige**, and **Sancerre Vendange du 10 octobre** (which is produced only in very good vintages)—one rosé, **Pinot Rosé**, and two reds from Pinot Noir, **La Croix du Roy** and **LC Cuvée Prestige Rouge.** Most but not all of these wines are available for purchase in the United States.

Wines of Sancerre

Sancerre and Pouilly-Fumé are the two most well-known appellations in the Central Vineyard Region of France's Loire Valley. The Central Vineyards (so named because of the location in the center of France, not because they are in the center of the Loire Valley) are comprised of the departments of the Cher, the Indre, and parts of the Loire, Nièvre, and Loir-et-Cher departments.

The appellation of Sancerre is centered around the town of Sancerre in the Cher department on the western bank of the Loire River in the region known as Le Berry. Fourteen villages are permitted to produce wine under the Sancerre appellation, the most famous of which is Chavignol. Two grapes are allowed in Sancerre: Sauvignon Blanc and Pinot Noir. White wine from Sauvignon Blanc accounts for approximately 80 percent of production. Pinot Noir is used for red and rosé wines (12 percent and 8 percent of production, respectively). The AOC for Sancerre Blanc was awarded in 1936. Sancerre Rouge and Rosé received it in 1959.

Foods of Sancerre

While the food of Sancerre is impacted by its western neighbors the Touraine and Sologne with their abundance of agricultural products, game, and fish, it is predominantly defined by its Berrichonne heritage.

Historically a deeply agricultural region, the cuisine of the Berry is plentiful and filling, characterized by hearty stews and rich, blood-thickened sauces. Additionally, there is a bounty of vegetables and fruits including asparagus, cornichons, and strawberries, and freshwater fish from rivers and lakes. Pork is very popular, and although lamb no longer figures heavily in the cuisine of Sancerre and the region of Berry, cheese from the region is primarily goat, and some lamb dishes remain. As in the nearby Allier and Auvergne, potatoes and cream also play large roles. Regional specialties include:

Poultry

Poule Noire du Berry: A highly sought-after breed of chicken from Berry. It is prized for its small size and its fine white flesh.

Coq au Vin à la Berrichonne: Found throughout France, this fricassée is best made with an old rooster (good luck finding one) but can be made with an old chicken or a stewing fowl. In this case, a wine from one of the Berry appellations is used.

Poulet en Barbouille: One of the most famous dishes of the region, *Poulet en Barbouille* is a chicken cooked in brandy served in a blood-thickened sauce of cream, egg yolks, and chopped liver. Said to be so delicious that it causes even the fastidious French to dig in and get their hands messy while eating it.

Meat

Boulettes: Pork, veal, or beef meatballs.

Crépinettes: Pork sausage wrapped in caul fat and coated in fine breadcrumbs before being fried in butter until crisp and cooked through.

Saupiquet: Shallot, tarragon, cream, and wine-braised ham.

Viau au Vin: Veal sautéed in red wine.

Seven-hour Lamb: Although not as common as it once was on local tables, this recipe that calls for slow cooking the lamb for seven hours is still quite popular.

Civet de Lièvre: Hare stewed in red wine. This famous recipe comes from the neighboring Sologne, but it appears so frequently on menus in Sancerre and Berry that it is considered a standard-bearer for the region.

Ris et Rognons à la Berichonne en Croûte: Veal or lamb sweetbreads and kidneys cooked in a pastry crust.

Pâté Berrichon (Pâté de Pâques [Easter Pâté]): Puff pastry wrapped pork pâté. The inclusion of a hard-boiled egg in the center of the meat mixture is de rigueur. As the name implies, this is a highlight of the Easter table in Berry.

Riches from the Rivers and Lakes of Sologne and Brenne

The Sologne to the west and the Brenne to the south (there are more than 2,500 small lakes and ponds in the Brenne) furnish a wealth of fish and other wiggly creatures. Carp, pike, perch, pikeperch, lamprey, eel, frogs, and snails are readily available throughout the region and figure quite heavily in local cuisine.

Stuffed Carp from Brenne: Local carp is stuffed with a farce of sausage, fish roe, milk-soaked bread, mushrooms, and aromatic herbs before being sewn closed. It is then baked on a bed of mushrooms, aromatics, white wine, and butter.

Matelotes: Winey, blood-thickened stews featuring eel or lamprey from local rivers.

Flambéed Frogs' Legs with Garlic Parsley Cream: *Grenouilles* (*Guernouilles* in the local dialect) cooked in a parsley and garlic cream sauce, and flambéed right before serving.

Petit Gris de Cluis: Cultivated snails from the village of Cluis in the Indre in southern Berry, these small gray farm-raised snails are prized for their delicate texture and flavor.

Fricassée of Lumas à la Berrichonne: a regional treat featuring Petit Gris, garlic, and parsley sautéed in butter and simmered in a pan with white wine until the snails soften and the sauce thickens.

Other Regional Foods and Dishes

Black Truffles of Berry: The prized *Tuber Melanosporum,* while not found in as dense quantities as in the Dordogne, is a highly sought-after delicacy in the clay limestone soils of Champagne Berrichonne—a region that begins at the Loire River just south of Sancerre and extends to the west past Bourges, Issoudun, and Chateauroux.

Green Lentils of Berry: These small legumes are prized for their sweet chestnut flavor.

Crème de Lentilles Vertes du Berry aux Truffes: Cream of green lentil soup with black truffles.

Lentil Salad with Warm Goat Cheese: Lentils of Berry tossed in a creamy vinaigrette and topped with a round of warm goat cheese.

Tourte Berrichonne or Pâté de Pommes de Terre: As in Saint Pourçain to the south, this is more of a potato tart than a pâté, with potatoes, onions, and crème fraîche baked in a flaky crust and an opening at the top to allow steam to escape. More thick, rich crème fraîche is poured through the hole in the crust during the last ten minutes of baking. Delicious!

Pâté à la Citrouille: Similar to the potato tart above but without the cream, this is a savory pumpkin pie served throughout fall and winter in the Berry.

Chaussons de Berry: Pastry turnovers filled with cheese instead of the traditional apple filling.

Vinegar from Orléans: Oak-aged vinegar.

Goat Cheeses

Goat cheese abounds in this part of France, and its pairing with crisp, minerally, grassy Sauvignon Blanc is one of the world's great classics. Luckily, there are a whole lot of both to go around!

Crottin de Chavignol: Some say the name comes from the shape, which is reminiscent of the base of an oil lamp. Some say it's from *crotte,* slang for goat droppings. Yikes! I'll leave you to choose which version you prefer. Either way, the popularity of this little goat cheese from Chavignol is undeniable. Small, flat, and round, approximately an inch-and-a-half tall and the same distance across, Crottin is made from whole goat's milk. The minimum aging requirement is ten days, although twenty is more standard. It starts out quite soft in its fresh stage, but as it ages it gets considerably firmer. The taste echoes this progression, with the younger cheeses being milder while, with age, the tart acidity increases along with strength of the flavors of hay and nuts. Old Crottin de Chavignol is very dry, firm, and extremely powerful.

My first experience with Crottin de Chavignol dates back to my first wine trip to Chavignol a million years ago. We were driving slowly through the village looking for our destination when we happened to spy a vending machine off the small square in the middle of town (more of a crossroads really). It was one of those vending machines where you put in your money and press a button until your choice of item appears in the window. Then you slide a plastic shield back to remove your item. We were amused to see that rather than selling sodas or packages of crackers (or decades-old cinnamon rolls, as one would have encountered in the US), this machine dispensed a Crottin de Chavignol for your five Francs. (Yes, I said Francs! I did tell you it was a million years ago!) I can assure you that the vending machine Crottin was not the best example of that cheese that I have ever had, but it is a funny memory!

Other well-known goat cheeses from the region include: **Pouligny-Saint-Pierre, Pyramide de Valençay, Selles-sur-Cher.**

Salade Berrichonne: This composed salad has a whole lot going on. It consists of a piece of warm goat cheese on toast that is perched on top of a poached egg, bacon, tomatoes, and walnuts that are dressed with cider vinegar, walnut oil, and mustard.

Desserts

Clafoutis: A pastry made from thick crêpe batter, studded with fresh fruit, and baked in the oven. (see Clafoutis recipe, page 403.)

Pithivier: Puff pastry almond tart.

Tarte Tatin: From the nearby town of Orléans in Sologne, this upside-down apple tart is traditionally made with Reine de Reinette apples (a firm orangish red apple). Tarte Tatin is one of the quintessential French desserts.

Tarte Berriaude: Apple tart with a cinnamon cream sauce.

Poirat: Local pear tart made with pears, sugar, eau de vie, and cream.

Sanciaux: A thick-battered crêpe.

Croquets de Charost: Almond Biscuits.

Forestines des Bourges: A thin, hard-shelled sweet candy filled with a soft hazelnut, almond, or chocolate filling.

Sablé de Nançay: A crunchy, sweet cookie. According to the official website, the original recipe for the Sablé was a mistake made by the baker's son, Jacques. Rather than waste the failed dough, they made sample cookies from it to give out to customers. The cookies were so popular, that they made the same "mistake" the next day, and the next. Sixty years later, this recipe is the basis for the famed Sablé de Nançay.

Jams: Preserves made from all types of fruits are popular with quince, apple (especially Reine de Reinettes), and pear being the most well known.

Dinner with Laurence

My second visit to Domaine Lucien Crochet had less to do with tasting wine than with understanding the food culture of one of my favorite wineries. Laurence Crochet and I had really hit it off at my first visit and had corresponded about food and wine pairings a couple of times in the interim. In fact, our rapport was so amicable right from the start that when she heard that I had eaten at a mediocre restaurant in Sancerre the evening before my first visit to them, she chided me for not calling them and inviting myself to dinner! It seemed logical that when I began to think of cooking with winemakers and their families, Laurence was one of the first people who came to mind.

Medium height and trim in the way of many French women, Laurence is dark-haired with a slender face. Upon first acquaintance, she gives the appearance of quiet, friendly competence. Further time spent together solidifies the impression of quietness, but her friendliness shines more brightly with familiarity. I was quite taken with her enthusiasm in describing their wines and the life that she and Gilles had together. As with my previous visit, Gilles was away on a trip when I arrived at the winery, prompting me to tease Laurence that he was actually a figment of everyone's imagination.

After tasting through a good number of the current vintages of their wines as well as some back vintages for comparison, I set off to Chavignol to check into my hotel before rendezvousing at Laurence's home for dinner. (It was a good thing I did, because although there aren't a lot of turns between Bué and Sancerre and from Sancerre to Chavignol, it is a four-mile trip on narrow hilltop lanes and one that I was glad not to have to make for the first time after nightfall in the fog and rain.)

I arrived at the Crochet home while it was still daylight (another good thing because I'm not sure I would have a) found it, or b) believed that such a structure could exist in a remote area of central France—the clean architectural design of their lovely modern gray weathered wooden house seemingly more typical of the Northwestern United States). The interior decor revealed sleek modern lines, the soothing gray tones accessorized with splashes of vibrant red; the quiet modern furniture accented with African and Far Eastern statues and artifacts. A long dining room table adorned with a modern pottery vase filled with pristine white roses was framed on two sides by floor-to-ceiling windows revealing a large wooden deck surrounded by trees and flowers,

with the steeple and slate rooftop of the church in Bué framed in the green limbs of the trees. There was a serenity and charm to the ambiance that echoed my sense of Laurence's personality. This feeling was in no way marred by the unexpected arrival of her daughter, Esther, home sick from school in nearby Tours. Laurence accepted Esther's arrival calmly, dispensing comfort to her sick offspring, serenely searching out remedies while brewing tea and starting supper.

While preparing dinner, we chatted about the complications of feeding a family when one lives in a remote part of France. Bué is a small village of approximately 350 inhabitants. Both Gilles and Laurence are very busy with work at the winery, and yet she cooks lunch for the two of them every day when he is in town. They rarely drink at lunchtime. Come dinnertime, she cooks a more involved meal, and they drink a glass or two of wine, although it is seldom one of their own wines. Gilles is good friends with many other vignerons, and they tend to drink wines from those friends. She explained that they taste their own wines so often, they find it diverting to taste other wines.

Food shopping is a real task and involves significant strategizing. There are no shops in Bué, which necessitates traveling a bit to get provisions. For major shopping, Bourges (twenty-six miles southwest of Bué) is the most convenient if not the closest. It has more stores than Sancerre and several excellent farmer's markets on most days. She buys her meat at a butcher closer to home and goes to the Thursday farmer's market in Saint-Satur, four miles away. Clearly, there is no such thing as jumping in the car and running to your local grocery store to pick up a lemon.

At harvest time, although they have a lovely kitchen in the winery, they hire a caterer to feed the workers, as everyone is amply occupied with the demands of harvest.

As for holidays, Laurence counts herself lucky to have a well-respected chef in the family. Her brother-in-law is Gilles Tournadre, chef-proprietor of the excellent Restaurant Gill in Rouen, Normandy. He frequently brings supplies for Christmas and other celebrations: turkey, roasting chickens, oysters from Normandy, and other delicacies. As with other special events, the family celebrates these meals with special bottles from Gilles and Lucien Crochet's cellars—their own wines and those of valued friends.

Their tastes in food combine seasonal items from the neighboring area with specialties of other regions. Our dinner began with chilled *Crevettes Grises,* small gray shrimp served with slices of baguette and salted Normandy butter paired with the 2010 Crochet Sancerre. The briny shrimp were fabulous with the bright acidity of the wine. I've always liked these little shrimp. They are eaten whole—shell and all—and I love their crunchy texture. We followed that with fresh local spring asparagus served with a light creamy mustard sauce and a glass of 2010 Croix du Roy.

Continuing the local theme, Laurence showed me a favorite dish of hers, incorporating thinly sliced white button mushrooms and Crottin de Chavignol. After arranging the mushroom slices on chilled salad plates, we painted them with a dressing made from the juice of oranges, lemons, and limes flavored with crushed coriander seeds,

parsley, salt, pepper, and a generous splash of good olive oil. This cooks the mushrooms similarly to how citrus in ceviche cooks the fish, softening the mushrooms slightly and taking away the raw flavor so dominant in uncooked mushrooms. At the last minute, we shaved Crottin de Chavignol on top of the salad. I was thrilled with this dish. Simple to make, it is a complex

blend of clean flavors, the trio of citrus, the earthiness of the mushrooms, the spice of the coriander and pepper, the fruity olive oil, and the high-toned, bright, grassy notes of the cheese. It was a study in acidity and umami, and it was genius. The addition of the minerally Sauvignon Blanc was perfect.

For our main course, Laurence had tasked her fishmonger in Bourges with picking out whatever looked good to him. I was pretty happy he chose Dover Sole—a particular weakness of mine. Laurence skillfully pan fried it in butter and served it with parsley and lemon and accompanied by crispy butter fried baby potatoes.

I am a huge sucker for Dover Sole, and I was so impressed with her execution of the dish. The luxuriousness of the golden brown sole and the crunchy potatoes called for something a little richer wine-wise, in this case a 2010 Cul du Beaujeu. Unlike most of the Crochet vineyards that are on *Caillottes* soil in Bué, Le Cul du Beaujeu is one of the most famous vineyards in Chavignol located on *Terres Blanches* soils. The added richness from the Kimmeridgian soil encouraged Gilles to depart from the Domaine's traditional stainless-steel regimen, and Le Cul du Beaujeu is partially aged in large oak. It was a lovely pairing, both the sole and the wine evidencing flavors of brine—logical, considering sole is a salt water fish and the soil of the vineyards is heavily laden with fossils of sea creatures. The richness of the brown butter and the flavors of slight oak aging matched seamlessly, as well.

Dessert skewed local again, as we macerated *Mara des Bois*, wild forest strawberries, with sugar and a touch of red wine. Laurence served a small amount of Cuvée Prestige Rouge, their oak-aged Sancerre Rouge made from Pinot Noir, with the strawberries. As she poured it, she admitted that she was experimenting, as she was unsure if the wine would stand up to the sweetness of the strawberries. While it might not have been the best pairing of the night, it was a fun experiment.

Over the course of the evening, Esther popped in and out of the kitchen, clad in an over-size sweatshirt, yoga pants, and Uggs-style boots—exactly what an American teenager her age would have worn. Although she refused to eat, nibbling only a bit, she consented to be dosed with cold medicine and submitted to a maternal hand to her forehead to check her temperature. The interplay was quite amusing to me, as it recalled times with my son, Bryce, when he was sick as a teenager and reminded me that although people may think they are different when they come from different countries, kids are kids and parents are parents. The accents may be different, but family doesn't change.

The Winemaker Recommends: Dover Sole with Lucien Crochet Sancerre Cul de Beaujeu.

Mushroom Salad
with Crottin de Chavignol

Yield: Serves 4 as a first course | Ease of Preparation: Simple | Ease of Sourcing: Moderate
Wine Pairing: Lucien Crochet Sancerre

Laurence Crochet of Domaine Lucien Crochet and I made this dish in her lovely kitchen in Bué. Simple to make, it is a complex blend of clean flavors, the trio of citrus, the earthiness of the mushrooms, the spice of the coriander and pepper, the fruity olive oil, and the high-toned bright grassy notes of the cheese. It was a study in acidity and umami—total genius.

INGREDIENTS

1 tsp. kosher salt

1 tsp. coriander seeds

½ tsp. black peppercorns

½ cup fresh squeezed orange juice

¼ cup fresh squeezed lemon juice

¼ cup fresh squeezed lime juice

1 Tbsp. minced flat leaf parsley

⅓ cup extra-virgin olive oil

12 ounces white button mushrooms

2 pieces Crottin de Chavignol cheese

WHAT YOU'LL NEED

Mortar and pestle

Pastry brush

Cheese plane

TIMING 30 minutes

PROCESS

Rough crush kosher salt, coriander seeds, and black peppercorns with the mortar and pestle.

Whisk orange, lemon, lime juice, and olive oil together with the parsley and the salt and coriander mixture.

Slice the white button mushrooms in ⅛-inch slices. Arrange in a round pattern on a platter. Use the pastry brush to paint dressing on the mushrooms to lightly coat them. They should be moist. A little dressing can seep through to the bottom of the platter, but the mushrooms should not be standing in a sea of dressing. Before serving, use the cheese plane to shave the Crottin over the mushrooms.

Note

Crottin de Chavignol is a small goat cheese from the Sancerrois village of Chavignol. It is available in various stages of aging. When it is fresh, it is moist and soft and weighs approximately 4 ounces; as it ages, it dries out and the flavor becomes more pronounced—it also reduces in size with the loss of moisture. In the case of this salad, it is preferable that you have a firm dry cheese so that it is easier to shave with the cheese plane. Most Crottin de Chavignol you find in the US will be aged sufficiently that they will be dry enough to shave easily. If Crottin de Chavignol is not available, use the firmest goat cheese you can find.

Sole Meunière

Yield: 2–3 people as a main course | Ease of Preparation: Moderate | Ease of Sourcing: Difficult.
Wine Pairing: Lucien Crochet Sancerre Cul de Beaujeu, or White Burgundy

Sole Meunière is one of my all-time favorite dishes. The full name Sole à la Meunière is French for Sole in the style of the miller's wife. Meunière is defined as something that is coated in flour and sautéed in butter—which makes sense, since a miller's wife would definitely have flour. Although it is frequently made with sole fillets, the traditional (and more showy) version uses whole sole. The presentation of a whole head-on sole, sautéed to golden loveliness, drizzled with lemon, parsley, and butter, is classically striking—a definite crowd pleaser.

Sole is a bit of a dichotomy—the flesh is firm and extremely delicate at the same time. It is also hideously expensive, which might explain why despite the simplicity of preparation, it is found more frequently in restaurants than in home kitchens. It is the rare home cook who risks cooking a product this dear, one that requires a certain financial comfort and a clear amount of cooking confidence. I was honored that Laurence Crochet prepared this for me when I joined her for dinner at her home. She is a composed, unfussy cook, supremely calm and friendly, even when working with such a prized ingredient. I suspect some of her aplomb comes from having cooked with her brother-in-law, Gilles Tournadre, chef-proprietor of the excellent Restaurant Gill in Rouen, Normandy, from where Sole Meunière hails, but a good part of it is Laurence's own self possession. It was a perfect choice to pair with the richness of her 2010 Crochet Cul de Beaujeu.

INGREDIENTS

2 one-lb. Dover Sole, cleaned and
    gutted, fin, tails, gills, and skin
    removed
2 cups all-purpose flour
1 Tbsp. kosher salt for breading
6 Tbsp. + 3 Tbsp. unsalted butter
2 Tbsp. lemon juice
2 Tbsp. finely minced parsley
Kosher salt for the butter sauce
Lemon wedges

TIMING

Prep Time: 15 minutes
Cooking Time: 20–25 minutes

WHAT YOU'LL NEED

Skillet large enough for two Dover Sole
    or two smaller skillets large enough
    for one sole each.
Long fish spatula (or any long spatula)
Oval platter large enough for two sole
    or two large oval dishes
Breading container large enough to
    hold 2 cups of flour and one whole
    fish
Tongs
Paper towels
Butter knife
Two serving spoons

PROCESS

Rinse and pat the fish dry.

Mix the flour and kosher salt in the breading container. Coat the fish on both sides with the flour. Pat off any excess flour.

Melt 6 tablespoons butter in the large skillet (or 3 tablespoons in each smaller skillet) over medium heat. When it begins to bubble, place the fish in the pan. Allow it to cook for 6–10 minutes before checking it. Carefully lift the fish with the spatula to see if it is golden brown. If you are satisfied with the color, carefully turn the fish. If not, leave it on that side until it is beautifully golden brown. I know I keep using the word "carefully," but this is a delicate fish and you do not want to break it. Once you have turned it, continue cooking until it is golden brown on the other side and firm to the touch. The flesh should be snowy white and firm all the way through under the crust. This will take between 10 and 15 minutes total time, depending on the thickness of the fish.

Laurence had a neat trick for removing the fine layer of bones on the outside edge of the fish. Once the fish was done, she separated the bones from the fish by using the edge of the spatula to cut a line along the point where the bones meet the fish and dragged the row of small bones away.

Remove the fish to the platter (or the two plates) and keep in a warm place. Fold a couple of paper towels and grasp them with the kitchen tongs. Working quickly, use the paper towels to wipe out the skillet, put the remaining 3 Tbsp. of butter in the skillet, and heat it until it bubbles and turns light golden brown. Turn off the heat and add the lemon juice, parsley, and kosher salt to taste. Stir to combine and pour over the sole.

Garnish the dish with lemon wedges and serve immediately.

Notes

#1. Dover Sole is a flat fish with both eyes on the same side of its body. The side with the eyes has rough dark gray skin, while the underside (the one without the eyes) has white, more delicate skin. In additional to Dover Sole being hideously expensive, it is also somewhat seasonal with best availability between January and March. If you have a dedicated fishmonger, you should be able to find it. Definitely ask them to clean it for you—taking off the skin, fins, tails, gills, and removing the innards. If they only have fillets, go for it. It will still be delicious. If you cannot find sole or quite understandably do not want to spring for this extravagance, try the same preparation with flounder or trout fillets. I would not recommend using trout for the whole fish preparation, since it is not a flatfish and therefore has a completely different shape. If you use fillets rather than the whole fish, adjust your timing accordingly.

#2. As I said, this is a showy dish made even flashier by serving it whole and plating it at the table. To serve it, gently slide a butter knife or serving spoon along the center bone of the fish, sliding the two fillets apart. Use the spoons to lift the fillet up and serve. Repeat with the other top fillet. Carefully lift the skeleton, making every effort to leave the bottom fillets intact. Discard the bones and serve the bottom fillets. Repeat with the second fish, serving half a fish per person. Although there aren't many bones in the main part of the fillet, the edges have a feathery row of small bones. Either cut them away, as Laurence did, or make sure to warn your guests about these.

Crispy Baby Potatoes

Yield: Serves 4–6 as a side dish | Ease of Preparation: Simple | Ease of Sourcing: Simple
Wine Pairing: Match the wine for this dish according to the accompanying main course

Laurence Crochet served this simple dish with Sole à la Meunière. The secret to making it is to be patient. If you cook them very slowly, the potatoes develop a lovely crumbly yet crispy crust.

INGREDIENTS

4 Tbsp. unsalted butter
2 lb. baby potatoes, cleaned and cut in half
Kosher salt to taste
Finely ground black pepper
Optional: Finely minced parsley or chives

WHAT YOU'LL NEED

Large flat-bottomed sauté pan big enough to hold the potatoes in one layer (or two medium skillets)
Metal spatula

TIMING

Prep Time: 5 minutes
Cooking Time: 30 minutes

PROCESS

Melt the butter in the sauté pan over medium heat. Reduce the heat to low and place the potatoes cut side down on the pan. Cook very slowly until the potatoes are deep golden brown. Once they are beautifully browned, turn them over and cook the other side. The extremely slow cooking allows the butter and heat to sink into the surface. If the heat is too high, it makes the surface of the potatoes too rigid and they brown too fast. (Laurence took almost 30 minutes to cook her baby potatoes.) Once the potatoes are done, add salt, pepper, and optional minced herbs if desired.

Strawberries Marinated
in Red Wine

Yield: 4–6 servings | Ease of Preparation: Simple | Ease of Sourcing: Simple when strawberries are in season.
Wine Pairing: Rosé d'Anjou or Demi-sec or Doux Rosé Champagne

What to serve for dessert? It's a dilemma for many people when they entertain. You want to serve something, but frequently by the end of a meal people are too full to do it justice and all the work you have put into your lovely dessert goes to waste. Laurence Crochet's Red Wine-Marinated Strawberries are a simple, elegant, and delicious solution.

INGREDIENTS

1½ lbs. ripe strawberries, hulls
    removed, cut in bite-size pieces
1 cup reasonably priced Pinot Noir or
    Beaujolais
2 Tbsp. granulated sugar

WHAT YOU'LL NEED

Paring knife
Bowl for strawberries
Small bowl
Whisk or fork
Rubber spatula or large spoon

TIMING

Prep Time: 15 minutes
Marinating Time: 1 hour

PROCESS

Rinse the strawberries. Remove the hulls, cut the strawberries in halves or quarters, and place them in the bowl.

Using a whisk or fork, stir the red wine and granulated sugar until the sugar dissolves.

Pour the wine mixture over the strawberries and mix to coat them. Marinate for at least an hour, stirring periodically to rotate the strawberries.

Note

Strawberries in season are amazing! Out of season, they are like tomatoes—totally lacking in flavor. I recommend eating your fill during strawberry season and moving on when the season is past. This dish is also delicious with blackberries, mulberries, and black raspberries. I do not like it nearly as much with red raspberries. I find the tartness of red raspberries accentuates the acidity of the wine.

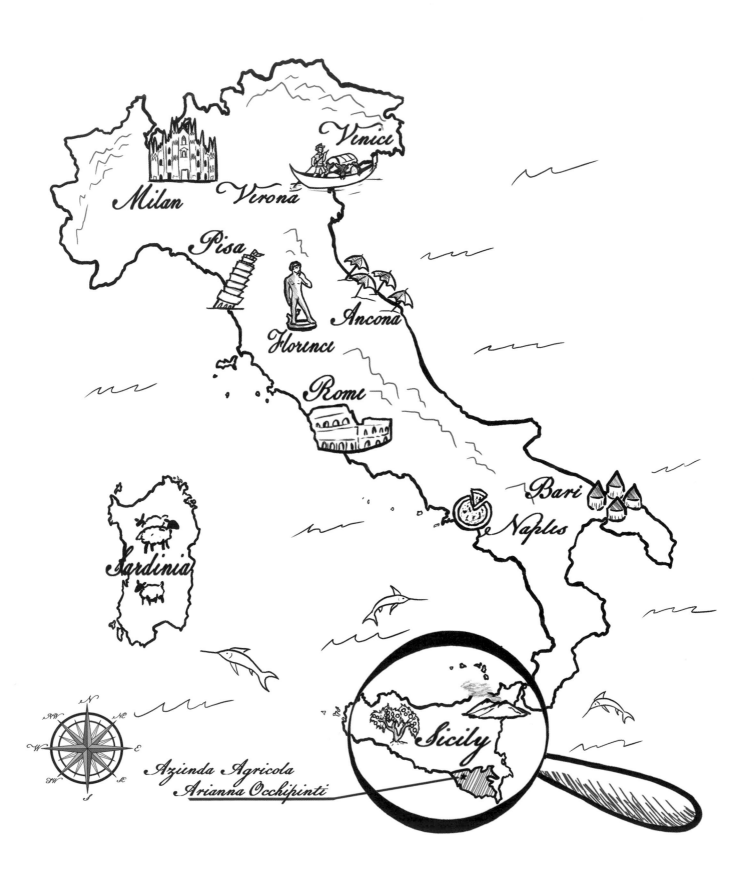

Milan

Verona

Vinice

Pisa

Florenci

Ancona

Rome

Bari

Naples

Sardinia

Sicily

Azinda Agricola
Arianna Occhipinti

"A Bellwether Named Paco"
A Visit with Arianna Occhipinti
Vittoria, Sicily, Italy

Italy's largest region, Sicily is earthy and mysterious—impacted by ancient civilizations and maritime traditions—its very essence defined by its agricultural heritage—oranges, olives, and grapes. It feels inaccurate to describe it as isolated. Its history teems with a diverse collection of settlers and invaders—Greeks, Arabs, Phoenicians, Romans, and Normans—a veritable murderer's row of conquerors. And yet, it is this conglomeration of influences that differentiates Sicilians from their ostensible countrymen. They are clearly Sicilian first and Italian second, and their culture reflects this—perhaps more so than any other region in Italy, a country that prides itself on the varied characteristics of the denizens of its individual regions. Nowhere was this more evident to me than when I visited Arianna Occhipinti, the world-renowned winemaker from Vittoria in the Iblean foothills near Ragusa in southeastern Sicily.

Arianna is in her early thirties. A media phenom, she has received multiple rave reviews from the *New York Times* and, despite her young age, is widely recognized to be on the

Arianna Occhipinti
Photo credit: Arianna Occhipinti

forefront of the natural wine movement. Her autobiographical book, *Natural Woman,* describes her path to the present.

Even though I had met her several times at tastings in New York and had tasted her wines many times over the last several years, I was still intrigued at the complex combination of incredibly serious, contemplative farmer and winemaker and the joyful young woman who reveled in the flowers gracing the field near her vines—one who picked plums straight from the tree, handing some down for me to taste, her foot still wedged in the crook of the tree, before jumping down to lead me through her vineyards, discussing soil types, climate, and the viticultural practices needed to produce balanced wines with little or no chemical intervention.

Some people become winemakers because it is the family business. Some come to it later in life, their passion for winemaking propelling them to a second career. Arianna's path began quite early for someone who was not raised by winemaker parents. Although she was born in Marsala on the western coast of Sicily, she was raised in Vittoria, a town of 63,000 people about seventeen miles from Ragusa, the regional capital. At the age of seventeen, her uncle Giusto Occhipinti, co-owner of COS, the well-respected biodynamic winery in Vittoria, asked her if she would like to help pour wine at his stand at Vinitaly, the annual wine fair in Verona. Arianna jumped at the chance—although she does admit that her motives were driven as much by the opportunity to skip four days of school as by helping Giusto, whom she adored. Upon returning from Verona, she worked two harvests at COS, and when the time came to choose a course of study after high school, she enrolled at the Oenology School in Milan with her Uncle Giusto's encouragement.

With the example of Giusto at COS, Arianna was already conversant with organic and biodynamic winemaking, and the lessons she had learned from him contrasted sharply with the "technical winemaking" she was being taught at school. Those differences troubled her. She felt they were being instructed to follow broad rules that did not take individual vineyard, soil, and vine needs into consideration—decisions made from afar by oenologists unfamiliar with the particularities of each location. On weekend breaks, she visited wineries on the forefront of natural winemaking (Foradori, Radikon, Rinaldi, and Gravner, to name a few). What she saw there cemented what she had already seen at COS and set her on her course to make artisanal, natural wines.

Arianna returned home in 2003 and began farming a two-acre plot owned by her parents in the Fossa di Lupo contrada of Vittoria. She made her first wine in 2004 at the age of 21. That first winter, with her wines quietly aging in three barrels, she got bored and went to London to work in restaurants for a change of scenery. This was yet another

form of education, seeing things from the sommelier's perspective. (Ironically, one of the restaurants where she worked is currently a customer of hers, although she has never mentioned that to them.) In subsequent years, she acquired another twenty-two acres from her parents and rented five acres of fifty-five-year-old vineyards from a neighbor.

Although she is well known in the realm of natural winemaking, over the course of her twelve-year career Arianna has come to the realization that it is not natural winemaking that drives her. Rather, she is dedicated to indigenous Sicilian grape varieties (Frappato, Nero d'Avola, Albanello, and Zibibbo) and her own plots of land. As she told me, what is important are "these varieties, with this soil."

Five years ago, Arianna purchased an old farm with seventeen acres of abandoned vineyards. She replanted the vineyards using *Massale Selection* (see Wine Terms, page 473). She built a new winery and cellar in 2012.

On a tour of her new winery, she makes a point of stopping in front of a subterranean white limestone wall, resting her hand on it. "This is our treasure," she says. "The white salt-rich rock comes from the sea and keeps moisture in the soil." The idea of terroir-driven wines is hardly new, but it is this concept that inspires her. Does she use natural techniques to arrive at this? Yes. Is she making certified organic wines? Yes, but she doesn't do it to make natural or organic wines; she does it to make the best wines from *her* plot of land, from *her* terroir.

Located between mountains and sun, it is the elevation of the mountains and the cooling winds (with nighttime and daytime temperature differences of as much as 35 degrees) that enables the winemakers of Vittoria to produce wines that are fresh and elegant. While the effects of the wind combined with incredibly low annual-rainfall totals (sometimes as low as sixteen inches) make treatment for mold and insects less important, the almost drought-like conditions mandate extremely careful soil management. Frequent manual working of the soil around the base of the vines forces the roots to grow down into the ground instead of growing along the surface of the vineyard. The deeper the roots go, the fresher, more complex are the wines. Working the soil also helps minimize water evaporation, as does the spontaneous vegetation of Mediterranean plants that help to maintain soil humidity. Arianna plants fava beans between rows of vines and plows them under when they flower. This practice, known as *sovescio* or green manure, is a natural form of vegetable-based fertilization and enables her to eschew traditional animal-based fertilizers.

Arianna is extremely happy with the new winery, allowing that it makes it much easier to produce clean wines. While much of the modern winery is underground, the offices, tasting room, and the winery kitchen are above ground and partially constructed from

Old limestone palmento in Arianna's winery.

an old limestone palmento purchased with the property. The winery is designed to be sustainable, with solar panels for electricity and heating provided by burning olive pits.

Wines of Sicily

Winemaking in Sicily dates back to the Greek settlement of the island in the 8th century BC, and a detailed history of viticulture in Sicily and all of its ebbs and flows could fill a chapter itself, if not a book.

In the 19th and most of the 20th century, the focus was on producing bulk wine to be shipped to mainland Italy rather than on the quality of the wines that were made. Recently, however, there has been added emphasis on improving the caliber of the wines, and according to *The Oxford*

Palmento Once found on almost every farmholding in Sicily, *palmenti* are the precursors to modern wineries—with rooms for bringing in the grapes, foot treading the grapes, and storing the wines—all equipped with passages to move the grapes and then the wine from one area to the next by use of gravity. Currently illegal for use in the winemaking process because of sanitary concerns, *palmenti* represent the history of winemaking in Sicily. Arianna's restoration of her *palmento* evidences her commitment to preserving local traditions and her respect for her region.

Companion to Wine, in 2013 Sicily was the second largest Italian wine-producing region (after the Veneto), with considerable amelioration in quality.

Sicily is a huge island, and its climate is quite varied, with conditions ranging from the almost Alpine Mt. Etna with its high elevation and volcanic soils to the subtropical Pantelleria. Depending on the location, high elevation or strong winds can be very helpful to cool the grapes and discourage pests and mold. Major DOCs in Sicily include:

Sicilia DOC: Raised to DOC status in 2011 with very few production regulations or requirements that the wines be bottled in the region of origin of the grapes. DOC Sicilia can be made from fifteen different white wine grapes of which Grillo, Catarratto, and Chardonnay are most common and sixteen different red wine grapes, the most common being Nero d'Avola, Frappato, and Perricone. There are no minimum aging requirements for Sicilia DOC wines.

Terre Siciliane IGT: Established in 2011, IGT Terre Siciliane encompasses the whole island of Sicily and can be made from twenty-four white grapes and twenty-two red grapes. There are no minimum aging requirements for Terre Siciliane IGT. Grape yields for Terre Siciliane wines are higher than for Sicilia DOC, and the minimum alcohol by volume is lower.

Etna Rosso and Etna Bianco: Wines from the area surrounding Mt. Etna are some of the most interesting wines coming from Sicily. Reds and rosés from Nerello Mascalese, Nerello Cappuccio, and Nocera, and whites from Carricante are garnering a loyal following. There is a considerable amount of investment in the region, and the quality levels can be extremely high.

Cerasuolo di Vittoria DOCG: Sicily's only DOCG is produced in the region surrounding the southern Sicilian town of Vittoria from equal parts Frappato and Nero d'Avola. Arianna's wines and those of her uncle Giusto's COS are recognized as quality leaders in the DOCG.

Arianna's Wines

Arianna produces six wines from her own property under the Arianna Occhipinti label and three Tami wines from a joint venture with a good friend. With the exception of Grotte Alte, her Cerasuolo di Vittoria DOCG, Arianna's wines are all labeled Terre Siciliane IGT. Despite the fact that her yields are extremely low (which often results in increased ripeness), Arianna's emphasis on natural agriculture produces lower alcohol wines with levels below the minimum requirement for Sicilia DOC. Additionally, her SP68 Rosso uses 70 percent Frappato and 30 percent Nero d'Avola instead of the 50 percent each necessary to allow the use of the Cerasuolo di Vittoria DOCG designation.

Azienda Agricola Arianna Occhipinti

SP68 Bianco, Terre Siciliane IGT; and SP68 Rosso, Terre Siciliane IGT: Arianna has two wines that she named SP68 for the road that passes in front of her property, Stradale Provinciale 68. These wines are fermented and aged in cement tanks and are her most forward, early drinking wines. The white is made from 60 percent Moscato d'Alessandria (a.k.a. Zibibbo) and 40 percent Albanello. The red is made from 70 percent Frappato and 30 percent Nero d'Avola.

Il Frappato, Terre Siciliane IGT: This wine is produced from 40-year-old Frappato vines grown on red sand and chalk soils with deep limestone subsoils. It is a wine with peasant origins, expressive of the land where it is grown and combining elegance with rustic, bitter, and sanguineous notes.

Siccagno, Terre Siciliane IGT: Siccagno is produced from thirty-five-year-old Nero d'Avola vines grown on the same kind of soils as the Frappato (*Siccagna* means Nero d'Avola in the local dialect). Siccagno is amazingly fresh and elegant for a grape that can sometimes be stewed in its flavor profile. It is red-fruited and noble but with a deep side that is dark and almost brooding.

Grotte Alte, Cerasuolo di Vittoria DOCG: Named Grotte Alte for the limestone ridge upon which the town of Vittoria is built, this is Arianna's Cerasuolo di Vittoria DOCG (the only DOCG in Sicily). It is a fifty-fifty blend of Nero d'Avola and Frappato di Vittoria from forty-year-old vineyards. It is fermented in concrete and aged thirty months in large, old, Slovonian oak barrels. It is elegant and benefits from the combination of the two indigenous grapes.

Passo Nero, Passito Terre Siciliane IGT: Made from 100 percent Nero d'Avola from fifteen-year-old vines, this Passito is a bit of an experiment. Arianna was curious to track the evolution of the Nero d'Avola grape when it was allowed to dry and shrivel. The Passo Nero is a moderately dry version of a Passito (a wine made from grapes allowed to dry, either on the vine or in drying racks in the winery before being pressed, with the resulting juice vinified to the desired sweetness level).

Grappa di Frappato: Although she doesn't make it herself, Arianna sends the pressed skins and seeds from her grapes to a local distiller to make her grappa.

Tami

Tami is both a retail wine store in Siracusa owned by Arianna and her friend Francesco and a line of natural wines that she produces with grapes from a friend's vineyard. She oversees not only the vineyards, but the winemaking, as well. Her intent with Tami is to produce quaffable, natural terroir-driven wines in order to introduce good affordable natural Sicilian wines to a younger, less well-heeled audience. She produces one Tami white made from the Grillo grape and two Tami reds, a Frappato and a Nero d'Avola.

Culture and Foods of Sicily

Located in the central Mediterranean Sea separated from the boot-shaped Italian peninsula by a mere two-mile span at the Strait of Messina, the island of Sicily with its five million people boasts the fourth largest population of any region in Italy. Its most prominent landmark is Mt. Etna, the striking peak with a continuous trail of smoke billowing from its crest, the tallest active volcano in Europe. Triangular in shape, Sicily covers 9,927 square miles of hilly terrain with the highest mountains on the northern side of the island and the slightly lower elevation Iblean mountain range to the south. A typically Mediterranean climate with hot, dry summers and mild moist winters makes this a prime location for agriculture.

Mount Etna

The history of Sicily, evidenced by ruins of its many colonizing civilizations, is diverse, rich, and fascinating—the natural landscape an appropriate backdrop for said ruins. Picturesque fishing villages dot the coastlines, their harbors and ports home to mariners for countless years. The pristine clear blue-green waters lap beaches, some sandy, others pebbly, while in still other locales the sea crashes against rocky outcrops or limestone cliffs with breathtaking formations carved by countless waves. Farther inland, mountains, plateaux, and rivers define the terrain and local culture. Sicily is varied, both scenically and culturally. A person could easily spend a few months exploring and still feel as if they had only begun to scratch the surface of Sicily.

Inherent to this culture is the food of Sicily. Many people are familiar with some of Sicily's more famous dishes: *Arancini* (fried rice balls), *Pasta con le Sarde* (pasta with sardines), *Pasta alla Norma* (pasta with eggplant and ricotta salata), *Caponata* (sweet-and-sour eggplant paste), Grilled Tuna and Swordfish, *Bottarga* (dried fish roe), Pistachio Gelato (best made with pistachios from Bronte near Mt. Etna), and *Cannoli* (pastry tubes stuffed with sweetened ricotta cheese studded with chocolate bits or pistachios), to name just a sampling.

Foods of Ragusa

The foods from Arianna's home region of Ragusa are less sea-focused and more land-based. Even though the town of Ragusa is only thirteen miles from the sea, cattle breeding and farming play major roles in the local economy. Thus, in addition to seafood, meat, cheese, and vegetables figure prominently in the cuisine of the region; and Ragusa's rich heritage is evidenced by the number of Designated Products to which it lays claim, more than any other region of Sicily, a number of them Slow Food Presidia.

Slow Food Presidia in Ragusa

Ispica Sesame: Small, strongly flavored sesame seeds.

Giarratana Onions: Large onions (weighing between one and five pounds) with a slightly squashed appearance, brown skin, and white flesh.

Modicana Cows: Pasture-raised from nearby Modica, these dark red cattle are known for producing high-quality beef and excellent milk (used in the production of Ragusano DOP cheese).

Typical Specialties of Ragusa

As a whole, the region is well known for olives, grapes, citrus fruits, wheat, Iblean honey, and a variety of vegetables.

Meats

While beef is very common in the region, white meats—pork, chicken, and rabbit—are also quite popular in local cuisine, with pork showing up in the form of aspics, sausages, and stuffed chops. I had a delicious mixed grill for dinner at a great local trattoria in Ragusa featuring both pork and beef.

Rabbit Pattuisa: Braised rabbit, usually with tomatoes and olives.

Turcinuna: Lamb intestines baked in a casserole.

L'Abbuttanata: Leg of lamb stuffed with minced meat, chopped salami, boiled eggs, and potatoes.

Stuffed Breads/Pastries

There are many versions of breads and round or crescent pies filled with meats in Ragusa. The fact that there are quite a few different names for similar dishes can be a bit confusing.

Pastieri/Mpanate/Scacce/Teste di Turco

I Pastieri: Small round pastries filled with beef and peas. The dough is folded in pleat-like fashion, leaving a small opening at the top.

Mpanate di Agnello: (*Mpanate ri Agnieddu* in the local dialect. *Mpanare* means to wrap, fold, or coat in bread.) Meat pies stuffed with lamb, garlic, parsley, salt, and olive oil (and sometimes sundried tomatoes). They are a traditional Easter dish in Ragusa.

Scaccia: (Plural: Scacce) Made from dough that has already risen twice and thus does not rise again when it is baked, Scaccia is most frequently a flat bread that is topped with a number of different things—eggplant, cauliflower, cheese, sausages, ricotta, onions, and tomato sauce—before being folded over on itself to form a packet. It is also seen in Ragusa simply smeared with tomato sauce and sprinkled with Caciocavallo cheese. It is then folded multiple times to form a lasagne-like loaf and baked. In either form, it is an important street food in Ragusa.

Tommasini: (Sometimes also called *Teste di Turco,* although there is also a sweet pastry of the same name.) These small ricotta cheese and sausage pastries are shaped like turbans—thus the name "Heads of the Turk."

Pasta

Though one can find many of the standard Sicilian pastas like Pasta alla Norma and Pasta con le Sarde, Ravioli with Pork Sauce, and Ricotta-stuffed Ravioli in Ragusa, seasonal vegetable pastas like *Pasta Ca Tinnirumi*, a midsummer dish of pasta featuring green zucchini leaves in broth, are very popular in Ragusa.

Cheeses

Ragusano DOP: A firm stretched curd cow's milk cheese made from the milk of Modicana cattle raised solely on fresh grass or hay in the provinces of Ragusa and Siracusa.

Caciocavallo: Whole milk firm cow's milk cheese.

Provola: Made from whole cow's milk, Provola is usually formed into a bulb, and then suspended from a ribbon or string for aging. This gives it a pear shape, with each bulb weighing two pounds or less. In general, the more mature the Provola, the deeper yellow its rind.

Ricotta Iblea in Cavagna: Cow's milk ricotta stored in *cavagna* (conical tubes made from cane).

Desserts

Cassateddi: A ricotta and cinnamon cake.

Pasta Reale or Martovana: Almond paste sweets in the form of various fruits.

Bianco Mangiare: A milk and almond pudding dating back to the Middle Ages.

Citrus Cakes: Cakes made with all of Sicily's famed citrus fruits—oranges, blood oranges, and mandarins.

Mucatoli: S-shaped cookies filled with figs and walnuts, although other dried fruits and nuts can also be used.

Mustata and Mustaccioli of Vin Cotto: Cookies and sweetened breads made with *Vin Cotto*. Literally "cooked wine," Vin Cotto is grape must boiled down with orange peels to form a sweet syrup.

Almond Biscuits

Cannoli

Iblean Honey: Produced in a very small area of Sicily, Hyblaean wildflower honey has been famous since ancient times. The local flora (local flowers, thyme, and carob trees) greatly influences the flavors. Iblean honey is dark-colored with good acidity.

Monte Iblei Olive Oil: Made from the Tonda Iblea variety of olive.

She Doesn't Just Make Wine!

Olive Oils: Even though the majority of her time is spent with her vines, Arianna is also extremely well known for her excellent organic olive oils. She produces two single cultivar oils. (A cultivar is a type of olive, just as a variety is a type of grape.)

Gheta is produced from the Nocellara del Belice olive trees owned by her grandmother Margherita (whom she called Gheta) on family property in the Valle del Belice in western Sicily.

Panterei is made from Tonda Iblea olives from Chiaramonte Gulfi.

In addition to her vineyards and olive groves, the property she purchased in 2012 included an old orange grove, and Arianna has an extensive garden at her house. During the summer, she plants tomatoes, green beans, eggplant, zucchini, mint, and basil. She is growing tumminia, an ancient Sicilian variety of durum wheat. Also known as marzuolo because it is planted in March, tummunia has a short growing season and is quite resistant to drought. It is used in fresh pastas and to make the famed Black Bread of Castelvetrano (itself a Slow Food Presidium). She also has her own beehives that yield about fifty kilos of honey each year.

Pasta with Pesto Trapanese

As in much of Italy, spontaneous rosemary and oregano abound. What food she does not grow herself, she tries to purchase at organic markets or from friends.

When Jeff and I arrived at Arianna's house that afternoon in July, we found her working on the irrigation lines for her orange groves. Not surprisingly, with all that she does, she rarely has any down time. She enjoys entertaining, although with her work schedule she is not able to do so as much as she would like these days. She is "super focused" on finishing her winery building. After that is accomplished, she will tackle the house attached to the winery. She already has a great outdoor barbecue in place. She loves to cook, however, and when she does entertain, she makes "pure food" using recipes she learned from her mother, who, according to Arianna (and many others), is a great cook.

Arianna is an intensely enthusiastic person. Despite her packed schedule, she threw herself fully into our visit, giving us a tour of the vineyards and winery before leading the way to the fantastic new kitchen in the palmento section of the winery. She immediately put me to work cleaning fresh sardines for *Sarde a Linguato,* and while I had not expected to be gutting and deboning fresh fish by hand (and I do mean by hand—they were too small to use a knife), I was perfectly content to oblige. Once done with the sardines, we munched on Noto almonds and Pecorino Pepato (a local black pepper-studded sheep milk cheese) and sipped chilled SP68 Bianco while continuing to cook—the citrus and floral notes of the wine a superb foil to the sharp spicy cheese and the nutty almonds.

Our lunch was a perfect example of how her food culture is just an extension of her philosophy as a whole, featuring local food from her region—terroir-based cuisine, if you will. Again, I know the word terroir is bandied about quite frequently nowadays, but Arianna defines it. We started with *Pasta with Pesto Trapanese* (made with small amounts of tomato and basil, Noto almonds instead of pine nuts, and Pecorino Pepato in place of the Parmigiano Reggiano you would find in northern Italy), before moving on to the *Sarde a Linguata,* breaded and fried sardines from the Mediterranean (her winery is only twelve miles from the sea) accompanied by a room temperature salad of her own green beans with baby potatoes and red onions dressed with apple cider vinegar, her own olive oil, wild oregano from her garden, and sea salt from Trapani. We switched to SP68 Rosso with the sardines and salad.

While dining, we continued to discuss the way she approaches food and wine. Although we were having wine at lunch, entertaining guests is really the only time she drinks. She lives alone and works practically nonstop, so she prefers to drink only if others are with her. During harvest, she has ten pickers in addition to four interns and her own employees who supervise the pickers. She has two employees in the cellar with

her. Everyone used to eat together during harvest at umbrella-shaded tables in the garden, but as they have gotten busier, the pickers stay in the vineyards for lunch and her employees cook and eat as they have time. At the end of harvest, they have a big lunch together to celebrate.

Arianna Occhipinti is educated and well traveled, and yet there is an earthy side to her, one that resonates with an affinity for her land, and it is this affinity that rules her decisions. In spite of all of the technology available to her, it is the land and the rhythm of the seasons in this particular part of Sicily that guide her. She told me that although there are many technical ways of determining when to harvest, she holds to the lessons from the old folks of the region who remind one that grapes are a fall fruit—a harvest of autumn's bounty. She employs common sense practices gleaned from observing neighbors with many years of experience. She may be a young phenom but she takes advice from those with more seasoning, and as visionary as she might be, there is a common sense side to her personality—one that pays attention to the patterns and cycles of the land she loves (she never begins harvest before September 22, looks for a bit of rain in early September to revitalize her wines after the heat and lack of precipitation during the summer months, and notes that her older vineyards are not as affected by drought because the roots are very deep), employing traditions that work, and only changing things to improve the wine, not just for the sake of modernization.

Arianna does not adhere to a set-in-stone harvest date, dictated by faraway oenologists, nor to complicated measurements of sugar content in the grapes—her harvest bellwether comes in the form of a yellow Labrador Retriever named Paco. When Paco begins eating the grapes off the vines, everyone knows the grapes are ready and harvest starts. Simple—naturally.

The Winemaker Recommends: Arianna recommends serving sardines with Nero d'Avola. She believes they have a real affinity for each other. When we had lunch together, she served fried sardines with SP68 Rosso, which is 50 percent Nero d'Avola.

Fried Sardines
Sarde a Linguata

Yield: 4–6 appetizer servings
Ease of Sourcing: Difficult/Extremely Difficult (depending on your access to a good fishmonger)
Ease of Preparation: Difficult if you clean the sardines yourself.
Simple if you purchase them already cleaned.
Wine Pairing: Occhipinti SP68 Rosso or Occhipinti Siccagno Nero d'Avola

Had you asked me before my visit with Arianna Occhipinti if I expected to be cleaning a bunch of fresh sardines by hand, I would have said no. Likewise, I would not have expected to pair those sardines with a full-bodied red wine. In both instances, I would have been wrong, and that's why cooking with winemakers is so important to me. You learn the unexpected, and the surprises are at the very least educational (as in the case of cleaning fresh sardines so tiny that you could not use a knife, just your fingers) and, in the case of pairing Nero d'Avola with crunchy, salty fried sardines, delicious, as well! Arianna believes that sardines have a natural affinity with Nero d'Avola because they share the same salty, maritime flavors. This is a prime example of one of my favorite pairing tips—listen to the winemaker, they know best what food goes with their wine.

INGREDIENTS

2 lbs. fresh sardines (12–18 depending
on the size of the fish), gutted, head,
fins, and bones removed
1½ cup white wine vinegar
2 cups finely ground durum wheat
semolina flour, preferably labeled
Rimacinata (see notes)
1 tsp. kosher salt
3–4 cups extra-virgin oil
Maldon or medium sea salt (Arianna
used sea salt from the nearby
Trapani Salt Ponds)
2 lemons, quartered

TIMING

Sardine cleaning time (if necessary):
30–45 minutes
Soaking Time: 10 minutes
Frying Time: 5–10 minutes

WHAT YOU'LL NEED

Dish large enough to hold the sardines
in a single or double layer
Medium paper or gallon plastic bag
Wok, 3-inch-deep frying pan, or
electric fryer
Spider or slotted spoon
Paper towel-lined platter

Equipment to Clean Sardines
(if necessary):

Sharp knife
Cutting board
Running water
Paper towels

PROCESS

Hopefully, your fishmonger will clean your sardines for you. (Ask them to clean, gut, and remove the head, bones, and fins.) If not, you will need a sharp knife, cutting board, paper towels, and running water.

Cleaning Sardines:

If your sardines are whole, you must first remove the head. If it is small, you can just twist it off. Larger fish will require that you cut it off. Once that is done, run your knife down the belly of the fish and remove the guts. Rinse the fish well. Find the fin on the back of the fish and insert your knife between the backbone and the bottom edge of the fin and cut about ¼ to ½ way up. Once you have done this, grab the fin and pull toward the head end of the sardine. The fin and small deeper bones will come out easily, leaving a small slit along the backbone of the fish.

Turn the fish on its back and slide the tip of your knife under the top of the spine and along the bones on both sides of the spine, separating the flesh of the fish from the bones. Be careful doing this—you are trying to remove the bones and leave the flesh intact. Once you have the separation started, grasp the bones between your thumb and forefinger on one hand and slide the tip of your forefinger on the other hand between bones and flesh. Slowly pull while continuing to slide your finger along the fish to separate the flesh from bone. Use your knife to trim away any remaining bones and clean up the shape of the fish. It may take a bit of time to get the hang of this, but once you get it, it moves pretty quickly.

Marinating and Frying the Sardines:

Place the cleaned sardines in your dish. Once all the sardines are cleaned and in the dish, add enough vinegar to just cover the sardines. (You may not need to use all of the vinegar.) Let them marinate for 10 minutes (no more, or the vinegar will overpower the dish).

Put 2 cups of flour and salt in the bag. Shake to combine.

Add enough olive oil to your frying vessel until the level is 1½ inches deep. You may not need to use all of your oil. Make sure you leave at least a 1½ inch space at the top of your pan so that the oil does not bubble over during the frying process.

After the sardines have marinated 8 minutes, begin heating the oil over medium-high heat. If you have an electric fryer, set the temperature to 350° F. If you don't have a fryer, drop a bit of flour in the oil to test the temperature. (When the flour sizzles but does not immediately burn, it is perfect for frying. If it doesn't sizzle, keep heating. If it burns the flour, turn the heat down a bit.)

After 10 minutes, remove the sardines from the vinegar and shake off any excess liquid. Add the sardines to the bag with the flour and salt. Shake well to coat the sardines.

When the oil has reached the correct temperature, remove the sardines from the bag. Pat them to remove any excess flour and place them in the heated oil. Do not crowd your pan to the extent that the oil is in danger of bubbling over. You may need to fry in several batches. Use your spider to turn the sardines over. Fry until golden brown (approximately 3–4 minutes). Remove the sardines to the paper towel-covered platter and sprinkle with a little medium grain sea salt—preferably from Trapani on the western coast of Sicily.

Serve with lemon wedges.

Notes

#1. The sardines at Arianna's house were quite small—the size of anchovies. They were incredibly fresh, having come straight from the local fish market that morning. Because of their size, they were quite easy to clean. Ideally, we would all live within a couple of hours of a sea teeming with sardines. That way, fresh sardines would be readily available.

Unfortunately, that is not the case for most of us. If you live in an area with a good fish market, you will likely be able to get fresh sardines. In Washington DC, we have access to a large variety of seafood. I checked with Blacksalt, my local fishmonger, and they have fresh sardines from Portugal available pretty much year-round, as does the Organic Butcher in McLean, Virginia. Check with your local fishmonger or butcher. They may have them, as well. Call ahead to make sure they have them, as they sell out quickly. With sizes starting at around 3 ounces, sardines from Portugal are larger and, unfortunately, harder to clean. Ask your fishmonger to clean, gut, and debone them for you. They may charge you a fee, but, believe me, it is totally worth it. As a last resort, if there is a good fish/seafood restaurant in your town, ask them if they can get fresh sardines and see if they will order some for you. You would be surprised how many restaurants are willing to do this. Of course, it helps if you are already a regular customer. You will likely have to clean these sardines yourself. If you cannot find sardines, but can find fresh anchovies, they are a good substitute.

#2. Semolina is high-gluten flour made from the endosperm of hard durum wheat. It is traditionally used to make pasta but when combined with other flours can also be used to make delicious bread. Depending on the intended use, it can be coarse or fine ground. *Rimacinata* is the Italian term for semolina flour that has been milled an additional time to produce an extremely fine flour. Arianna uses *Rimacinata* semolina flour to bread her sardines because she likes the fine yet crunchy texture it produces. *Rimacinata* is available in Italian and gourmet specialty markets or online—I found mine at the Italian Store in Arlington, Virginia, for $3.99 for a one-kilo (2.2 lb.) bag. Amazon sells Caputo brand *Rimacinata*. If you can't find it, substitute all-purpose flour.

Pesto Trapanese
Trapani-style Pesto

Yield: 2 cups of pesto, enough to serve 6 as a first course | Ease of Preparation: Simple | Ease of Sourcing: Simple
Wine Pairing: SP68 Terre Siciliane Bianco, Tami Grillo, or a Sicilian White Wine

Arianna Occhipinti's mother is from Marsala, just south of Trapani on the western shore of Sicily. Her mother's recipe for Pesto Trapanese calls for mint and a larger proportion of almonds to basil than the traditional basil/pine nut proportion in Pesto Genovese. The use of mint lends a bright note, while the higher almond to basil ratio renders it nuttier and more subtle than what many of us are used to. I really like this combination, as I sometimes find the green pungency of the basil in traditional pesto to be a bit overpowering, especially when paired with wine. The addition of the sharper Pecorino Pepato adds a note of interest—balancing the creaminess of the almonds with the tang of peppery raw sheep's milk cheese.

INGREDIENTS

½ cup basil

½ cup mint

2 large cloves garlic

6 cherry or grape tomatoes cut in half
(or one small tomato, quartered)

¾ cup blanched almonds, unsalted

¾ cup grated Pecorino Pepato + ½ cup
reserved

¾ cup high quality extra-virgin olive oil

½ Tbsp. kosher salt

¼ tsp. coarse ground black pepper

WHAT YOU'LL NEED

Food processor
Cheese grater
Rubber spatula

TIMING

15 minutes

PROCESS

Process basil, mint, garlic, and tomatoes in the food processor. Scrape down the sides of the processor bowl. Add almonds and process until they are the size of a grain of rice, scraping periodically. Add ¾ cup Pecorino Pepato and process lightly. With the processor running, add the olive oil. Taste. Add salt and black pepper.

Notes

#1. Pecorino Pepato is a Sicilian Pecorino (sheep's milk cheese) studded with whole black peppercorns. If you do not have Pecorino Pepato, use Pecorino Romano and add extra black pepper.

#2. Arianna and I blanched and peeled our almonds. You may certainly do this, but blanched almonds are easy enough to find if you wish to go that route.

Green Beans, Baby Potatoes, and Red Onion Salad

Yield: Serves 4 | Ease of Preparation: Simple | Ease of Sourcing: Simple
Wine Pairing: Occhipinti SP68 Rosso, Frappato, or a light fruity red wine

I loved all of the food Arianna and I prepared. Each dish was a great example of Wine Table cooking—very few yet perfect ingredients prepared simply and served in a warm casual setting with good conversation and a great glass of wine. During summer months, one trip to the farmer's market will arm you with the produce needed to make this delicious salad.

Between six to eight full-time employees (including Karina and Guillaume) run the property throughout the year. During harvest, this number swells to twenty-five or thirty, some of whom (like me) are housed in the *gîte*, some of whom live on the property in a yurt—a semipermanent tent structure—while still others live in Miramas.

Purchased in 2004 with the help of relatives, the property (then known as Château de Sulauze) was not making the caliber of wines to which Guillaume and Karina aspired. Upon acquisition of the property, they immediately stopped all use of chemicals. By 2006, they began the push toward organic certification, with full certification coming in 2008. Early on, they had realized that all of the wines that they liked were biodynamic, and they decided to make biodynamic wines (see Wine Terms, page 472). As difficult as it was to change winery practices, changing the reputation of Château de Sulauze was even more challenging. They made the decision to drop the word "Château" from the name and use the word Domaine instead—feeling that this engendered a sense of artisanality. The work in the fields and winery, the movement to organics and biodynamics, and their association with other like-minded winemakers who opened avenues for them to sell their wine have paid off, and they are in the enviable position of being able to sell all the wine that they make. Positive reviews in the wine press have helped their cause. In fact, at this point, demand for their wines outstrips production, with 70 percent of their wines sold for export and 30 percent for domestic consumption in France.

Their commitment to organics and considerate treatment of the earth extends to their food culture and their day-to-day behavior. When I visited Karina and Guillaume, they were already quite self-sufficient with regards to food for the Domaine, but in the last couple of years they have become almost completely autonomous. In addition to the grapes for wine, grain for beer and bread, and olives, they have an extensive organic kitchen garden, and an orchard with fruit and almond trees. Every scrap produced from cooking serves as feed for the colorful brood of chickens that roam freely about the property, and the bounty of eggs is quickly incorporated into the cakes and desserts that Karina whips out for the family and the harvesters. Although they raise their own chickens, cattle, pigs, and sheep, Karina barters wine for meat with her next-door neighbor, who raises Taureau de Camargue, the famed regional cattle. The very few things not grown on the property are purchased from a local organic co-op.

Not content with simply farming organically, eating responsibly, and respecting the land and the environment themselves, Karina and Guillaume have recently established a WWOOFing program at Domaine de Sulauze. WWOOF stands for World Wide Opportunities on Organic Farms and is a network of national organizations that coordinates homestay opportunities on organic farms throughout the world in an effort to teach people about Permaculture, the practice of sustainable farming, and ecosystems.

I see a lot of people in my travels and in my daily life in the Washington, DC area. Some people talk a good game about being local, seasonal, organic, and kind to the environment. Karina and Guillaume back it up with action. (Don't get me wrong. I do not insist that everyone eat locally or organically. That doesn't work for certain people, and who am I to force my views on them? But for me, if you say it, you should do it. Phew! Now I'm exhausted.)

Originally from Brazil, Karina is an incredible athlete. When I was there, she was training for a big competition called a "Raid d'Aventure" that incorporated running, strength, and endurance in the wilderness—kind of a mountain triathalon, if you will. She swims, and both plays and coaches basketball. The day she picked me up at the train station, she had already run ten miles. Later that day, she went rollerblading for half an hour. In the meantime, she helped her mother put the finishing touches on the Feijoada—the black bean and meat stew that is the national dish of Brazil—they were serving the harvesters for lunch. Although Guillaume is athletic as well, when I was there, his attention was completely turned toward the harvest. For years, Guillaume was in charge of the fields and the winery while Karina took care of the commercial side of things, but recently she has given up her office work and is instead using horses to work the vineyards, an occupation that seems much more suited to her athletic personality.

I spent a very interesting morning in the winery with Guillaume and his winery workers (for the most part permanent, full-time employees). Like picking grapes in the fields, working in the winery is a busy, physically active job. I watched them bring in the freshly picked grapes and run them through the press. After pressing, the grapes were transferred to stainless-steel fermentation tanks. Guillaume tested each tank frequently, checking the progress and meticulously recording the results in a log.

I was struck by the massive amount of cleaning that went on in the winery. Guillaume and his staff were constantly hosing down the winery floors, machinery, even the spigots of the tanks after each sample was taken. Guillaume said that cleaning is a huge part of winemaking, especially during harvest. It is of particular importance in an organic winery located in an area as hot as Côteaux d'Aix-en-Provence given the need to produce their wines without additives. Additionally, it helps eliminate problems with flies and other insects. As rigorous as the work was, Guillaume and his staff were incredibly tolerant of my questions and all the photos I was taking.

One morning Carmen, Karina and Guillaume's six-year-old daughter, caught sight of me walking by on my way to the winery and asked me to take her with me. Since she was barefoot and still in her nightgown, she actually wanted me to carry her, which I did. Once we got to the winery, I set her on her feet and transferred responsibility for her to her dad. She asked Guillaume for a small glass of grape juice from one of the tanks. As she sipped it, she told Guillaume she could taste the difference from the previous day—that she could tell fermentation had begun because of the prickle of gas on her tongue. She's pretty amazing to have a grasp of the concept of fermentation at such a tender age.

Given their athleticism and their emphasis on organics and care about their food, I initially found it surprising how many sweets the family and harvesters consumed. Dessert was a part of each meal, and sweets played a starring role in the casse-croûte, the morning snack that Karina took down to the harvesters and winery workers.

Surprise on my part should not be mistaken for disapproval: a) Because it is none of my business, and b) Because it is hard to argue with the success evident before my eyes. The family (and really everyone I encountered at Domaine de Sulauze) was fit—lean, strong, and glowing with good health. My theory is that if you eat sugar in conjunction with a healthy diet—a diet almost totally lacking in processed food—and maintain an athletic lifestyle, you can still be very fit. I mean in the United States, where we have huge problems with obesity and the resultant health problems, we publicly revile sugar. I contend that if we ate some sugar but fewer processed foods, limited our portions, and exercised more, as a nation we would be much healthier. (I know, I know, you heard it here last.)

Guillaume is very proud of this philosophy, even going so far as to refuse a store-bought burger bun because it contained too much sugar, stating that "he liked *his* bread made from *his* own flour, baked in *his* own oven." It is hard to argue with the concept of diet based on well-sourced, local ingredients. This is what Provençal food is all about, emphasizing few but perfect ingredients. (Sounds like everything I believe in, right?)

Foods of Provence

Vegetables

Warm sunny weather provides a long growing season for the vegetables for which the region is so famous. Olives, eggplant, tomatoes, zucchini, onions, artichokes, green beans, and garlic—all of these vegetables have a prominent place in the cuisine of the region.

Olives and Olive Oil: The oils of Provence are delicious and vary from bright fresh peppery oils from green olives, riper oils made from black ripe olives that have riper fruitier flavors, and oils made from late harvest, black ripe olives that are allowed to age several days in the mill before processing. (Because of this aging, the last oils are labeled "virgin oil" instead of "extra-virgin.") These oils from aged olives are rich and sweet with mushroom, dried fruit, and even cocoa notes.

My favorite and perhaps the best-known oils of Provence are those from Les Baux de Provence. Olive Oil Les Baux de Provence AOP is made from Salonenque, Beruguette, Verdale, and Grossane olives grown in the flat lands below the starkly beautiful hill town of Les Baux-de-Provence. I highly recommend buying these oils if you happen to find them.

Cavaillon Melons: The most famous melons of Provence hail from the small town of Cavaillon in the Vaucluse. The dry, hot, sunny weather is perfect for growing the Charentais variety of melons—small melons, their creamy yellow skin striped with bluish green lines, the interior orange, moist, and juicy.

Vegetable Dishes

It's pretty easy to be a vegetarian in Provence—or at the very least a pescatarian. Some of the most famous dishes of the regions feature vegetables in a starring role.

Anchoïade: A thick paste of anchovies, garlic, and olive oil. It's fantastic served with bread or brightly colored, crisp vegetables.

Tapenade: A lovely tangy paste made of olives, capers, garlic, anchovies, and olive oil. Tapenade is basically anchoïade with olives and capers added. Both are delicious served with a glass of chilled Provençal Rosé.

Ratatouille: One of the most classic Provençal dishes, Ratatouille is a hearty vegetable dish of eggplant, zucchini, bell peppers, onions, tomatoes, garlic, and olive oil. (Although in some circles, the addition of bell peppers is up for debate.) Ratatouille is cooked until the vegetables are soft but not falling apart and can be served warm or cold.

Tomatoes Provençal: Tomato halves stuffed with garlic, breadcrumbs, herbs, and olive oil, and then baked until just soft. The crunchy breadcrumbs and the juicy tomatoes are a perfect foil for each other.

Artichokes Barigoule: Tender young artichokes braised on a bed of onions, shallots, carrots, white wine, olive oil, and garlic. As with many ancient recipes, there are many variations of this traditional dish, including the use of mushrooms, bacons, chives, breadcrumbs, and butter.

Panisses: This is probably my favorite discovery in Provence in recent years. Panisses are chickpea pancakes lightly fried in olive oil and garnished simply with crunchy salt and freshly cracked pepper. Panisses + Rosé = Provençal heaven.

Soupe au Pistou: Fresh vegetable and bean soup garnished with basil pesto and flavorful Provençal extra-virgin olive oil.

Aioli: The word Aioli comes from the combination of garlic and oil in the Provençal dialect. I'm not trying to be the Aioli Police or anything, but Aioli is NOT the flavored mayonnaise that you find on every menu trying to be trendy throughout the world. It isn't even garlic mayonnaise. It is easy to understand why some confuse it with garlic mayonnaise, since it is an emulsion of garlic and oil. There is no mustard in aioli. The only possible cheat to aid in the emulsion is the use of either an egg or a boiled potato. Garlic is the ONLY flavor of aioli there is. Full stop. (Phew! Sorry, but obviously I feel strongly about this.) There *is* a dish called aioli that you find frequently on the Provençal table. The dish Aioli is a room temperature salad of boiled salt cod, boiled potatoes, steamed carrots, *haricots verts* (pencil thin French green beans), and hard-boiled eggs accompanied by a bowl of aioli sauce.

Fish and Seafood

The proximity to the Mediterranean makes seafood an inescapable pleasure. A stroll along the Quai des Belges in Marseille's Vieux Port with its morning fish market will net you some interesting photos of local fish and crustaceans, although over the years the number of fishmongers and selection at the market seem to have diminished. Still, seeing scorpion fish, rascasse, sardines, sea urchin, conger eel, and whole monkfish is quite a sight for those unused to such an array of Mediterranean products. Lucky shoppers may find a fisherman selling *Oeil de Sainte Lucie*. Literally the Eye of Saint Lucie, this orange mother-of-pearl disk is the lid from the opening of a certain type of sea snail. Fishermen and sailors consider it good luck. I'm not sure about that. I managed to lose mine before I could take a photo of it.

All of this bounty finds its way into many of the most famous dishes of Provence.

Bouillabaisse: Arguably the most famous fish stew in the world, there are as many recipes for Bouillabaisse as there are restaurants in Provence. So many, in fact, that a Charter of Bouillabaisse was formed in 1980 by chefs in Marseille to protect the integrity of the dish (later expanded to include restaurants between Marseille and Cassis). While some variables still exist, there are certain inviolable rules. The soup base always includes tomatoes, onions, garlic, fennel, saffron, and olive oil, although potatoes, cumin, and, in some cases, pastis can be added. As for the fish itself, although some variation regarding type of fish is acceptable, there is no argument that the only fish permitted in bouillabaisse are fish from the Mediterranean.

Even the service of Bouillabaisse is bound by tradition. To begin, the waiter will bring a tray of fresh fish to your table—these are *your* fish—before whisking them away to the kitchen and into the pot. Bouillabaisse is traditionally served in two courses: First, a tureen with thick, garlicky, rust-colored fish soup appears with a tray of bread croutons and rouille sauce, a rust-colored garlic and pepper sauce similar in consistency to aioli. (I cannot stress this enough—no matter

Soupe de Poisson, Restaurant Le Miramar, Marseille, France

how delicious the fish soup is—do not have seconds. Should you ignore my warning, you will not have room for what comes next.)

Second, a platter with all of *your* fish is brought to your table, and your extremely talented waiter will carefully debone it for you tableside. A new bowl of soup is placed in front of you, and your perfectly deboned fish is added to this second bowl of soup. Fantastic! I advise ordering a bottle of chilled Provençal Rosé to go with it. Oh, and finally, bring a friend and don't plan anything for later in the day. This is a meal to relax over. Eat slowly and enjoy. Your only remaining decision is whether to order a second bottle of rosé. I vote yes.

Other notable fish dishes include:

Brandade de Morue: This aromatic appetizer is made by puréeing salt-cod, milk, garlic, olive oil, and boiled potatoes. The texture is creamy yet fibrous—the flavors, salty, rich, and maritime with strong notes of garlic and olive oil. Spread it on crisp baguette slices and share with good friends. (A certain familiarity is needed given the elevated levels of garlic and fish.)

Grilled Fish: Especially sardines—delicious when freshly grilled.

Poutargues: West of Marseille, the fishing port of Martigues is known for *Poutargues* (the Italians call it *Bottarga*), dried sets of salted and cured fish roe (generally grey mullet or tuna). Approximately six inches long and three inches wide, *Poutargues* are found throughout the Mediterranean. *Poutargues* taste like the best of the sea, salty with a sweet clean fishy quality. It is traditionally shaved or grated over finished dishes.

Encornet: Small squid bodies stuffed with ground pork and aromatics. Served in a light tomato sauce. I should mention that like Bouillabaisse, Encornet also have their own Charter to regulate the standards of the dish.

Meat

Taureau de Camargue: Although Taureau means bull, this is actually a breed of cattle from the Camargue. Karina and Guillaume's next-door neighbors raise Taureau de Camargue to sell for their meat. Sausages from Taureau de Camargue are delicious, definitely gamier than traditional beef sausages.

Sisteron Lamb: My friend Chef Elisabeth Bourgeois of Mas Tourteron in Gordes swears by the superiority of the lamb from Sisteron. Raised in the hills in the foothills of the Alps, Sisteron lamb is pasture-raised, grazing on a flavorful diet of wild rosemary and thyme. The meat is tender and mild.

Daube à la Provençale: Traditional winter fare in Provence, Daube is beef stew made with red wine, onions, carrots, garlic, and Herbes de Provence.

Pied et Pacquets: A stew made from pig's feet and tripe "packages" stuffed with a farce of garlic, parsley, minced *ventrèche* (dry cured pork belly which the Italians call *pancetta*), and black pepper. The feet and packages are slow braised in a tomato, onion, and garlic sauce.

Goat Cheese

Provence is justifiably well known for its goat cheese.

Banon: The most famous goat cheese of Provence, Banon is a soft, unpasteurized cheese. Shaped like a disk, it is easily recognized by its wrapping of fresh chestnut leaves.

Picodon: This small round cheese can be light and fresh with a creamy texture in its youth. Give it some age, however, and the complexity begins to shine. The color of the crust changes to a creamy yellow and the texture becomes drier and chalkier and the flavor deepens, becoming spicy and tangy.

Brousse du Rove: This small soft fresh goat cheese has been recognized as a Slow Food Presidium. Although many imitate it, real Brousse du Rove can only be produced by eight shepherds following very strict guidelines:

- The milk must come from Rove goats with their long, lyre-shaped horns. This breed is particularly well suited to drought and heat, and although they do not produce large quantities of milk, what they do produce is rich and flavorful.
- The Rove sheep must be allowed at least six hours daily of free pasture time year-round.
- The sheep must only graze in certain delineated areas of the Bouches-du-Rhône, the Vaucluse, and the Var. These areas are home to two distinct scrubby plants: Thorny Broom and Kermes Oak, both of which give Brousse du Rove its distinctive and persistent flavor—a rare quality in a cheese meant to be eaten within 5 days of production.

Other Provençal Specialties

Truffles: Winter black truffles of the *tuber melanosporum* variety are one of Provence's main claims to fame. Found mainly in the Vaucluse, they are incredibly fragrant and obviously quite sought after. The main market for black truffles in Provence is in Carpentras, but they can also be found at the *Maison de la Truffe* (House of Truffles) in Ménerbes. I was lucky enough to cook there with my friend Elisabeth Bourgeois at an event that the Mayor of Ménerbes hosted for members of the *Académie Française*, the preeminent council responsible for all things pertaining to the French language. They may be some of the most well-respected intellectuals in France, but that didn't stop them from devouring Elisabeth's *Brouillade aux Truffes* (custardy scrambled eggs with truly sick amounts of truffles mixed in). Or maybe that is just further proof of their intelligence.

Herbes de Provence: An herb blend made from thyme, rosemary, basil, oregano, and savory. Its use is ubiquitous in Provençal cooking and has spread to many other corners of the world.

Sel de Camargue: Evidence of salt production in the Camargue town of Aigues-Mortes can be traced back to the 4th century BC. Currently there are ten *sauniers* (salt workers) in the salt marshes of the Camargue taking advantage of the perfect combination of wind, water, and sun that makes sea salt possible. In addition to maintaining the salt ponds, tracking salinity levels, and harvesting the salt, *sauniers* (a.k.a. *paludiers*) are responsible for safeguarding the biodiversity of the region. Sea salt of the Camargue and the more prized Fleur de Sel de Camargue are known throughout the world for their quality. Fleur de Sel is particularly noteworthy. Pure white crystals form on the surface of the ponds in the summer when the winds lessen. Harvested by hand, the crystals are slightly moist with a distinctive crystal shape, size, and flavor. Fleur de Sel de Camargue tends to be a bit saltier and a little less fine than its Atlantic cousin, Fleur de Sel de Guérande.

Lavender: Well known for its beauty and cosmetic applications, lavender also flavors regional vegetable dishes, custards, sorbets, and cookies. Lavender-flavored honey is particularly delicious.

Desserts

Navettes: Long, orange blossom-scented cookies from Marseille.

Calissons d'Aix: Almond shaped candies from Aix-en-Provence, Calissons d'Aix consist of a fruit paste made from melons, oranges, and almonds. The paste has a texture similar to marzipan and is topped with royal icing glaze. The production of Calissons in Provence dates back six centuries.

Pastis: This famed anise-flavored liquor is ubiquitous in Provence and is somewhat divisive. If you like anise, you'll probably love it. Not a fan of anise? Probably not so much. Either way, one can hardly visit Provence without trying it at least once. Aficionados swear by its thirst-quenching properties. Pastis is traditionally drunk with one or two ice cubes (not more) in a ratio of one part pastis to five or six parts water. The most famous brands are Ricard and Pernod. Be careful, the alcohol content can sneak up on you!

Wines of Provence

The dry, sunny, and hot climate, along with strong winds and nutrient-poor but well-drained soil make Provence a hospitable area for growing grapes. The three largest AOCs (Côtes de Provence, Côteaux d'Aix-en-Provence, and Côteaux Varois en Provence) make up 96 percent of the region's wine production, and since 80 percent of Provençal wines are rosé, it is clear that the vignerons in Provence have hung their hat on the rosé peg. These beautiful pale pink wines (with colors ranging from pink to salmon) are dry, low in alcohol, and supremely quaffable.

The most common grape varieties:

Rosé and Red: Grenache, Cinsault, Mourvedre, Counoise, Syrah, Carignan, and Cabernet Sauvignon. Carignan and Cabernet Sauvignon may not account for more than 30 percent of the blend.

White: Rolle (a.k.a. Vermentino), Ugni Blanc, Clairette, Semillon, and Bourboulenc Blanc.

Côteaux d'Aix-en-Provence where Domaine de Sulauze is located is in the western part of Provence. Its four most important characteristics are abundance of sun (2,900 average hours of sun per year), its limestone soils, the strong *mistral* winds, and the low rainfall quantities (between 21 and 26 inches per year with the majority falling during the spring and fall). Grenache is the most widely planted grape, followed by Cinsault and Carignan. Historically a region of moderate quality levels, there are some very good producers in Côteaux d'Aix-en-Provence, and organic viticulture has become a significant practice in the region.

Wines of Domaine de Sulauze

At Domaine de Sulauze, Guillaume and Karina produce ten wines: seven still dry wines, two dessert wines, and a sparkling wine in three different bottle sizes. The following are excerpts from the Domaine de Sulauze website with rather amusing editorial descriptions:

Dry Still Wines

Pomponette: AOP Côteaux d'Aix-en-Provence Rosé, "which makes the women amorous." Grapes: Grenache Noir, Cinsault, Syrah, Mourvèdre, and Vermentino.

Galinette: AOP Côteaux d'Aix-en-Provence Blanc, "Excellent." Grapes: Grenache Blanc, Ugni Blanc, Clairette, and Vermentino.

Lauze: AOP Côteaux d'Aix-en-Provence Rouge, "Strapping and well made, Thanks Vines!" Grapes: Cabernet Sauvignon, Syrah, and Mourvèdre.

Les Amis: Côteaux d'Aix-en-Provence Rouge, "Unique, it's a delight!" Grapes: Small-berry Syrah and Grenache Noir.

Liane: Côteaux d'Aix-en-Provence Rouge, "Friendly!" Grapes: Grenache and Syrah.

Chapelle Laïque: Côteaux d'Aix-en-Provence Rouge, "Magnifique!" Grapes: Cinsault from the vineyard behind the ancient chapel.

Cochon: Vin de France Rouge, "A light wine for all occasions: All is good in the pig!" (*Cochon* means pig in French.)

The still wines are fermented without added yeast or filtration and with little to no added sulphur.

Dessert Wines

Amaury: a late-harvest dessert wine made from Marselan (a cross between Cabernet Sauvignon and Grenache).

Suce Miel: Vin de France. Sweet wine made from dried Vermentino and Clairette grapes.

Sparkling Wines

The Pét-Nats:

Modeste (33cl bottle), **Super Modeste** (75cl bottle), and **Hyper Modeste** (magnum). These sparkling wines are made in the Pétillant Naturel or Ancestrale method. This means unfinished wine (still fermenting) is bottled, and as the sugars continue to ferment, bubbles develop. Pét-Nats vary from lightly sweet to dry.

The amusing wine names and descriptions hint at another side of Karina and Guillaume's personalities. While very serious about the quality and origins of their food, they were not the least bit stuffy. The opposite was true. In the midst of harvest, Karina playfully varied the menu for the workers—serving Feijoada one day and a dinner of bruschetta from leftovers the next. I made large pork roasts, their accompanying potatoes stewed in the same roasting pan to soak up the juices. We prepared lots of crunchy vegetarian salads, fruit pies, and my mom's peanut butter

cookies (a special request from Karina, a fond memory from her days as an exchange student in Texas). Panisses, the savory yet simple fried chickpea cakes so traditional to Provence, became an immediate favorite of mine.

The beer keg at the gîte flowed—another amenity—with organic beer brewed right at the Domaine. I had always kind of disdained the rather cutesy phrase "It takes a lot of beer to make good wine." My experience at Domaine de Sulauze (as well as the other wineries on my harvest trip) convinced me of its validity. Harvest is hard manual labor, and a cold beer tastes really great after that.

Growing grapes and making wine can be quite stressful, especially if the weather does not cooperate. Late at night, Guillaume and the harvesters drank beer and played music around the big farm table, unwinding after the long days that began with cool weather early in the morning but quickly became extremely hot with the arrival of midday sun. Likewise, as they trickled in from the fields, the beer keg at the gîte was one of the first stops the harvesters made—a bracingly cold and welcome respite after the hot physical effort of picking grapes.

This is not Germany, however, or even the US. There were no beer steins or mugs. They were using wine glasses for the beer, and as anyone who has ever drawn beer from a tap knows, you have to let the first little bit of beer escape to get rid of the foam. That meant a considerable amount of beer, was wasted for each 4-oz. glass of beer, and they were going through kegs faster than a college fraternity on homecoming weekend.

After watching the harvesters run out of beer the second night in a row, I suggested that they use a pitcher to capture the beer and pour it into their wine glasses from there. The young gentlemen explained to me in a polite yet somewhat condescending fashion that beer needed to be drunk quickly to retain its bubbles. They didn't come right out and say it, but they were clearly thinking, "What does this spoiled American woman know about drinking beer from a keg?" Equally polite, I suppressed my three-word answer—"Kansas State University." Drinking beer wasn't my major in college, but I did devote several block periods of time per week to the pursuit. I also didn't mention that I was the beer buyer for a short amount of time at Comet Ping Pong—the pizza and craft beer restaurant where I had worked in DC. (Frankly, there is only so much interfering that you can do when you are the guest, whether you are cooking for them or not.)

Harvest Lunch

The final harvest lunch was quite celebratory, with workers gathered around the table, special bottles of wine sharing space with glasses of beer, and plates filled with roasted Taureau de Camargue, crisp bright salads, fruit tarts and simple cakes.

Beer shortages and hard work notwithstanding, Guillaume and Karina provided a hospitable and relaxing environment for the people doing the important yet seasonal task of bringing in the grapes in the heat of a Provençal September. Having an organic brewery on-site was an appreciated added bonus.

Karina, in blue; Guillaume, to her right

The Winemaker Recommends: Panisses with Domaine de Sulauze Côteaux d'Aix-en-Provence Rosé.

Panisses

Yield: Serves 6 as a first course or 12 for cocktails | Ease of Preparation: Moderate
Ease of Sourcing: Moderate | Wine Pairing: Domaine de Sulauze Côteaux d'Aix-en-Provence
Rosé or other Provençal rosé

Panisses were one of the first dishes I ate when I arrived at Domaine de Sulauze in Côteaux d'Aix-en-Provence. Panisses are fried cakes made from chickpea flour. Karina explained that not only is it a Provençal staple, it is also a mainstay at the Domaine during harvest because they invariably have a considerable number of vegans working the harvest, and Panisses are good source of protein, fiber, and vitamins. They are also gluten free. Crunchy and salty on the outside and creamy on the inside, they are a perfect snack to accompany a glass of Provençal Rosé. It's great when tradition is practical and at the same time delicious!

INGREDIENTS

1 quart water
1½ cups extra-virgin olive oil
1 Tbsp. kosher salt
2 cups chickpea flour
Fleur de Sel
Coarse ground pepper

TIMING

Cooking Time:10 minutes
Chilling Time: 1 hour
Frying Time: 10 minutes

WHAT YOU'LL NEED

9 x 13-inch cake pan
Sifter
Large saucepan
Whisk
Wooden spoon
Rubber spatula
Large skillet
Metal spatula
Paper towel covered tray
Decorative platter

PROCESS

Cover the bottom and sides of the cake pan with a thin layer of olive oil.

Sift the chickpea flour to remove any lumps and aerate it.

Heat the water, 1 tablespoon olive oil, and kosher salt until the water is just boiling. Whisk the flour in a little at a time. Be careful not to whisk it in too quickly or it will get lumpy. Once all the chickpea flour is incorporated, switch to the wooden spoon and vigorously stir over low heat for approximately 7–8 minutes. You are trying to remove as many lumps as possible. It may not be possible to remove them all. This is fine. Small lumps melt away during the frying process. When the mixture is extremely thick and big bubbles begin to appear, turn off the heat.

Quickly use the spatula to scrape the chickpea batter into the oiled cake pan. Smooth it out as best you can. Chill until solid, at least one hour.

Slice the Panisses in 1 x 2-inch rectangles.

Add ⅛ inch of olive oil to the large skillet. Heat it on medium-high heat until it shimmers. Add the Panisses to the oil and fry them until golden brown on one side. Use the metal spatula to turn them over and fry on the other side. Depending on the size of your skillet, you may have to fry in batches.

Transfer the fried Panisses to the paper towel-covered tray and sprinkle with Fleur de Sel and coarse ground pepper.

Serve warm with a chilled glass of rosé preferably on a sun-drenched patio.

Notes

#1. Chickpea flour (also called garbanzo bean flour or in Italian *farina di ceci*) was not always easy to find, but in recent years it has become more readily available. Most organic markets (Whole Foods, etc.), specialty gourmet stores, and Italian markets carry it. Two excellent brands are Bob's Red Mill Garbanzo Bean Flour and Molino Zanone Farina di Ceci—both are available online through Amazon.

#2. I like to use really good extra-virgin olive oil to fry my Panisses. When making them at Domaine de Sulauze one evening, one of the young harvest workers was horrified at that thought. She wanted to use canola oil because she believed that there were health risks from heating olive oil to a temperature high enough to fry with it. I didn't agree at the time and I still don't. It was not the only nutritional area where she and I were not in agreement. She was vegan. I clearly am not. (She also lives in a yurt, by the way, so we are fairly far apart philosophically.) That being said, I liked her quite a bit, and her Panisses were really good. I certainly didn't hesitate to eat them. I just think they taste even better fried in good olive oil.

Cucumber Salad
with Crème Fraîche and Yoghurt

Yield: Serves 4 as a side dish | Ease of Preparation: Simple | Ease of Sourcing: Simple
Wine Pairing: Côteaux d'Aix-en-Provence Blanc, Muscadet Sèvre et Maine Sur Lie or a crisp unoaked white

Harvesting grapes in the South of France is incredibly hard, hot work, and working in the winery isn't much better—in fact, the hours are even longer. Karina Lefèvre knows that the food she serves the harvesters needs to be bright, flavorful, filling, and easy to eat. It also helps to have a lot of salads to help cool the harvesters down. This cucumber salad, dressed simply with a mixture of yoghurt, crème fraîche, and fresh herbs, fits the bill. It is chilled, tasty, and the yoghurt is an alternate source of protein, especially important when you consider the number of vegetarians working at Domaine de Sulauze. Long a favorite of mine, I was very pleased to see this on her harvest table. She used an assortment of fresh herbs: basil, parsley, and mint. Feel free to use whatever combination you have on hand.

INGREDIENTS

1 lb. cucumbers

½ cup crème fraîche

1 cup plain whole milk yoghurt

3 Tbsp. finely minced fresh green herbs (i.e., parsley, mint, basil, dill, chives, or cilantro)

½ tsp. kosher salt

Finely ground white pepper to taste

WHAT YOU'LL NEED

Vegetable peeler

Sharp kitchen knife or mandolin to slice the cucumbers

Rubber spatula

Medium size kitchen bowl

Optional: decorative serving bowl

TIMING

Prep Time: 15 minutes

Chilling Time: 30 minutes

PROCESS

Peel and thinly slice the cucumbers.

Add the crème fraîche and yoghurt and mix well with the spatula. Add the herbs. Taste the mixture and add kosher salt and white pepper to taste.

Chill well before serving.

Notes

#1. I like to use small cucumbers for this. The larger the cucumbers, the more seeds there are. If seeds bother you, after peeling the cucumbers, slice them in half lengthwise and remove the seeds with a spoon before slicing.

#2. This recipe calls for whole milk yoghurt. If you wish to substitute fat-free or reduced fat yoghurt, feel free.

Quinoa Tabouleh

Yield: 2 quarts | Ease of Preparation: Moderate | Ease of Sourcing: Easy
Wine Pairing: Crisp Provençal white or rosé

Many of the harvesters at Domaine de Sulauze were vegetarians, and although neither Karina nor Guillaume is vegetarian, healthy eating is of paramount importance to them. Not only is this fresh, bright salad delicious and refreshing, the substitution of quinoa for bulgur ups the protein content considerably—super helpful for hard-working vegetarians. You can play around with the proportions if you wish—some folks like a bit more mint and parsley—but this is how Karina made it.

INGREDIENTS

1 cup quinoa
2 cups water
1 tsp. kosher salt
½ cup diced red onion
2 cups peeled and diced cucumber
2 cups diced cherry tomatoes
½ cup mint, sliced in very thin strips
½ cup parsley, finely minced
¼ cup lemon juice
¼ cup high-quality extra-virgin olive oil
Kosher salt
Black pepper

WHAT YOU'LL NEED

Baking sheet
2½ quart saucepan
Large salad bowl

TIMING

1 hour

PROCESS

Preheat oven to 350° F.

Spread the quinoa on the baking sheet and toast it in the oven for 3 minutes. Toasting it enhances the nuttiness of the dish.

Place two cups water, the quinoa, and 1 teaspoon kosher salt in the saucepan. Bring it to a boil, then reduce the heat to a low simmer. Cook covered between 10 to 15 minutes. The quinoa is done when it is still lightly al dente and rings form around the outside of each seed. Strain any excess water and set aside to cool.

Dice the onions, cucumbers, and tomatoes. The onion dices should be half the size of the cucumbers and tomatoes. I like to use cherry tomatoes, as I find they are less messy to cut. Mix the vegetables with the cooled quinoa in the large salad bowl. Add the herbs and stir. Add the lemon juice and the olive oil. Stir and taste for seasoning. Add more lemon juice or salt and pepper to suit your taste.

I like this salad at room temperature, but in heat of the summer you might want to chill it.

Notes

#1. Quinoa comes in different colors—white, red, and black are the most common. I like using red quinoa for this recipe because it makes the dish more colorful. Quinoa is a complete protein—meaning it contains all essential amino acids. Additionally, because it is a seed, not a grain, it is gluten free.

#2. Some brands of quinoa require rinsing. The brand I buy states you do not need to rinse it. I like to lightly toast my quinoa before cooking it. I find it enhances the nuttiness of the dish.

Karina's Apple Cake

Yield: One 8 x 12-inch cake | Ease of Preparation: Simple | Ease of Sourcing: Simple
Wine Pairing: Lightly sweet white dessert wine (still or sparkling)

This wonderfully simple cake recipe (the French version of a pound cake) was a mainstay of the morning snack "casse-croûte" Karina Lefèvre prepared each morning for the harvest workers at Domaine de Sulauze. Using a base recipe, she varied the fruits and flavoring agents—using apples one day and poppy seeds the next. It's lightly sweet, incredibly moist, and lends itself perfectly to seasonal cooking—allowing you to take advantage of what fruits are available at the moment. I've made it with quince, peaches, cherries, and rhubarb—you get the idea.

INGREDIENTS

1½ lbs. pie apples
Juice of one lemon
2 sticks softened butter (8 oz.) + 1 to 2
    Tbsp. to butter the cake pan
1 cup granulated sugar
4 large eggs
1 cup all-purpose flour + ¼ cup to
    flour the cake pan
¾ tsp. kosher salt

WHAT YOU'LL NEED

Electric mixer
Potato peeler
Rubber spatula
8 x 12-inch cake pan
Toothpick or wooden skewer
Cookie sheet
Decorative platter

TIMING

Prep Time: 30 minutes
Baking Time: 45 minutes
Cooling Time: 1 hour

PROCESS

Preheat the oven to 350° F, preferably on the convection bake setting.

Cream softened butter and sugar on medium-high speed until the sugar has melted—approximately 10 minutes. Do not shortcut this important step. Creaming the butter and sugar until it is fluffy and has lightened in color will make your cake lighter. Stop the mixer periodically and use the spatula to scrape down the sides of the bowl.

While the butter and sugar are creaming, peel your apples, cut them in quarters, remove the cores, and cut each quarter in half again lengthwise. Toss the pieces in lemon juice and continue with the next apple.

Once the butter and sugar are light and fluffy (test the texture of the mixture; if it no longer feels granular, you are good to go), add one egg at a time and continue mixing on medium high. Once the eggs have been incorporated and the batter is fluffy again, shut off the mixer and add the salt and ¼ of the flour. Mix on slow until it is blended, scrape down the sides of the bowl, and add another ¼ of the flour. Continue until all the flour is mixed in.

While the batter is mixing, butter and flour the cake pan.

Cover the bottom of the cake pan with a layer of batter (approximately half the batter). Drain the apple slices, making sure there is no excess lemon juice. Arrange a layer of apples on the batter in the cake pan. Scrape the remaining batter over the apple slices. Gently shake the cake pan to even out the batter. It's fine if a few apple slices peek out from the batter.

Bake for 40 to 45 minutes, turning twice during the baking process. After 40 minutes, check to see if the cake is done. First, use your skewer to verify that the apples are cooked. If they are soft, insert the skewer into the cake to see if the batter is fully cooked. If the skewer comes back clean, the cake is done. If not, cook it a little more.

Cool the cake for 15 to 20 minutes on a cake rack. Run a butter knife around the inside of the pan to loosen the cake. Place a cookie sheet upside down on the cake pan and flip the cake to unmold. Center your decorative platter face down on the cake and flip it again to return the cake to the presentation side.

Note

I like to use tart apples for this cake for the contrast of the sweet cake and the lightly tart apples.

Champagne
Ligras & Haas

Mont
Saint-Michel

Rouen

Tours

Nantes

Lyon

Bordeaux

Marseilles

Corsica

"Burgers, Beer, and Brut Champagne"
Harvest at Champagne Legras & Haas
Chouilly, France

I can't help but smile when I think of the first time I met Jérôme Legras. Arrowine & Cheese in Arlington, Virginia, was hosting an after-hours private tasting of Legras & Haas Champagne, and I was scheduled to "work" the tasting. There's really not a whole lot of work involved. Basically, you pour wine for people and listen to the winemaker talk about his or her wines. In this case, the wines in question happened to be Grand Cru Champagne, and the winemaker was a charming guy in his early thirties, a bon vivant of sorts who recounted his family's story with dedication and engaging enthusiasm. I wouldn't call Jérôme bubbly, but his manner is so upbeat it is infectious, and yet there is a very serious wine professional underneath.

Champagne Legras & Haas

As the tasting progressed, Jérôme described his family's winery in Chouilly, France. Before they were winemakers, the Legras family grew grapes on their polycultural farm in Chouilly. For three generations, the family made Champagne from their grapes,

Photo credit: Michael Boudot

and in 1991, husband and wife team François Legras and Brigitte Haas Legras founded Champagne Legras & Haas.

François and Brigitte's philosophy is that "making wine without growing grapes makes no sense," and they believe that "winemaking starts in the vineyards and that it is crucial to know the history and background of a vineyard or a hill to make the best Champagne possible." While most of their wines are made solely from their own grapes, several cuvées incorporate grapes from long-term relationships with trustworthy growers. Their three sons, Rémi, Olivier, and Jérôme, join François and Brigitte in the family business.

Legras & Haas produces five white Champagnes and one rosé.

Brut Tradition: Their entry-level Champagne is a delicious blend of Chardonnay, Pinot Meunier, and Pinot Noir and is a particular pride of patriarch François Legras, who understands that this is the cuvée upon which a Champagne house is most frequently judged.

Left to Right, Jérôme, Olivier, and Rémi
Photo credit: Champagne Legras & Haas.

Blanc de Blancs Brut: Chardonnay Grand Cru. 100 percent Chardonnay from Chouilly.

Blanc de Blancs Extra Brut: As with the previous wine, The Blanc de Blancs Grand Cru is made from 100 percent Chardonnay from Chouilly but in an even drier style than the Brut. It is also aged a little longer than the two previous wines.

Blanc de Blancs Millésime: This wine is made from Grand Cru Chardonnay from selected vineyard sites from a single year's harvest. It is fuller and richer than the non-vintage wines and can stand up to more full-bodied foods.

Exigence: This wine is a blend of equal parts Grand Cru Chardonnay from Chouilly and Grand Cru Pinot Noir from Ay in the Vallée de la Marne. It is full and very complex and only made in exceptional vintages, as befits its name. *Exigence* means demand or requirement in French and connotes a high-quality standard.

Rosé: The Legras & Haas Rosé contains a large proportion of Chardonnay (50 percent) to ensure a markedly high acidity level to accompany the red fruit and buttery notes of the red grapes with 25 percent each of both Pinot Noir and Pinot Meunier.

With the exception of the Extra Brut, all of the Legras & Haas cuvées have 7g/l of residual sugar. This level is on the lower or drier side for a Brut-level wine.

That evening at the end of the Arrowine tasting, while things were winding down, I was chatting with Jérôme about harvest at their winery—specifically the provisions for feeding the staff during harvest. He told me that for years his mother had cooked for the winery staff, but that recently she had begun to hire a catering company to provide the food even though she had a new kitchen at the winery. When I asked how that was going, he admitted in a rueful fashion that it was nowhere near as good as when his mother had been doing the cooking. I mentioned to Jérôme that it was a dream of mine to cook at a winery in France during harvest. He replied, "Don't say that or I'll take you up on it." I teased back, "No. Don't *you* say that or I'll take *you* up on it." This joking exchange continued until we discovered that we were both serious and started comparing schedules. Realizing it might actually work out, Jérôme said he would speak with his mother about it and get back to me.

In addition to being a great cook, Jérôme's mother, Brigitte, is first and foremost a businesswoman. She and her husband François founded Legras & Haas twenty-five years ago with him in charge of the vineyards and the winemaking and her in charge of the commercial side of things. She has not grown her very successful business by making rash decisions. Since my project was not going to be long-term, she didn't want to endanger her relationship with the local caterer, so she invited me to come and cook dinner for three days at the beginning of harvest. That way she could keep the caterer for lunchtime and not jeopardize things when I had to leave.

I arrived at Champagne Legras & Haas in Chouilly late on a September afternoon. Jérôme had arranged to meet me there to take me on a tour of the winery and to introduce me his mother, Madame Legras. Chouilly, a small village (pop. 1,000) in the Côte des Blancs district of Champagne three miles east of Epernay, is designated a Grand Cru Village in the *Échelle des Crus*. (See the box Champagne Production and the Échelle des Crus, p. 378.) The winery and its offices are located across the road from each other in the middle of town. While we were touring the winery we determined that although I would stay with Brigitte and François Legras at their incredibly lovely home in nearby Plivot, I would be cooking at Jérôme's home in Chouilly. The new kitchen at the winery was perfect for heating and serving already-prepared food, but to prepare a full meal would have been a challenge, especially since the kitchen would be in use full-time to serve lunch and for morning and afternoon coffee breaks. During the course of our acquaintance, it had become obvious that Jérôme is a total foodie, so I wasn't surprised to learn that he has a brand new gourmet kitchen in his home a couple of blocks from the winery. Since he would be in the fields supervising pickers or working in the winery, it was perfect for my needs because I would have space to cook and it was close by. Plus it gave me access to his garden filled with tomatoes, peppers, and tons of fresh herbs—kind of a win-win, if you ask me. It also enabled Jérôme, when working nearby at the winery or on his way back from the fields, to pop in a grab a coffee with me and sneak a taste of whatever I was cooking.

By the time we finished meeting with Madame Legras, it was time for dinner. Jérôme proposed eating dinner together in Epernay with his friend Raf, who was here from the Loire Valley to help with the harvest. I was somewhat shocked to find out that our restaurant in Epernay was a burger and beer joint! Not at all what I would expect to find in the center of one of the most prestigious wine regions in the world.

Likewise, it would never have crossed my mind that Jérôme and Raf would spend dinner picking my brain about grilling, burgers, and barbecue! It soon became evident that Jérôme loves barbecue of all kinds. Over truly delicious burgers, loaded with some pretty unusual toppings (because it's France), we touched on the differences in regional barbecue traditions in the US. (Being from Kansas, I have a clear preference for Kansas City Barbecue, but I can be objective if I must!)

Early the next morning, I enjoyed a lovely breakfast that Madame Legras had left for

Jérôme sampling meatballs

me, made even better by having it in her showcase kitchen. Seriously, I almost swooned when I saw her double oven French Blue Cornue Range. It was huge, with four burners, a grill, and a large circular French cooktop. It was the stove of my dreams sitting right next to where I was having my morning tea!

After a little time spent planning my menus, I met up with Madame Legras, who took me around Chouilly and Epernay to purchase supplies for dinner that evening. German by birth, Brigitte Haas-Legras is a handsome blonde woman whose presence demands attention and respect. Her demeanor, while kind, is more reserved than that of her gregarious youngest son. Clearly, she is well-thought-of in town, with each merchant greeting her warmly but with deference, calling her Madame Legras and seeing to her needs immediately. She introduced me to local merchants, instructing them to put my future purchases on her account, and gave me directions to the Cueillette d'Aulnay sur Marne—a pick-your-own farm several miles outside of town. (*Cueillir* means to gather or pick and generally refers to picking fruits and vegetables or flowers.)

During harvest time, the workforce at Legras & Haas swells to almost one hundred people. Hand harvesting, as is required by Champagne law, takes a considerable number of people in the fields, and at this busy time the crew at the winery itself numbers almost twenty. The folks harvesting the grapes stayed in nearby campgrounds or local housing and provided their own food.

Jérôme and his family furnish food for the winery staff beginning with coffee at seven a.m., followed by a *Casse-Croûte* (snack) in the morning around nine a.m. comprised of savory charcuterie, cheese, fruit tarts, coffee, and red wine. Lunchtime is between noon and one p.m. and is a moderately sized meal. Coffee in the afternoon is served quickly for those who are interested. The biggest meal comes in the evening around seven p.m. Dinner is more relaxed than the other meals, with a first course, a main course, cheese, and dessert. Although I'm not sure how feasible it would be on a long-term basis, I derived a distinct pleasure not only in cooking the food, but in the knowledge that I had personally harvested almost all of the fruits and vegetables that I used in the meal—whether from the Cueillette or from the garden in Jérôme's back yard. (There was even one vegetarian on staff, so I was doubly happy to be able to offer a variety of meatless options.)

Over the course of my days in Chouilly I cooked:

1. A Spaghetti and Meatball dinner (a special request from Jérôme) with a colorful Cannellini Bean Salad and Quetsche Clafoutis for dessert. (Clafoutis is one of my go-to desserts. Made from a thick crêpe-type batter, this classic dessert traditionally uses dark cherries—pit included)—but what I love about it is you can substitute almost any firm fruit that is in season. In this case, I substituted quetsche plums that I had picked at the Cueillette.)

2. A meal featuring two classic French salads (Beets in Lemon Vinaigrette and Shredded Carrots in Walnut Vinaigrette), *Coq au Champagne* (which is a variation on *Coq au Vin*, Chicken Braised in Wine, but the aforementioned wine is Champagne. So that's a special treat!), and an Apple Crumble.

3. And on the final night, a Gruyère flan with gorgeous heirloom tomatoes and basil from the Jérôme's garden and the Cueillette, a Roast Pork Loin cooked in Champagne with potatoes and onions roasted in the pan juices along with the pork, and a Strawberry Rhubarb Tart with fruit from the Cueillette. Every night, Jérôme pulled out all the stops, opening wines from his cellar: Bordeaux, Red and White Burgundy. He, like I, has a fondness for Chablis, and it was a real treat to share those wines with him, his family, and their staff.

Harvesting at the Cueillette d'Aulnay sur Marne

When the time came to take the food to the winery every evening, Jérôme would crawl into the back of a winery truck to hold everything in place for the short ride from his house to the winery where people would be waiting to help us carry it in. The crew was friendly and intelligent. Each night Jérôme's parents, his brothers, Rémi and Olivier (the general manager of the winery), and Hélène Vollereaux, Olivier's fiancée, would round out the crowd. Hélène and her family own Champagnes Vollereaux in nearby Pierry. While chatting with the family, I was able to get a sense their property and wines, of the region as a whole, and in particular food traditions among the vignerons of Champagne.

Although the Champagne-Ardenne region (bordered on the west by the Ile de France, on the north by Belgium, on the south by Burgundy, and on the east by the Mosel, Alsace, and Lorraine) is comprised of four departments—Marne, Haute-Marne, Aube, and Ardennes—most people think of the Marne when they think of Champagne. Reims and Epernay are the main towns in the Marne region. The Montagne de Reims, Côte des Blancs, and Vallée de la Marne, famous for Pinot Noir, Chardonnay, and Pinot Meunier, respectively, make up a huge proportion of Champagne production and are located in the Marne, as is the Côte de Sézanne, some thirty miles south of Epernay. The Côte des Bar, the fifth Champagne-producing district, is located in the Aube seventy miles south of Epernay.

The main river of the region, the Marne runs right through Epernay in the heart of Champagne, dividing the Montagne de Reims from the Côte des Blancs with the vineyards of the Vallée de la Marne on both sides of the river. Further to the south, the Aube and Seine Rivers are the major influences in the Aube district of Champagne.

Industry in the region is predominantly agricultural. Farming accounts for 61 percent of the land use in Champagne with viticulture, cereals (wheat and corn), sugar beets, fruits, and poultry (mainly for foie gras) playing the largest roles. Nonagricultural industries include metallurgy and the automotive sector.

Foods of Champagne

While there is some influence on the cuisine of the region from neighboring Belgium (*Carbonnade*, the beef and beer stew for which Belgium is famous, appears on many Champenois menus) and Alsace/Lorraine (think Choucroute), the cuisine of Champagne can actually be described as traditionally northern French *Cuisine du Terroir*, Cooking of the Land.

Regional specialties include:

Meat, Poultry, and Fish

Boudin Blanc: From the small town of Rethel, Boudin Blanc is a delicate, moist, white sausage made from a mixture of finely minced white meat pork, veal and/or chicken, bread, eggs, shallots, cream, marjoram, and sage. The mixture is stuffed into casing and cooked very slowly to retain its delicacy. It is generally browned in butter and served with apple compote or with purée or sauté of potatoes. It is perfect served with a glass (or two) of Champagne.

La Joute (Potée Champenoise): The local version of a *Pot-au-Feu*, a rustic main dish consisting of a brothy vegetable soup made from smoked ham, cabbage, chicken, and local sausages along with other fresh vegetables like carrots, turnips, and potatoes. As with many similar recipes, there are as many versions of *La Joute* as there are cooks making it; however, what seems to distinguish *La Joute* from the *Pot-au-Feu* of other regions is the addition of chicken (preferably a young rooster) and the predominance of cabbage in the vegetable mixture.

Pig Trotters of Sainte-Menehould: This dish takes a really long time to make *and to eat*! First the pig's feet are gently simmered in a flavorful stock for hours until tender. Then they are breaded in breadcrumbs and fried in butter before being served with a garlic and chive garnish. Picking the meat and gelatinous bits from the bones takes a good amount of time, but it is worth it since it's delicious. Grab a glass of Rosé Champagne, relax, and enjoy.

Andouillette of Troyes AAAAA: Association Amicale des Amateurs d'Andouillette Authentique (Friendly Association of Authentic Andouillette Lovers), or the A.A.A.A.A., gets together several times a year to celebrate this regional specialty. The A.A.A.A.A. designation that frequently appears on menus throughout France serving Andouillette gets its name from this association. Possibly the most famous dish of the Aube in southern Champagne, this sausage is made from carefully selected pork intestines and stomach seasoned with onions, herbs, salt, and pepper and stuffed in casing. (see Soil and Soul, page 431.)

Trout: Although there is no seafood in this landlocked region, river fish, trout in particular, are quite popular, especially when served with a Champagne butter sauce.

Escargots Champenois: These large white snails from the Marne region are farm raised. The most traditional recipe involves stuffing the shells with butter, garlic, shallots, and parsley, much like in Burgundy.

Poultry: Geese, ducks, chicken, and Red Turkey of Ardennes are popular in the cooking of the region, with some geese and ducks being bred specifically to produce foie gras.

Wild Boar: Game from the forests of the Ardennes is quite popular in Champagne, particularly Wild Boar Ragout.

Mushrooms, Fruits, and Vegetables

Mushrooms: Just like hunting, foraging for mushrooms and truffles is popular in the forests of the region.

Fruits and Vegetables:

Champagne's northern climate makes it a perfect place to grow potatoes, leeks, turnips, carrots, beets, beans, and cabbage. In full summer, tomatoes and peppers also flourish. At the Cueillette d'Aulnay sur Marne, there were tomatoes, bell peppers, rhubarb, and even hydroponic strawberries available even in late September/early October.

La Cueillette d'Aulnay sur Marne

Lentillons Champenois: These small pink lentils with a delicate almost sweet flavor are popular served with fish.

White Asparagus: This elegant favorite is available for a short time in the spring.

Cheeses

Champagne is cow's milk country. Its most famous cheeses are **Chaource,** a creamy soft cheese with a white bloomy rind, and **Langres,** a small soft cylindrical orange cheese whose rind is washed with a brine solution and then rubbed with *raccou,* a natural colorant from a tropical shrub. As it ages, the top of the cylinder sinks slightly, making a perfect receptacle for a little dose of Champagne—so good! Although **Brie de Meaux** is technically from Meaux, just over the border in Ile-de-France to the west, it is often claimed by the Champenois.

Other Regional Specialties

Reims Mustard: While not as famous as its cousin from Dijon, *Moutarde de Reims* is piquant and delicious. It is available in a smoother fine version as well as the coarser whole grain *Moutarde à l'Ancienne.*

Champagne Sauce: One distinction in Champagne is that in other regions of France, dishes are frequently sauced with *Beurre Blanc,* a white wine and butter sauce, whereas the Champenois version incorporates Champagne instead of the white wine in the original recipe.

Desserts

Remember that although many think that Champagne is a dessert wine, when pairing wine with dessert, the wine must be sweeter than the dessert or it will taste tart. This is the time when I recommend drinking sweet Champagne. Look for the terms *Demi-Sec* to pair with a lightly sweet dessert and *Doux* when your dessert is on the sweeter side.

Biscuits Roses de Reims (Pink Lady Fingers from Reims): The best-known dessert of the region is a delicate cookie made from eggs, sugar, flour, vanilla, and carmine food coloring. These are a major component of a Charlotte, a dessert made by lining a special charlotte tin with the biscuits and filling it with custard or fruit purée. The dessert is then chilled until the custard or purée sets and is served cold.

Croquinoles: Another cookie from Reims, slightly drier than the Roses de Reims, it can be pink or white.

Shortbread: Often baked in the shape of a Champagne cork, the *pâte sablée* for these cookies contains ground almonds and Champagne.

Ratafia: Technically a *mistelle*—a fortified wine made from a combination of unfermented grape juice (typically Pinot Meunier juice) and *Marc de Champagne.* I tend to think of Regency England and Jane Austen when I hear of *Ratafia,* it being the drink that was served to ladies when the gentlemen were having Brandy. With the prices commanded by Champagne in today's market, production of *Ratafia* has fallen off in recent years.

Marc de Champagne: Unlike *Ratafia,* production of *Marc de Champagne* (Brandy of Champagne) is still strong. Since it is made from the pomace or remains of Champagne production (the stems, seeds and skins left after pressing), production of this distillate does not lower Champagne production.

After sharing several meals with the Legras family, I broached a topic about which I had been quite curious. This is not a region that only eats seafood, fish, or white meat. In fact, there is quite a lot of pork, game, and dark meat eaten in the region. What, I asked, do they drink when the meal calls for red wine? The consensus around the dinner table in the winery at Legras & Haas was that although some Côteaux de Champenois is produced in the region, for the most part, the Legras family drinks Bordeaux with red meat. They have friends in Bordeaux, and when the occasion calls for red wine with red meat, they most often drink those friends' wine.

It wasn't a question that came to me suddenly. In fact, the first night I arrived in Chouilly, when Jérôme and Raf took me out for burgers, they drank beer with their burgers. I wasn't in the mood for beer, and although it didn't make any sense with a messy burger, having finally arrived in Champagne, I wanted to drink Champagne. Would beer or Bordeaux have been more logical? Probably, but I could not be pushed off my desire for Champagne. I got the sense that Jérôme didn't mind at all. It is, after all, the wine of his home. So when he and Raf toasted me with beer, I raised a glass of Brut Champagne in return. Not all bubbles are the same, of course, and I am the first person to tell you that I do not need a celebration to drink Champagne. I think it is an amazing food wine and one that pairs well with so many different types of food, but on that evening in a hopping burger joint in Epernay, as I was toasting finally being in Champagne and embarking on my cooking adventure in Chouilly, I *was* celebrating, and Brut Champagne seemed the perfect choice!

The Winemaker Recommends: Jérôme really likes Sea Urchin with Legras & Haas Blanc de Blancs Extra Brut.

Champagne Production and the Échelle des Crus.

Let's get one thing straight. Not all sparkling wines are Champagne. There are quite a few strict regulations regarding Champagne production. Location is the number one requirement that sets it apart from all other sparkling wines. Champagne can only be produced in the region of Champagne in northeast France.

Champagne is the northernmost wine-producing region in France (49th parallel); and it is only due to the warming influence of the Atlantic Ocean, the Marne River, and the temperature-stabilizing regional forests that grapes are able to ripen there at all. These factors combine with the belemnite (sea fossil) chalky soils that absorb heat from the sun and provide excellent drainage to allow optimal ripeness of the relatively early maturing varieties of Pinot Noir, Chardonnay, and Pinot Meunier—ultimately achieving an equilibrium of ripe healthy grapes and the extremely high acidity so necessary in sparkling wine. This combination results in wines of finesse, elegance, power, and structure that are unlike any others.

Champagne is produced predominantly from three grapes, Chardonnay, Pinot Noir, and Pinot Meunier. (Four other grapes are also authorized but rarely used: Pinot Blanc, Arbanne, Fromonteau [Pinot Gris], and Petit Meslier.) For the most part, Champagne is a blended wine. It can be a blend of: grapes varieties, grapes from different vineyards or areas within Champagne, and/or vintages.

Champagne is produced in the *Méthode Champenoise. Méthode Champenoise* means that after undergoing alcoholic fermentation in a vat, the wine is bottled with added sugar and yeast (*liqueur de tirage*). This *tirage* of sugar and yeast causes a secondary fermentation in the bottle (that's what causes the bubbles). The wine then ages in bottle on the yeast sediment. (Yeast adds toasty, bread flavor as well as preventing oxidation.) When the wine has finished aging, the bottles are riddled (turned and tilted to capture the sediment in the neck of the bottle), and finally the yeast is removed by a process known as disgorgement. Disgorgement results in a slight loss of wine from the bottle. This loss of volume is rectified with the addition of *liqueur d'expédition* or *liqueur de dosage*. The amount of sugar in the *liqueur de dosage* determines the dryness level of the finished wine.

Finally, the champagne cork is inserted and the wire cage (*muselet)* is installed. As with the use of the name Champagne, only wines produced by this method ***in Champagne*** may employ the words *Méthode Champenoise*. Other sparkling wines produced this same way must use *Méthode Traditionelle or Méthode Classique*. Although some producers (mostly in the US) still use the term Champagne, sale of these wines is prohibited in the EU.

A handful of famous names and events have mightily influenced Champagne production:

Dom Pérignon: Cellar master at the Benedictine Abbey of Hautvilliers from 1668–1715. Contrary to wine lore, he did not invent sparkling wine. He was involved in viticultural improvements (lowering yields and increasing emphasis on Pinot Noir as a variety in the region) and is said to have encouraged development of stronger wine bottles to withstand the extreme pressure from carbon dioxide.

Madame Barbe-Nicole Ponsardin: THE Veuve (Widow) Clicquot was instrumental in developing *remuage,* or riddling, the process whereby sideways bottles are turned and tilted on *pupitres* (racks) until their upside-down position causes the sediment to settle in the neck of the bottle, promoting ease of sediment removal at disgorgement.

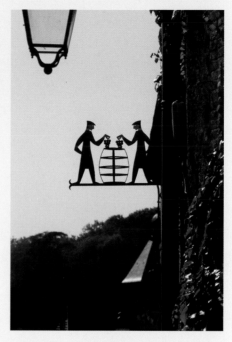

Hautvilliers, France

Jean-Antoine Chaptal: In 1801, this French chemist recognized the link between the sugar content in grapes and fermentation and proposed that in years with little sun (resulting in low sugar levels), wines could be improved with the addition of sugar. Chaptalization, the process of adding sugar to grape juice to increase alcohol content, is named after him.

Négociant System

Ameliorated bottle strength (prior to this, bottles frequently ruptured from the internal pressure of the bubbles) and cork technology improved Champagne bottling, but these enhancements came at a cost that was prohibitive to small growers. Consequently, Champagne production became something that only larger, wealthier producers could afford. Small grape farmers were left with no recourse but to sell their grapes to the larger houses, and the **Négociant** system was born.

As of 2016, there were approximately 15,800 grape growers in Champagne. These growers who own a lion's share of the land in the region sell their grapes to the 349 Champagne houses. Additionally, there are 100 cooperatives that sell processed grape must or finished wine to Champagne houses or finished wine to consumers.

Récoltant-Manipulant

There is a small but growing trend of estate bottling in the Champagne region. Champagne producers who grow all their own grapes and produce and bottle their own "Grower Champagnes" on their estates are known as *Récoltant-Manipulants*. An *RM* on the front label of these wines indicates Récoltant-Manipulants while an *NM* identifies Négociants.

Appellation Contrôlée and the CIVC

Champagne was originally delineated in 1908 (at the time this delineation did not include the Aube, although a large quantity of grapes from the Aube was used in Champagne production). With the outbreak of Phylloxera and World War I, many large houses purchased grapes from the Loire Valley and elsewhere, causing riots among growers in Champagne. Regulations were established to require that grapes used for Champagne wine be grown in the Champagne region. In 1927, the region was expanded to include the Aube, and in 1936 Champagne received Appellation Contrôlée status.

Count Robert-Jean de Vogüé: (Moët et Chandon). In 1941, De Vogüé assembled a broad consortium of growers, producers, and shippers to fight against the challenges of Nazi occupation, including their looting and forced appropriation of Champagne stocks. The **CIVC** (*Comité Interprofessionel du Vin de Champagne*) currently regulates Champagne production and mediates between large Champagne producers and the growers from whom they purchase their grapes.

Échelle des Crus:

In response to discord between négociants (those who buy grapes to produce Champagne) and growers, the CIVC established the **Échelle des Crus,** a village-rating scale to regulate prices of grapes. Villages are ranked on a quality level, with *Grand Cru* Villages receiving 100 percent. Those ranked 90–99 percent are rated *Premier Cru* and below that are simply *Cru* Villages, although the word *Cru* is rarely used. This rating was originally designed as a method of regulating grape prices to smooth negotiations between growers and producers. A standard grape price was set each year and farmers received a percentage of that price based on the *Échelle* rating of their village. In 1990, the *Échelle* system became more of a suggestion rather than an enforceable price, and in the early 2000s, the CIVC abolished the *Échelle* system altogether although producers in Grand Cru and Premier Cru villages understandably still continue to use the designation on their labels.

Duo of French Salads
Grated Carrots with Walnut Vinaigrette
Carottes Rapées

Yield: 5 cups | Ease of Preparation: Simple
Wine Pairing: Both salads pair well with crisp white wines and dry rosés

I was having dinner with a French family in Roussillon once and mentioned that one of the things I really missed in restaurants were traditional French salads (the French sometimes call them crudités) like Carottes Rapées or Salade de Betteraves. One of the teenage daughters told me I needed to go to an "auto-grill" or truck stop. I couldn't decide if I should be insulted (probably yes), or just take it as the truth. The basic salads that I love are not found in gourmet restaurants, but rather in simple cafés, local traiteurs (catering shops selling elegant to-go food), and, yes, in auto-grills throughout France. That's fine—they may not be haute cuisine, but they are delicious, fresh, and satisfying—a lovely way to start a meal.

INGREDIENTS

1 lb. carrots (preferably in a variety of colors)
3 Tbsp. Dijon mustard
¾ cup apple cider vinegar
½ cup walnut oil
½ cup neutral oil (canola or corn oil)
1 Tbsp. kosher salt
Pinch white pepper
2 Tbsp. finely chopped flat leaf parsley

WHAT YOU'LL NEED

Vegetable peeler
Box grater or a food processor with grating attachment
2-quart salad bowl
Large salad bowl
Whisk
Rubber spatula

TIMING

30 minutes if you are grating by hand, 20 if using the food processor

PROCESS

Peel and grate the carrots. If using a box grater, try to hold the carrots so that the pieces come out as long as possible. (I asked my dad to grate the carrots for me once. My dad is super strong—like Popeye—and he really put his muscles into the grating process. His carrot pieces were about ⅔ of an inch long—they tasted fine but were not quite as pretty.)

Whisk the mustard and cider vinegar until smooth. Whisk in the oils, salt, and pepper.

Place the carrots and parsley in the large salad bowl and toss to mix. Mix with the walnut dressing, adding a little at a time. Be careful not to overdress. Taste for seasoning before serving.

Diced Beets with Lemon Vinaigrette
Salade de Betteraves

Yield: 6 cups | Ease of Preparation: Moderate | Ease of Sourcing: Simple

I'll be honest. I almost prefer how beets look to how they taste. This is not as much a comment on their flavor as to how incredibly pretty I find this jewel-toned vegetable. There is almost no food more beautiful than a perfect beet glistening with oil. The more different colors of beets you are able to find for this salad, the more beautiful it will be.

INGREDIENTS

2 lbs. large beets (preferably at least two different colors)

4 Tbsp. kosher salt

Rosemary sprigs

Bay leaves

10 black peppercorns

Water

Extra-virgin olive oil

2 Tbsp. finely chopped parsley

1 cup of Lemon Vinaigrette (recipe below)

WHAT YOU'LL NEED

One ovenproof nonreactive baking dish for each color of beets

Aluminum foil

Paper towels

Latex gloves

Plastic cutting board

Medium salad bowl for each color of beets

TIMING

Baking time: 30 minutes to 1½ hours. See Note #1 below.

Peeling time: 10 minutes

Cutting time: 15 minutes

PROCESS

Preheat oven to 400° F.

First things first! Be careful! Beet juice bleeds and stains everything! Everything you use for this recipe should be stainproof. If you have more than one color of beets, separate the beets by color.

Remove the beet greens (if there are any) close to the beet itself—make sure you leave a little of the stalk; this will prevent the beet from bleeding too much. Place each color of beets in different baking dishes. Fill the dish with enough water to come halfway up the beets. Add 1 tablespoon of salt per pan, 1 large sprig rosemary, two bay leaves, and 5 black peppercorns. Add ¼ to ½ cup olive oil. It should form quarter-sized circles on the surface of the water—not a solid layer.

Cover each baking dish with aluminum foil and bake until just done. Start to check for doneness after 30 minutes by poking the largest beet with a fork. It should just slide to the center of the beet. If you have to press hard, it's not done. Put it back in and bake for 10 to 15 minutes before testing again. The beet will continue to cook a little when you take it out of the oven. Once the beets are done, remove the baking dishes from the oven and let them cool.

Now for the messy part! Put on your latex gloves. Begin with the lightest colored beets first. Use a paper towel to rub the beet. The skin should slip right off.

Slice the beets in ⅓- to ½-inch rounds. Line up the rounds and slice strips of beet the same width as the rounds. Line up the strips and cut in square cubes. Place the cubes in salad bowls separated by color. Once you have finished, add some parsley to each bowl and stir to combine. Dress each color of beets separately. Toss together at the last minute. The beets do not bleed as much once they are dressed, but keeping them separate until the last minute will ensure the colors stay as true as possible.

Notes

#1. Cooking time depends on the size of beets and how old they are. If they are very small or recently harvested, they take less time to cook. If they have been kept in a cellar for a while, they lose moisture and take longer. I have cooked the same size of beets at different times of the year with wildly different cooking times. Try not to overcook the beets: they lose structure and the color is not as vibrant—especially in lighter-colored beets.

#2. If you are lucky enough to find very small beets, you might not even need to cut them or you may choose to cut them in halves or quarters. This keeps the distinctive heart shape of the beet intact.

#3. If the beet greens look good, keep them to cook with, using them as you would use chard or kale.

Lemon Vinaigrette

Yield: 3 cups | Ease of Preparation: Simple | Ease of Sourcing: Simple

This is my favorite salad dressing. I like quite a bit of garlic, and the combination of garlic, lemon, and Dijon mustard blends so well with the greenness of the parsley and olive oil. I like to make a batch at the beginning of the week so that I have dressing all week long. I find the use of lemon juice instead of vinegar makes it considerably more wine-friendly.

INGREDIENTS

4 medium cloves garlic, chopped
¼ cup chopped parsley
½ cup lemon juice
1 Tbsp. Dijon mustard
1 Tbsp. kosher salt
1 tsp. pepper
2 cups extra-virgin olive oil

WHAT YOU'LL NEED

Blender
Rubber spatula

TIMING

10 minutes

PROCESS

Put the garlic, parsley, lemon, mustard, kosher salt, and pepper in the blender. Process for one minute until it is well chopped and blended together. Push down with a spatula. Process again and with the motor running, add oil very quickly. Do not go slowly or it will become too thick. Shut off the blender as soon as all of the oil is added. Taste for seasoning and if necessary add more salt, pepper or lemon juice.

Keeps its maximum quality for a week to 10 days in the refrigerator.

Notes

#1. The use of a blender is optional. If you are like me and prefer chopping more than cleaning your blender, sharpen your knife and finely mince the garlic and the parsley, put all the ingredients in a jar with a tight-fitting lid, and shake the dressing until it emulsifies.

#2. This dressing tastes quite salty on its own. This is intentional. The dressing is intended to eliminate the need for further salt in the salad.

Gruyère Flan
with Heirloom Tomatoes

Yield: one large flan | Ease of Preparation: Simple | Ease of Sourcing: Simple
Wine Pairing: Brut Champagne or young White Burgundy

This savory cheese flan is creamy and delicate. I like to serve it with ripe heirloom tomatoes as a first course at dinner or a main course at lunch with a green salad. Although I use Gruyère, you may substitute any easy-melting cheese in this recipe. Because this dish has so few ingredients, I recommend using the best eggs, cream, and Gruyère you can find.

INGREDIENTS

4 eggs

2 cups heavy cream

1 cup finely shredded Gruyère

1 tsp. kosher salt

¼ tsp. finely ground white pepper

Pinch freshly grated nutmeg

½ tsp. Piment d'Espelette

Warm water

Optional: one lb. heirloom tomatoes
(preferably different sizes and colors)

WHAT YOU'LL NEED

Rotary cheese grater or box grater

Large mixing bowl

Metal whisk

Oven-safe Pyrex baking dish
(at least 1½ quart capacity)

Scissors

Parchment paper

Pan spray

Aluminum foil

Oven-safe pan large enough to hold the
baking dish

Butter knife

Serving platter

TIMING

Prep Time: 10 minutes

Baking Time: 2¼ hours

Cooling Time: 30 minutes

PROCESS

Preheat oven to 350° F.

Break the eggs into the mixing bowl and whisk until completely homogenous. Whisk in the cream, grated cheese, kosher salt, white pepper, nutmeg, and Piment d'Espelette.

Cut a piece of parchment paper into a circle the size of the bottom of the baking dish. This circle should cover only the bottom of the dish. It should not move up the sides.

Spray the baking dish with pan spray.

Place the parchment in the baking dish and press out any bubbles.

Pour the cream mixture into the baking dish. Cover it with foil. Line the bottom of the large oven-safe pan with a kitchen towel. Place the flan-filled dish on the towel. Pour enough warm water into the oven pan to come about 1 inch up the side of the dish containing the flan. This water bath will keep the flan from forming bubbles while it cooks. I like to place the pan in the oven first, allowing one corner to stick outside the oven, and then pour the water into it. Then slide the pan fully into the oven. Be very careful not to get any water into the flan.

After 1½ hours, remove the pan from the oven and check to see if the flan has set by shaking it gently. If it is not totally set, return it to the oven and continue baking until it is firm and set up. Do not undercook. The flan will not firm up later. If in doubt, insert the tip of a paring knife in the center of the flan and pull it to the side. If there is a clear division, the flan is set. If it is still liquid or if your knife comes back coated in flan batter, continue cooking it for 10 more minutes and test it again. Repeat until the flan is set.

Cool the finished flan on a baking rack for 30 minutes.

After 30 minutes, the flan should be ready to unmold. Run a knife around the outside of the flan to loosen it from the dish. Invert your platter over the baking dish, hold both the platter and the baking dish securely, and flip it over. The flan should plop down onto your platter. If it doesn't, shake it a bit. Don't panic if it doesn't fall right away. It will eventually succumb to gravity and drop down. Remove the parchment paper and discard.

Serve with colorful heirloom tomatoes.

Note

Piment d'Espelette is a red pepper grown in and around the picturesque Basque town of Espelette in the French Pyrénées mountains. It is most frequently found in dried ground form. Piment d'Espelette is sweet and slightly spicy. If you cannot find it, you could substitute cayenne pepper, but keep in mind that cayenne is much hotter than Piment d'Espelette, so a pinch or two of cayenne will be plenty.

Cannellini Bean Salad
with Peppers and Onions

Yield: 3 cups | Ease of Preparation: Simple | Ease of Sourcing: Simple
Wine Pairing: Crisp, dry white wine or a young, fresh unoaked red

I love this salad. It is easy to prepare and so colorful—the bright bell peppers and red onions, a confetti-like splash against the pale almond-colored background of the beans. It brightens up the table, and best of all it is vegan and a good source of protein, helpful when you need to feed a crowd of hungry vegetarians who've been working in the field or winery as I did at Domaine de Sulauze and Champagne LeGras & Haas.

INGREDIENTS

15½-ounce can cannellini beans
½ cup red bell peppers, in ¼-inch dice
½ cup orange or yellow bell peppers, in ¼-inch dice
¼ cup red onions, in ¼-inch dice
½–⅔ cup lemon vinaigrette (page 384)
¼ cup finely minced flat leaf parsley
Kosher salt
Finely ground black pepper

WHAT YOU'LL NEED

Can opener
Fine mesh strainer
Medium bowl
Decorative bowl

TIMING

Prep Time: 30 minutes
Chilling Time: 30 minutes

PROCESS

Open the can of cannellini beans. Using the mesh strainer, strain and rinse them well to remove the cloudy liquid from the can. Shake off the excess liquid and pour into your bowl. Add the bell peppers and red onions and stir.

This next part is a matter of personal preference. Add ¼ cup of vinaigrette, stir, and taste a bit of the salad. If you are satisfied with the amount of dressing, you are good. If you prefer a little more dressing, add a bit more. Once you have reached your preferred ratio of dressing to salad, add the minced parsley and check for seasoning. Depending on your salt tolerance, you may need to add a little more salt and pepper.

If you wish, serve the salad at room temperature, but I prefer it to be chilled a little bit. Serve it in a decorative bowl.

Notes

#1. If you cannot find cannellini beans, any white bean will do. Beans are one of the few canned products that I use with regularity. If you wish to cook your beans from scratch, feel free.

#2. I like the look of this salad with the different colors of peppers and red onions. If you can only find one color of pepper, that's fine, use one cup of that. If you don't have red onions, substitute yellow onions. Be aware that using green peppers will add pronounced green notes to the dish and that some yellow onions are stronger than others. Either way, it will still be delicious!

Classic Fennel Meatballs
in Marinara Sauce

Yield: 40 golf ball-size meatballs | Ease of Preparation: Moderate
Ease of Sourcing: Easy | Wine Pairing: Chianti, Barbera, Valpolicella or Montefalco Rosso

The day I arrived at Champagne Legras & Haas, Jérôme mentioned that he had promised to make Spaghetti and Meatballs for the winery staff the next evening. I was happy to volunteer to take on the task. I am aware that in Italy, Spaghetti and Meatballs is a no-no. You either get spaghetti tossed in meat sauce with a grating of Parmigiano Reggiano, or Polpette (Italian for meatballs) with a light tomato sauce and shaved Parmigiano Reggiano, but not both. Spaghetti and Meatballs is an Italo-American invention. Does that mean that it is not good? No! And was that what Jérôme and his staff had a hankering for that first day of harvest? Yes. So, Spaghetti and Meatballs it was! They also make a tasty appetizer course or a snack at a cocktail party.

INGREDIENTS

For the Meatballs:

1½ cups day-old bread cubes, or 5 to 6 inches of dry baguette cut in one-inch slices

1 cup water

3 Tbsp. olive oil

1 tsp. fennel seeds

¾ cup fresh fennel, finely chopped

¾ cup yellow onion, finely chopped

3 cloves garlic, finely chopped

1½ tsp. dried oregano

1 bay leaf

1 Tbsp. kosher salt

1 lb. ground beef

1 lb. ground pork

3 large eggs

1 cup grated Parmigiano Reggiano + extra for garnish

¼ cup finely chopped fresh parsley

½ tsp. black pepper

For the Marinara Sauce:

2 28-oz. cans whole peeled San Marzano DOP tomatoes

½ cup extra-virgin olive oil

6 cloves thinly sliced garlic

½ cup fresh basil leaves sliced in ½-in. strips

½ tsp. crushed red pepper flakes (optional)

Kosher salt to taste

2 lbs. excellent-quality dry spaghetti (optional)

WHAT YOU'LL NEED

Dish to soak the bread

Medium-sized sauté pan

Electric mixer with paddle attachment

Small fry pan

Parchment paper

2 half-sheet trays

Disposable latex kitchen gloves
(optional)

Metal spatula or kitchen tongs to turn the
meatballs

Large bowl

6-quart saucepan

Box grater (optional)

Cheese grater

TIMING

Prep Time: 30 minutes

Mixing Time: 5 minutes

Meatball Rolling Time: 30 minutes

Cooking Time: 30 minutes

PROCESS

Preheat oven to 425° F.

For the Meatballs:

Soak bread in water until it begins to soften—no more than a couple of minutes. Squeeze the water out very well. This is very important. Do not to leave any excess water in the bread or your meat mixture will be quite mushy, and that makes them very difficult to roll into balls.

In a sauté pan, toast fennel seeds in 3 tablespoons of olive oil over medium heat. Add chopped fennel, onions, garlic, oregano, and bay leaf. Add 1 teaspoon kosher salt and cook until onions and fennel are softened, but not browned. Remove bay leaf and discard. Allow the onion mixture to cool.

Use the paddle attachment on your mixer and mix the cooled onion mixture and all of the remaining meatball ingredients (ground beef, ground pork, eggs, parmesan, parsley, black pepper, and the remaining salt) for 5 minutes until sticky.

Fry a small amount to taste for seasoning. Add more salt if necessary. Shape into golf ball-size balls and place on a sheet tray lined with parchment paper, leaving a small space between each meatball so they do not stick together. (I know it is fussy on my part, but I use latex gloves when I roll out my meatballs. That's up to you.)

Bake in a 425° F degree oven for 5 minutes, then turn the meatballs to make sure they do not flatten out too much. At this point, I sometimes have to use two spoons to reshape the meatballs if I haven't squeezed all of the water out of the bread. Lower the heat to 400° F and continue cooking until lightly browned and cooked through, continuing to turn the meatballs every five minutes (approximately 20 minutes total). The meatballs are cooked when they are firm when you press on them. If in doubt, cut one open to see if it is done. (The meatballs may exude some liquid during this process. Don't worry, that's fine.)

For the Marinara Sauce:

This sauce could not be any easier. Dump the contents of the cans of San Marzano tomatoes into your large bowl and squeeze them between your fingers to break them up. Be careful or you will end up wearing the tomatoes.

Place the saucepan on medium heat and add a half cup of extra-virgin olive oil. Some people use less oil than this, but I like the flavor. Add the garlic and cook for a minute or so, stirring constantly until the garlic is golden but not brown. Do not burn it! Lower the heat and add the basil. Stir for 30 seconds and then add the tomatoes and the optional crushed red pepper flakes. Simmer over low heat until the tomatoes are broken down into a sauce (approximately 30 minutes). If it begins to cook dry, add ¼ cup of water and lower the heat even more. Add extra salt if needed.

At this point, you may sauce the meatballs in a sauté pan and serve them as a main course with a light grating of extremely good Parmigiano Reggiano. If you wish to go the classic Italian American Spaghetti and Meatballs route, cook your spaghetti according to the package instructions for the number of guests you are serving. Pull the pasta while it is still al dente. Toss it in a little olive oil and twirl it in the center of your pasta bowl. Top with the meatballs in marinara sauce and garnish with a healthy sprinkling of Parmigiano Reggiano.

Notes

#1. This recipe calls for grated Parmigiano Reggiano. If you are purchasing it pregrated at your local store, remember grated is different from shredded. Grated is the powdery texture; shredded is small strips of cheese. If you are grating it at home on a box grater, use the side of the box grater that looks like little metal spurs or stars.

#2. Why San Marzano tomatoes? These deep red tomatoes are Italian plum tomatoes with a pedigree. With their low acidity, high pulp-to-seed ratio, and sweet, ripe flavor, San Marzano DOP (*Denominazione di Origine Protetta*) tomatoes grown in the volcanic soils at the foot of Mount Vesuvius are universally recognized as fantastic sauce tomatoes. Unfortunately, there are a lot of fake San Marzanos on the market. Make sure the tomatoes you buy actually say San Marzano DOP on the label. If you cannot find them, Muir Glen brand whole peeled tomatoes are very good. If you grow your own tomatoes, feel free to use them, but make sure they are very ripe and allow extra cooking time, since canned tomatoes are already partially cooked.

Pork Loin
with Potatoes and Onions

Yield: Serves 6 to 8 | Ease of Preparation: Moderate | Ease of Sourcing: Simple
Wine Pairing: Champagne, White Burgundy, or Dry Vouvray or Montlouis

When I packed my bags to go to France to cook for harvest workers a couple of years ago, I knew that I would likely use this recipe. A long-time favorite of mine, pork loin roasted with potatoes and onions in white wine and butter is simple yet very flavorful. I cooked this dish for the harvest workers at Domaine de Sulauze and also for the winery workers at Champagne Legras & Haas. Try to get a pork loin with some fat left on the outside—it enhances the flavor of the final dish.

INGREDIENTS

4 lb. loin of pork

Kosher salt

Freshly ground black pepper

6 Tbsp. unsalted butter, divided into
    2 and 4 Tbsp.

6–8 medium Russet potatoes
    (approximately 1½ lbs.), peeled and
    sliced in ¼-inch slices

1 large yellow onion, peeled and sliced
    in ⅛-inch slices

2 cloves garlic, peeled and sliced thin

2 bay leaves

½ Tbsp. kosher salt

½ tsp. freshly ground black pepper

1½ cup dry white wine

1 cup water

⅓ cup finely minced fresh flat leaf
    parsley

WHAT YOU'LL NEED

Butcher's twine

Roasting pan safe for stovetop use

Tongs

Skewer or instant read meat
    thermometer

TIMING

Prep Time: 30 minutes

Cook Time: 1½ hours

Rest Time: 15 minutes

PROCESS

Preheat the oven to 350° F.

Use a sharp knife to remove the silver skin from the outside of your pork loin, being careful to leave the fat. I like my pork roast tied with butcher's twine. You can tie it yourself in 1½ inch intervals or ask your butcher to do it. This is optional, but I like the way the meat looks when it is tied.

Rub kosher salt and fresh ground pepper on the outside of the pork loin.

Melt 2 tablespoons of unsalted butter in the roasting pan over medium heat. Raise the heat to medium high. Brown the pork loin until it is golden brown on all sides. Take the time to do this well. It makes all the difference in the world when it comes to the flavor of the final dish.

Place the roasting pan in your preheated oven and roast for 15 minutes.

At the end of the 15 minutes, add the potatoes, onions, garlic, bay leaves, ½ tablespoon salt, and ½ teaspoon pepper to the pan and stir them in the juices from the meat. Add the remaining 4 tablespoons butter, white wine, and water and return the pan to the oven.

Continue roasting for 1 hour, stirring the potatoes periodically. Test the pork for doneness by inserting a skewer into the loin. If the juices run clear, the meat is done. Alternately, you may use an instant read meat thermometer. When the meat is done to your satisfaction, remove the meat to a cutting board and hold it in a warm part of the kitchen so it does not get too cold. Check the doneness of the potatoes. They should be soft and have absorbed some of the cooking juices. If they are not quite done, return them to the oven to finish cooking.

When the potatoes are fully cooked, remove the bay leaves and check for seasoning, adding more salt and pepper if necessary. Stir the minced parsley in with the potatoes and onions. Slice the pork and serve with the potatoes either on individual plates or family style on a large decorative platter. Pass a small pitcher with the pan juices so guests can put a little of the flavorful juice on their portion.

Notes

#1. This dish can be made with all types of pork roasts. I've even made it at Christmastime with a Crown Pork Roast. The one exception is pork tenderloin—I do not recommend it. I find it cooks too quickly and does not allow for the development of flavor you get with a thicker piece of meat. If you use a different type pork roast, you will need to adjust the cooking time.

#2. Pork temperature. In 2011, the USDA released new temperature guidelines for cooking pork that lowered the recommended cooking temperature by 15° F from 160° F to 145° F. If you prefer to use a meat thermometer to check the temperature of your pork, slide the thermometer in the roast. Remove the roast from the oven when the temperature reads 140° F to 142° F and let it rest for 5 minutes. The final temperature will rise to 145° F during the rest time. This is sometimes called carryover cooking.

#3. I like Russet potatoes or another starchy variety for this dish. Starchy potatoes absorb liquid and soften nicely. You want the potatoes to really soak up the meat and wine juices. If all you have are waxy potatoes, you can use them; they just don't take on as much flavor as starchy ones.

Coq au Champagne

Yield: Serves 4 | Ease of Preparation: Moderately difficult | Ease of Sourcing: Moderately easy, but expensive
Wine Pairing: Champagne: Blanc or Rosé, preferably with some age on it.

I make Coq au Vin quite often. It feels homey yet luxurious at the same time. Substituting Champagne for the traditional Bourgogne Rouge changes the flavor profile from dark and a bit brooding to a somewhat lighter, more lifted dish. I made this for the winery workers at Champagne Legras & Haas in Chouilly, Champagne.

INGREDIENTS

For the Garnish:

18 white or yellow pearl onions

4 Tbsp. unsalted butter, divided in two

Kosher salt

4 sprigs thyme

¼ cup reasonably priced Champagne

1 cup chicken stock, preferably
    homemade

10 oz. small white button mushrooms

¼ lb. slab pancetta or ventrèche (see Note
    #3 below)

For the Chicken:

4 chicken leg quarters

Kosher salt

White pepper

3 Tbsp. unsalted butter

2 garlic cloves, puréed

2 cups reasonably priced Champagne

2 cups chicken stock, preferably
    homemade

2 bay leaves

2 Tbsp. minced parsley

For the noodles:

1 package dry egg noodles

2 Tbsp. butter

¼ cup minced parsley

WHAT YOU'LL NEED

Paring knife

Chef's knife

Slotted spoon or spider

Skillet large enough to hold 8 pieces of
    chicken

3 medium skillets for the garnish (or use
    one and wash it between ingredients)

Large pot for cooking pasta

Large strainer

Large bowl

TIMING

For the garnish: 45 minutes

For the chicken: 45 minutes

PROCESS

For the Garnish:

I generally make the garnishes ahead of time. That way, if I get interrupted while making the chicken, the garnishes are already done. One of my pet peeves is when people overcook the chicken on this dish.

Pearl Onions:

Use the paring knife to cut a shallow *x* on the root side of the pearl onions.

Bring two cups of water to a rolling boil and blanche the pearl onions for two minutes. Use the slotted spoon to remove the onions from the water and let them cool. When they are cool, peel the skin off the onions.

Melt 2 tablespoons butter in the medium skillet and brown the onions until they are golden, swirling the pan periodically to get an even color. Add ¼ teaspoon kosher salt, 2 sprigs thyme, ¼ cup Champagne, and enough chicken stock to come half way up the onions and simmer covered until the onions are tender and the sauce has thickened. You may need to add a little extra stock as the level evaporates. Place the onions to the side for use in final plating.

Sautéed Mushrooms:

Depending on the size of your mushrooms, either half or quarter them. Ideally, you would find mushrooms the same size as the pearl onions, but I rarely do, so cut them to approximately the same size as the onions.

Melt 2 tablespoons butter in the medium skillet. Once it is melted, add the mushrooms and two sprigs thyme. DO NOT ADD SALT. Adding salt causes mushrooms to exude liquid. This will flood your pan, giving you boiled mushrooms instead of sautéed ones. Sauté until the mushrooms are golden brown on all sides and set aside.

Lardons:

Peel the paper from the pancetta or ventrèche and roll it out. It should look like a thick slab of bacon. Cut the slab into ⅓-inch slices. Turn the slices on the side and cut ⅓-inch strips. This is a lardon. It should be approximately the same thickness all around. Cook the lardons in a medium skillet until they are brown and cooked through. They do not need to be crispy all the way through. Set aside.

For the Chicken:

Rinse the chicken pieces and pat dry. Separate the leg from the thigh. Lightly salt and pepper each piece.

Melt 3 tablespoons butter in the large skillet over medium-high heat. When it is melted, place the chicken skin side down on the skillet. Brown the chicken on both sides. Take the time to get good golden color on the skin. When you are satisfied with the color, add the garlic and stir it quickly until it turns light golden, being careful not to burn it. This only takes about 5 seconds. Once it is golden, add 2 cups Champagne and 1 cup chicken stock to the pan. The liquid level should come half way up the sides of the chicken pieces. If it isn't high enough, add more stock. Add the bay leaves and lower the heat. Simmer covered for approximately 20 minutes. The chicken should be done at this point. Remove the lid and raise the heat level to medium high to reduce the sauce. Turn the chicken in the sauce to coat the pieces. There should be a glazed coating of sauce on the chicken.

Prepare the egg noodles per the package instructions. Strain the cooked pasta into a large bowl. Toss with 2 tablespoons butter, salt, white pepper, and ¼ cup minced parsley.

Combine the onions, mushrooms, and lardons in a skillet and warm them through.

Arrange the chicken with sauce on a decorative serving platter and garnish with the onions, mushrooms, lardons, and 2 tablespoons minced parsley. Serve with buttered egg noodles.

Notes

#1. I know that it is traditional to make Coq au Vin with an old rooster, but even though I have farmer friends who raise poultry, I can't get a rooster. I use free-range local chickens, preferably a heritage breed that has some texture to the meat. Use the best-quality chicken you can source.

#2. I like dark meat chicken for this dish. I find that it stays moister than white meat. If you have a white meat chicken lover in your family, by all means use both light and dark meat. Remember that white meat cooks faster than dark meat.

#3. *Ventrèche* vs. *Pancetta* vs. Bacon. *Ventrèche* and *Pancetta* are the same thing, dry-cured pork belly. It is available at most gourmet stores, Italian markets, and online through Amazon and d'Artagnan (d'Artagnan calls it *ventrèche*). Although it is often available sliced thin, it can be found in a rolled-up version—that's what you want for this recipe. If you cannot find it, you may substitute the most neutral-flavored slab bacon you can find. If your bacon is strongly flavored or smoky, blanche it for a minute or two in simmering water, drain it well, and dry it thoroughly. I will warn you, smoky bacon will totally ruin the delicacy of this dish. You have gone to the trouble and expense of buying Champagne. Don't mess it up by using overpowering bacon. You would be better off leaving it out than putting smoky bacon in your Coq au Champagne.

#4. Champagne vs. sparkling wine. I love Champagne, so that's what I use in this dish—usually a cheaper Champagne for cooking and a more expensive Champagne to drink. If you wish to substitute a sparkling wine, try to find a traditional method wine. Good examples are Franciacorta, Cava, or American Traditional Method Sparkling wine. These wines are aged on yeast and have a richer flavor. Prosecco is not aged on yeast and does not have the same complexity of flavor.

Apple Crumble

Yield: 10 cups of crumble topping—enough for one 9 x 13-inch dish, or 12 individual ramekins
Ease of Preparation: Simple | Ease of Sourcing: Simple
Wine Pairing: Depending on the fruit, either a white, red, or rosé dessert wine

I love desserts that can be adapted to use seasonal fruits all year long. Crumble is a perfect example of this. The topping is simple to make and keeps well. One trip to the farmer's market or local pick-your-own farm, and you've got a sweet end to a meal that will make people swear your grandmother came to visit. I prepared apple crumble for the winery workers at Champagne Legras & Haas with apples I picked at the Cueillette de d'Aulnay sur Marne (a pick-your-own-fruit and vegetable farm about five miles from the winery). Feel free to substitute your favorite fruit.

INGREDIENTS

For the Crumble:

1 lb. light brown sugar
4 cups rolled oats
1 Tbsp. kosher salt
½ cup all-purpose flour
1 lb. cold unsalted butter, cut in ¾-in.
    cubes

For the Apple Filling:

5 lbs. baking apples, peeled, cored,
    and sliced into twelve pieces
¼ cup lemon juice
¼ cup sugar
¼ cup cinnamon
½ tsp. kosher salt
Vanilla or crème fraîche ice cream to
    garnish

WHAT YOU'LL NEED

Electric mixer with paddle attachment
9 x 13-inch baking dish
Vegetable peeler
Wooden skewer

TIMING

For the crumble topping: 10 minutes
Baking time: 45 minutes to 1 hour

PROCESS

For the Crumble Topping:

Place the brown sugar, oats, kosher salt, and flour in the bowl of your mixer and mix on the lowest setting until well blended. There should be no lumps of brown sugar. Add the cold cubed butter and mix on the lowest setting until the butter pieces have reduced to the size of a small grape and they are fully coated with the sugar oat mixture. **Do not step away**. Do not continue beating until the butter is completely broken down and blended in. (Depending on the size of your mixer bowl, you may need to place a clean kitchen towel over the mixer to prevent the contents of the bowl from shooting around the room.) This method produces a crispy-textured crumble topping when baked. The topping can be made ahead of time and stored in the refrigerator for a week.

For the Apple Crumble:

Preheat the oven to 350° F.

After peeling and slicing the apples, add lemon juice to keep them from browning. Add the sugar, cinnamon, and kosher salt to the apples. Place the apples in the bottom of the baking dish. Press down to make sure there is a solid layer of apples.

Cover the apples with a generous layer of crumble—between ½ to ¾ inch thick.

Bake in the preheated oven for 45 minutes, turning once. After 45 minutes, use a wooden skewer to poke through the crumble topping to see if the apples are soft. If they are still firm, return the crumble to the oven and continue baking until the apples are soft.

Serve warm with vanilla or crème fraîche ice cream.

Notes

#1. Make sure you use pie apples. They are crisp and hold their shape well. Examples of pie apples are McIntosh, Jonathan, Jonagold, Pippin, Braeburn, and Honeycrisp. These are just a few suggestions. Ask your local farmer what they recommend.

#2. This dish is fantastic with all sorts of fruit. You may need to add a bit of cornstarch or flour to the fruit mixture depending on the moisture content of the fruit. Adjust the amount of sugar based on the tartness level of the fruit. Depending on which fruit you use, you may also wish to omit the cinnamon.

Clafoutis

Yield: 12 individual or 1 large Clafoutis | Ease of Preparation: Moderate
Ease of Sourcing: Simple if cherries, berries, or plums are in season. | Wine Pairing: Light-bodied dessert wine

Although I first had this dish when visiting the Faugier family of Domaine des Hautes Chassis in Crozes-Hermitage, it became a spring and summer staple on my menu at Buck's Fishing & Camping. Naturally, I took the recipe with me when I packed my bags to cook the harvest in France. It's easy, the ingredients are easy to come by, and you can change the fruit depending on what's available. Traditionally made with dark cherries with the pits still in them, I served it with Quetsche plums for the winery workers at Legras & Haas. I never really know how to describe Clafoutis. It isn't custard, nor is it a cake. It is as if you took a thick crêpe batter and poured it over fruit—giving you a texture that is thicker than custard and less crumbly than cake. Whatever. It's delicious!

INGREDIENTS

Butter

1 cup all-purpose flour

¼ tsp. kosher salt

½ cup granulated sugar

4 large eggs (5 if medium or small),
    beaten very well until homogenous

2½ cups whole milk

1 tsp. vanilla extract

1 tsp. orange zest

2 to 3 pints fruit (raspberries, cherries,
    blackberries, blueberries, or plums,
    your choice) + extra for garnish

WHAT YOU'LL NEED

12 four-oz. ramekins or 1 ten-inch
    straight-sided tart or casserole pan

2 medium mixing bowls

Fine mesh strainer

Quart sized pitcher (if making
    individual Clafoutis)

Sheet tray (if making individual
    Clafoutis)

TIMING

Prep Time: 15 minutes

Batter Resting Time: 15 minutes

Baking Time: 20 minutes or 40–50
    minutes depending on whether you
    make 12 individual tarts or a single
    large one.

Resting Time: 15 minutes

PROCESS

Preheat oven to 375° F, preferably on convection setting.

Liberally butter ramekins or tart pan. If using individual ramekins, place them on a half sheet tray.

Mix dry ingredients.

Mix wet ingredients until homogenous.

Pour wet ingredients into dry and mix well. Add orange zest. Set aside in refrigerator for at least 15 minutes. This allows the starch molecules of the flour to be absorbed into the liquid and makes the Clafoutis more tender. It also gives the flavors of the orange zest time to develop. While the batter is resting, scatter fruit in bottom of the buttered ramekins or tart pan.

Remove the batter from the refrigerator. Whisk batter well and strain it into your quart pitcher to remove lumps and orange zest. (I like to use a pitcher for the batter because it is easier to pour it into the ramekins. If you are making a full-sized Clafoutis, you can strain the batter directly into the fruit-filled tart pan.)

Pour the batter over the fruit.

Bake 20 minutes for ramekins, turning once after 10 minutes. The tart will take 40 to 50 minutes total; turn it twice during the baking process. Clafoutis should look puffy and brown and be almost firm to the touch. It should be jiggly in the center and just barely opaque, but there should not be standing liquid on the top anywhere. Be careful not to cook it until it is totally solid. This will make it tough.

If using ramekins, let the Clafoutis rest 15 minutes before unmolding. To remove, run a butter knife along the inside of the ramekin to loosen it. Take the time to do this right. Use the rounded side of the knife to really pull the Clafoutis away from the sides. Shake the Clafoutis out into your hand. Flip it right side up on a plate. Sprinkle with confectioner's sugar, add extra fruit and unsweetened lightly whipped cream. (I think it is prettier to unmold the small Clafoutis, but if you are nervous about this, by all means, serve them in the ramekins.)

If using a tart pan, you still need to let it rest at least 15 minutes after baking, but you do not need to unmold it. Present it in the tart pan before cutting and plating individual servings with a sprinkle of confectioner's sugar, a dollop of unsweetened lightly whipped cream, and some berries.

Note

As I mentioned above, in France, dark unpitted cherries are typically used. The pit adds a note of bitterness (and therefore interest) to the dessert. I never had the temerity to serve it this way at Buck's but would totally serve it that way for friends at home. I love using all types of berries and plums (without the pits) in Clafoutis with the exception of strawberries. I find that strawberries' tendency to exude liquid messes up the batter because it makes it too thin and the color bleeds, turning the Clafoutis pink.

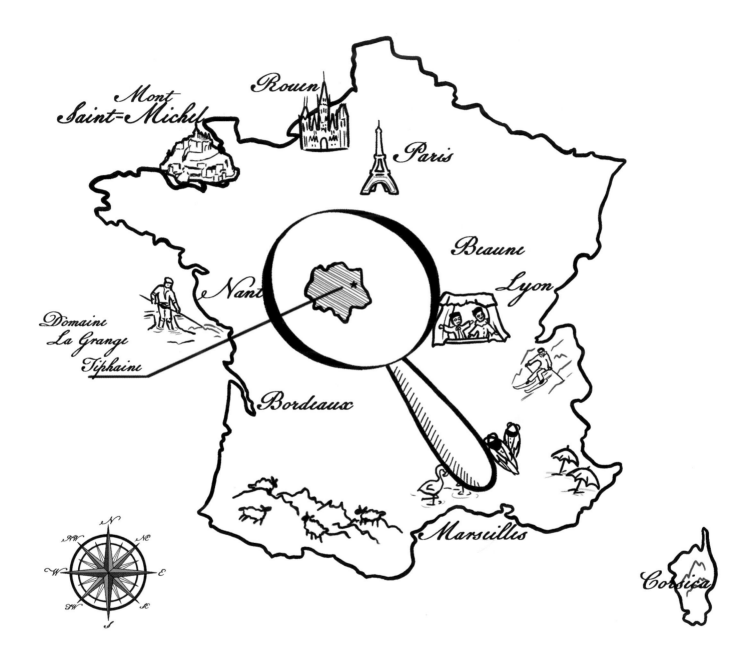

Mont
Saint-Michel

Rouen

Paris

Beaune

Lyon

Nantes

Domaine
La Grange
Tiphaine

Bordeaux

Marseilles

Corsica

N
NW NE
W E
SW SE
S

"Roots, Rillettes, and Chenin Blanc"
A Visit with Damien Delecheneau
La Grange Tiphaine, Montlouis-sur-Loire, France

My very first memories of France aren't of a trip I took there, but rather of a place of dreams: Chambord, an immense château with a rectangular keep and four massive round towers, its rooftop skyline so whimsically reminiscent of an Italian village that it caused Henry James to observe "the towers, cupolas, the gables, the lanterns, the chimneys, look more like the spires of a city than the salient points of a single building." A picture of Chambord with its spires, gables, and chimneys graced the cover of my first French textbook in high school, and the spell it cast upon me lasts to this day. This obsession with Chambord drew me to the Loire Valley on my first trip to France and on many subsequent visits, especially once the obsession broadened to include the region as a whole. The Loire Valley, with its perfect, unaccented French, its lovely mild climate, and a delicate yet homey cuisine characterized by seemingly unlimited supplies of delicious food products, kept pulling me back as if to a long lost home.

I did my first "real" wine tasting at a tasting room in Vouvray and nibbled on Pork Rillettes every chance I got. Even though I have added to my list of wine favorites, my first

wine love was Loire Valley Chenin Blanc. After seeing my family name on a marker in a churchyard near Tours, I felt compelled to start researching my lineage, convinced that my ancestors must be from there. Sadly, I have never found any evidence to support that fantasy. Still, the Loire is the homeland of my heart.

Obviously, I'm crazy about all things Loire Valley. At the top of that list is my love for Pork Rillettes. (My screen name in several chat rooms is Loire Lover only because Rillettes Lover was already taken.) Seriously, my obsession with Rillettes is pretty out of control. I mean, how could I not love something so delicious that the famous gourmand Honoré de Balzac nicknamed it "brown pig jam"?

I spent years perfecting my recipe for Rillettes and many of my friends were tasked with consuming my experiments until I got it right. (They tell me there are worse things in life.) It isn't just that I wanted to learn to make Rillettes. A good number of people make Rillettes. In fact, for a while, it seemed like you couldn't go into a French or wine-centric restaurant anywhere in DC without finding Rillettes of some sort on a charcuterie plate. I needed to make Rillettes like those I had eaten in the Loire. The meat and fat had to have a brown slow-cooked flavor—the concentrated meat juices mingling with the silky savoriness of the pork fat, the flavors cohesive. All of that can only be achieved by cooking it slow and low.

There should be no experimentation with the flavors of Rillettes, no twists, and by that I mean no overt Christmas cookie spices or riffs on Asian cooking, and please, no fast cooking it and beating it in a mixer to break up the chunks. It's a classic for a reason, and the flavors should not be tampered with.

According to Jacqueline Friedrich, author of the fabulous book *A Wine and Food Guide to the Loire* (a definite must-read for those interested in the Loire Valley), there are two types of Pork Rillettes from the Loire Valley—Rillettes de Tours (from the central Loire region of Touraine, specifically Vouvray) and Rillettes du Mans (from Le Mans). Rillettes de Tours tend to be burnished and more finely textured, while Rillettes du Mans are chunkier and pale.

For years I made the style from Tours, but after a lunchtime cooking session with Damien Delecheneau in the farmhouse kitchen of his winery home, I have adjusted my way of thinking about and cooking Pork Rillettes. His combines the burnished brown quality of Rillettes de Tours with the chunkiness of Rillettes du Mans. Before going to his house for lunch that day, I had stopped at Hardouin in Vouvray and picked up a pot of what I had always considered the gold standard of Rillettes to offer as a host gift. Damien's pot blew my gold standard out of the water (sorry, Hardouin). There were morsels of brown pork—some as large as my thumb, some smaller, finer shreds—"dressed" in amber, savory, slightly gelatinous fat. Damien hastened to assure me that the color of his Rillettes comes not from adding caramel coloring, but from slow cooking.

Ha! Vindication! Slow cooking, as I had discovered years ago through my own efforts, is the secret to making good Rillettes. Where Damien's differed from mine was in the size of the chunks of meat that, because of the slow cooking process that both he and I prefer, lent texture to the spread and yet still melted in your mouth. When combined with his organic Montlouis-sur-Loire (my favorite with Rillettes is La Grange Tiphaine La Grenouillières, a demi-sec Chenin Blanc from sandy soils), it was as if my little French soul had come home.

Foods of Touraine

One thing I have noticed (and Jacqueline Friedrich mentioned it in her book, as well) is that for the most part the cuisine of the Touraine seems to be traditional "French Food." By that I mean the specialties of the region are what many of us think of as simply French—foods that would logically appear on a menu anywhere in France or in any French restaurant throughout the world. It seems as if the abundance of produce and products and the mild climate lends itself to balanced, lovely, somewhat delicate food. In addition to my favorite Rillettes, Tourangelle cuisine features:

Rillons (a.k.a. Rillauds, Grillons): Cubed pork cooked in its own fat for a couple of hours until fork tender. I often prepare an extra large batch of pork cubes when I make Rillettes and pull some out after a couple of hours *et voilà*—Rillons! They can be eaten at room temperature on a salad, but I like to serve them warm with fried potatoes or over rice with a green salad. They are also delicious as a snack smashed onto a baguette.

Noisettes de Porc au Pruneaux: Pork medallions in a prune and wine sauce. Prunes feature heavily in central Loire cooking. It makes sense that they are combined with pork in the dish, since "Monsieur Pig," as he is fondly called, is the king of meats in the Loire Valley.

Matelote of Eel: Prunes also make an appearance in this traditional red wine-based eel stew garnished with prunes, hard-boiled eggs, and bread croutons fried in walnut oil.

Coq au Vin: Chicken in red wine with lardons, button mushrooms, and pearl onions. Traditionally, Coq au Vin is made with an old rooster, but given the lack of roosters for sale nowadays, substitute a free-range, heritage breed chicken. You are looking for a chicken with texture that can stand up to the braising process without falling apart.

Salmon with Beurre Blanc: Although technically from Nantes, Beurre Blanc (or Beurre Nantais) sauces fish just fine no matter where you find it.

Lièvre à la Royale: This famed dish is labor intensive and incredibly rich. It calls for placing pieces of hare with red wine, red wine vinegar, shallots, garlic, and herbs in a casserole that has been sealed with luting dough and cooking it for a very long time (See Food Terms, page 471.) Subsequently, a concoction of the innards of the hare—heart, lungs, liver—mashed up with red wine and lard are added to the casserole and it is returned to the oven for another hour. Finally, the sauce is thickened with blood before serving.

Fouace: According to Rabelais, the recipe for Fouace includes "fine butter, fine egg yolks, fine saffron, and fine spices." This brioche-type roll can include cinnamon, bergamot, saffron, or orange water and is frequently studded with walnuts.

Macarons de l'Abbaye de Cormery: Although there are records of Macarons dating back to the Middle Ages, legend has it that Marcarons were invented in the Abbaye de Cormery, south of Tours. These ring-shaped cookies made from almond powder, sugar, and egg whites, should not be mistaken for Macarons of Paris, which are brightly colored and have a ganache or jam filling. Legend has it that the shape of Macarons de l'Abbaye de Cormery was inspired by a monk's navel.

Cheese: Goat cheeses from the Touraine rank as some of the best goat cheeses in the world, with Pouligny-St.-Pierre, Valençay, Sainte-Maure, and Selles-sur-Cher being the best known. Small quantities of cow and sheep milk cheeses are also produced.

Tarte au Fruit: Because of the abundance of tree fruits, fruit tarts of all types are found throughout the Loire Valley.

Eau de Vie and Fruit Wine: As with the tarts, the vast selection of fruit in the region means there is a booming *eau de vie* and fruit wine industry with *eaux de vie* from pears, plums, quetsche, and cherries and wines from peaches and sloe berries (*épines*) frequently served at the end of the meal.

La Grange Tiphaine

Located on a crest two miles to the south of the town of Amboise (famous for its elegant medieval château overlooking the Loire River) in the central Loire Valley region of Touraine, Domaine La Grange Tiphaine has been in Damien Delecheneau's family for four generations. Touraine is both a wine region and one of the historic French provinces. When the country was reorganized in 1790, the Touraine was divided into the departments of Indre-et-Loire, Loir-et-Cher, and Indre. Its bordering provinces are: to the northeast, the Orleannais; to the southeast, the Berry; to the southwest, Poitou; to the west, Anjou; and to the north, the Maine. Part of the famed Paris Basin, with its sedimentary geology ideally suited to viticulture, the Touraine is dominated by the Loire River and its tributaries, the Cher, the Indre, and the Vienne.

Damien and his wife, Coralie, both graduates of the School of Oenology in Bordeaux, own the seventy-seven-acre Domaine La Grange Tiphaine. For much of the year, Coralie is in charge of the commercial side of the business, while Damien oversees the vineyards and the cellar work. During harvest, when the workload confines Damien to the vineyards, Coralie works in the cellar. They produce wines in three appellations: Montlouis-sur-Loire, Touraine, and Touraine-Amboise.

Montlouis-sur-Loire is an appellation for white wine made solely from Chenin Blanc. The wines can be still or sparkling. Sparkling wines are made using either the traditional method or the Pétillant Naturel *méthode ancestrale,* where a partially fermented wine finishes fermentation in bottle without the addition of added yeast or sugar. Pét-Nat wines frequently exhibit fewer bubbles than traditional method sparkling wine and often have some residual sugar, although the "Nouveau Nez," the Pét-Nat from La Grange Tiphaine, is vinified extra dry with less than 2g/l of residual sugar.

Located on the southern bank of the Loire River across from its more famous sibling, Vouvray, Montlouis-sur-Loire received its AOC certification in 1938. The region covers approximately 1,100 acres, and over 40 percent of its 50 producers are certified organic.

Touraine is a large appellation in the central Loire Valley—its 13,950 noncontiguous acres stretching approximately fifty miles from the eastern edge of the Anjou region to the town of Blois. White, rosé, and red still wines and white and rosé sparkling wines are made. Allowed grape varieties are Chenin Blanc, Sauvignon Blanc, Chardonnay, and Menu Pineau for white; Gamay, Cabernet Franc, Grolleau, Pineau d'Aunis, Côt (Malbec), Cabernet Sauvignon, and Pinot Noir for red and rosé; and Chenin Blanc, Menu Pineau, and Chardonnay for sparkling.

Touraine-Amboise is one of the subappellations of the Touraine. It is named after the village of Amboise on the southern bank of the Loire River. Touraine-Amboise covers 544 acres of flinty clay and clay limestone soils on both sides of the Loire River. White wine from Chenin Blanc and rosé and red wines from Gamay, Cabernet Franc, and Côt are produced under the Touraine-Amboise appellation. Sweet white wines from Chenin Blanc are also produced.

The climate in Montlouis-sur-Loire, Touraine, and Touraine-Amboise is influenced by the Atlantic Ocean on the western side turning to a more continental climate on the eastern side.

Making Wine at La Grange Tiphaine

La Grange Tiphaine is certified organic, and Damien and Coralie employ biodynamic practices—made easier by the fact that theirs are the only vineyards in the immediate area and therefore not in danger of contamination from a neighboring farm. Their approach to life and winemaking is very holistic. Damien believes that everything is interrelated and makes every effort to be kind to the environment—for example, relying on Percheron horses rather than tractors to work the vines when possible. Of their seventy-seven acres, forty acres are covered in prairie, and Damien trades his organically grown hay to his neighbor who raises organic cattle. In turn, the neighbor gives Damien organic cow manure to use as fertilizer in the vineyards.

All of the wines from La Grange Tiphaine are certified both organic and biodynamic by ECOCERT and BIODYVIN. All of the red wines of the Domaine are dry wines. La

Photo credit: Domaine La Grange Tiphaine

Grange Tiphaine produces the following wines (included in the descriptions are quotes from their website):

Montlouis-sur-Loire

In keeping with Montlouis-sur-Loire AOC regulations, all of their Montlouis-sur-Loires are made from 100 percent Chenin Blanc planted on well-drained sand and flinty clay soil with limestone subsoils:

Clef de Sol Blanc, Sec (Dry): Eighty-year-old vines. Alcoholic fermentation and aging in barriques on the lees until bottling. "Expression of minerals," an homage to the "grand terroir" of Montlouis-sur-Loire and Chenin Blanc.

Les Epinays, Sec (Dry): Ten-year-old vines. Alcoholic fermentation in large barrels without racking or sulfur. Fruity, spicy, floral wine with balance of fruit and acidity.

Les Grenouillères, Demi-Sec (Off Dry): Eighty-year-old vines. Alcoholic fermentation in barriques. "The perfect balance" of residual sugar and acidity with an accent on the fruit.

L'Equilibriste, Moelleux (sweet): Eighty-year-old vines. Alcoholic fermentation in tank and barrel (50/50) for eight months. This "Tightrope walker's wine" offers a "world of sensations" of the balancing act between sugar and acidity.

Nouveau Nez Pétillant Naturel, Sec (Dry) and sparkling: Ten-year-old vines. To drink on its own as an aperitif, after dinner, or to accompany fish or poultry.

Touraine-Amboise

The vineyards for the Touraine-Amboise and Touraine from La Grange Tiphaine are planted on red clay flinty soils over an outcrop of limestone bedrock.

White wine:

Bel Air, Chenin Blanc, Sec: Seventy-year-old vines. Three months lees aging in cement tanks. "Freshness, tension, and limestone."

Red wines:

Bécarré, Cabernet Franc: Twenty-year-old vines. Fermentation in cement tanks and aged nine months in barriques. "Sociable Cabernet Franc"—generous and drinkable. Good with dark meat or game.

Côt Vieilles Vignes, Côt: 115-to-200-year-old vines. Fifteen-day maceration on the skins in cement. Aged in egg-shaped concrete tanks and 225-liter barriques (50/50) for nine months.

Clef de Sol Rouge, Côt and Cabernet Franc: Sixty-year-old vines. Maceration and fermentation with indigenous yeasts in cement tanks. Aging in barriques of 225 and 400 liters with no racking and only light filtration. "A wine to age (to age . . . or to drink!)." Dark and serious, good with stewed meats or "winter dishes."

Touraine

White Wine:

Quatre Mains, Sauvignon, Sec: Fifty-year-old vines. Long fermentation in barrel with indigenous yeasts. "Excellence of Terroir," Racy and elegant, the expression of "osmosis between a grape type and its terroir of choice," in this case, Sauvignon and flint soils.

Red Wine:

Ad Libitum, Côt, Cabernet Franc, and Gamay: Fifteen-to-forty-five-year-old vines. Each variety of grape is fermented separately in cement tank before being blended and aged in cement for four months. "True greed," a full expression of voluptuous fruit, volume, and the way these three Touraine grape varieties compliment each other.

Vin de Table:

Rosa, Rosé, Rosam, Pétillant Naturel Rosé, Gamay, Grolleau, Côt, Cabernet Franc: Seventy-to-eighty-year-old vines. "The simple pleasure of fruity and refreshing bubbles."

I first met Damien and Coralie at the Salon des Vins de Loire—the Loire Valley Wine Fair held annually in Angers. They were pouring their wines, and I was impressed with the wines and with the dedication and thoughtfulness of the attractive young couple. Unfortunately, when I returned the next year to visit and cook lunch at the winery, Coralie was in Paris at a tasting of independent wine producers, so I was unable to renew our acquaintance. Damien was just as I had remembered him, scruffily handsome, quietly charming, friendly yet serious, seemingly shy yet very passionate about his métier, his family, and their way of life.

Spring 2013 was treacherous for winemakers in France, with extremely rainy wet conditions. The day that I was scheduled to visit Damien, he had to postpone because it was the first day in a month without rain and he had to treat his vines with organic methods to prevent mildew and rot. Completely understandable, the vines come first. I took the opportunity to wander around Amboise, to have tea and a pastry at Pâtisserie Bigot, and to have dinner at a local restaurant. Given that Damien doesn't like being late or rushed (he feels that being late causes one to rush and that rushing compromises the quality of the work you are doing), the fact that he had to get all of his treating done in one day emphasizes the severity of the weather that year and illustrates the life of a vigneron.

The next day, after a tour of the winery and vineyards, Damien and I prepared lunch in their lovely farmhouse kitchen, its space dominated by a large wooden table with childrens' drawings stacked at the end of the table, a glass vase with cheery daisies sharing space with a colorful bouquet of hand-cut construction-paper flowers. I peeled and julienned carrots, tossing the peels and scraps directly out the open kitchen window to the

chickens grazing in the flower-filled yard while Damien unwrapped pork chops from the organic pig purchased and slaughtered earlier that year. We sipped chilled Montlouis as we cooked and discussed their lives and food philosophy.

Family is of utmost importance to Coralie and Damien. They have no television, and involving the children in the working life of the farm and cooking together are ways

Paul Delecheneau, Urbane the horse, and Lou the dog
Photo credit: Domaine La Grange Tiphaine

of spending time together. Although Coralie does more of the day-to-day cooking, Damien is very involved in the family's eating habits. He makes his own yoghurt and goes to the farmer's markets in Amboise and Tours with the kids, and when time allows (after all, they have vineyards to tend and a winery to run), they spend the day cooking together. At the time of my visit, their sons, Camille and Paul, were six and four years old and at such young ages already knew the recipe for making Madeleines—the famed Proustian little cakes—by heart.

As a family, they eat locally from what he calls "real" producers. Each year they purchase an organic pig from a neighbor and slaughter it themselves—providing meat for the year for family (including for the delicious aforementioned Rillettes). He has a casual network of friends, all of whom grow and trade food. They purchase crottin-style goat cheeses called Gargilesse in quantity from an organic producer from the department of Indre to the south. They get together and purchase pallets of organic fruit and vegetables from Spain (oranges, lemons, limes, figs, and avocados). Even though these products do not grow locally, it is important for Damien and Coralie to make sure that they purchase them from organic growers whom they trust.

Damien and I sat down to lunch. Our first course was a taste test of the two Rillettes (and we already know how that turned out) followed by pork chops with julienned carrots and a side dish of creamy sautéed mushrooms and onions. While we ate, we tasted through a selection of the Domaine's wines—crisp dry Chenin Blancs from Montlou-

is-sur-Loire, mineral-driven cherry-flavored, earthy Cabernet Franc and Côt (Malbec) from Touraine. He heated thin slices of baguette on a griddle, topped them with organic Gargilesse cheese and local honey, and served them with his demi-sec La Grenouillières, all the while answering my questions and sharing some recipes for favorite dishes that weren't currently in season, like a spring favorite, radish and carrot frond soup. Damien said that they although they do drink wine, they do not drink on a regular basis, as he believes that one should moderate their alcohol consumption. When they do drink, they often drink wines from other like-minded winemakers from around France.

At harvest, with Damien and Coralie occupied in the fields and the winery, Damien's mother, Martine, is in charge of feeding everyone—preparing two large family-style meals every day for the family and harvest workers alike. An accomplished cook, she takes great pride in never repeating the same dish twice in one year.

Although the family is dedicated to eating locally, they do splurge on special occasions like Christmas, visiting the various vendors at Les Halles de Tours, the large daily covered market some 17 miles away, purchasing oysters from Cancale, Brittany, and a massive marbled *Côte de Boeuf* (a thick bone-in rib steak).

After coffee I had to take my leave. I was due in Sancerre later that day and there was rain in the forecast, so I needed to get on the road. This was the first visit of my new project researching *The Wine Table,* and it was exactly what I had hoped it would be. It seems extraordinarily fitting that it should take place over a glass of Loire Valley Chenin Blanc with a pot of Pork Rillettes in the central Loire Valley less than an hour from Château Chambord. I had come full circle back to the site of my spiritual roots. Emotionally grounded, I was ready to take off on my new adventure.

The Winemaker Recommends: Coralie loves the pairing of Pork Rillettes and La Grange Tiphaine Montlouis-sur-Loire "Les Grenouillères."

Springtime Radish and Carrot Frond Soup

Yield: six 8-ounce servings | Ease of Preparation: Simple | Ease of Sourcing: Moderate.
Wine Pairing: La Grange Tiphaine Touraine-Amboise "Bel Air," Montlouis-sur-Loire Sec

As with a lot of Wine Table cooking, the secret to this delicate soup is sourcing and season. Damien Delecheneau stressed that this is an early springtime soup because that is when the green aboveground part (a.k.a. fronds) of the radishes and carrots are most tender and sweet. Although it makes a wonderful first course, I like to serve it as a main course at lunch with warm chunks of baguette and salted butter. Follow it with a platter of well-ripened cheeses—so good!

INGREDIENTS

1 quart chopped radish fronds
1 cup chopped carrot fronds
1 clove garlic
1 cup peeled, diced potatoes
2 quarts water
Kosher salt
Black pepper, fresh ground
Crème fraîche
Optional garnish: julienne of radishes, radish sprouts

WHAT YOU'LL NEED

4-quart saucepan
Blender
4-quart bowl
Salad spinner (optional but recommended)

TIMING

Prep Time: 15 minutes
Cook Time: 20 minutes
Purée time: 10 minutes

PROCESS

The hardest part about this recipe is cleaning the fronds, which just goes to show you how easy the recipe really is. Take the time to clean them well, preferably in a salad spinner. You don't want any grit left to spoil the texture of this delicate soup.

Tear or lightly chop the fronds. Put the fronds, garlic clove, and cubed potatoes in the saucepan. Add enough water to just cover the vegetables (you may not need the full 2 quarts). Season with 2 teaspoons kosher salt and a couple of grinds of black pepper. Bring to a boil and then reduce to a simmer. Simmer until the potatoes are very soft.

At this point the soup is done except for the puréeing. The amount of time you purée it is a matter of personal preference. I have processed it lightly so that there were small flecks of green and little tiny chunks of potatoes remaining to give it a bit of texture. I have also puréed it until it was completely smooth. If you are making it your main course, a little texture might be preferable, but whichever you choose is fine. Process it in batches, placing the freshly processed soup in the 4-quart bowl.

Once you achieve your desired level of smoothness for the whole batch of soup, quickly wash the saucepan, transfer the soup back into the saucepan, and return it to the stove. Reheat the soup on medium-high heat. Once it is hot, taste for seasoning and adjust it to your liking.

Serve it with a grind of fresh cracked pepper, a dollop of crème fraîche, and, if you like, a garnish of julienned radishes or radish sprouts.

Notes

#1. Blenders are incredibly convenient, but they can also be dangerous—and not for the reason you might think. Overfill the blender bowl and the contents can splash out, making a complete mess; and if that liquid is hot—wow! It is a recipe for a bad burn. (I could enclose a photo of one of my cooks with hot mushroom soup on his chest, but that wouldn't be nice. Or maybe it would, since he was kind of cute!) Anyway, let your soup mixture cool slightly and do not overfill the blender bowl. It may take a minute or two longer, but you'll avoid both a messy clean-up and a trip to the ER to treat the burns!

#2. Even if you do not plan to eat the soup right away, it is best to reheat it after puréeing it so that you can check the seasoning while it is hot. When food is cold, the salt contents taste muted. If you salt it while it is cold, you run the risk of it tasting too salty when it is warmed to serving temperature.

Pork Rillettes

Yield: 1 large terrine | Ease of Preparation: Moderate but time-consuming | Ease of Sourcing: Moderate
Wine Pairing: La Grange Tiphaine Montlouis-sur-Loire "Les Grenouillères,"
Demi-Sec Vouvray, or other off-dry Loire Valley Chenin Blanc

Pork Rillettes is one of my all-time favorite dishes to cook. In fact, I used to give jars of Rillettes to friends for the holidays each year. I first had it when I was nineteen years old on my initial exchange trip to France. I have loved it ever since, and over the years I thought the Pork Rillettes from La Maison Hardouin in Vouvray were the best there were. That was until I had Damien Delecheneau's Rillettes. There was no comparison. Damien's were so much better, and I was happy to realize that mine had many similarities with his—brown and moist with chunks of meltingly tender meat held together in a suspension of pork fat and gelatinous meat juices. Take the time to brown the meat well. It makes all the difference in the world.

INGREDIENTS

⅓ cup kosher salt

2 bay leaves

2 tsp. dried thyme

⅛ tsp. ground mace

⅛ tsp. ground cinnamon

1 tsp. dried sage

½ tsp. dried marjoram

1 tsp. dried basil

⅛ tsp. ground nutmeg

2 cloves

½ tsp. freshly ground black pepper

3 cloves garlic

5 lbs. marbled pork shoulder cut in
    1½ inch pieces, large morsels of fat separated out
    (see Note #1 below)

½ bottle demi-sec Montlouis-sur-Loire or Vouvray

Water

1 tsp. Piment d'Espelette

WHAT YOU'LL NEED

Small kitchen bowl

Large plastic container to hold pork cubes

Large Dutch oven (big enough to hold all
of the pieces of pork) with lid

Separate container large enough to hold
the pork cubes

Small container for rendered pork fat

Tongs

Strainer

Aluminum foil

Kitchen spoon

Terrine large enough to hold all of the pork
or a combination of terrines and jars

TIMING

Prep Time: 1 hour

Salt-curing Time: 4 hours or overnight

Browning Time: 1 hour

Braising Time: Between 6–8 hours

Chilling Time: Overnight

PROCESS

Combine the salt, spices, herbs, and garlic cloves together in the small kitchen bowl.

Rub the pork with the salt/spice mixture and refrigerate the pork along with the garlic cloves for at least 4 hours, preferably overnight.

After the resting period, remove the pork from the refrigerator and pat it dry with paper towels. Separate the pieces of pork that are fat only. Cut the fat morsels into ½-inch pieces. Remove the garlic cloves and set them aside.

Place the Dutch oven on the stove over medium heat.

Brown the fat morsels. Once they are browned, remove them to the second container. Strain the resulting grease and reserve. Work in batches to brown all of the pork—do not overcrowd the pan. If you crowd the pan, the meat will not brown. Continue browning and removing the browned pork to the second container until the pieces of pork are browned. Make sure you brown them well. This is what will give flavor to the dish.

Once all pieces of meats are browned, return the meat, fat, and garlic cloves to the Dutch oven. Add one half bottle of wine and enough water to come three-quarters of the way up the level of the pork. Stir the contents of the Dutch oven.

Place a piece of aluminum foil directly down on the pork and wine mixture. This aluminum foil will force the liquid back down into the pork itself. Cover with the lid and simmer the pork mixture. Depending on the size and strength of your burner, you might have to adjust the heat of your stove. You want this to simmer, not boil. Stir the contents periodically (every 15 minutes or so). The level of liquid will begin to reduce. You will need to add more water if the pan begins to boil dry. Continue cooking for between 6–8 hours, replenishing water during this period.

Rillettes are finished when the meat chunks are smaller than their original size, tender, and falling apart. Remove the Dutch oven from the heat. Remove the bay leaves and the cloves if you see them. Stir periodically to help the meat mixture cool. During the course of this stirring, the meat will break apart. Do not overmix. Leave some small pork chunks if you can. You do not want to make pork paste. When the meat comes to room temperature, add 1 teaspoon Piment d'Espelette to the Rillettes. Taste for seasoning. You may need to add a little salt to finished Rillettes.

Transfer the Rillettes into the large terrine or the smaller terrines and the jars. Smooth the top of the meat and clean the edges of the terrine and/or jars. Heat the reserved pork fat and pour a layer of melted fat on top of the Rillettes. Cover and chill overnight.

The next day, prior to serving, remove the Rillettes from the refrigerator for at least thirty minutes before serving. This allows the fat to soften and makes the Rillettes texture more silky and spreadable.

Notes

#1. Use the best pork possible—either organic or local—preferably a heritage breed from a farmer you know. It is important to have pork with a good amount of fat and/or marbling. If you can only find lean pork, you should use a bit of pork belly to add fat to the Rillettes. If you do not have enough pork fat to melt and pour over the finished Rillettes, substitute duck fat. Hopefully you have some left over from previous recipes!

#2. Pork Rillettes will keep for at least seven days in the refrigerator. It can be frozen, although the texture suffers very slightly. I am not big into canning, so I usually make a batch for a party, a catering event, or to give to friends. If you wish to preserve it, there are many books available on canning.

#3. If, when you have finished cooking the Rillettes and are tasting for seasoning, you decide that they are extremely oversalted for your taste, peel a potato, put it into the Rillettes with one cup water, put it back on the stove, and cook on medium heat until the potato is done. The potato will absorb excess salt from the mixture. (This works for soups and sauces too!) Remember, though, the Rillettes will be served at room temperature (or possibly cold) and the salt content be more muted than if they were served hot, so you want them to taste a little salty when they are hot.

#4. Rillons or Rillauds. These braised chunks of pork are actually the intermediate stage of Pork Rillettes when the meat is cooked all the way through—browned, incredibly tender, but not yet falling apart. They are often eaten at room temperature on a green salad or sautéed potatoes. Like Rillettes, they can be preserved in jars or cans for later use.

Creamy Sautéed Mushrooms and Onions

Yield: Serves 4 as a side dish, or 2 as a main course over rice
Ease of Preparation: Simple | Ease of Sourcing: Simple
Wine Pairing: Dry or off-dry Chenin Blanc (Montlouis, Vouvray, or Saumur)

Damien Delecheneau served these at lunch with his Pan-Roasted Pork Chops and Julienned Carrots. The umami of the mushrooms combines with the sweetness of the onions and cream for a lovely side dish. You could also serve it over rice or egg noodles for a vegetarian main course.

INGREDIENTS

2 Tbsp. unsalted butter

1 medium yellow onion, halved and thinly sliced

Kosher salt

10 oz. white button mushrooms, cleaned and sliced in ⅛-inch slices

1 tsp. fresh thyme leaves

White pepper, finely ground

½ cup heavy cream

WHAT YOU'LL NEED

Thick-bottomed 10-inch skillet

TIMING

Prep Time: 15 minutes
Cook Time: 20 minutes

PROCESS

Heat the butter in the skillet on medium heat. When the butter is melted, add the onions, stirring to coat with the butter. Add a pinch of salt. Stir and cook for 3 minutes until the onions begin to soften but not change color.

Add the mushrooms to the onions and cook continuing to stir until the mushrooms just begin to brown a bit, approximately 5 minutes. Add the thyme, a pinch of salt, and a grind of finely ground white pepper. Stir again to combine well and add the heavy cream. Heat through while continuing to stir. Allow the cream to reduce for approximately 5 minutes. This will give the cream time to absorb the mushroom and onion flavors. Taste for seasoning and correct if necessary.

Set aside off the heat until ready to serve. Just before serving, reheat slightly, being careful not to burn the cream.

Pan-Roasted Pork Chops
with Julienned Carrots

Yield: 4 servings | Degree of Difficulty: Moderate | Ease of Sourcing: Simple
Wine Pairing: Dry or off-dry Loire Valley Chenin Blanc (Montlouis or Vouvray)

This dish is simple yet comforting. The key to cooking and eating for Damien Delecheneau is not just how good food tastes, but the wholesome quality of careful sourcing. He and Coralie buy a whole pig from a friend who raises organic pork and butcher it themselves—thereby ensuring that the family has healthy local pork for the year. As with all the vegetables that he does not grow himself, the carrots were purchased at the local farmer's market in Amboise. It was midspring, and the carrots were tender and sweet. Pan-Roasted in the same nonstick pan with the pork chops, using only the fat rendered from the pork, the carrots were just tender and delicately flavored with juices from the meat.

INGREDIENTS

3 cups peeled and julienned carrots
Four 6 to 8 oz. bone-in pork loin chops
    (approximately ¾ to 1-inch thick)
Kosher salt
Black pepper, finely ground
Optional: 1 to 2 Tbsp. canola oil

WHAT YOU'LL NEED

Vegetable peeler
Extremely sharp knife
Nonstick skillet large enough to hold
    4 pork chops comfortably with
    room to spare for the carrots.
Tongs
Optional: Food processor with julienne
    attachment.
Optional: Instant read meat
    thermometer

TIMING

Prep Time: 10–30 minutes (Depending
    on your knife skills, it may be
    longer or shorter, as all the prep
    entails is peeling and julienning the
    carrots.) If you decide to use a food
    processor, it will probably take you
    longer to assemble, disassemble, and
    wash the processor than to actually
    julienne the carrots.
Cook Time: 15–20 minutes

PROCESS

Once you have peeled the carrots, either julienne them by hand with your sharp knife or use the food processor to produce fine matchstick-sized carrot sticks.

Turn the heat to medium high under the nonstick skillet. If you do not have a skillet large enough to hold all four pork chops *and* the carrots, you will need to use two pans or work in batches. Lightly salt and pepper the pork chops. Place the chops in the pan. Cook for several minutes until some of the fat begins to render. You may need to use your tongs to turn the chops on their side to render the fat from the edge of the chop. Move the chops around so the rendered fat and juices form a thin layer on the pan. (If your chops are very lean, there may not be much fat to render. In that case, add 1 to 2 tablesoons of canola oil to the pan.) Add the carrots. Lightly salt and pepper the carrots. Periodically turn the carrots. After 5–7 minutes, check to see that the chops have developed a golden-brown color. If they have not browned, leave them on that side until they do. Once you are satisfied with the color, turn the chops and cook until the opposite side is brown, as well. Press the chops with your finger. If the meat is firm to the touch, it is done.

By the time the chops are cooked, the carrots should also be done. You want them to be just soft—not mushy, but not crunchy, either—there should still be some texture to them. Remove the chops to a warm side dish for a moment. Taste the carrots for seasoning and adjust if necessary. If you wish to serve family style, plate the carrots on a serving platter and arrange the chops on top of them. If you wish to plate individually, arrange a mound of carrots on one side of the plate and lean the golden chop on it.

Serve with Creamy Sautéed Mushrooms and Onions (page 424).

Notes

#1. Pork temperature. In 2011, the USDA released new temperature guidelines for cooking pork that lowered the recommended cooking temperature by 15° F from 160° F to 145° F. If you prefer to use a meat thermometer to check the temperature of your pork, slide the thermometer in the meaty side of the chop. Do not touch the bone with the thermometer, as this will interfere with a correct temperature reading. Remove the chop from the pan when the temperature reads 140° F and let it rest for 5 minutes. The final temperature will rise to 145° F during the rest time. This is sometimes called carryover cooking.

#2. Wine pairing. Pork is one of those dishes where I can go either way when pairing— red or white. In this case, the sweetness of the carrots marries extraordinarily well with Chenin Blanc like a La Grange Tiphaine Montlouis-sur-Loire, and the high acidity of the wine cuts nicely through the fat of the pork chop.

#3. Eat with your eyes! Orange carrots are fine, but if you have access to multicolored carrots, this dish will be even more striking. There are so many colors available: pale yellow, light orange, salmon pink, even dark purple. Careful, though! Some of those purple ones are just a tease, with purple skin only. They are plain old orange when you peel them. Look for the Purple Rain carrots. They are purple all the way through. The varied colors don't actually make the dish taste any better, but they are really pretty!!

Gargilesse de l'Indre Toast
with Local Honey

Yield: Serves 4 as a cheese course or light dessert | Ease of Preparation: Simple | Ease of Sourcing: Moderate
Wine Pairing: Delecheneau Montlouis-sur-Loire Demi-Sec, other Demi-Sec Loire Valley Chenin Blanc

I am generally not a huge fan of honey, but this simple cheese course made a convert of me. Softened Loire Valley goat cheese perched atop a griddled baguette slice with a drizzle of delicate honey made a perfect end to my lunch with Damien. The tangy notes of the cheese melded superbly with the sweet floral honey and the toasted flavors of the lightly crunchy bread—three ingredients, total satisfaction.

INGREDIENTS

Baguette

4 Gargilesse de L'Indre, Crottin de
Chavignol, or other dry Loire Valley
Goat Cheese

High-quality honey, preferably
wildflower

WHAT YOU'LL NEED

Bread knife
Cutting board
Paring knife
Griddle
Metal spatula
Decorative platter or 4 small plates
Teaspoon

TIMING

Prep Time: 5 minutes
Cooking Time: 10 minutes

PROCESS

Slice the baguette in ½-inch rounds.

Cut the goat cheese in quarters and then cut each quarter in half.

Place 16 baguette slices on the griddle. Arrange 2 pieces of goat cheese on each slice of bread and turn the heat under the griddle on low. After 5 to 10 minutes, the cheese will have softened, and the bottom of the toast will be golden brown and crisp. The cheese should have changed color, going from a chalky white to a translucent pale gold. That's what you are looking for.

Use the spatula to remove the toast to the decorative platter (or the individual plates).

Stir the honey and drizzle a teaspoon of honey over each cheese-covered toast.

Serve immediately.

Notes

#1. Gargilesse de l'Indre. Damien and Coralie are committed to purchasing local and organic food. They belong to a network of like-minded friends who barter and/or purchase products in bulk for their families. One such product is Gargilesse de l'Indre, a small-production farmstead raw-milk goat cheese from Gargilesse-Dampierre, a town that is eighty-five miles away in the nearby department of L'Indre. The Delecheneaux and their friends purchase a couple of cases of Gargilesse at a time to split among them. Gargilesse is not available in the United States. I recommend substituting Crottin de Chavignol, Valençay, or Saint-Maure. The important thing is that the cheese be on the dry side, if possible. That enables it to hold its shape during the heating process.

#2. As always, when so few ingredients are involved in a recipe, it is important that every element be of the highest quality. Use a flavorful, local honey to top the cheese after toasting. Some honeys have strong flavors. In this case, I recommend a delicate floral honey.

Mont-
Saint=Michel

Rouen

Par

Champagne Roses
de Jeanne

Tours

Nantes

Bordeaux

Marseilles

Corsica

N
NW   NE
W   E
SW   SE
S

Mont
Saint-Michel

Rouen

Par

Champagne Roses
de Jeanne

Tours

Nantes

Bordeaux

Marseilles

Corsica

"Soil and Soul"
A Visit with Cédric and Emilie Bouchard, Champagne Roses de Jeanne, Celles-sur-Ource, France

Although I have mentioned that I was standing in the kitchen at Domaine Weinbach when the idea of cooking the harvest for winemakers came to me, I did have a crazy dream about it once, shortly after my first visit to Cédric Bouchard in Celles-sur-Ource in 2009. Of course, as with many dreams, this one was filled with odd details, like the fact that I was obsessively stressed that I had to cook in a t-shirt, jeans, and tennis shoes instead of my chef's coat, pants, and kitchen clogs. Still, it was the first nascent glimmer of this book.

My first visit with Cédric (the real one, not the dream) was unlike any other wine visit I had ever had. First, although his winemaking odyssey was quite young (as was he), I had known of his wines for several years and they were already some of my very favorites. Second, at the time he did not even have his own winery. He made and cellared his wines in a small part of his father's winery.

We stood at the bottom of Les Ursules, the first vineyard he bought (a 2.2 acre north-facing plot of Pinot Noir) on an extremely windy March day and discussed the soil, the grapes, how he planted each young vine, how he worked the soil, harvested grapes, vinified, and bottled his wines. The visit went on and on—shockingly long—five hours at least. I've been at long tastings before, but those have generally been with larger groups or included a meal. In this case, it was the two of us, touring Les Ursules and the small part of his father's winery where he worked, and tasting in the barrel room where he stored his still wines. I was fascinated. The visit would have continued longer if I hadn't realized that if I didn't leave, I wouldn't make it to my hotel in Colombey-les-Deux-Eglises an hour away before nightfall. (And, whether or not I was spitting the wine as I tasted—which completely broke my heart, by the way—I needed

to depart at a somewhat reasonable hour, since I did have to drive and wasn't exactly sure of the way.)

Cédric is an interesting character, attractive in a very bohemian kind of way—with dark eyes and lean expressive features, his dark brown hair looking as if he has been dragging his fingers through it for much of the day. His manner is deceptive, though. His affability belies an intensity and drive that have enabled him to become a cutting-edge vigneron with revolutionary ideas in the small provincial southern Champenois town where he grew up. In 2008, these traits resulted in Gault Milau naming him the finest winemaker in Champagne that year.

Celles-sur-Ource is located in the Barsequennais region of the Aube—an area known as the Côtes des Bars. The Aube region is planted mostly to Pinot Noir and is known for its Kimmeridgian soils. (See the box on next page.) In 1911, when the official delineations of the wine-growing region of Champagne were first drawn up, they focused on the region of the Marne and excluded the Aube. Even though the Aube is geographically part of Champagne, and Troyes was once the provincial capital of Champagne, historically much of its grape production was sold to the Grande Marque Champagne houses in Reims and Epernay. It wasn't until 1927 that, after considerable protest, the borders of Champagne production were expanded to include the Aube. Currently, although a sizeable amount of grapes is still sold and sent up north, there is an emerging movement in the Aube of *Récoltant-Manipulants* (see Burgers, Beer, and Brut Champagne, page 380)—producers who grow and estate bottle their own Champagnes. Although he was not the first *Récoltant-Manipulant* (RM), Cédric Bouchard and his success at Roses de Jeanne have helped bring the wines of the region and in particular those of Celles-sur-Ource into the international spotlight.

The son of Jean-Pierre Bouchard, a commercially successful *Récoltant-Manipulant* from Celles-sur-Ource, Cédric attended the wine school in Beaune for four years but left before graduating. He returned home and began working with his father, but it soon became evident that their winemaking philosophies were not compatible. Shortly thereafter, Cédric moved to Paris to spend time with his graphic designer girlfriend Emilie (now his wife), finding work in a wine shop where exposure to winemakers working organically and biodynamically opened his eyes to a myriad of winemaking ideas.

Inspired by these connections, Cédric returned home and in 2000 began Roses de Jeanne with his father's somewhat reluctant help. He purchased a small number of tiny vineyards that he farms and bottles under the Roses de Jeanne label and rented several small plots from his father for his Inflorescence label. Jean-Pierre has since retired, and

Kimmeridgian Soil. The first time I met Cédric Bouchard, I was on a Kimmeridgian pilgrimage of sorts. Early on in my exploration of wine, the high acid, mineral-driven wines of Chablis and Sancerre emerged as favorites of mine. I was aware that despite their different grape varieties, they seemed to have more in common with each other than with the wines of their own titular regions of Burgundy and the Loire Valley. The Pinot Noir-based Champagnes of the Aube soon joined my list of favorites, and I was determined to explore the wines of that narrow vein of Kimmeridgian soil whence all three came.

Kimmeridgian soil is widely lauded as one of the premier soils in the world of wine. It should be noted that the name Kimmeridgian is based on a period of time. The Kimmeridgian age covers a five-million-year span of the late Jurassic Period. Although it is often called Kimmeridgian clay because the soil in the village of Kimmeridge in southern England where it was first identified has an elevated clay content, the Kimmeridgian soils of France have high levels of sea fossil-studded limestone. It is on this geological outcrop of Kimmeridgian soil on the south side of the Paris Basin (once covered by a shallow sea brimming with marine life) that the great vineyards of the Aube, Chablis, and Sancerre produce some of the world's finest mineral-driven wines—all within 150 miles of one another.

To further understand Kimmeridgian soil, I suggest you read *The Kimmeridgian Exposed and Explained,* an excellent article by Wayne Belding, MS, of the Boulder Wine Merchant in the July 1, 2014, online edition of *The Wine Review.*

Cédric has brought all Inflorescence vineyards under the Roses de Jeanne label for a total of eleven acres.

Champagne has long been known as a blended wine, utilizing grapes from different parcels (at times even from different parts of the Champagne region), different grape varieties, and different vintages to produce a standard "house" style of wine. Cédric's wines are a complete departure from this tradition, his approach more Burgundian. He bottles single varietal, single parcel, single vintage wines, and while he is not the only winemaker to do this, he was definitely one of the first and most adamant proponents of the practice.

This philosophy exposed him to criticism from the old guard winemakers in his hometown. Likewise, his minuscule yields (less than 25hl/ha compared to the 85hl/ha allowed in Champagne), his practice of leaving grass very long in his young vineyards, and even the way he planted new vineyards—requiring the nurserymen from whom he purchased his baby vines to grow them extra long so that he could plant them several feet deep, thereby giving the roots a head start at reaching deep down to the minerally Kimmeridgian subsoil—all caused raised eyebrows from his older neighbors. I mean, look at it from their point of view. Here they were making good money, raising grapes for large producers up north, or even if they were bottling their own rather ordinary wines, they were wealthy and liked their life. He had to be crazy, this young upstart, planting deep roots, with waist-high grass, bottling single vineyard, single varietal, single vintage Champagnes with no added yeasts, no fining, no filtering, no dosage. Who did he think he was?

Cédric was confident and committed to his philosophy, and he had no interest in arguing winemaking techniques down at the local café, so much so that very early on he stopped discussing his practices with his neighbors. He went quietly about his work, never revealing to them the extraordinarily high prices that he was receiving for his wines or the accolades that were piling up in the wine press. For example, in 2008, his 2004 La Haute Lemblé, a cuvée from a plot of two-year-old Chardonnay vines, received a review of 97 points from Antonio Galloni in *The Wine Advocate*, the highest of any Champagne reviewed by that publication that year. The review only increased the clamor for his already sold-out wines.

Oddly, for someone who makes some of the most sought-after Champagnes in the world, Cédric does not like bubbles. He feels they distract from the wine itself. He advocates drinking his wines from a white wine glass, prefers them at cellar temperature, and even recommends decanting them and drinking them over the course of several days to observe the progression of the wine. He bottles his wines at lower atmosphere 4.5 bar/kilo, compared to the traditional ratio of 6 bar/kilo. (Atmosphere levels are what make sparkling wines bubbly. The higher the atmosphere, the more bubbles in the wine.) This lower atmosphere, combined with the long, cool conditions that slow secondary fermentation, results in a wine with small, fine, less effervescent bubbles.

He has a new project in Molesmes near Chitry, where he intends to produce still Pinot Noir. Ideally, he would love to do this anonymously, but he is aware that given the demand for his wines, that likely will not be possible, and he fears that the prices of his Bourgogne Rouge will skyrocket because of the price of his Champagnes.

Cédric farms organically, but his farm is not certified organic. Emilie's cousin Guillaume helps in the vineyards and the winery, and Emilie manages the day-to-day business side of things. During harvest it is all hands on deck, with the addition of twenty harvest workers. He admits that his laid-back persona disappears every year during harvest—the focused side of his personality leaving little room for bonhomie in his haste to harvest his grapes quickly and correctly at the moment of absolutely perfect ripeness.

He uses only indigenous yeasts for both alcoholic and malolactic fermentation and employs no stabilization, no fining, no filtration, no chaptalization, and no dosage at disgorgement. (To further understand the Champagne production process, see Burgers, Beer, and Brut Champagne, page 367). With the exception of his still wine, an oak-aged Côteaux Champenois Blanc, all of the Roses de Jeanne wines are aged in stainless steel. Despite the fact that he is extremely fond of both Red and White Burgundy with their traditional oak regimen, he eschews the use of wood for his sparkling wines, preferring to emphasize the distinctive pure fruit and mineral aspects of the wines.

Although Cédric and Emilie have a new home and cellar in nearby Landreville, wine production still takes place at his father's former winery in Celles-sur-Ource. The facility in Celles was becoming too small for their operation, but Cédric was leery of changing anything. He is familiar with the conditions there—the heat, humidity, the indigenous yeasts—and does not want to take the risk that moving production to Landreville would impact the wine in a negative fashion. Cédric believes that positivity and negativity affect wines and strives to keep things in balance to protect them. Everything from harvest to disgorgement and recorking happens in Celles-sur-Ource, and then the wines are aged in Landreville in a subterranean cellar that is dug right into the ground—its walls a mass of solid rock and earth—the climate perfect and totally natural.

The cellar is accessed by an industrial elevator operated by a switch hanging from a cable (à la *Terminator*). As the elevator creakingly descends, so too does the temperature, dropping 15 to 20° F by the time you arrive in the cellar with its metal cages of unlabeled bottles, untreated oak shelves holding the very limited library of back vintages of Roses de Jeanne wines, and a packaging area where bottles are labeled, wrapped in tissue paper, and packaged by hand. Each cuvée has a different tissue paper wrapping that Emilie designed with a map of the parcel describing the location, grape variety, planting density, and yield. Because they have had issues with black market sales of their wines in the past, each bottle is now numerically coded, and meticulous records are kept to prevent this from occurring or, if it does occur, to track the distributor and deal with them. With the exception of the Côte de Val Vilaine, each cuvée is packaged in six-bottle wooden cases. This adds considerably to his costs, but Cédric says, "The pleasure of his wines deserves wooden boxes."

All of his wines are hand riddled on wooden *pupitres* (racks). He experimented with a gyropalette (an automatic riddling machine) early in his career, but given his small

production quantities, he doesn't see the point. He also said, "Man sleeps, gyropalettes do not." Maybe he thinks his wines need to rest, too!

Cédric owns eleven acres of vineyards, although he farms only seven-and-a-half of them (because he doesn't like the other three-and-a-half acres) to make his seven Champagnes. He took me on a tour of his vineyards pointing out exposition, slope, microclimate, and the minuscule size of the vineyards. I can honestly say that taking notes while he wrangled his farm truck on the roads leading to the different vineyards was quite challenging, to say the least.

Roses de Jeanne Wines

Les Ursules is a 2.2-acre vineyard of Pinot Noir located quite close to the winery in Celles-sur-Ource. The vineyard is north facing and rather flat with clay limestone soils.

La Haute Lemblé is a 0.27-acre south-facing vineyard near Celles-sur-Ource with Kimmeridgian soils. It is planted with five specially selected Burgundian Chardonnay clones chosen for low yields and high quality.

La Bolorée is a half-acre vineyard of old vine Pinot Blanc near Landreville. South facing with a couple of feet of clay sandy soil and chalk subsoil, La Bolorée is a rarity and a source of pride for Cédric.

In 2005, when the opportunity to purchase the vineyard arose, Cédric agreed to purchase it with two friends. The vineyard was comprised of one-third Chardonnay, one-third Pinot Noir, and one-third Pinot Blanc grapes. At the time, Cédric was totally disinterested in the Pinot Blanc, but the agreement was made that they would draw straws to see who got what part of the vineyard, and Cédric drew the short stick. Disappointed at the time, he is now quite happy with his highly unusual Pinot Blanc.

La Presle is Cédric's newest vineyard (planted in 2007). Located in a forest near Celles-sur-Ource, the 0.617 acre vineyard is planted on Kimmeridgian soil and is the coolest of all his vineyards and, therefore, the last to be harvested. It is comprised of fifteen very short rows planted with ten different Burgundian clones of Pinot Noir, all selected for very low yields.

This was the vineyard that he described on my first visit where he planted extremely tall baby vines very deep in the ground and left waist-high grass to compete with the new vines to force the roots even deeper. Many of the baby plants died in the first year, some of which he replanted. Currently, he has no grass in any of his fields because with deep roots, low-yielding clones, and meticulous working of the soils in the vineyards, the vines don't need extra competition.

Creux d'Enfer is a 0.17-acre west-facing vineyard planted on Kimmeridgian soils near Celles-sur-Ource, of which three rows of vines—yep, you read that correctly, three rows or 0.079 acres are Pinot Noir. Cédric uses this Pinot Noir for his Creux d'Enfer Rosé. His only rosé, the grapes for Creux d'Enfer are foot crushed. This method leaves whole clusters and grapes that are then allowed to macerate for 24 hours.

He uses only *saignée* method free run juice. (See "Vickie Dreams of Aligot," page 183.) This a total departure from traditional Champagne practices. *Saignée* method is where juice is "bled" off from the fermentation tank to produce a rosé wine. (The traditional method for making Rosé Champagne is the addition of a small amount of still red Côteaux Champenois to still white wine to make rosé before secondary fermentation. Champagne is the only appellation in France allowed to make rosé with this blended method.)

I could not believe it when Cédric admitted that depending how he feels, some years he doesn't make Creux d'Enfer Rosé at all.

The remaining 0.096 acres of Creux d'Enfer are planted to Chardonnay, and Cédric makes Côteaux Champenois Blanc from this, albeit as with the rosé above, not every year.

Once part of the Inflorescence line, with the retirement of Cédric's father, the final two wines have been brought under the Roses de Jeanne umbrella.

Côte de Val Vilaine: The wine formerly known as Inflorescence is from a 3.68-acre Pinot Noir (enormous by Roses de Jeanne standards) vineyard in nearby Polisy (two miles southwest of Celles-sur-Ource). The vineyard was his father's but now is Cédric's.

Côte de Béchalin: was previously bottled as Inflorescence "La Parcelle" and is from a 1.24-acre parcel of Pinot Noir also in Polisy. Although I know I should not play favorites, Roses de Jeanne Côte de Béchalin is probably my favorite wine on earth. If only he made more of it!

As I neared the end of my research for this book, I knew that I wanted to visit Cédric and Emilie again. My fondness for the Roses de Jeanne wines coupled with the real sense of camaraderie I had felt on my first visit convinced me that cooking with them would be the perfect final chapter for my book.

One thing you learn working in restaurants and even writing a book like this with so many diverse personalities and moving parts is that different people communicate differently. As a chef, I memorized which staff members texted, which ones preferred email, and which rare few liked to talk on the phone or in person. I'm pretty easy that way, totally comfortable switching communication methods. Cédric is a phone guy. Over the years I have

Picturesque buildings in Troyes

emailed him, and it's a toss-up whether he will respond. If I really need to get in touch with him, I contact his broker, my good friend Tom Calder.

Tom is an American wine broker who lives in Paris. Over the years, he has long-sufferingly consented to my dragging him to bistros and brasseries throughout Paris, Angers, and Bordeaux when he would rather be tasting wine at his office or whatever wine fair we are attending. He has corrected my French in emails I was sending to winemakers, once comparing an extremely involved sentence with an accident victim—bloody and mangled. (He has such a nice a way with words!) In June 2016, Tom sent a letter to Cédric about my plans to visit Celles-sur-Ource and my desire to cook with Emilie and him.

Cédric responded to me immediately, "What a superb project! Thank you for thinking of us!" That's the fastest he has ever responded by email. (I've since learned that if you want to speak with Cédric himself, you need to call him on his cell phone. If his hands are free, he'll answer. My other cheat is to email Emilie, who is definitely more responsive.)

We agreed on a date for my visit, and then I didn't hear anything for several weeks. I was traveling in Brittany and I sent periodic updates with my arrival time and where I would be staying in Troyes, the provincial capital of the Aube. Troyes features a charming old quarter with one of the most extensive collections of sixteenth-century half-timbered buildings still in existence today. It is a lively tourist center with narrow streets, a cathedral, hotels, restaurants, and shops.

My phone rang as I checked into Relais Saint Jean, a hotel housed in several half-timbered buildings on a tiny street right off the lovely main square in the old section of Troyes. It was Cédric, friendly as ever, laughing, "Sorry I haven't emailed. I've been busy, but we are really excited about doing this." We decided that we would cook some of their favorite foods. They love fresh foods—seasonal vegetables, ripe fruits, and crisp salads. They particularly love risotto with crunchy vegetables. And they wanted to share a favorite recipe of Emilie's for *Pintade* (Guinea Fowl).

The stumbling block was shopping for the food. Celles-sur-Ource and Landreville are tiny villages with less than 1,000 inhabitants between them. There are no grocery stores. Bar-sur-Seine (population 3,233) has a very small grocery store, and market day is Friday. Since it was already Saturday, the best place to shop for our meal was at the Halles de Troyes—the daily covered market in Troyes. Happily, I was staying in Troyes, and visiting markets is one of my favorite pastimes. We compiled a list and agreed to meet at their home at 10:00 a.m. on Monday. Even had I not been shopping for ingredients to cook for lunch at Cédric and Emilie's home, I would have been at the Halles de Troyes on Sunday morning anyway because it's in my DNA to explore the food culture of whatever locale I am visiting. What can I say, some people go antiquing, I visit food markets.

Foods of the Aube

The Aube is the southwesternmost of the four departments of the Champagne-Ardenne Region (the other three are The Marne and Ardennes to the north and the Haute Marne to the east). While it shares many food specialties with the Marne (see "Burgers, Beer, and Brut Champagne," page 367), the Aube prides itself on specific local delicacies:

Andouillettes AAAAA de Troyes: The most famous dish of the Aube, this sausage is made from carefully selected pork large intestines (*chaudins*) and stomach (*panses*) seasoned with onions, herbs, salt, and pepper stuffed in casing. The recipe dates back to the Middle Ages. These strong-tasting sausages (a little too strong for some tastes, mine included) are frequently served with a sauce of coarse mustard and cream or a Chaource cheese sauce. In 1970, a group of butchers created an association to protect the tradition of Andouillette of Troyes. This group, known as the Association Amicale des Amateurs d'Andouillette Authentique (Friendly Association of Authentic Andouillette Lovers) or the A.A.A.A.A., gets together several times a year to celebrate this regional specialty. The A.A.A.A.A. designation that frequently appears on menus throughout France serving Andouillette gets its name from this association.

Andouillettes à la Ficelle: Refers to a specific method of stuffing the casings whereby a *ficelle* (thread) is tied around twelve strips of innards (generally ⅔ *chaudins* and ⅓ *panses*) and then the thread is carefully hand pulled through the sausage casing to stuff the sausage. This artisanal method is rarely practiced nowadays, and the resulting Andouillettes—produced in minuscule quantities—are highly prized for their texture and authenticity.

Chaource Cheese: This double cream cow's milk cheese is from the town of the same name. It has a white bloomy rind and a pale butter-colored paste. From the outside it resembles Brie that has been shoved into a taller, narrower mold. It received AOC status in 1977 and is taller than it is wide. It was traditionally molded using a ladle. The flavors are creamy and delicate with a hint of white button mushrooms.

Sauerkraut (Choucroute): Choucroute is both a name of a dish (see "Tending the Fire in Alsace," page 31) and an ingredient—in French it means sauerkraut. The Aube ranks #2 in France (after Alsace) for production of sauerkraut, and there are several fine artisanal Choucrouteries around Troyes.

Escargot Gris: North of Troyes, in the village of Longsols along the Longsol River, the Escargotière des Lacs de Longsols (that's a mouthful!) produces approximately 200,000 large gray snails a year. This type of snails is prized for its robust flavorful qualities.

Honey: Honey from the Aube is prized in kitchens throughout France. Not surprisingly, many honey producers also sell beeswax products.

Pascal Caffet Chocolates: Pascal Caffet was born in Troyes and joined his father at the family store "Le Palais de Chocolat" at a young age. Since then, he has devoted his life to chocolate and pastries, has opened stores throughout France and the world, and has racked up an amazing list of awards, including Meilleur Ouvrier de France Patisserie 1989 (Best Worker in France—the top French distinction for artisans in France); Best Chocolate Maker in France 2009; and two Gold Medal Pastry and Chocolate World Championships, Lyon, France 2003 and Milan, Italy 1996. Have I mentioned how delicious his chocolates are? They are fantastic, with specialties like chocolate covered pralines, macarons, and an array of filled

Meilleur Ouvrier de France is a prestigious award given to craftsmen in a variety of artisan and trade specialties. The competition is held every four years and is an extremely rigorous trial, pitting the top professionals in each discipline against one another with the aim of encouraging continued excellence in trade and crafts. Disciplines include: Hospitality, Building, Clothing and Accessories, Beauty and Aesthetics, Textile Industries, Home Decoration, Metallic Structures, Industries, Precision Techniques, Synthetic Materials Arts and Techniques, Leathers and Skins, Ceramics and Glassworks, Graphic Arts and Trade, Artistic Metal Works, and Flowers and Countrysides.

chocolates—not to mention all of the delicious pastries—definitely a must when you are in Troyes, or Paris, or Tokyo.

Apples and Apple Cider of Pays d'Othe: Apples grown in the Pays d'Othe, a small region between Troyes and Auxerre, produce ciders renowned for their sweet yet flinty (they call it "firestone") flavors. They use ten heirloom apple varieties (with such names as flat nose and cat's nose) to produce cider. After crushing, the ciders undergo fermentation for several months in chestnut or oak barrels. Apples and jams are also well reputed in the region.

Prunelle de Troyes: Troyes sloe berry liquor is a historic specialty of Troyes. Prunelle has been made since 1840 using the same original recipe in the Cellier Saint Pierre distillery, opposite Troyes cathedral. The distillery building dates from the late 1100s and was originally called the tithe store. The shop where you can taste and purchase Prunelle de Troyes is a Canon's residence built in the 17th century with a tunnel connecting the cellar to the cathedral. Prunelle is produced by crushing the pits of the sloe berry, soaking them in alcohol, and then double distilling them. Prunelle de Troyes contains 40 percent alcohol and is drunk as an aperitif, a disgestif, in a Champagne cocktail called a "*Trou Champenois*," and poured over sorbet.

Rosé de Riceys: This wine appellation with only seventy-five acres of Pinot Noir from three villages in the Southern Aube makes serious rosé. The wines are produced using the *saignée* method and are darker than the rosés found in southern France. Its flavors and aromas are smoky and mushroomy with forest floor notes mingling with red cherry fruit—very clearly Pinot Noir.

These local specialties as well as many other products from France and around the world are easily found in grocery stores, local outdoor markets, and permanent covered markets (Halles) throughout the region. As I have said, I adore food markets. I would rather shop for food and wine than anything else (except maybe shoes), so it was no imposition to go Les Halles de Troyes to purchase our provisions. Luckily, I went around 11:00 a.m. because although the website indicated that the Halles was open all day Sunday, I quickly found out many of the vendors were closing at 12:30 and only a smattering of them would be open the next day, which meant I had to hurry with my shopping. Challenge accepted.

Clearly the hardest purchase was going to be the Guinea Fowl leg quarters. I had had the forethought to check the minifridge in my hotel and had already determined that if it could not adequately chill bottled drinks, storing poultry in it would not be a stellar idea. I found a vendor who not only had Guinea Fowl, but, although not "officially" open on Monday, planned to have an employee there for a short amount of time the next morning—perfect!

I had my eye on one particular vegetable stand where the produce looked amazing but soon learned he wasn't going to be open the next day. Another nearby stand had some beautiful ochre-colored girolle mushrooms and English peas and promised to be open the next day. While shopping for nonperishables like Arborio rice, I determined that no cheesemongers would be open the next day, either. I purchased my Parmigiano Reggiano, some Brittany butter (from Jean-Yves Bordier, a genius butter producer from Saint-Malo), and Camembert—taking the chance that the fridge in my hotel room would work adequately for that. (I should probably have apologized to the next occupant of the room—the drinks that shared space with it in the minibar smelled pretty heavily of extremely ripe Camembert by the time I left the next morning.)

When I finished my shopping, it was late enough that I stopped at the Crieurs de Vin stall and grabbed a glass of their private cuvée Champagne to sip with six Fine de Claire

oysters from the fishmonger next door. You can say all you want about Wheaties being the breakfast of champions. My money is on oysters and Champagne. (Crieurs de Vin is a really great wine shop and funky restaurant in Troyes. Their stall at the Halles in Troyes, while not as well stocked as the main store, is a great source for grower Champagnes and estate-bottled wines.)

Monday morning, I arrived at Les Halles right as they opened and grabbed my Guinea Fowl before heading over to the vegetable stand. I was disheartened to discover that apparently everyone else had liked the looks of the girolles, as well—so much so that they were completely sold out. Such a disappointment! As I looked around trying to decide what to buy for my risotto, I noticed there was someone at the stand that had been my first choice the day before. I asked the gentlemen if he was open and he said no, then he asked what I wanted. When I mentioned girolles and favas, he went downstairs, returning with cases of each from which I could choose. They were even prettier than the ones I had seen the day before! That guy was my hero! In fact, everyone at the market had been incredibly helpful, and I left fully stocked with everything I needed for my cooking adventure with the Bouchards.

When I first met Cédric in 2009, he and Emilie lived in Celles-sur-Ource, but with two children and the need for more space at the winery, they purchased a property in Landreville, a small village four miles away. Their new home is lovely. Hidden behind an ornate verdigris grillwork gate, the 300-year-old property is made up of a stately red brick and gray stucco three-story main house with dormer windows, a balcony with stone balustrades, a first floor with a grand arched window, and an outdoor patio with a retractable awning. Several out buildings (including the all-important new cellar) cluster around the main house. The whole property abounds with plants: climbing ivy, hydrangeas, boxwoods of all sizes, several massive wisterias, and a child's swing set. The expanse of yard is divided by the buildings and grillwork and sports small fruit trees, a flower-filled erstwhile water well, an old watering trough filled with lily pads, and stuck out of the way in the corner, a well-used Weber kettle barbecue grill. It is absolutely clear that this is a family's home, not simply a place of business.

As I pulled into the limestone gravel inner courtyard, Cédric bounded out of the house to meet me, hugging me and talking nonstop. Clad in dark cargo shorts, a heather gray Henley, and Birkenstock sandals, he began grabbing groceries and ushering me into the house, all the while delivering a casual deluge of words, as if it had only been days since we had last seen each other rather than seven years. He introduced me to Emilie and Emma, their five-year-old daughter, as we unloaded groceries in their large lovely kitchen.

As with the yard, this is a home, not a showplace. It was clean but cluttered. The counter was covered with the requisite paraphernalia accumulated in a home with small children—pacifiers, crayons, and toys. Likewise, the small corner kitchen table was covered with children's books. This is a family completely comfortable in their own skin. There were shoes on the floor everywhere, as if they had been kicked off in preparation to sit on the floor and play with toys. The Disney presence was huge, most notably from Disney's

Frozen movie in the form of books, coloring books, and a favored doll. The fact that they had not spruced things up made me feel more comfortable than if everything had been spotless and meticulously arranged.

We unpacked the groceries, doing an inventory of my purchases as well as their pantry supplies. Not knowing for sure if Guillaume (Emilie's cousin) or other family members would be joining us, I had purchased a little extra of everything. Guillaume couldn't join us, so Emilie immediately called her mother, Maryse (who lives nearby), to come for lunch. After taking stock of everything, we decided to go with the *Pintade* (Guinea Fowl), spring vegetable risotto, a green salad, a selection of cheeses, and fruit for dessert. Before getting started, Cédric went downstairs to grab a couple of bottles of Champagne for us to drink. While we cooked, we discussed Roses de Jeanne and my book, which of course led me to ask questions about their philosophies on food, eating, and shopping.

While quality is important to Emilie and Cédric, I would not describe them as food-obsessed. The success of Roses de Jeanne, the new project in Molesmes, and the fact that they have two small children (their younger daughter, Violette, was at a local nursery school class the day I visited) means their time is limited and they are more interested in ensuring that their food is fresh, wholesome, and relatively easy to prepare. And, as evidenced by their request for risotto, they do not limit their selections to only foods from their small corner of France. After all, they both lived in Paris and, as I found out later, they were married in Las Vegas! Cédric has traveled quite a bit, and he is quite fascinated with California. They like crunchy vegetables, salads, and simple classic sweets (mostly for the girls).

Because of their busy work and family life, Cédric and Emilie do not drink wine at every meal, but when they do drink, they drink Burgundy—usually that of a friend—and holidays like Christmas and times of celebration call for opening special bottles of Burgundy from the cellar.

At harvest time, given the small vineyard size and relatively limited staff, they celebrate the end of harvest with a dinner with the family and the families who help with the harvest.

Emilie is more quiet than her gregarious husband. She is definitely friendly—but not as outgoing as he is. She is of medium height and quite trim with long silky, sable-colored hair, and a quiet but ready smile. Cédric was much as I had remembered him—slender and medium height with thin mobile features. He has wiry dark hair, dark eyes, tons of laugh lines, a winning smile, and an intense manner. I'm not sure how someone can be so intense and yet so zen at the same time, but Cédric accomplishes it. Their daughter Emma is a beautiful combination of both of her parents with silky hair and delicate features like Emilie, and an intense manner similar to Cédric's. Clearly, they both dote on her (as does Grandma Maryse). She is slightly spoiled—completely normal for a child so loved. She definitely wanted their attention but at the same time was happy playing independently, clad in a cute summer dress and rain boots for the task of filling her water bucket (adorned with likenesses of Elsa, Anna, and Olaf the snowman of Disney's *Frozen* fame) from an outdoor water spigot or playing with her Elsa doll.

I always enjoy cooking, but I confess, cooking while drinking Cédric's 2008 Bolorée was quite a treat. I will admit that watching Cédric use Roses de Jeanne Champagne that had been open several days to make risotto almost stopped my heart, but that has more to do with how carefully I husband my supply of his wines than anything else. Emilie's parchment-wrapped roasted *pintade* was as easy as Cédric had described and just as delicious! Set-up for

lunch was accomplished in a laid-back fashion, with Maryse and Emilie setting a simple table outside under the awning and Emilie, Cédric, and I putting finishing touches on the food. No fuss, delicious, and accompanied by crazy good wines—beginning with the Pinot Blanc La Bolorée with the Pea, Fava Bean, and Girolle Risotto and continuing with a bottle of Creux d'Enfer Rosé! (I can't help it! Two hundred bottles-made-per-year Rosé Champagne from my favorite producer affects me this way!) He also opened a bottle of Claude Dugat Gevrey-Chambertin to go with the *pintade*. I could not have been happier. The risotto was creamy yet crunchy, with al dente rice and crispy vegetables. The *pintade* was perfectly cooked—tender meat with a crisp sticky quality to the skin, the tangy flavor of Dijon mustard, blending with the garlic, thyme, and dark meat juices—classic and simple with a small number of well-sourced perfect ingredients.

I left their home eight hours after I had arrived and headed back to Troyes. Our conversations had been so interesting and lively that I had almost lost my voice. I have always said that some of the best times in my life have been spent at a winemaker's table, eating good, simply prepared food and drinking good wine. This had definitely been that.

Make no mistake. Cédric Bouchard is not your run-of-the-mill winemaker. He is a revolutionary winemaker making meticulous revolutionary wine in abso-

lutely minuscule quantities and a media darling with nine articles about him in the past ten years in the *New York Times* alone. He is also a family man (he named his winery Roses de Jeanne after his Polish Grandmother Janika) and, according to him, a taskmaster when it comes to his vineyards and his wines. Looking at him, you would never know this. He could easily be mistaken for the front man of an indie rock band (whose daughter plays with *Frozen* dolls).

In reality, Cédric is comfortable in his own skin, and he spends much of his waking time working to ensure—to show the world—the soul of the soil where he has staked his claim.

The Winemaker Recommends: Guinea Fowl en Papillote with Roses de Jeanne Creux d'Enfer Rosé or Gevrey-Chambertin.

Guinea Fowl en Papillote
Pintade en Papillote

Yield: Serves 8 | Ease of Preparation: Moderate | Ease of Sourcing: Difficult
Wine Pairing: Roses de Jeanne Creux d'Enfer Rosé (good luck with that!), Rosé Champagne, or Red Burgundy.

When Cédric and Emilie were brainstorming about what we should cook together, they immediately thought of this simple dish. As Cédric described it, it has rich, deep flavors, and a nice crunchy skin. I totally agree! On top of that, other than the difficulty of sourcing Guinea Fowl thighs (see my note below), it has relatively few ingredients, and once you get the hang of folding the papillote—the parchment paper packet—it is super easy to make. The benefit of cooking en papillote is it locks in the moisture and flavors of your ingredients, and when you open your packet, you have a moist, delicious dish! It's also a kind of flashy way to impress your friends—you don't have to tell them how easy it really is.

INGREDIENTS

8 Guinea Fowl leg quarters
Kosher salt
Freshly ground black pepper
1 cup Dijon mustard
24 sprigs fresh thyme
16 unpeeled garlic cloves
8 Tbsp. unsalted butter

WHAT YOU'LL NEED

8 sheets parchment paper (12 x 14 inch)
Scissors
Pan spray
Pastry brush
Two baking sheets

TIMING

Prep Time: 30 minutes
Baking Time: 40 minutes

PROCESS

Preheat oven to 425° F, preferably on convection setting.

Cutting the Parchment into a Heart Shape:

Fold the parchment sheets in half on the 14-inch side so that the folded paper measures 12 x 7 inches. Cut the paper into a tear drop shape such that when you open the paper it is in the shape of a heart.

Assembling the Packets:

Open the parchment and generously spray one half of the heart with pan spray.

Salt and pepper the skin side of a Guinea Fowl thigh then brush it with mustard and place the thigh skin side down on the spray-covered parchment paper. Paint mustard on the other side of the thigh. Place 3 sprigs of thyme and 2 cloves of garlic on top of the mustard. Sprinkle with a dash of salt and black pepper. Cut a tablespoon of butter into three pieces and place on top of the thigh.

To close the parchment, fold the parchment over the Guinea Fowl thigh. Begin at the indented end of the heart and tightly fold the edges to close the package. Continue folding in small increments until you reach the pointed end of the heart. Twist the end of the parchment and fold it under. Make sure you leave some extra room inside the packet, as air will cause the packet to expand during the baking process. Place the packet on the baking sheet.

Repeat the process for each thigh. When all eight packets are assembled, place the baking sheets in the oven. Cook for 40 minutes.

After 40 minutes, remove the baking sheets from the oven. If you wish to allow your guests to open their *papillote* themselves, place each packet on an individual plate and serve. If you don't want to go for this option, slice open the top of the packets. Serve one thigh per person. Drizzle any juices over the thigh.

> **Note**
>
> Unlike in France where Guinea Fowl (or Guinea Hen) is quite common, it is not an everyday ingredient in the United States. The meat of Guinea Fowl is darker than chicken and quite lean. Ask your local butcher or gourmet food store if they can get Guinea Fowl thighs. If they cannot, they are available online through d'Artagnan or Grimaud Farms (www.grimaudfarms.com).

Crème Caramel

Yield: Serves 6–8 | Ease of Preparation: Moderate | Ease of Sourcing: Simple
Wine Pairing: White Dessert Wine, Sauternes or Quarts de Chaume

This simple recipe is a favorite of Emilie Bouchard's. It's a French classic—creamy custard, lightly sweet with a delicate wobbly texture, the dark almost bitter caramel its perfect foil. Emilie claims not to be much of a cook, but her notes for this recipe belie this notion—the casual instruction "make a caramel from 60 grams of sugar and coat the inside of the baking dish" an indication of her comfort in the kitchen. I'm doubly happy with the recipe, as Crème Caramel, despite (or maybe because of) its simplicity, has long been a favorite of mine. As usual, with so few ingredients, I recommend using the best eggs and milk you can find!

INGREDIENTS

For the Caramel:

⅓ cup granulated sugar
2 Tbsp. water

For the Custard:

1 vanilla bean
2¾ cups whole milk
⅓ cup granulated sugar
Pinch salt
4 large eggs, beaten very well
Several quarts of warm water

WHAT YOU'LL NEED

2-quart saucepan
Small whisk
4-quart saucepan
8-inch-diameter deep cake, casserole
    or soufflé dish (approximately
    3 inches tall)
Ladle
Medium size mixing bowl
Rubber spatula
Medium fine strainer
Oven-safe pan large enough to hold the
    cake dish
Kitchen towel
Large decorative platter

TIMING

Caramel: 10 minutes
Custard: 10 minutes
Baking Time: 50–60 minutes
Cooling Time: 4½ hours to overnight

PROCESS

For the Caramel:

Melt ⅓ cup sugar and 2 tablespoons water in the small saucepan over very low heat. Whisk until it is completely dissolved. Raise the heat to medium high. Once you raise the heat, do not whisk. Bring the sugar and water to a boil. Continue boiling it, moving the pan to swirl the mixture periodically. Keep cooking it until it becomes a medium-amber color. This takes between 5 to 8 minutes. The darker the color, the more bitter the flavor of the caramel. I like to stop at medium amber, but if you like things on the bitter side, continue until it is dark amber or brown. Pour the caramel into your baking dish. Work quickly, spinning the dish to cover the bottom with caramel. Use a rubber spatula to clean out the pan and use the excess to fill in any blank spots. The darker your caramel, the more quickly it solidifies. BE CAREFUL! Caramel is like Napalm, and if you get it on yourself, it will produce an impressive burn.

For the Custard:

Preheat the oven to 360° F.

Slice the vanilla bean open lengthwise, being careful not to slice it in two. You are basically opening the vanilla bean like a pouch. Drag your knife down the length of the inside of the bean to collect the black specks. Scrape these specks into the milk.

Heat the vanilla-flavored milk, ⅓ cup sugar, and a pinch of salt in the larger saucepan until the sugar is dissolved and the mixture is very hot and begins to bubble on the edge. Do not boil it.

Place your beaten eggs in the mixing bowl and whisk one ladle full of hot milk into the eggs. This will temper the eggs. Continue adding the milk. Do not do it in the other direction! If you put the eggs into the hot milk, they will curdle! Once the milk and eggs are combined, use the strainer to carefully strain them into the caramel-coated baking dish.

Line the bottom of the large oven-safe pan with a kitchen towel. Place the custard-filled dish on the towel. Pour enough warm water into the oven pan to come about 1 inch up the side of the dish containing the custard. This water bath will keep the custard from forming bubbles while it cooks. I like to place the pan in the oven first, allowing one corner to stick outside the oven and then pour the water into it. Then I slide the pan fully into the oven. Be very careful not to get any water into the custard.

Bake the custard for 50 to 60 minutes. Fully baked custard looks a little wobbly when you shake it, but it is no longer liquid. If in doubt, make a small incision with a knife. The custard is done when you can tilt the knife to one side and see a clear division in the custard. If it is still liquid or if your knife comes back coated in custard batter, continue cooking it for 10 more minutes and test it again.

Remove the baking pan from the oven, being careful not to spill the water. Remove the custard dish from the water bath and allow it to cool for 30 minutes. After 30 minutes, place it in the refrigerator and chill for at least 4 hours.

When you are ready to serve it, run a knife around the outside of the custard to loosen it from the dish. Invert your platter on the custard dish, hold both the platter and the custard dish securely, and flip it over. The crème caramel should plop down onto your platter. If it doesn't, shake it a bit. Don't panic if it doesn't fall right away. It will eventually succumb to gravity and drop down.

Serve on individual plates garnished with a spoonful of caramel.

Notes

#1. If you do not have vanilla beans, substitute ¾ teaspoon vanilla extract.

#2. This is a basic recipe. You can add different flavors to the dish by adding flavored extracts or by steeping ingredients, lavender or saffron, for example, into the milk.

SECTION THREE
WINE TABLE FAVORITES

I am often asked my opinion on places I like—favorites for eating, drinking, and shopping—both from my travels and at home. The following is a list of my favorite restaurants, wine bars, specialty stores, and farmer's markets. Additionally, because some of the ingredients in this book may be a bit challenging to find, I am including a list of helpful online shopping websites.

Restaurants, Wine Bars, and Shops

France

Paris

L'Avant Comptoir, 3 Carrefour de l'Odéon, 6th arrondissement. Located next door to Yves Camdebord's acclaimed restaurant, **Le Comptoir du Relais**, this pork-centric small bites and natural wine bar takes no reservations and has no seats. You've heard of standing room only? This is standing only. You just belly up to the bar elbow-to-elbow with other patrons who are sharing from the communal jars of cornichons, Dijon mustard, and salty chunks of Bordier butter. It is my favorite place to hang out and grab a quick bite when I'm in Paris. Lines are very long, so I recommend going at noon right when they open or in the middle of the afternoon. I make a habit of stopping there at noon for a small snack and a glass of champagne (or two) on my way to the airport as I leave Paris. It makes the ordeal of traveling through Charles de Gaulle and the long flight to Washington more bearable.

L'Avant Comptoir de la Mer, 9 Carrefour de l'Odéon, 6th arrondissement. The sister to L'Avant Comptoir, this spot next door focuses on the bounty of the sea.

Semilla, 54 Rue de Seine, 6th arrondissement. Fantastic restaurant with excellent, well-sourced products, prepared carefully in an unfussy fashion. Outstanding wine list.

Wine Table Favorites   457

La Dernière Goutte, 6 Rue de Bourbon le Château, 6th arrondissement. This small wine shop, from the owners of Semilla restaurant, specializes in terroir-driven, estate-bottled wines, many of which are organic and biodynamic. They have a particularly good selection of Récoltant-Manipulant Champagnes.

Bordeaux

La Tupina, 6 Rue Porte de la Monnaie. The flagship restaurant of Jean-Pierre Xiradakis specializes in the cuisine of Southwest France, especially foie gras and duck. There is a strong emphasis on local products and an extensive wine list. Dishes cooked on a spit in the open hearth are a real treat. Whole duck breast on the bone, when featured as a daily special, is not to be missed. It is fantastic. In addition to La

Tupina, Xiradakis owns **Kuzina,** a Cretan/Mediterranean fish restaurant, **Au Comestible,** a gourmet grocery store, and **Maison Fredon,** a guesthouse. The street has been dubbed **"*Rue Gourmande,*"** and Xiradakis and some friends have established *Défense et Sauvegarde des Traditions du Sud-Ouest*, an organization to "protect traditions of southwestern France."

Le Petit Commerce, 22 Rue Parlement Saint Pierre. Fantastic seafood restaurant with an excellent wine list on a quaint street in *Vieux Bordeaux,* old Bordeaux.

Wine More Time, 8 Rue Saint-James. A combination wine bar/natural wine store in *Vieux Bordeaux,* whose outdoor seating offers a fantastic view of the *Grosse Cloche*

(The Great Clock), is a must for wine geeks. Small plates are available to accompany the thoughtful wine selection.

L'Oenolimit, 2 Rue des Ayres. Another fantastic wine bar in *Vieux Bordeaux* featuring cheese, charcuterie, and small plates.

Le Comptoir Bordelais, 1 Rue Piliers du Tutelle. Small, well-stocked gourmet store specializing in products from Southwest France.

Canelés Baillardran, twelve locations throughout Bordeaux. Canelés are a Bordelais specialty. I first heard of these little fluted cakes on my first trip to Bordeaux as an exchange student. Canelés have a crispy, caramelized exterior and an extremely moist soft interior flavored with your choice of rum or vanilla. They are completely addictive.

Provence

Mas Tourteron, Chemin de Sainte Blaise Les Imberts, Gordes. Lovely elegant country restaurant in the rolling hills outside of Gordes. Owned by my good friends, wife and husband team Elisabeth Bourgeois and Philippe Baique, the peaceful lush garden and warmly decorated interior create the ideal setting for Elisabeth's acclaimed Provençal cuisine. Philippe's thoughtful wine list is a perfect foil for Elisabeth's food. Do not miss her famous dessert table, laden with traditional French desserts. Reservations suggested.

Bistrot du Paradou, 57 Avenue de la Vallée des Baux, Paradou. This classic Provençal bistrot at the foot of the famous hill town Les Baux de Provence sports simple delicious food and one of the best cheese boards I have ever seen! Reservation required. After lunch at Le Paradou, stop by the **Mas de la Dame Tasting Room** directly below the cliffs of Les Baux de Provence. The tasting room in this winery offers wine tastings and the opportunity to purchase not only the wines of the Domaine, but also its incredible olive oils.

Lyon

Au Petit Bouchon Chez Georges, 8 Rue du Garet. Extremely small Lyonnais bouchon (traditional worker's restaurant in Lyon). Reservations a must!

Brasserie Le Nord, 18 Rue Neuve. My favorite of the eight Brasseries owned by Paul Bocuse, this classic Brasserie is elegant and welcoming—Dover Sole filleted tableside is a standout offering.

Huilerie Beaujolaise, 29 Rue des Echarmeux Beaujeu. While not actually in Lyon, this oil producer in the small Beaujolais town of Beaujeu has gained the patronage of many of the most well-respected chefs in France. Jean-Marc Montegottero produces a large range of nut and seed oils (almond, grilled peanut, pumpkin seed, pine nut, pecan, walnut, pistachio, hazelnut, toasted sesame, grilled rapeseed, turnip seed, poppy seed, and argan), extra virgin olive oils, and wine and flavored vinegars.

Troyes

Aux Crieurs de Vin, 4 place Jean-Jaurès. Rustic restaurant located in the back rooms of the Crieurs de Vin wine shop featuring local, rustic fare and extremely interesting by-the-glass wines. Prefer something by the bottle? Choose a wine from the wine shop and chef/owner Jean-Michel Wilmes will be happy to open it for you. The Crieurs de Vin Special Champagne Cuvée, produced by my friends at Champagne Pierre Gerbais, is a great way to start your meal. A smaller shop/kiosk is located in the Halles de Troyes covered market. The selection is thoughtful, albeit not as large as the main store. Grab a glass of wine and a seat at the nearby fishmonger—they will be happy to shuck some fresh oysters to go with your wine.

Burgundy

Ma Cuisine, Passage Sainte-Hélène, Beaune. Extremely popular small restaurant in a passageway off Beaune's main square, featuring impeccably prepared classic French fare and an extensive Burgundy wine list. Reservations essential.

Cellier Volnaysien, 2 Place de l'Eglise, Volnay. Jean-Pierre Charlot from Domaine Joseph Voillot highly recommends the Cellier Volnaysien—so do I. Their brick-vaulted dining room, decorated with winemaking paraphernalia, is charming. The menu serves gold-standard Burgundian dishes and offers a wonderful wine list. Reservations recommended.

Hostellerie des Clos, 18 Rue Jules Rathier, Chablis. Lovely gourmet restaurant and hotel located in the former *Hospice de Chablis* building. Fantastic food, great service, and a superb list of Chablis.

Alsace

Sézanne, 30 Grand Rue, Colmar. This small gourmet/wine shop has a fantastic little wine bar featuring natural wines, meats, cheeses, and local dishes. Unusual hours (9:00 a.m. to 7:00 p.m.).

Restaurant au Pont Corbeau, 21 quai St.-Nicolas, Strasbourg. Traditional Alsatian restaurant with warm décor, local classic Alsatian food, and a broad selection of local wines.

Italy

Rome

Roscioli, Via dei Giubbonari, 21/22. If you only have time for one meal in Rome, I beg you to have it at Roscioli. This small store/restaurant features an amazing array of cured meats, cheeses, foodstuffs, and well-chosen wines. Forty seats at small tables squeezed up against wine bottle-lined shelves, along the bar, and in the wine cellar in the basement afford the opportunity to taste the shop's wares as well as indulging in a true Roman meal, featuring classic pastas, and local dishes. I have Arianna Occhipinti to thank for the recommendation, and I can only echo her advice: "Have the *Cacio e Pepe* (pasta in cheese and black pepper sauce)!" It was an epiphany. Equally delicious are the pizzas, breads, and baked goods available from their bakery, **Roscioli Forno** across the street at Via dei Chiavari, 34. Reservations recommended for the restaurant.

Armando al Pantheon, Salita dei Crescenzi, 31. Traditional Roman restaurant next to the Pantheon. Wonderful service and great Roman dishes. Reservations recommended.

La Prosciutteria, three locations in Rome: Trastevere, Piazza Navona, and Via della Panetteria. Fantastic cured meats, cheeses, drop-dead-good Porchetta, and interesting wines by the glass.

Trapizzino, two locations: Via Giovanni Branca, 88; Piazzale di Ponte Milvio. Hand-held thick pizza, cut into triangles and stuffed with traditional toppings and Roman specialties.

Venice

Al Covo, Calle de la Pescaria, 3968. Elegant classic Venetian food in a rustic, intimate, and warm ambiance. Outdoor seating available. Reservations necessary.

Ristorante Oniga, Dorsoduro, 2852. Small casual restaurant with creative, local food.

Enogastronomica Pantagruelica, Calle Lunga S. Barnaba. Fantastic gourmet food shop in Venice specializing in organic food. Wine tastings, and cheese and meat samplers available.

Verona

Osteria Sottoriva, Via Sottoriva, 9/A. My wonderful friend Ludovica Fabbri of Savignola Paolina and I spent several evenings at this warm, casual, extremely wine-centric restaurant under the porticos near the river in Verona. Sensational wine list—especially champagne!

Bologna

Trattoria Gianni, Via Clavature, 18. Small family-owned traditional trattoria on a narrow street off the Piazza Maggiore in Bologna. If you are there in the winter, the *Tortellini in Brodo,* chicken soup with tortellini pasta, is a must!

Senigallia

Ristorante Da Carlo, Lungomare Dante Alighieri. Senigallia might not be a household name when one thinks of towns on the Adriatic coast of Italy, but if you are in the Marche, I definitely recommend this family-owned restaurant with its array of fresh, locally caught seafood. Reservations recommended on weekends and holidays.

Catania

Osteria Antica Marina, Via Pardo, 29, Catania, Sicily (inside Catania's famed Pescheria Market). This fish restaurant serves bounty from the sea prepared in traditional Sicilian fashion. Try the *Frittura di Paranza,* a plate of fried small whole fish and baby calamari fresh from the market.

Frittura di Paranza, Osteria Antica Marina, Catania, Sicily

United States

Washington, DC and Virginia

Because I live in Arlington, Virginia, right across the Potomac River from Washington, DC, I frequent establishments in both Virginia and Washington, DC, as well.

Buck's Fishing & Camping and **Comet Ping Pong.** 5031 and 5037 Connecticut Avenue NW, Washington DC. These two restaurants are the type of places where everyone knows your name and the neighborhood feel is definitely part of their charm. I should mention that I worked at both Buck's and Comet and am still friends with James Alefantis, the owner, and many of the staff. My particular favorite is Bryce, the general manager of Comet Ping Pong (he is also my son). All of that explains *why I feel so comfortable there*, but both restaurants are familiar haunts of patrons from all over the city, as well. **Buck's** focuses on local ingredients in a warm, rustic yet artsy environment and features a thoughtful, Old World wine list. Try the wood-grilled Buck's Steak (one pound of prime strip steak), the grilled pork chop, fried oysters, and onion rings with spicy mayonnaise. **Comet Ping Pong** specializes in artisanal pizzas and salads made from local ingredients, killer jerk-style wings, and an extensive craft beer list in a hip, industrial environment. Ping pong and live bands on the weekend are frosting on the cake.

Daikaya Ramen and Izakaya, 705 6th Street NW, Washington DC. This combination restaurant (Sapporo-style Ramen on the first floor, Izakaya on the second) is one of my go-to Ramen and brunch spots.

Izakaya Seki, 1117 V Street NW, Washington DC. Father/daughter team, Hiroshi and Cizuka Seki's intimate Japanese restaurant is an absolute gem. Hiroshi's incredibly pristine sashimi and grilled and fried specialties are made even better when paired with Cizuka's sake, soju, and craft beer list.

Taco Bamba, 2190 Pimmit Dr., Falls Church, Virginia. Fast casual Mexican storefront restaurant tucked away in a small shopping center featuring both classic and original combinations of tacos, sopes, tortas, flautas, and tamales.

Arrowine and Cheese, 4508 Lee Highway, Arlington, Virginia. Doug Rosen and Shem Hassen have created not just an award-winning wine and cheese shop, but also a neighborhood gathering place. They stock a large number of interesting wines (many sourced by Doug himself from his travels to the wine-producing regions of the world), and an extensive selection of cheeses and cured meats, and bring local denizens together on the weekends with a series of wine, beer, and cheese tastings. I spent nine years as an

Arrowine and Cheese, Arlington, Virginia

employee at Arrowine and still shop there multiple times a week. The staff in the deli has been instrumental in helping me source hard-to-find ingredients for this book. **Arrowine and Spirits,** Doug and Shem's Washington, DC location, carries a great selection of craft spirits in addition to wine and beer.

Black Salt Fish Market, 4883 MacArthur Boulevard NW, Washington DC. The fish and seafood counter at Black Salt stocks an impressive array of fresh seafood coupled with attentive service and a willingness to special order unusual, hard-to-find ingredients.

Broad Branch Market and **Soapstone Market,** 5608 Broad Branch Road NW, Washington, DC and 4465 Connecticut Avenue NW, Washington DC. Located in a stand-alone house in the Chevy Chase neighborhood of Washington DC, **Broad Branch Market** is a corner store with gourmet sensibilities. With its in-house butcher, prepared food counter, a small but well-stocked grocery section, craft beers both in bottles, cans, and growlers, and a really nice wine section, Broad Branch Market (owned by Tracy Stannard and her partner John Fielding) provides all the groceries you need on a daily basis. The ice cream shop, candy store, and coffee nook located in one of the side rooms make it popular with neighborhood children and parents alike. **Soapstone Market,** the newer, larger sibling of Broad Branch Market carries many of the same products as the original and features a wine bar and table seating where customers can enjoy their purchases.

Italian Store, Two locations. 3123 Lee Highway and 5837 Washington Boulevard, Arlington, Virginia. Bob Tramonte's paean to all things Italian. Stop in for a sandwich, or a slice of pizza—leave with a basket of Italian food and wine.

Dolcezza Gelato, eight store locations in Washington DC, Virginia, and Maryland, two farmer's market stands, and a large factory and store. In my opinion, husband and wife team, Robb Duncan and Violetta Edelman, make the best gelato in town. Their gelato and coffee shops feature gelato and sorbet made with local ingredients. (Every one says that, but given the fact that I first met Robb when we were both buying flats of blackberries at an early morning farmer's market, I know it to be true.)

Wagshal's Market, two locations. Spring Valley Market, 4845 Massachusetts Avenue NW and Wagshal's on New Mexico, 3201 New Mexico Avenue NW. Family-owned stores featuring prime beef, Iberico di Bellota pork, seafood, produce, and gourmet products. Ask for Pam "the Butcher" Ginsberg; she has never steered me wrong!

Organic Butcher, 6712 Old Dominion Drive, McLean, Virginia. Small, well-run butcher shop specializing in local, organic meats and fresh seafood. I appreciate their willingness to provide special cuts and clean fish, and to source hard-to-find products.

Via Umbria, 1525 Wisconsin Avenue NW, Washington DC. Bill and Suzy Menard's ode to Umbria features gorgeous Deruta Ceramics, Umbrian linens, Italian foodstuffs, Italian wine, and a full-service deli. A private dining room upstairs offers weekly dinners and wine tasting events.

German Gourmet, 5838 Columbia Pike, Falls Church, Virginia. When I need items for Choucroute, I head straight to the German Gourmet. They offer sausages, mustards, and hard-to-find items in an old world setting.

Market Streets and Covered Markets

The following are my favorite covered markets, food market streets (streets with a large concentration of food shops), and weekly outdoor markets. The list is not all-inclusive, but rather focuses on places of which I am particularly fond.

France

Paris

Rue de Buci, 6th arrondissement. Picturesque market street in Saint-German-des-Prés.

Rue Cler, 7th arrondissement. This popular market street is a few blocks from the Eiffel Tower—a perfect location to stock up for a picnic with a world-class view. Although not actually on Rue Cler, make sure not to miss Marie-Anne Cantin's cheese shop or L'Epicerie Fine, the well-stocked gourmet store next door, both located just around the corner on Rue Champ-de-Mars.

Rue Mouffetard, 5th arrondissement. A quaint historic market street with food stands, grocery stores, small restaurants, and cute bohemian clothing and jewelry shops.

Marché Boulevard Raspail, 6th arrondissement. Large outdoor market (Tuesday-Friday mornings). The Sunday morning market is devoted to organic producers.

Marché Saxe-Breteuil, 7th arrondissement. Tuesday and Saturday. Beautiful outdoor market with an amazing number of vendors.

Isle-sur-la-Sorgue

Sunday's morning market in the picture-perfect town of Isle-sur-la-Sorgue is the largest and arguably the most famous market in Provence's Luberon region. It is a combination food market and flea market, but what really separates it from the rest of the Provençal markets is the large number of antique vendors. In addition to the antique vendors that set up only on Sunday, numerous brick-and-mortar antique shops line the streets across from the market. Purchase the makings for a picnic and then wander the stands and stores until it is time to eat. One warning: if you have a hankering for a roast chicken

Sunday Market, Isle-sur-la-Sorgue

from the rotisserie stand, place your order when you arrive at the market. They sell out early—way before they are even close to being cooked. Ask me how I know!

Lyon

Les Halles de Lyon Paul Bocuse, 102 Cours Lafayette, Lyon. Shops open daily. Over 60 vendors including butchers, bakers, fishmongers, and wine shops (sorry, no candlestick makers) offer all you could possibly want to prepare the perfect Lyonnais meal or picnic. I suggest getting there early and wandering around. When you get tired, take a break at one of the great restaurants scattered amidst the vendors. My go-to is a seafood stand for a dozen oysters and a glass of Muscadet.

Troyes

Marché des Halles de Troyes, Place Hôtel de Ville, Troyes. Open daily: Monday through Thursday, 8:00 a.m. to 12:45 p.m., 3:30 p.m. to 7:00 p.m.; Friday and Saturday, 7:00 a.m. to 7:00 p.m.; and Sunday, 9:00 a.m. to 1:00 p.m. Thirty-five vendors specializing in products of the Aube but stocked with regional foods from elsewhere in France and the world.

Italy

Rome

Campo de' Fiori is one of the most famous and scenic daily markets in Rome. Even if you don't have a place to cook, it warrants a visit, if only to stroll around looking at vendors. It is also an ideal spot to grab something to snack on while sitting on the banks of the nearby Tiber River. In recent years, I have noticed that some of the stands have become somewhat touristy, selling packaged pastas and sauces, but the atmosphere remains so charming, it is still definitely worth a visit.

Testaccio Market, Via Beniamino Franklin, Testaccio. More than sixty merchant stands selling meats, fish, fruits and vegetables, breads, groceries, wines, prepared foods, clothing, leather goods, and household products. This is my new favorite market in Rome. I went there in search of the *Polpette di Bollito,* fried shredded meat patties, at **Mordi e Vai** (which loosely translates to Eat and Run), a popular food stand that focuses on sandwiches stuffed with traditional Roman dishes like tripe Roman-style, beef with chicory, sausages with broccoli rabe, grandma's meatball, and artichokes with pecorino. Also of note: **Strit Fud,** a stand on the outside of the market featuring street food like *fritto misto* (mixed fried seafood), *arancini* (fried rice balls), *panini,* daily specials, and some delicious crisp wines by the glass; and **Antico Forno,** a bakery inside the market where I had the best slice of thin-crust tomato pizza I've ever had. It was simple and delicious, just a crispy, slightly charred crust and a delicious thin layer of tomato sauce.

Bologna

Via Pescherie Vecchie and Via Clavature: Located just to the east of Piazza Maggiore, these narrow streets teem with food shops and stands. Bologna is considered by many to be the Gastronomic Capital of Italy, and the array of local foods available in the stores lining this quarter is out of this world. DO NOT LEAVE without trying the *mortadella*—a far cry from Oscar Meyer Bologna. It is silky and awe-inspiring, and I'm totally in love with it.

Catania, Sicily

Pescheria di Catania: (*Piscaria* in Sicilian Dialect) Catania's historic fish market still bustles six days a week in the old section of town a few blocks away from the harbor. Fishmongers hail customers, touting the quality of their multicolored selection of today's catch, fresh from the Mediterranean, the cacophony of their cries accompanied by smells of salt water and the sea. Stands are not limited to seafood; butchers, fruit and vegetable vendors, bakers, and grocers offer an impressive array of local products.

With Me, It's All about the Farmers

Whether the farmers grow grapes or other vegetables, raise farm animals, or make their own cheese, I feel a special connection to them. I spend an inordinate amount of time at local farmer's markets when I'm home, whether I need to purchase food or not. The relationships I have forged with my farmer friends are important to me. They make me feel grounded—connected to the land somehow—even if I live in a large metropolitan area.

Leedstown Farm: Leedstown, Virginia. One of my first stops on Friday mornings at the McLean Farmer's Market in McLean, Virginia, is Bob Jochum's stand. Bob works his small farm, producing local fruits and vegetables. Some items, figs and fava beans, for example, are available only in very small quantities, necessitating getting to the market early if you want to take some home. His English peas, sugar cube melons, watermelons, white corn, and heirloom tomatoes are excellent, and his folksy banter and weekly offer of a little bunch of complimentary basil make the experience all the more personal.

Rettland Farm: Gettysburg, Pennsylvania. Beau Ramsburg and his family raise Berkshire Pork and pastured poultry (which they process in their own on-farm, very small, low-volume, USDA-inspected poultry slaughtering plant) and make cheese on their family farm.

Blue Ridge Dairy: Sterling, Virginia. I stop by this stand every Saturday morning to stock up on local yoghurt, fresh mozzarella, ricotta, and butter from cheesemaker, Jack Clagett and his adorable daughter Jane.

How often does the daughter of the person helping you at a big box store (trick question: no one helps you at a big box store) give you a hand-drawn picture to put on your fridge? It's a little bonus to go with their fabulous products!

Martin's Angus Beef: The Plains, Virginia. Bill and Holly Martin specialize in locally raised, grass-fed, grain-finished lamb and thirty-day, dry-aged Prime Angus beef.

Whitmore Farm: Emmitsburg, Maryland. Owned by my good friends Will Morrow and Kent Ozkum, Whitmore Farm raises some of the most perfect pork, lamb, and chickens you will ever taste. Although they are phasing out their production before moving on to other things, I will never forget the quality of their products and their love for their animals.

Vendor Websites

d'Artagnan: www.dartagnan.com Purveyor of gourmet meats and food products.

Heritage Foods USA: www.heritagefoodsusa.com Farm-to-table online butcher dedicated to supporting family farmers raising livestock with old-school genetics on pasture.

Grimaud Farms: www.grimaudfarms.com Purveyor of Muscovy Duck and Guinea Fowl.

German Gourmet: www.germangourmet.com The online store of my go-to place for sausage and smoked meats for Choucroute is a little pricey when you add in the shipping cost, but the products are first-rate.

Smoking Goose: www.smokinggoose.com Purveyor of salumi, smoked and cured meats, fresh sausages, and leaf lard.

Penzeys Spices: www.penzeys.com Excellent source for hard-to-find spices.

Amazon: www.amazon.com If in doubt, it's a good idea to search Amazon for difficult-to-source food items.

APPENDIX

Food Terms

While most food terms in this book are probably self-explanatory, following are a few words that might need explanation:

Braise: To lightly brown food in fat and then slowly cook in a covered pan with a small amount of liquid.

Chiffonade: Finely shredded or finely cut leaf vegetables, frequently used as a garnish.

Deglaze: To add liquid (usually stock or wine) to a pan where meat has been roasted or sautéed in order to loosen and/or dissolve food particles that remain in the bottom of a pan.

Farce: A stuffing that is usually made out of meat, which distinguishes it from the bread-based stuffings that we use in the United States.

Fricassée: Meat, especially chicken or veal, browned lightly, stewed, and served in a sauce made with its own stock.

Lardons: A small strip or cube of pork fat used to flavor savory foods and salads.

Lute: To seal the lid on a dish with a flour and water paste (luting) or to seal a pastry lid onto a pie dish with an extra strip of pastry.

Sauté: To fry quickly in a small amount of hot fat. *Sauté* means "jumped" in French and refers to the action of flipping the ingredients in the pan, in essence making them jump.

Season to Taste/Check for Seasoning: To add as much salt or pepper or as much of a spice or herb as one likes so something tastes good.

Wine terms

Alcohol by Volume (ABV): A standard measure of how much alcohol is contained in a given volume of an alcoholic beverage (expressed as a percentage).

Appellation Contrôlée (AOC): A designation awarded to a French wine guaranteeing that it has been produced in the region specified, using vines and production methods that adhere to rules set forth by the regulating body.

Barriques: The French term for a small wine barrel usually made of oak. Barrique sizes vary and are expressed in liters. The most common barrique sizes are Bordeaux, 225 liters; and Burgundy, 228 liters.

Biodynamics: An enhanced method of organic farming that involves the implementation of various concepts from Austrian philosopher, Rudolf Steiner (1861–1925). Biodynamics emphasizes the health of the vines and vineyard as one whole organism. The aim of biodynamics is to harness beneficial forces by observing lunar phases and planetary cycles for all of the work in the vineyards and the winery and by using herbal and mineral tinctures and preparations.

Botrytis cinerea (Noble Rot): It seems odd to think that a fungus could be beneficial, but in the case of *botrytis cinerea,* that is absolutely true. *Botrytis cinerea* affects fruit following damp conditions. It is called Nobel Rot because it causes the grapes to shrivel and concentrates the juices without actually destroying the grapes. Although grapes affected with *botrytis cinerea* can be used in the production of dry wines, they are more commonly used to produce sweet wines. Some of the most famous sweet wines in the world are the result of *botrytis cinerea,* including sweet wines from Bordeaux (of which Sauternes is the most well known), Alsace, Austria, Germany, and the Loire Valley.

Charmat Method: A method for producing sparkling wine. In the Charmat (or Tank) Method, the secondary fermentation that produces bubbles takes place in a closed tank rather than in bottle, as with the Traditional Method. (To better understand Traditional Method Sparkling Wine Production, see "Burgers, Beer, and Brut Champagne," page 367.)

Cloning: The process of vine propagation where clones are produced from a single "mother" vine. Each cloned vine has DNA and characteristics identical to those of the mother vine.

Denominazione di Origine Controllata (DOC): The Italian counterpart of the French Appellation Contrôlée system. In Italy, there are two levels: Denominazione di Origine Controllata (DOC) and Denominazione di Origine Controllata e Garantita

(DOCG). The latter is a stricter designation and involves a guarantee from the regulatory authority that the wines adhere to the more stringent guidelines. DOGCs are usually sourced from smaller regions than DOCs. Indicazione Geografica Tipica (IGT) is a broad designation established by the Italian wine regulating body for wines that do not adhere to DOC or DOCG regulations. These wines can be of extremely high quality.

Disgorgement: The process of removing the dead yeast cells that have settled in the neck of a bottle of traditional method sparkling wine.

Filtration: The process of filtering liquid from solid particles in a finished wine to obtain a clear final product.

Fining: The clarification of a finished wine wherein a clarifying agent is suspended into the finished wine that attaches to unwanted particles. After several days, the clarification agent and the attached unwanted particles settle to the bottom of the wine storage vessel and are removed.

Lees/Lies: Lees are dead yeast cells, stem, and skin fragments that remain after the fermentation process in finished. **Lees contact** is the process of leaving fermented wine in contact with the lees, adding flavor and preservative qualities (frequently used in traditional method sparkling wine production). **Sur Lie:** a process during white wine production whereby wines are produced with lees contact. *Sur Lie* is an official designation in Muscadet, France.

Massale Selection: A method of selecting the source of new vine plants. Massale Selection involves taking cuttings from a number of outstanding old vines from a vineyard and then propagating new vines from these cuttings. This is done to protect the diversity of the vineyards and to encourage a continuation of the preferred characteristics of the old vines.

Monopole: A Burgundian term for a contiguous vineyard wholly owned by a single winery that is (usually) considered historically special or granted its own place in the AOC system. For example, Clos de Tart is a Burgundy Grand Cru that is owned entirely by one producer.

Must: Freshly pressed grape juice that contains the skin, seeds, and stems of the fruit.

Passerillage/Passito: The process of drying grapes to concentrate their flavors before pressing them and producing wine. Typically used in sweet wine production.

Pump Over: Pumping wine from the bottom of the tank over the grape must at the top of the tank.

Punch Down: The process of breaking up the thick layer of skins, stems, and seeds that forms at the surface of fermenting red wine and submerging it to extract color, tannins, flavor, and aromas from the grape solids.

Phylloxera: A louse that attacks the roots of vines and kills the plant. Phylloxera caused catastrophic damage to the vineyards of France in the 1860s before spreading throughout Europe and to the New World. The industry was saved by grafting its vines onto American rootstock, which is not susceptible to the louse. Phylloxera is still a danger to vines throughout the world to this day.

Racking: The process of moving wine from one barrel to another by gravity. Racking results in clearer wine by leaving the sediment in the bottom of the original barrel.

Residual Sugar: The amount of sugar that remains in a wine after fermentation is complete, usually stated in grams per liter (g/l).

Terroir: I like the definition on the Guild Somm website (www.guildsomm.com): "The complete system of the living vine." This takes into account: location, topography, soil, climate, and aspect (degree and direction of slope).

Varietal: A descriptive term for a wine named after the main grape variety from which it is made.

Variety: A type of grape or grapevine.

Vieilles Vignes: Old Vines.

Yeast: Microscopic fungi that when combined with the sugar in grape juice cause fermentation.

Yield: The volume of wine that is produced per unit surface of vineyard. In Europe, this yield is stated in hectoliters per hectare (hl/ha).

ACKNOWLEDGMENTS

Many authors say they could not have written or published their book without help from other people. In my case, given that this is a book about my experiences visiting winemakers, this is particularly true. I would like to thank the wonderful winemakers that I visited: Monique, Ugo, Pietro, and Franco Gussalli Beretta; Colette, Catherine, Laurence, and Théo Faller; Natalia, Giuseppe, and Giancarlo Nicolis and Martina Fornaser; Giorgio Colutta; Jean-François and Isabelle Coquard; Jean-Marc and Christelle Grussaute; Philippe, Denise, and Julien Teulier; Jean Pierre Charlot; Marc and Geneviève Ollivier; Ludovica Fabbri; Gabriele Buondonno; Stefano Grandi; Roberto and Marilena Pucci; Denis, Monique, and Brian Barbara; Laurence and Gilles Crochet; Arianna Occhipinti; Guillaume and Karina Lefèvre; François, Brigitte, Jérôme, Rémi, and Olivier Legras; Damien and Coralie Delecheneau; and Cédric and Emilie Bouchard. I am also grateful to Stéphane Chetrit and Michela, Francesca, and Piera Spalla Selvatico for their warm welcome.

To my dear wine friends who fact-checked my wine descriptions, I owe you a debt of gratitude: Michael Muller, Jim Cutts, Brian Forsgren, Jean-François Coquard, Ed Addiss, Brennan Downey, Evan Carlson, Roy Cloud, Mike Daniels, Kevin McKenna, and Nicolas Mestre. Thanks as well to Kevin McKenna, Alberto Panella, Ryne Hazzard, Peg Downey, and Matthew Tucker for helping to arrange winery visits; and very special thanks to Tom Calder for checking my facts, writing letters and emails, and making phone calls to winemakers on my behalf.

Patty Kaplan and Corrine Sidener, I thank you both for proofing so many drafts of documents for me.

Either a friend or family member tested every recipe in this book at least once. I am forever indebted to all of those who helped with this: Hannah Rose, Elise Hoffmann, Alice Bergen Phillips, Evan Carlson, Kristin Wiley, Margie Davis, Lucy Whiting, Nathaniel Fink-Humes, Bill McKenney, Alison Rittenberg Ricketts, Genevieve Bentz, Corrine and Ron Sidener, Shereen Herbert, Bryce Reh, Milena Aradski, Jodie Steiner (who is also my Italian language expert), and special thanks to Shelby and Evan Pushchak, and my sister Lori Rock. These last three tested large numbers of recipes with extremely hard-to-find ingredients—many before I had even sold the book.

To Hannah Rose for creating the maps, end papers, and the koala bear drawing for the book. You are a wonderful artist, and I had a fantastic time collaborating with you.

Thanks to Linda Roth and Elli Benchimol for the help and friendship, and to Rutger de Vink and Jarad Slipp for their kindness and for waiting until next time!

To the gang at Arrowine and Cheese: Doug Rosen, Shem Hassen, Kathleen Calnan, Jim Cutts, Michelle Petree, Bill Watts, Nathaniel Fink-Humes, Badr Adam Abaichi, Todd Himes, Jim Parlett, Neal Kennedy, David Baum Rojas, and Emily Auer, thanks for your assistance.

I owe a huge debt of gratitude to the wonderful people at Buck's Fishing & Camping and Comet Ping Pong—employees and customers alike—for their support and encouragement. To James Alefantis, thank you for your faith in me and to James Rexroad, thanks for the laughs, the special orders, and your gougères recipe.

To Shereen Herbert, you have been a lifesaver, helping me through all of my computer ineptitude, taking photographs, and being such a good friend.

Thank you to Barton Seaver who encouraged me early on and told me that I was the only one who could tell "my story."

To my agent, Peter Riva, and my editor, Leah Zarra. Thank you for everything.

Finally, to Bryce and Jeff: I love you both. I could not have written this book without you two. You believed in and supported me from the beginning to the end of this endeavor. Bryce, thanks for testing recipes despite my helicoptering, for photography and computer advice, and for being such a wonderful son.

Jeff, you've been wonderful throughout this whole process. You've been such a trooper, bearing up under the trials of tasting all those wines and dishes, traveling with me to crazy parts of France and Italy—like Burgundy, Tuscany, and Sicily—taking tons of photos and proofing my book. Seriously, though, we may not always agree on comma usage, but your loving support has been incalculable, and I owe you so much. I'll bet you can't wait to hear my idea for the next book!

BIBLIOGRAPHY

Although much of the research for this book was done during my visits to the wineries in *The Wine Table* and through follow-up emails and telephone calls, following are additional sources that I used during my research. I have broken the sources out by books, magazines, and websites.

Books

Bastianich, Joseph and Lynch, David, *Vino Italiano, The Regional Wines of Italy,* New York: Clarkson N. Potter, 2002.

Child, Julia, *The Way to Cook,* New York: Alfred A. Knopf, 1989.

Friedrich, Jacqueline, *Wine and Food Guide to the Loire,* New York: Henry Holt and Company, 1996.

———, *Earthly Delights from the Garden of France—Wines of the Loire, Volume I, The Kingdom of Sauvignon Blanc, Sancerre, Pouilly Fumé and the Sauvignon Satellites,* Paris: Jacqueline Friedrich, 2011.

Fromageot, Geneviève C., *Les Recettes Bourguignonnes de Tante Margot,* Rennes: Edilarge, 1995.

Ingram, Christine, *Cooking Ingredients, The Ultimate Photographic Reference Guide for Cooks and Food Lovers,* New York: Hermes House, 2002.

Lallemand, Roger, *Le Bourbonnais, La Vraie Cuisine à Travers La France,* Paris: Editions Lanore.

Millo, François, *Those Provence Rosé Moments,* Paris: Hachette Livre, 2010.

Millo, François and Todorovka, Viktorija, *Provence Food and Wine, The Art of Living,* Chicago: Surrey Books, 2014.

Pitiot, Sylvain and Sevant, Jean-Charles, *The Wines of Burgundy,* Paris: Collection Pierre Poupon, 14th edition, 2010.

Robinson, Jancis and Harding, Julia, *The Oxford Companion to Wine, Fourth Edition,* Oxford: Oxford University Press, 2015.

Robinson, Jancis, Harding, Julia and Vouillamoz, José, *Wine Grapes, A complete guide to 1,368 wine varieties, including their origin and flavors,* New York: Harper Collins, 2012.

Roeckel, Didier, *Savoury Specialities from Alsace,* Bernardswiller: I.D. L'Edition, 2012.

Magazine Articles

Harmon Jenkins, Nancy, "Home Cooking in Sicily," *Saveur,* March 21, 2011, 136.

Gollner, Adam Leith, "Eating the Arab Roots of Sicilian Cuisine," *Saveur,* March 17, 2016, 182.

Online Articles

Belding, Wayne, M.S., *The Kimmeridgian Exposed and Explained,* www.Wine Review Online.com, July 1, 2014.

Hemming, Richard, M.W., *New Crus for Muscadet,* www.JancisRobinson.com, September 8, 2011.

Websites

www.agricolaocchipinti.com

www.agricolegussalliberetta.com

www.allier-auvergne-tourisme.com

www.aoc-marcillac.com

www.aube-champagne.com

www.behind-the-french-menu.blogspot.com

www.caminlarredya.com

www.chambersstwines.com

www.champagne.fr

www.chianticlassico.com

www.colliorientali.com

www.colutta.it

www.consorziovalpolicella.it

www.consorziovarzi.it

www.cru-gorges.com

www.davidlebovitz.com

www.domainedelapepiere.com

www.domainedesulauze.com

www.domaine-du-cros.com

www.domaine-grosbot-barbara.com

www.domainevollot.com

www.domaineweinbach.com

www.elegancedesvolnay.com

www.finedininglovers.com

www.franciacorta.net
www.guildsomm.com
www.italia.it
www.italianwinecentral.com
www.italymagazine.com
www.lagrangetiphaine.com
www.legras-et-haas.com
www.loirevalleywine.com
www.louisdressner.com
www.lucien-crochet.com
www.made-in-italy.com
www.marvellous-provence.com
www.ossau-iraty.com
www.ragusaospitalitadiffusa.it
www.rdj.com
www.regions-of-france.com
www.salumificiomagrotti.it
www.sanvincenti.it
www.savignolapaolina.com
www.sicily.co.uk
www.slowfood.com
www.tenuta-mazzolino.com
www.turismofvg.it
www.tourisme-aveyron.com
www.vigneronsdupallet.com
www.vinclisson.com
www.viniesaporidilambardi.it
www.vininicolis.com
www.vinoltrepo.org
www.vinsalsace.com
www.vinsdeprovence.com
www.vins-jurancon.fr
www.vinsmontlouissurloire.fr
www.volnay.com
www.winesofalsace.com
www.winesofsicily.com

INDEX

CONVERSION CHARTS

Metric and Imperial Conversions
(These conversions are rounded for convenience)

Ingredient	Cups/Tablespoons/Teaspoons	Ounces	Grams/Milliliters
Butter	1 cup/16 tablespoons/2 sticks	8 ounces	230 grams
Cheese, shredded	1 cup	4 ounces	110 grams
Cream cheese	1 tablespoon	0.5 ounce	14.5 grams
Cornstarch	1 tablespoon	0.3 ounce	8 grams
Flour, all-purpose	1 cup/1 tablespoon	4.5 ounces/0.3 ounce	125 grams/8 grams
Flour, whole wheat	1 cup	4 ounces	120 grams
Fruit, dried	1 cup	4 ounces	120 grams
Fruits or veggies, chopped	1 cup	5 to 7 ounces	145 to 200 grams
Fruits or veggies, puréed	1 cup	8.5 ounces	245 grams
Honey, maple syrup, or corn syrup	1 tablespoon	.75 ounce	20 grams
Liquids: cream, milk, water, or juice	1 cup	8 fluid ounces	240 milliliters
Oats	1 cup	5.5 ounces	150 grams
Salt	1 teaspoon	0.2 ounce	6 grams
Spices: cinnamon, cloves, ginger, or nutmeg (ground)	1 teaspoon	0.2 ounce	5 milliliters
Sugar, brown, firmly packed	1 cup	7 ounces	200 grams
Sugar, white	1 cup/1 tablespoon	7 ounces/0.5 ounce	200 grams/12.5 grams
Vanilla extract	1 teaspoon	0.2 ounce	4 grams

Oven Temperatures

Fahrenheit	Celsius	Gas Mark
225°	110°	¼
250°	120°	½
275°	140°	1
300°	150°	2
325°	160°	3
350°	180°	4
375°	190°	5
400°	200°	6
425°	220°	7
450°	230°	8

Domaine du Cros

Forte Masso

Tenuta Mazzolino

Giorgio Colutta

Domaine de Sulauze

Domaine de la Pépière

Azienda Agricola Lo Sparviere

Orlandi Contucci Ponno

Tenuta San Vincenti

Domaine Legras & Haas

Camin Larredya